EVERYMAN'S LIBRARY

771

BIOGRAPHY

Everyman, I will go with thee, and be thy guide,
In thy most need to go by thy side

SAMUEL JOHNSON, born at Lichfield in 1709, the son of a bookseller. His poverty induced him to leave Oxford before taking a degree. Became an usher and a school-teacher, but in 1737 went to London and devoted himself to journalism and literature generally. Made a number of important friendships, but it was not until 1762 that he became settled financially. Met Boswell, 1763. Died on 13th December 1784.

SAMUEL JOHNSON
LIVES OF
THE ENGLISH POETS

IN TWO VOLUMES · VOLUME TWO
CONGREVE TO GRAY

INTRODUCTION BY
L. ARCHER HIND

LONDON J. M. DENT & SONS LTD
NEW YORK E. P. DUTTON & CO INC

CONTENTS

52902

LIVES OF THE ENGLISH POETS

WILLIAM CONGREVE

1670—1728-29

Born at Bardsey in Yorkshire—Educated at Kilkenny and Dublin—
Entered of the Middle Temple—Early Appearance as a Poet—His first
Dramatic Labour—Obtains the Patronage of Halifax—Writes *The Double
Dealer*, *Love for Love*, and *The Mourning Bride*—His Controversy with
Collier—His last Play, and high Poetical Reputation—His Government
Situations—Death, and Burial in Westminster Abbey—Works and
Character.

WILLIAM CONGREVE descended from a family in Staffordshire,
of so great antiquity that it claims a place among the few that
extend their line beyond the Norman Conquest; and was the
son of William Congreve, second son of Richard Congreve of
Congreve and Stratton. He visited, once at least, the residence
of his ancestors; and, I believe, more places than one are still
shown, in groves and gardens, where he is related to have written
his *Old Bachelor*.

Neither the time nor place of his birth are certainly known;
if the inscription upon his monument be true, he was born in
1672. For the place, it was said by himself that he owed his
nativity to England, and by everybody else that he was born in
Ireland. Southerne mentioned him with sharp censure, as a man
that meanly disowned his native country. The biographers
assigned his nativity to Bardsa, near Leeds in Yorkshire, from
the account given by himself, as they suppose, to Jacob.

To doubt whether a man of eminence has told the truth
about his own birth, is, in appearance, to be very deficient in
candour; yet nobody can live long without knowing that falsehoods of convenience or vanity, falsehoods from which no evil
immediately visible ensues, except the general degradation of
human testimony, are very lightly uttered, and once uttered
are sullenly supported. Boileau, who desired to be thought
a rigorous and steady moralist, having told a pretty lie to

Louis XIV., continued it afterwards by false dates; thinking himself obliged *in honour*, says his admirer, to maintain what, when he said it, was so well received.

Wherever Congreve was born, he was educated first at Kilkenny, and afterwards at Dublin, his father having some military employment that stationed him in Ireland: but after having passed through the usual preparatory studies, as may be reasonably supposed, with great celerity and success, his father thought it proper to assign him a profession, by which something might be gotten; and about the time of the Revolution sent him, at the age of sixteen, to study law in the Middle Temple, where he lived for many years, but with very little attention to Statutes or Reports.

His disposition to become an author appeared very early, as he very early felt that force of imagination, and possessed that copiousness of sentiment, by which intellectual pleasure can be given. His first performance was a novel, called *Incognita, or Love and Duty reconciled*. It is praised by the biographers, who quote some part of the Preface, that is indeed, for such a time of life, uncommonly judicious. I would rather praise it than read it.

His first dramatic labour was the *Old Bachelor*; of which he says, in his defence against Collier, "that comedy was written, as several know, some years before it was acted. When I wrote it, I had little thoughts of the stage; but did it, to amuse myself in a slow recovery from a fit of sickness. Afterwards, through my indiscretion, it was seen, and in some little time more it was acted; and I, through the remainder of my indiscretion, suffered myself to be drawn in to the prosecution of a difficult and thankless study, and to be involved in a perpetual war with knaves and fools."

There seems to be a strange affectation in authors of appearing to have done everything by chance. The *Old Bachelor* was written for amusement, in the languor of convalescence. Yet it is apparently composed with great elaborateness of dialogue, and incessant ambition of wit. The age of the writer considered, it is indeed a very wonderful performance; for, whenever written, it was acted (January 1692-3) when he was not more than twenty-one [four] years old; and was then recommended by Mr. Dryden, Mr. Southerne, and Mr. Maynwaring. Dryden said that he never had seen such a first play; but they found it deficient in some things requisite to the success of its exhibition, and by their greater experience fitted it for the stage.

Southerne used to relate of one comedy, probably of this, that when Congreve read it to the players, he pronounced it so wretchedly, that they had almost rejected it; but they were afterwards so well persuaded of its excellence, that, for half a year before it was acted, the manager allowed its author the privilege of the house.

Few plays have ever been so beneficial to the writer; for it procured him the patronage of Halifax, who immediately made him one of the commissioners for licensing coaches, and soon after gave him a place in the Pipe Office, and another in the Customs of 600*l.* a year. Congreve's conversation must surely have been at least equally pleasing with his writings.

Such a comedy, written at such an age, requires some consideration. As the lighter species of dramatic poetry professes the imitation of common life, of real manners, and daily incidents, it apparently presupposes a familiar knowledge of many characters, and exact observation of the passing world; the difficulty therefore is, to conceive how this knowledge can be obtained by a boy.

But if the *Old Bachelor* be more nearly examined, it will be found to be one of those comedies which may be made by a mind vigorous and acute, and furnished with comic characters by the perusal of other poets, without much actual commerce with mankind. The dialogue is one constant reciprocation of conceits, or clash of wit, in which nothing flows necessarily from the occasion, or is dictated by nature. The characters both of men and women are either fictitious and artificial, as those of Heartwell and the ladies; or easy and common, as Wittol a tame idiot, Bluff a swaggering coward, and Fondlewife a jealous Puritan; and the catastrophe arises from a mistake not very probably produced, by marrying a woman in a mask.

Yet this gay comedy, when all these deductions are made, will still remain the work of very powerful and fertile faculties: the dialogue is quick and sparkling, the incidents such as seize the attention, and the wit so exuberant that it "o'er-informs its tenement."

Next year he gave another specimen of his abilities in *The Double Dealer*, which was not received with equal kindness. He writes to his patron the Lord Halifax a Dedication, in which he endeavours to reconcile the reader to that which found few friends among the audience. These apologies are always useless: "de gustibus non est disputandum"; men may be convinced, but they cannot be pleased against their will. But though taste is obstinate, it is very variable, and time often prevails when arguments have failed.

Queen Mary conferred upon both those plays the honour of her presence; and when she died, soon after, Congreve testified his gratitude by a despicable effusion of elegiac pastoral; a composition in which all is unnatural, and yet nothing is new.

In another year (1695) his prolific pen produced *Love for Love*; a comedy of nearer alliance to life, and exhibiting more real manners, than either of the former. The character of Foresight was then common. Dryden calculated nativities; both Cromwell and King William had their lucky days; and Shaftesbury himself, though he had no religion, was said to regard predictions. The Sailor is not accounted very natural, but he is very pleasant.

With this play was opened the New Theatre, under the direction of Betterton the tragedian; where he exhibited two years afterwards (1697) *The Mourning Bride*, a tragedy, so written as to show him sufficiently qualified for either kind of dramatic poetry.

In this play, of which, when he afterwards revised it, he reduced the versification to greater regularity, there is more bustle than sentiment; the plot is busy and intricate, and the events take hold on the attention; but, except a very few passages, we are rather amused with noise, and perplexed with stratagem, than entertained with any true delineation of natural characters. This, however, was received with more benevolence than any other of his works, and still continues to be acted and applauded.

But whatever objections may be made either to his comic or tragic excellence, they are lost at once in the blaze of admiration, when it is remembered that he had produced these four plays before he had passed his twenty-fifth year, before other men, even such as are some time to shine in eminence, have passed their probation of literature, or presume to hope for any other notice than such as is bestowed on diligence and inquiry. Among all the efforts of early genius which literary history records, I doubt whether anyone can be produced that more surpasses the common limits of nature than the plays of Congreve.

About this time began the long-continued controversy between Collier and the poets. In the reign of Charles the First the Puritans had raised a violent clamour against the drama, which

they considered as an entertainment not lawful to Christians—
an opinion held by them in common with the Church of Rome;
and Prynne published *Histrio-mastix*, a huge volume, in which
stage plays were censured. The outrages and crimes of the
Puritans brought afterwards their whole system of doctrine into
disrepute, and from the Restoration the poets and players were
left at quiet; for to have molested them would have had the
appearance of tendency to puritanical malignity.

This danger, however, was worn away by time; and Collier,
a fierce and implacable Non-juror, knew that an attack upon
the theatre would never make him suspected for a Puritan; he
therefore (1698) published *A short View of the Immorality and
Profaneness of the English Stage*, I believe with no other motive
than religious zeal and honest indignation. He was formed for a
controvertist: with sufficient learning; with diction vehement
and pointed, though often vulgar and incorrect; with unconquerable pertinacity; with wit in the highest degree keen and
sarcastic; and with all those powers exalted and invigorated by
just confidence in his cause.

Thus qualified, and thus incited, he walked out to battle, and
assailed at once most of the living writers, from Dryden to
D'Urfey. His onset was violent: those passages which while
they stood single had passed with little notice, when they were
accumulated and exposed together, excited horror; the wise
and the pious caught the alarm, and the nation wondered
why it had so long suffered irreligion and licentiousness to
be openly taught at the public charge.

Nothing now remained for the poets but to resist or fly.
Dryden's conscience, or his prudence, angry as he was, withheld
him from the conflict: Congreve and Vanbrugh attempted
answers. Congreve, a very young man, elated with success, and
impatient of censure, assumed an air of confidence and security.
His chief artifice of controversy is to retort upon his adversary
his own words: he is very angry, and, hoping to conquer Collier
with his own weapons, allows himself in the use of every term
of contumely and contempt; but he has the sword without the
arm of Scanderbeg; he has his antagonist's coarseness, but not
his strength. Collier replied; for contest was his delight—he
was not to be frighted from his purpose or his prey.

The cause of Congreve was not tenable: whatever glosses he
might use for the defence or palliation of single passages, the
general tenor and tendency of his plays must always be condemned. It is acknowledged, with universal conviction, that

the perusal of his works will make no man better; and that their ultimate effect is to represent pleasure in alliance with vice, and to relax those obligations by which life ought to be regulated.

The stage found other advocates, and the dispute was protracted through ten years: but at last Comedy grew more modest; and Collier lived to see the reward of his labour in the reformation of the theatre.

Of the powers by which this important victory was achieved, a quotation from *Love for Love*, and the remark upon it, may afford a specimen.

"*Sir Samps.*—Sampson's a very good name; for your Sampsons were strong dogs from the beginning.

"*Angel.*—Have a care—if you remember, the strongest Sampson of your name pull'd an old house over his head at last.

"Here you have the Sacred History burlesqued; and Sampson once more brought into the house of Dagon, to make sport for the Philistines!"

Congreve's last play was *The Way of the World* ; which, though as he hints in his Dedication it was written with great labour and much thought, was received with so little favour, that, being in a high degree offended and disgusted, he resolved to commit his quiet and his fame no more to the caprices of an audience.

From this time his life ceased to be public; he lived for himself and for his friends; and among his friends was able to name every man of his time whom wit and elegance had raised to reputation. It may be therefore reasonably supposed that his manners were polite and his conversation pleasing.

He seems not to have taken much pleasure in writing, as he contributed nothing to *The Spectator*, and only one paper to *The Tatler*, though published by men with whom he might be supposed willing to associate; and though he lived many years after the publication of his *Miscellaneous Poems*, yet he added nothing to them, but lived on in literary indolence; engaged in no controversy, contending with no rival, neither soliciting flattery by public commendations, nor provoking enmity by malignant criticism, but passing his time among the great and splendid, in the placid enjoyment of his fame and fortune.

Having owed his fortune to Halifax, he continued always of his patron's party, but, as it seems, without violence or acrimony; and his firmness was naturally esteemed, as his abilities were reverenced. His security, therefore, was never violated; and when, upon the extrusion of the Whigs, some intercession was used lest Congreve should be displaced, the Earl of Oxford made this answer:

Non obtusa adeo gestamus pectora Pœni,
Nec tam aversus equos Tyriâ sol jungit ab urbe.

He that was thus honoured by the adverse party, might naturally expect to be advanced when his friends returned to power, and he was accordingly made Secretary for the Island of Jamaica; a place, I suppose, without trust or care, but which, with his post in the Customs, is said to have afforded him 1200*l*. a year.

His honours were yet far greater than his profits. Every writer mentioned him with respect; and, among other testimonies to his merit, Steele made him the patron of his *Miscellany*, and Pope inscribed to him the translation of the Iliad.

But he treated the Muses with ingratitude; for, having long conversed familiarly with the great, he wished to be considered rather as a man of fashion than of wit; and, when he received a visit from Voltaire, disgusted him by the despicable foppery of desiring to be considered not as an author, but a gentleman; to which the Frenchman replied, "that if he had been only a gentleman, he should not have come to visit him."

In his retirement he may be supposed to have applied himself to books; for he discovers more literature than the poets have commonly attained. But his studies were in his latter days obstructed by cataracts in his eyes, which at last terminated in blindness. This melancholy state was aggravated by the gout, for which he sought relief by a journey to Bath; but being overturned in his chariot, complained from that time of a pain in his side, and died, at his house in Surrey-street in the Strand, Jan. 19, 1728-9. Having lain in state in the Jerusalem Chamber, he was buried in Westminster Abbey, where a monument is erected to his memory by Henrietta, Duchess of Marlborough, to whom, for reasons either not known or not mentioned, he bequeathed a legacy of about 10,000*l*.; the accumulation of attentive parsimony, which, though to her superfluous and useless, might have given great assistance to the ancient family from which he descended, at that time by the imprudence of his relation reduced to difficulties and distress.

Congreve has merit of the highest kind; he is an original

writer, who borrowed neither the models of his plot, nor the manner of his dialogue. Of his plays I cannot speak distinctly; for since I inspected them many years have passed; but what remains upon my memory is, that his characters are commonly fictitious and artificial, with very little of nature, and not much of life. He formed a peculiar idea of comic excellence, which he supposed to consist in gay remarks and unexpected answers; but that which he endeavoured, he seldom failed of performing. His scenes exhibit not much of humour, imagery, or passion: his personages are a kind of intellectual gladiators; every sentence is to ward or strike; the contest of smartness is never intermitted; his wit is a meteor playing to and fro with alternate coruscations. His comedies have therefore, in some degree, the operation of tragedies; they surprise rather than divert, and raise admiration oftener than merriment. But they are the works of a mind replete with images, and quick in combination.

Of his miscellaneous poetry I cannot say anything very favourable. The powers of Congreve seem to desert him when he leaves the stage, as Antæus was no longer strong than when he could touch the ground. It cannot be observed without wonder, that a mind so vigorous and fertile in dramatic compositions should on any other occasion discover nothing but impotence and poverty. He has in these little pieces neither elevation of fancy, selection of language, nor skill in versification: yet if I were required to select from the whole mass of English poetry the most poetical paragraph, I know not what I could prefer to an exclamation in *The Mourning Bride*:

ALMERIA
It was a fancied noise; for all is hush'd.

LEONORA
It bore the accent of a human voice.

ALMERIA
It was thy fear, or else some transient wind
Whistling thro' hollows of this vaulted aisle:
We'll listen——

LEONORA
Hark!

ALMERIA
No: all is hush'd and still as death.—'Tis dreadful!
How reverend is the face of this tall pile,
Whose ancient pillars rear their marble heads,
To bear aloft its arch'd and ponderous roof,
By its own weight made stedfast and immoveable,

> Looking tranquillity! It strikes an awe
> And terror on my aching sight; the tombs
> And monumental caves of death look cold,
> And shoot a chillness to my trembling heart.
> Give me thy hand, and let me hear thy voice;
> Nay, quickly speak to me, and let me hear
> Thy voice—my own affrights me with its echoes.

He who reads these lines enjoys for a moment the powers of a poet; he feels what he remembers to have felt before, but he feels it with great increase of sensibility; he recognises a familiar image, but meets it again amplified and expanded, embellished with beauty, and enlarged with majesty.

Yet could the author, who appears here to have enjoyed the confidence of nature, lament the death of Queen Mary in lines like these:

> The rocks are cleft, and new-descending rills
> Furrow the brows of all th' impending hills.
> The water-gods to floods their rivulets turn,
> And each, with streaming eyes, supplies his wanting urn.
> The Fauns forsake the woods, the Nymphs the grove,
> And round the plain in sad distractions rove:
> In prickly brakes their tender limbs they tear,
> And leave on thorns their locks of golden hair.
> With their sharp nails, themselves the Satyrs wound,
> And tug their shaggy beards, and bite with grief the ground.
> Lo! Pan himself, beneath a blasted oak
> Dejected lies, his pipe in pieces broke.
> See Pales weeping too, in wild despair,
> And to the piercing winds her bosom bare.
> And see yon fading myrtle, where appears
> The Queen of Love, all bath'd in flowing tears;
> See how she wrings her hands and beats her breast,
> And tears her useless girdle from her waist:
> Hear the sad murmurs of her sighing doves!
> For grief they sigh, forgetful of their loves.

And, many years after [1703], he gave no proof that time had improved his wisdom or his wit; for, on the death of the Marquis of Blandford, this was his song:

> And now the winds, which had so long been still,
> Began the swelling air with sighs to fill;
> The water-nymphs, who motionless remain'd,
> Like images of ice, while she complain'd,
> Now loos'd their streams: as when descending rains
> Roll the steep torrents headlong o'er the plains.
> The prone creation, who so long had gaz'd,
> Charm'd with her cries, and at her griefs amaz'd,
> Began to roar and howl with horrid yell,
> Dismal to hear, and horrible to tell!
> Nothing but groans and sighs were heard around,
> And Echo multiplied each mournful sound.

In both these funeral poems, when he has *yelled* out many

syllables of senseless *dolour*, he dismisses his reader with senseless consolation: from the grave of Pastora rises a light that
forms a star; and where Amaryllis wept for Amyntas, from
every tear sprung up a violet.

But William is his hero, and of William he will sing:

> The hovering winds on downy wings shall wait around,
> And catch, and waft to foreign lands, the flying sound.

It cannot but be proper to show what they shall have to catch
and carry:

> 'Twas now, when flowery lawns the prospect made,
> And flowing brooks beneath a forest's shade,
> A lowing heifer, loveliest of the herd,
> Stood feeding by; while two fierce bulls prepar'd
> Their armed heads for fight; by fate of war to prove
> The victor worthy of the fair one's love.
> Unthought presage of what met next my view;
> For soon the shady scene withdrew.
> And now, for woods, and fields, and springing flowers,
> Behold a town arise, bulwark'd with walls and lofty towers;
> Two rival armies all the plain o'erspread,
> Each in battalia rang'd, and shining arms array'd;
> With eager eyes beholding both from far
> Namur, the prize and mistress of the war.

The *Birth of the Muse* is a miserable fiction. One good line
it has, which was borrowed from Dryden. The concluding
verses are these:

> This said, no more remain'd. Th' etherial host
> Again impatient crowd the crystal coast.
> The father, now, within his spacious hands
> Encompass'd all the mingled mass of seas and lands;
> And, having heav'd aloft the ponderous sphere,
> He launch'd the world to float in ambient air.

Of his irregular poems, that to Mrs. Arabella Hunt seems to
be the best: his ode for Cecilia's Day, however, has some lines
which Pope had in his mind when he wrote his own.

His imitations of Horace are feebly paraphrastical, and the
additions which he makes are of little value. He sometimes
retains what were more properly omitted, as when he talks of
vervain and *gums* to propitiate Venus.

Of his translations, the satire of Juvenal was written very
early, and may therefore be forgiven, though it had not the
massiness and vigour of the original. In all his versions strength
and sprightliness are wanting: his *Hymn to Venus*, from Homer,
is perhaps the best. His lines are weakened with expletives, and
his rhymes are frequently imperfect.

His petty poems are seldom worth the cost of criticism; sometimes the thoughts are false, and sometimes common. In his verses on Lady Gethin, the latter part is an imitation of Dryden's ode on Mrs. Killigrew; and *Doris*, that has been so lavishly flattered by Steele, has indeed some lively stanzas, but the expression might be mended; and the most striking part of the character had been already shown in *Love for Love*. His *Art of Pleasing* is founded on a vulgar, but perhaps impracticable principle, and the staleness of the sense is not concealed by any novelty of illustration or elegance of diction.

This tissue of poetry, from which he seems to have hoped a lasting name, is totally neglected, and knownonly as it is appended to his plays.

While comedy or while tragedy is regarded, his plays are likely to be read; but, except what relates to the stage, I know not that he has ever written a stanza that is sung, or a couplet that is quoted. The general character of his *Miscellanies* is, that they show little wit, and little virtue.

Yet to him it must be confessed that we are indebted for the correction of a national error, and for the cure of our Pindaric madness. He first taught the English writers that Pindar's odes were regular; and though certainly he had not the fire requisite for the higher species of lyric poetry, he has shown us that enthusiasm has its rules, and that in mere confusion there is neither grace nor greatness.

SIR RICHARD BLACKMORE

1658?–1729

Born at Corsham, in Wiltshire—Educated at Westminster and Oxford—Becomes a Fellow of the College of Physicians—His first work an Heroic Poem—*Prince Arthur*—*King Arthur*—Attacked by Dennis—His *Satire against Wit* and Quarrel with Dryden—His other Poems—His Religious Life—Death and Burial at Boxted, in Essex—Works and Character.

SIR RICHARD BLACKMORE is one of those men whose writings have attracted much notice, but of whose life and manners very little has been communicated, and whose lot it has been to be much oftener mentioned by enemies than by friends.

He was the son of Robert Blackmore, of Corsham, in Wiltshire, styled by Wood *gentleman*, and supposed to have been an attorney. Having been for some time educated in a country school, he was sent at thirteen to Westminster; and in 1668 was entered at Edmund Hall, in Oxford, where he took the degree of M.A., June 3, 1676, and resided thirteen years—a much longer time than it is usual to spend at the university, and which he seems to have passed with very little attention to the business of the place; for, in his poems, the ancient names of nations or places which he often introduces are pronounced by chance. He afterwards travelled: at Padua he was made Doctor of Physic; and, after having wandered about a year and a half on the Continent, returned home.

In some part of his life, it is not known when, his indigence compelled him to teach a school—an humiliation with which, though it certainly lasted but a little while, his enemies did not forget to reproach him when he became conspicuous enough to excite malevolence; and let it be remembered for his honour, that to have been once a schoolmaster is the only reproach which all the perspicacity of malice, animated by wit, has ever fixed upon his private life.

When he first engaged in the study of physic, he inquired, as he says, of Dr. Sydenham what authors he should read, and was directed by Sydenham to *Don Quixote*, "which," said he, "is a very good book; I read it still." The perverseness of mankind makes it often mischievous in men of eminence to give way to merriment; the idle and the illiterate will long shelter themselves under this foolish apophthegm.

Whether he rested satisfied with this direction or sought for better, he commenced physician, and obtained high eminence and extensive practice. He became Fellow of the College of Physicians, April 12, 1687, being one of the thirty which, by the new charter of King James, were added to the former Fellows. His residence was in Cheapside, and his friends were chiefly in the city. In the early part of Blackmore's time a citizen was a term of reproach; and his place of abode was another topic to which his adversaries had recourse in the penury of scandal.

Blackmore, therefore, was made a poet not by necessity but inclination, and wrote not for a livelihood but for fame; or, if he may tell his own motives, for a nobler purpose, to engage poetry in the cause of virtue.

I believe it is peculiar to him, that his first public work was an heroic poem. He was not known as a maker of verses till he published (in 1695) *Prince Arthur*, in ten books, written, as he relates, "by such catches and starts, and in such occasional uncertain hours as his profession afforded, and for the greatest part in coffee-houses, or in passing up and down the streets." For the latter part of this apology he was accused of writing "to the rumbling of his chariot-wheels." He had read, he says, "but little poetry throughout his whole life; and for fifteen years before had not written an hundred verses, except one copy of Latin verses in praise of a friend's book."

He thinks, and with some reason, that from such a performance perfection cannot be expected; but he finds another reason for the severity of his censurers, which he expresses in language such as Cheapside easily furnished. "I am not free of the Poets' Company, having never kissed their governor's hands, nor made the least court to the committee that sits in Covent-Garden [Will's Coffee-house]; mine is, therefore, not so much as a permission-poem, but a pure, downright interloper. Those gentlemen who carry on their poetical trade in a joint-stock would certainly do what they could to sink and ruin an unlicensed adventurer, notwithstanding I disturbed none of their factories, nor imported any goods they had ever dealt in." He had lived in the city till he had learned its note.

That *Prince Arthur* found many readers is certain; for in two years it had three editions—a very uncommon instance of favourable reception, at a time when literary curiosity was yet confined to particular classes of the nation. Such success naturally raised animosity; and Dennis attacked it [1696] by a formal criticism, more tedious and disgusting than the work which he condemns. To this censure may be opposed the approbation of Locke and the admiration of Molyneux, which are found in their printed letters. Molyneux is particularly delighted with the song of Mopas, which is therefore subjoined to this narrative.

It is remarked by Pope, that what "raises the hero often sinks the man." Of Blackmore it may be said, that as the poet sinks the man rises; the animadversions of Dennis, insolent and contemptuous as they were, raised in him no implacable resentment: he and his critic were afterwards friends; and in one of his latter works he praises Dennis as "equal to Boileau in poetry, and superior to him in critical abilities."

He seems to have been more delighted with praise than pained by censure, and, instead of slackening, quickened his career. Having in two years produced ten books of *Prince Arthur*, in two years more (1697) he sent into the world *King Arthur* in twelve. The provocation was now doubled, and the resentment of wits and critics may be supposed to have increased in proportion. He found, however, advantages more than equivalent to all their outrages; he was this year made one of the physicians-in-ordinary to King William, and advanced by him to the honour of knighthood, with a present of a gold chain and medal.

The malignity of the wits attributed his knighthood to his new poem; but King William was not very studious of poetry, and Blackmore perhaps had other merit: for he says, in his Dedication to *Alfred*, that "he had a greater part in the succession of the house of Hanover than ever he had boasted."

What Blackmore could contribute to the succession, or what he imagined himself to have contributed, cannot now be known. That he had been of considerable use I doubt not but he believed, for I hold him to have been very honest; but he might easily make a false estimate of his own importance: those whom their virtue restrains from deceiving others are often disposed by their vanity to deceive themselves. Whether he promoted the succession or not, he at least approved it, and adhered invariably to his principles and party through his whole life.

His ardour of poetry still continued; and not long after

(1700) he published a *Paraphrase on the Book of Job,* and other parts of the Scripture. This performance Dryden, who pursued him with great malignity, lived long enough to ridicule in a prologue.

The wits easily confederated against him, as Dryden, whose favour they almost all courted, was his professed adversary. He had besides given them reason for resentment, as, in his Preface to *Prince Arthur,* he had said of the dramatic writers almost all that was alleged afterwards by Collier; but Blackmore's censure was cold and general, Collier's was personal and ardent; Blackmore taught his reader to dislike what Collier incited him to abhor.

In his Preface to *King Arthur* he endeavoured to gain at least one friend, and propitiated Congreve by higher praise of his *Mourning Bride* than it has obtained from any other critic.

The same year [1700] he published a *Satire against Wit*— a proclamation of defiance which united the poets almost all against him, and which brought upon him lampoons and ridicule from every side. This he doubtless foresaw, and evidently despised; nor should his dignity of mind be without its praise, had he not paid the homage to greatness which he denied to genius, and degraded himself by conferring that authority over the national taste, which he takes from the poets, upon men of high rank and wide influence, but of less wit, and not greater virtue.

Here is again discovered the inhabitant of Cheapside, whose head cannot keep his poetry unmingled with trade. To hinder that intellectual bankruptcy which he affects to fear, he will erect a *Bank for Wit.*

In this poem he justly censured Dryden's impurities, but praised his powers, though in a subsequent edition he retained the satire and omitted the praise. What was his reason I know not; Dryden was then no longer in his way.

His head still teemed with heroic poetry, and [July 1705] he published *Eliza* in ten books. I am afraid that the world was now weary of contending about Blackmore's heroes; for I do not remember that by any author, serious or comical, I have found *Eliza* either praised or blamed. She "dropped," as it seems, "dead-born from the press." It is never mentioned, and was never seen by me till I borrowed it for the present occasion. Jacob says, "it is corrected and revised for another impression"; but the labour of revision was thrown away.

From this time he turned some of his thoughts to the celebration of living characters, and wrote [1708] a poem on the

Kit-Cat Club, and [1706] *Advice to the Poets how to Celebrate
the Duke of Marlborough*; but on occasion of another year of
success, thinking himself qualified to give more instruction,
he again wrote [1709] a poem of *Advice to a Weaver of Tapestry*.
Steele was then publishing *The Tatler*; and looking round him
for something at which he might laugh, unluckily lighted on
Sir Richard's work, and treated it with such contempt, that,
as Fenton observes, he put an end to the species of writers
that gave "Advice to Painters."

Not long after (1712) he published *Creation, a Philosophical
Poem* [in seven books], which has been, by my recommendation, inserted in the late collection. Whoever judges of this by any
other of Blackmore's performances will do it injury. The praise
given it by Addison (*Spectator*, 339) is too well known to be
transcribed; but some notice is due to the testimony of Dennis,
who calls it a "philosophical poem, which has equalled that
of Lucretius in the beauty of its versification, and infinitely
surpassed it in the solidity and strength of its reasoning."

Why an author surpasses himself it is natural to inquire.
I have heard from Mr. Draper, an eminent bookseller, an
account received by him from Ambrose Philips, "That Blackmore, as he proceeded in this poem, laid his manuscript from
time to time before a club of wits with whom he associated;
and that every man contributed, as he could, either improvement or correction; so that," said Philips, "there are perhaps
nowhere in the book thirty lines together that now stand as
they were originally written."

The relation of Philips, I suppose, was true; but when all
reasonable, all credible allowance is made for this friendly revision, the author will still retain an ample dividend of praise;
for to him must always be assigned the plan of the work,
the distribution of its parts, the choice of topics, the train of
argument, and, what is yet more, the general predominance of
philosophical judgment and poetical spirit. Correction seldom
effects more than the suppression of faults: a happy line, or a
single elegance, may perhaps be added; but of a large work
the general character must always remain; the original constitution can be very little helped by local remedies; inherent and
radical dullness will never be much invigorated by extrinsic
animation.

This poem, if he had written nothing else, would have
transmitted him to posterity among the first favourites of
the English muse; but to make verses was his transcendent

pleasure, and as he was not deterred by censure, he was not satiated with praise.

He deviated, however, sometimes into other tracks of litera-ture, and condescended to entertain his readers with plain prose. When *The Spectator* stopped, he considered the polite world as destitute of entertainment; and in concert with Mr. Hughes, who wrote every third paper, published three times a week *The Lay Monastery*, founded on the supposition that some literary men, whose characters are described, had retired to a house in the country to enjoy philosophical leisure, and resolved to instruct the public by communicating their disquisi-tions and amusements. Whether any real persons were concealed under fictitious names is not known. The hero of the club is one Mr. Johnson—such a constellation of excellence, that his character shall not be suppressed, though there is no great genius in the design, nor skill in the delineation.

"The first I shall name is Mr. Johnson, a gentleman that owes to nature his excellent faculties and an elevated genius, and to industry and application many acquired accomplishments. His taste is distinguishing, just, and delicate; his judgment clear, and his reason strong, accompanied with an imagination full of spirit, of great compass, and stored with refined ideas. He is a critic of the first rank; and what is his peculiar ornament, he is delivered from the ostentation, malevolence, and supercilious temper, that so often blemish men of that character. His remarks result from the nature and reason of things, and are formed by a judgment free and unbiassed by the authority of those who have lazily followed each other in the same beaten track of thinking, and are arrived only at the reputation of acute gram-marians and commentators—men who have been copying one another many hundred years without any improvement; or, if they have ventured farther, have only applied in a mechanical manner the rules of ancient critics to modern writings, and with great labour discovered nothing but their own want of judgment and capacity. As Mr. Johnson penetrates to the bottom of his subject, by which means his observations are solid and natural, as well as delicate, so his design is always to bring to light some-thing useful and ornamental; whence his character is the reverse to theirs, who have eminent abilities in insignificant knowledge, and a great felicity in finding out trifles. He is no less industrious to search out the merit of an author than saga-cious in discerning his errors and defects, and takes more pleasure in commending the beauties than exposing the blemishes of a laudable writing; like Horace, in a long work he can bear some deformities, and justly lay them on the imperfection of human nature, which is incapable of faultless productions. When an excellent drama appears in public, and by its intrinsic worth attracts a general applause, he is not stung with envy and spleen, nor does he express a savage nature in fastening upon the celebrated author, dwelling upon his imaginary defects, and passing over his conspicuous excellences. He treats all writers upon the same impartial foot; and is not, like the little critics, taken up entirely in finding out only the beauties of the ancient and nothing but the errors of the modern writers. Never did anyone express more kindness and good nature to young and unfinished authors: he promotes their interests, protects their reputation, extenuates their faults, and sets off their virtues, and by his candour guards them from the severity of his judgment. He is not like those dry critics who are morose because they cannot write themselves, but is himself master of a good vein in poetry; and though he does not often employ it, yet he has sometimes entertained his friends with his unpublished performances."

The rest of the "Lay Monks" seem to be but feeble mortals in comparison with the gigantic Johnson, who yet, with all his abilities and the help of the fraternity, could drive the publication but to forty papers, which were afterwards collected into a volume, and called in the title *A Sequel to the Spectators*.

Some years afterwards (1716 and 1717) he published two volumes of Essays in prose, which can be commended only as they are written for the highest and noblest purpose, the promotion of religion. Blackmore's prose is not the prose of a poet, for it is languid, sluggish, and lifeless; his diction is neither daring nor exact, his flow neither rapid nor easy, and his periods neither smooth nor strong. His account of Wit will show with how little clearness he is content to think, and how little his thoughts are recommended by his language:

"As to its efficient cause, Wit owes its production to an extraordinary and peculiar temperament in the constitution of the possessors of it, in which is found a concurrence of regular and exalted ferments, and an affluence of animal spirits, refined and rectified to a great degree of purity; whence, being endowed with vivacity, brightness, and celerity, as well in their reflections as direct motions, they become proper instruments for the sprightly operations of the mind; by which means the imagination can with great facility range the wide field of nature, contemplate an infinite variety of objects, and, by observing the similitude and disagreement of their several qualities, single out and abstract, and then suit and unite, those ideas which will best serve its purpose. Hence beautiful allusions, surprising metaphors, and admirable sentiments, are always ready at hand; and while the fancy is full of images collected from innumerable objects, and their different qualities, relations, and habitudes, it can at pleasure dress a common notion in a strange but becoming garb, by which, as before observed, the same thought will appear a new one, to the great delight and wonder of the hearer. What we call *genius* results from this particular happy complexion in the first formation of the person that enjoys it, and is Nature's gift, but diversified by various specific characters and limitations, as its active fire is blended and allayed by different proportions of phlegm, or reduced and regulated by the contrast of opposite ferments. Therefore, as there happens in the composition of facetious genius a greater or less, though still an inferior, degree of judgment and prudence, one man of wit will be varied and distinguished from another."

In these essays he took little care to propitiate the wits, for he scorns to avert their malice at the expense of virtue or of truth.

"Several, in their books, have many sarcastical and spiteful strokes at religion in general, while others make themselves pleasant with the principles of the Christian. Of the last kind, this age has seen a most audacious example, in the book intitled *A Tale of a Tub*. Had his writing been published in a pagan or Popish nation, who are justly impatient of all indignity offered to the established religion of their country, no doubt but the author would have received the punishment he deserved. But the fate of this impious buffoon is very different; for in a Protestant kingdom, zealous of their civil and religious immunities, he has not only escaped affronts and the effects of public resentment, but has been caressed and patronised by persons of great figure, and of all denominations. Violent party-men, who differed in all things besides, agreed in their turn to show particular respect and friendship to this insolent derider of the worship of his country, till at last the reputed writer is not only gone off with impunity, but triumphs in his dignity and preferment. I do not know that any inquiry or search was ever made after this writing, or that any reward was ever offered for the discovery of the author, or that the infamous book was ever condemned to be burnt in public; whether this proceeds from the excessive esteem and love that men in power during the late reign [Queen Anne's] had for wit, or their defect of zeal and concern for the Christian religion, will be determined best by those who are best acquainted with their character."

In another place, he speaks with becoming abhorrence of a *godless author* who has burlesqued a psalm. This author was supposed to be Pope, who published a reward for anyone that would produce the coiner of the accusation, but never denied it; and was afterwards the perpetual and incessant enemy of Blackmore.

One of his essays is upon the Spleen, which is treated by him so much to his own satisfaction, that he has published the same thoughts in the same words—first in *The Lay Monastery*, then in the Essay, and then in the Preface to *A Medical Treatise on the Spleen*. One passage which I have found already twice, I will here exhibit, because I think it better imagined, and better expressed, than could be expected from the common tenor of his prose:

"As the several combinations of splenetic madness and folly produce an infinite variety of irregular understandings, so the amicable accommodation and alliance between several virtues and vices produce an equal diversity in the dispositions and manners of mankind; whence it comes to pass, that as many monstrous and absurd productions are found in the moral as in the intellectual world. How surprising is it to observe among the least culpable men some whose minds are attracted by heaven and earth with a seeming equal force—some who are proud of humility; others who are censorious and uncharitable, yet self-denying and devout; some who join contempt of the world with sordid avarice; and others who preserve a great degree of piety with ill-nature and ungoverned passions; nor are instances of this inconsistent mixture less frequent among bad men, where we often, with admiration, see persons at once generous and unjust, impious lovers of their country, and flagitious heroes, good-natured sharpers, immoral men of honour, and libertines who will sooner die than change their religion; and though it is true that repugnant coalitions of so high a degree are found but in a part of mankind, yet none of the whole mass, either good or bad, are entirely exempted from some absurd mixture."

He about this time (Aug. 22, 1716) became one of the Elects of the College of Physicians, and was soon after (Oct. 1) chosen

Censor. He seems to have arrived late, whatever was the reason, at his medical honours.

Having succeeded so well in his book on *Creation*, by which he established the great principle of all religion, he thought his undertaking imperfect unless he likewise forced the truth of revelation; and for that purpose added [1722] another poem on *Redemption*. He had likewise written, before his *Creation*, three books on the *Nature of Man*.

The lovers of musical devotion have always wished for a more happy metrical version than they have yet obtained of the book of Psalms: this wish the piety of Blackmore led him to gratify; and he produced (1721) *A New Version of the Psalms of David, fitted to the Tunes used in Churches*; which being recommended by the archbishops and many bishops, obtained a licence for its admission into public worship; but no admission has it yet obtained, nor has it any right to come where Brady and Tate have got possession. Blackmore's name must be added to those of many others who, by the same attempt, have obtained only the praise of meaning well.

He was not yet deterred from heroic poetry; there was another monarch of this island—for he did not fetch his heroes from foreign countries—whom he considered as worthy of the epic muse, and he dignified Alfred (1723) with twelve books. But the opinion of the nation was now settled; a hero introduced by Blackmore was not likely to find either respect or kindness; *Alfred* took his place by *Eliza* in silence and darkness: benevolence was ashamed to favour, and malice was weary of insulting. Of his four epic poems, the first had such reputation and popularity as enraged the critics; the second was at least known enough to be ridiculed; the two last had neither friends nor enemies.

Contempt is a kind of gangrene, which, if it seizes one part of a character, corrupts all the rest by degrees. Blackmore, being despised as a poet, was in time neglected as a physician; his practice, which was once invidiously great, forsook him in the latter part of his life; but being by nature, or by principle, averse from idleness, he employed his unwelcome leisure in writing books on physic, and teaching others to cure those whom he could himself cure no longer. I know not whether I can enumerate all the treatises by which he has endeavoured to diffuse the art of healing; for there is scarcely any distemper, of dreadful name, which he has not taught the reader how to oppose. He has written on the smallpox, with a vehement invective against inoculation; on consumptions, the spleen, the gout, the rheumatism, the king's evil, the dropsy, the jaundice, the stone, the diabetes, and the plague.

Of those books, if I had read them, it could not be expected that I should be able to give a critical account. I have been told that there is something in them of vexation and discontent, discovered by a perpetual attempt to degrade physic from its sublimity, and to represent it as attainable without much previous or concomitant learning. By the transient glances which I have thrown upon them, I have observed an affected contempt of the ancients, and a supercilious derision of transmitted knowledge. Of this indecent arrogance the following quotation from his Preface to the *Treatise on the Smallpox* will afford a specimen; in which, when the reader finds, what I fear is true, that when he was censuring Hippocrates he did not know the difference between *aphorism* and *apophthegm*, he will not pay much regard to his determinations concerning ancient learning.

"As for this book of aphorisms, it is like my Lord Bacon's of the same title, a book of jests, or a grave collection of trite and trifling observations of which, though many are true and certain, yet they signify nothing, and may afford diversion, but no instruction, most of them being much inferior to the sayings of the wise men of Greece, which yet are so low and mean that we are entertained every day with more valuable sentiments at the table-conversation of ingenious and learned men."

I am unwilling, however, to leave him in total disgrace, and will therefore quote from another preface a passage less reprehensible.

"Some gentlemen have been disingenuous and unjust to me, by wresting and forcing my meaning in the preface to another book, as if I condemned and exposed all learning, though they knew I declared that I greatly honoured and esteemed all men of superior literature and erudition, and that I only undervalued false or superficial learning, that signifies nothing for the service of mankind; and that as to physic I expressly affirmed that learning must be joined with native genius to make a physician of the first rank; but if those talents are separated, I asserted, and do still insist, that a man of native sagacity and diligence will prove a more able and useful practiser than a heavy notional scholar, encumbered with a heap of confused ideas."

He was not only a poet and a physician, but produced [1723] likewise a work of a different kind, *A True and Impartial History of the Conspiracy against King William of Glorious*

Memory, in the Year 1695. This I have never seen, but suppose it at least compiled with integrity. He engaged likewise in theological controversy, and wrote two books against the Arians —*Just Prejudices against the Arian Hypothesis,* and *Modern Arians Unmasked.* Another of his works is *Natural Theology, or Moral Duties considered apart from Positive; with some Observations on the Desirableness and Necessity of a Supernatural Revelation.* This was the last book that he published. He left behind him *The accomplished Preacher, or an Essay upon Divine Eloquence;* which was printed after his death by Mr. White of Nayland, in Essex, the minister who attended his death-bed, and testified the fervent piety of his last hours. He died on the 8th of October, 1729.

Blackmore, by the unremitted enmity of the wits, whom he provoked more by his virtue than his dullness, has been exposed to worse treatment than he deserved; his name was so long used to point every epigram upon dull writers, that it became at last a by-word of contempt: but it deserves observation, that malignity takes hold only of his writings, and that his life passed without reproach, even when his boldness of reprehension naturally turned upon him many eyes desirous to espy faults, which many tongues would have made haste to publish. But those who could not blame could at least forbear to praise, and therefore of his private life and domestic character there are no memorials.

As an author he may justly claim the honours of magnanimity. The incessant attacks of his enemies, whether serious or merry, are never discovered to have disturbed his quiet, or to have lessened his confidence in himself; they neither awed him to silence nor to caution; they neither provoked him to petulance, nor depressed him to complaint. While the distributors of literary fame were endeavouring to depreciate and degrade him, he either despised or defied them, wrote on as he had written before, and never turned aside to quiet them by civility, or repress them by confutation.

He depended with great security on his own powers, and perhaps was for that reason less diligent in perusing books. His literature was, I think, but small. What he knew of antiquity, I suspect him to have gathered from modern compilers: but, though he could not boast of much critical knowledge, his mind was stored with general principles, and he left minute researches to those whom he considered as little minds.

With this disposition he wrote most of his poems. Having

formed a magnificent design, he was careless of particular and subordinate elegances; he studied no niceties of versification; he waited for no felicities of fancy; but caught his first thoughts in his first words in which they were presented: nor does it appear that he saw beyond his own performances, or had ever elevated his ideas to that ideal perfection which every genius born to excel is condemned always to pursue, and never overtake. In the first suggestions of his imagination he acquiesced; he thought them good, and did not seek for better. His works may be read a long time without the occurrence of a single line that stands prominent from the rest.

The poem on *Creation* has, however, the appearance of more circumspection; it wants neither harmony of numbers, accuracy of thought, nor elegance of diction: it has either been written with great care, or, what cannot be imagined of so long a work, with such felicity as made care less necessary.

Its two constituent parts are ratiocination and description. To reason in verse is allowed to be difficult; but Blackmore not only reasons in verse, but very often reasons poetically, and finds the art of uniting ornament with strength, and ease with closeness. This is a skill which Pope might have condescended to learn from him, when he needed it so much in his *Moral Essays*.

In his descriptions both of life and nature, the poet and the philosopher happily co-operate; truth is recommended by elegance, and elegance sustained by truth.

In the structure and order of the poem, not only the greater parts are properly consecutive, but the didactic and illustrative paragraphs are so happily mingled, that labour is relieved by pleasure, and the attention is led on through a long succession of varied excellence to the original position, the fundamental principle of wisdom and of virtue.

As the heroic poems of Blackmore are now little read, it is thought proper to insert, as a specimen from *Prince Arthur*, the song of Mopas, mentioned by Molyneux.

> But that which Arthur with most pleasure heard
> Were noble strains, by Mopas sung the bard,
> Who to his harp in lofty verse began,
> And through the secret maze of Nature ran.
> He the great Spirit sung, that all things fill'd,
> That the tumultuous waves of Chaos still'd;
> Whose nod dispos'd the jarring seeds to peace,
> And made the wars of hostile Atoms cease.
> All Beings, we in fruitful Nature find,

Proceeded from the great Eternal Mind;
Streams of his unexhausted spring of power,
And, cherish'd with his influence, endure.
He spread the pure cerulean fields on high,
And arch'd the chambers of the vaulted sky,
Which he, to suit their glory with their height,
Adorn'd with globes, that reel, as drunk with light.
His hand directed all the tuneful spheres,
He turn'd their orbs, and polish'd all the stars.
He fill'd the Sun's vast lamp with golden light,
And bid the silver Moon adorn the night.
He spread the airy Ocean without shores,
Where birds are wafted with their feather'd oars.
Then sung the bard how the light vapours rise
From the warm earth, and cloud the smiling skies.
He sung how some, chill'd in their airy flight,
Fall scatter'd down in pearly dew by night.
How some, rais'd higher, sit in secret steams
On the reflected points of bounding beams;
Till, chill'd with cold, they shade th' etherial plain,
Then on the thirsty earth descend in rain.
How some, whose parts a slight contexture show,
Sink hovering through the air, in fleecy snow.
How part is spun in silken threads, and clings
Entangled in the grass in gluey strings.
How others stamped to stones, with rushing sound
Fall from their crystal quarries to the ground.
How some are laid in trains, that kindled fly
In harmless fires by night, about the sky.
How some in winds blow with impetuous force,
And carry ruin where they bend their course:
While some conspire to form a gentle breeze,
To fan the air, and play among the trees.
How some, enrag'd, grow turbulent and loud,
Pent in the bowels of a frowning cloud;
That cracks, as if the axis of the world
Was broke, and heaven's bright towers were downwards hurl'd
He sung how earth's wide ball, at Jove's command,
Did in the midst on airy columns stand;
And how the soul of plants, in prison held,
And bound with sluggish fetters, lies conceal'd,
Till with the spring's warm beams, almost releas'd
From the dull weight, with which it lay opprest,
Its vigour spreads, and makes the teeming earth
Heave up, and labour with the sprouting birth:
The active spirit freedom seeks in vain,
It only works and twists a stronger chain.
Urging its prison's sides to break a way,
It makes that wider, where 'tis forc'd to stay;
Till, having form'd its living house, it rears
Its head, and in a tender plant appears.
Hence springs the oak, the beauty of the grove,
Whose stately trunk fierce storms can scarcely move.
Hence grows the cedar, hence the swelling vine
Does round the elm its purple clusters twine.
Hence painted flowers the smiling gardens bless,
Both with their fragrant scent and gaudy dress.
Hence the white lily in full beauty grows,
Hence the blue violet, and blushing rose.

He sung how sun-beams brood upon the earth,
And in the glebe hatch such a numerous birth;
Which way the genial warmth in Summer storms
Turns putrid vapours to a bed of worms;
How rain, transform'd by this prolific power,
Falls from the clouds an animated shower.
He sung the embryo's growth within the womb,
And how the parts their various shapes assume.
With what rare art the wondrous structure's wrought,
From one crude mass to such perfection brought;
That no part useless, none misplac'd we see,
None are forgot, and more would monstrous be.

Prince Arthur, book iv.

ELIJAH FENTON

1683–1730

Born at Shelton, in Staffordshire—Educated at Cambridge, but leaves without taking a Degree—Becomes a Nonjuror—Secretary to the Earl of Orrery and Tutor to his Son—Acquires the Friendship of Southerne and Pope—Publishes his Poems—Assists Pope in the Odyssey—His Benevolence of Heart and Indolent Habits—Death and Burial at Easthampstead, Berks—Works and Character.

THE brevity with which I am to write the account of Elijah Fenton is not the effect of indifference or negligence. I have sought intelligence among his relations in his native country, but have not obtained it.

He was born near Newcastle in Staffordshire, of an ancient family, whose estate was very considerable; but he was the youngest of eleven children, and being therefore necessarily destined to some lucrative employment, was sent first to school and afterwards to Cambridge, but, with many other wise and other virtuous men who at that time of discord and debate consulted conscience, whether well or ill informed, more than interest, he doubted the legality of the government, and, refusing to qualify himself for public employment by the oaths required, left the university without a degree; but I never heard that the enthusiasm of opposition impelled him to separation from the Church.

By this perverseness of integrity he was driven out a commoner of Nature, excluded from the regular modes of profit and prosperity, and reduced to pick up a livelihood uncertain and fortuitous; but it must be remembered that he kept his name unsullied, and never suffered himself to be reduced, like too many of the same sect, to mean arts and dishonourable shifts. Whoever mentioned Fenton, mentioned him with honour.

The life that passes in penury must necessarily pass in obscurity. It is impossible to trace Fenton from year to year, or to discover what means he used for his support. He was a while secretary to Charles Earl of Orrery in Flanders, and tutor to his young son, who afterwards mentioned him with great esteem and tenderness. He was at one time assistant in the school of

Mr. Bonwicke, in Surrey; and at another kept a school for himself at Sevenoaks, in Kent, which he brought into reputation, but was persuaded to leave it (1710) by Mr. St. John, with promises of a more honourable employment.

His opinions, as he was a Nonjuror, seem not to have been remarkably rigid. He wrote with great zeal and affection the praises of Queen Anne, and very willingly and liberally extolled the Duke of Marlborough, when he was (1707) at the height of his glory.

He expressed still more attention to Marlborough and his family by an elegiac Pastoral on the Marquis of Blandford, which could be prompted only by respect or kindness, for neither the Duke nor Duchess desired the praise or liked the cost of patronage.

The elegance of his poetry entitled him to the company of the wits of his time, and the amiableness of his manners made him loved wherever he was known. Of his friendship to Southerne and Pope there are lasting monuments.

He published in 1717 a collection of Poems.

By Pope he was once placed in a station that might have been of great advantage. Craggs, when he was advanced to be Secretary of State (about 1720), feeling his own want of literature, desired Pope to procure him an instructor, by whose help he might supply the deficiencies of his education. Pope recommended Fenton, in whom Craggs found all that he was seeking. There was now a prospect of ease and plenty, for Fenton had merit, and Craggs had generosity: but the small-pox suddenly put an end to the pleasing expectation.

When Pope, after the great success of his Iliad, undertook the Odyssey, being, as it seems, weary of translating, he determined to engage auxiliaries. Twelve books he took to himself, and twelve he distributed between Broome and Fenton: the books allotted to Fenton were the first, the fourth, the nineteenth, and the twentieth. It is observable that he did not take the eleventh, which he had before translated into blank verse; neither did Pope claim it, but committed it to Broome. How the two associates performed their parts is well known to the readers of poetry, who have never been able to distinguish their books from those of Pope.

In 1723 was performed his tragedy of *Mariamne*; to which Southerne, at whose house it was written, is said to have contributed such hints as his theatrical experience supplied. When it was shown to Cibber it was rejected by him, with the additional insolence of advising Fenton to engage himself in some employment of honest labour by which he might obtain that support which he could never hope from his poetry. The play was acted at the other theatre, and the brutal petulance of Cibber was confuted, though perhaps not shamed, by general applause. Fenton's profits are said to have amounted to near a thousand pounds, with which he discharged a debt contracted by his attendance at court.

Fenton seems to have had some peculiar system of versification. *Mariamne* is written in lines of ten syllables, with few of those redundant terminations which the drama not only admits but requires, as more nearly approaching to real dialogue. The tenor of his verse is so uniform that it cannot be thought casual; and yet upon what principle he so constructed it is difficult to discover.

The mention of his play brings to my mind a very trifling occurrence. Fenton was one day in the company of Broome, his associate, and Ford, a clergyman, at that time too well known, whose abilities, instead of furnishing convivial merriment to the voluptuous and dissolute, might have enabled him to excel among the virtuous and the wise. They determined all to see the *Merry Wives of Windsor*, which was acted that night; and Fenton, as a dramatic poet, took them to the stage-door, where the doorkeeper, inquiring who they were, was told that they were three very necessary men, Ford, Broome, and Fenton. The name in the play, which Pope restored to *Brook*, was then *Broome*.

It was perhaps after this play that he undertook to revise the punctuation of Milton's Poems, which, as the author neither wrote the original copy nor corrected the press, was supposed capable of amendment. To this edition he prefixed a short and elegant account of Milton's Life, written at once with tenderness and integrity.

He published likewise (1729) a very splendid edition of Waller, with notes often useful, often entertaining, but too much extended by long quotations from Clarendon. Illustrations drawn from a book so easily consulted should be made by reference rather than transcription.

The latter part of his life was calm and pleasant. The relict of Sir William Trumbull invited him, by Pope's recommendation, to educate her son, whom he first instructed at home and then attended to Cambridge. The lady afterwards detained him with her as the auditor of her accounts. He often wandered to London and amused himself with the conversation of his friends.

He died in 1730, at Easthampstead, in Berkshire, the seat of Lady Trumbull; and Pope, who had been always his friend, honoured him with an epitaph, of which he borrowed the two first lines from Crashaw.

Fenton was tall and bulky, inclined to corpulence, which he did not lessen by much exercise; for he was very sluggish and sedentary, rose late, and when he had risen sat down to his books or papers. A woman that once waited on him in a lodging told him, as she said, that he would "lie a-bed and be fed with a spoon." This, however, was not the worst that might have been prognosticated; for Pope says, in his Letters, that "he died of indolence"; but his immediate distemper was the gout.

Of his morals and his conversation the account is uniform: he was never named but with praise and fondness, as a man in the highest degree amiable and excellent. Such was the character given him by the Earl of Orrery, his pupil; such is the testimony of Pope; and such were the suffrages of all who could boast of his acquaintance.

By a former writer of his Life a story is told which ought not to be forgotten. He used, in the latter part of his time, to pay his relations in the country a yearly visit. At an entertainment made for the family by his elder brother he observed that one of his sisters, who had married unfortunately, was absent; and found, upon inquiry, that distress had made her thought unworthy of invitation. As she was at no great distance, he refused to sit at the table till she was called; and, when she had taken her place, was careful to show her particular attention.

His collection of poems is now to be considered. The *Ode to the Sun* is written upon a common plan, without uncommon sentiments; but its greatest fault is its length. No poem should be long, of which the purpose is only to strike the fancy, without enlightening the understanding by precept, ratiocination, or narrative. A blaze first pleases and then tires the sight.

Of *Florelio* it is sufficient to say that it is an occasional pastoral, which implies something neither natural nor artificial, neither comic nor serious.

The next ode is irregular, and therefore defective. As the sentiments are pious, they cannot easily be new; for what can be added to topics on which successive ages have been employed?

Of the *Paraphrase on Isaiah* nothing very favourable can be said. Sublime and solemn prose gains little by a change to blank verse; and the paraphrast has deserted his original by admitting images not Asiatic, at least not Judaical:

—— Returning Peace
Dove-eyed, and rob'd in white.

Of his petty poems some are very trifling, without anything to be praised either in the thought or expression. He is unlucky in his competition; he tells the same idle tale with Congreve, and does not tell it so well. He translates from Ovid the same epistle as Pope; but, I am afraid, not with equal happiness.

To examine his performances one by one would be tedious. His translation from Homer into blank verse will find few readers while another can be had in rhyme. The piece addressed to Lambarde is no disagreeable specimen of epistolary poetry; and his ode to the Lord Gower was pronounced by Pope the next ode in the English language to Dryden's *Cecilia*. Fenton may be justly styled an excellent versifier and a good poet.

Whatever I have said of Fenton is confirmed by Pope in a letter by which he communicated to Broome an account of his death.

To the Revd. Mr. Broome

At Pulham, near Harlestone

Dᴿ Sɪʀ.   29 *August*, 1730.

I intended to write to you on this melancholy subject, the death of Mr. Fenton, before yʳˢ came; but stay'd to have inform'd myself & you of yᵉ circumstances of it. All I hear is, that he felt a Gradual Decay, tho so early in Life, & was declining for 5 or 6 months. It was not, as I apprehended, the Gout in his Stomach, but I believe rather a Complication first of Gross Humors, as he was naturally corpulent, not discharging themselves, as he used no sort of Exercise. No man better bore yᵉ approaches of his Dissolution (as I am told) or with less ostentation yielded up his Being. The great Modesty wᶜʰ you know was natural to him, and yᵉ great Contempt he had for all Sorts of Vanity & Parade, never appeared more than in his last moments: He had a conscious Satisfaction (no doubt) in acting right, in feeling himself honest, true, & un-pretending to more than was his own. So he dyed, as he lived, with that secret, yet sufficient, Contentment.

As to any Papers left behind him, I dare say they can be but few; for this reason, He never wrote out of Vanity, or thought much of the Applause of Men. I know an Instance where he did his utmost to conceal his own merit that way; and if we join to this his natural Love of Ease, I fancy we must expect little of this sort: at least I hear of none except some few further remarks on Waller (wᶜʰ his cautious integrity made him leave an order to be given to Mr.

Tonson) and perhaps, tho tis many years since I saw it, a Translation of yᵉ first Book of Oppian. He had begun a Tragedy of Dion, but made small progress in it.

As to his other Affairs, he dyed poor, but honest, leaving no Debts, or Legacies; except of a few pᵈˢ to Mr. Trumbull and my Lady, in token of respect, Gratefulness, & mutual Esteem.

I shall with pleasure take upon me to draw this amiable, quiet, deserving, unpretending Christian and Philosophical character, in His Epitaph. There Truth may be spoken in a few words: as for Flourish, & Oratory, & Poetry, I leave them to younger and more lively Writers, such as love writing for writing sake, & wᵈ rather show their own Fine Parts, yⁿ Report the valuable ones of any other man. So the Elegy I renounce.

I condole with you from my heart, on the loss of so worthy a man, and a Friend to us both. Now he is gone, I must tell you he has done you many a good office, & set your character in the fairest light, to some who either mistook you, or knew you not. I doubt not he has done the same for me.

Adieu: Let us love his Memory, and profit by his example. I am very sincerely

Dʀ Sɪʀ

Your affectionate

& real Servant

A. Pope.

JOHN GAY

1688–1732

Born at Barnstaple, in Devonshire—Apprenticed to a Silk-mercer—
Made Secretary to the Duchess of Monmouth—Publishes *The Shepherd's
Week*—Acquires the Friendship of Pope—His Court Disappointments—
His intimacy with Mrs. Howard and the Duchess of Queensberry—Writes
The Beggar's Opera—Its great success—His next Play prohibited—His
Fables—Death, Burial, and Monument in Westminster Abbey—Works
and Character.

JOHN GAY, descended from an old family that had been long
in possession of the manor of Goldworthy in Devonshire, was
born in 1688, at or near Barnstaple, where he was educated
by Mr. Luck, who taught the school of that town with good
reputation, and, a little before he retired from it, published a
volume of Latin and English verses. Under such a master he
was likely to form a taste for poetry. Being born without
prospect of hereditary riches, he was sent to London in his
youth, and placed apprentice with a silk-mercer.

How long he continued behind the counter, or with what
degree of softness and dexterity he received and accommodated
the ladies, as he probably took no delight in telling it, is not
known. The report is, that he was soon weary of either the
restraint or servility of his occupation, and easily persuaded
his master to discharge him.

The Duchess of Monmouth, remarkable for inflexible perseverance in her demand to be treated as a princess, in 1712
took Gay into her service as secretary: by quitting a shop for
such service, he might gain leisure, but he certainly advanced
little in the boast of independence. Of his leisure he made
so good use, that he published next year a poem on *Rural
Sports*, and inscribed it to Mr. Pope, who was then rising fast
into reputation. Pope was pleased with the honour; and when
he became acquainted with Gay, found such attractions in his
manners and conversation, that he seems to have received
him into his inmost confidence; and a friendship was formed

between them which lasted to their separation by death, without any known abatement on either part. Gay was the general favourite of the whole association of wits; but they regarded him as a play-fellow rather than a partner, and treated him with more fondness than respect.

Next year (1714) he published *The Shepherd's Week*, six English Pastorals, in which the images are drawn from real life, such as it appears among the rustics in parts of England remote from London. Steele, in some papers of *The Guardian*, had praised Ambrose Philips as the pastoral writer that yielded only to Theocritus, Virgil, and Spenser. Pope, who had also published Pastorals, not pleased to be overlooked, drew up a comparison of his own compositions with those of Philips, in which he covertly gave himself the preference, while he seemed to disown it. Not content with this, he is supposed to have incited Gay to write *The Shepherd's Week*, to show, that if it be necessary to copy nature with minuteness, rural life must be exhibited such as grossness and ignorance have made it. So far the plan was reasonable; but the Pastorals are introduced by a "Proeme," written with such imitation as they could attain of obsolete language, and by consequence in a style that was never spoken nor written in any language or in any place.

But the effect of reality and truth became conspicuous, even when the intention was to show them grovelling and degraded. These Pastorals became popular, and were read with delight as just representations of rural manners and occupations, by those who had no interest in the rivalry of the poets, nor knowledge of the critical dispute.

In 1713 he brought a comedy, called *The Wife of Bath*, upon the stage, but it received no applause: he printed it, however; and seventeen years after, having altered it, and, as he thought, adapted it more to the public taste, he offered it again to the town; but, though he was flushed with the success of *The Beggar's Opera*, had the mortification to see it again rejected.

In the last year of Queen Anne's life (1714) Gay was made secretary to the Earl of Clarendon, ambassador to the court of Hanover. This was a station that naturally gave him hopes of kindness from every party; but the Queen's death put an end to her favours, and he had dedicated his *Shepherd's Week* to Bolingbroke, which Swift considered as the crime that obstructed all kindness from the house of Hanover.

He did not, however, omit to improve the right which his

office had given him to the notice of the royal family. On the arrival of the Princess of Wales [1714-15], he wrote a poem, and obtained so much favour, that both the Prince and Princess went to see his *What d'ye call it*, a kind of mock-tragedy, in which the images were comic, and the action grave; so that, as Pope relates, Mr. Cromwell, who could not hear what was said, was at a loss how to reconcile the laughter of the audience with the solemnity of the scene.

Of this performance the value certainly is but little; but it was one of the lucky trifles that give pleasure by novelty, and was so much favoured by the audience, that envy appeared against it in the form of criticism; and Griffin, a player, in conjunction with Mr. Theobald, a man afterwards more remarkable, produced [1715] a pamphlet called *The Key to the What d'ye call it*; which, says Gay, "calls me a blockhead, and Mr. Pope a knave."

But Fortune has always been inconstant. Not long afterwards (1717) he endeavoured to entertain the town with *Three Hours after Marriage*; a comedy written, as there is sufficient reason for believing, by the joint assistance of Pope and Arbuthnot. One purpose of it was to bring into contempt Dr. Woodward the Fossilist, a man not really or justly contemptible. It had the fate which such outrages deserve: the scene in which Woodward was directly and apparently ridiculed, by the introduction of a mummy and a crocodile, disgusted the audience, and the performance was driven off the stage with general condemnation.

Gay is represented as a man easily incited to hope, and deeply depressed when his hopes were disappointed. This is not the character of a hero; but it may naturally imply something more generally welcome, a soft and civil companion. Whoever is apt to hope good from others is diligent to please them; but he that believes his powers strong enough to force their own way, commonly tries only to please himself.

He had been simple enough to imagine that those who laughed at the *What d'ye call it* would raise the fortune of its author; and, finding nothing done, sunk into dejection. His friends endeavoured to divert him. The Earl of Burlington [the architect] sent him (1716) into Devonshire; the year after, Mr. Pulteney [afterwards Earl of Bath] took him to Aix; and in the following year Lord Harcourt invited him to his seat [in Oxfordshire], where, during his visit, two rural lovers were killed with lightning, as is particularly told in Pope's Letters.

Being now generally known, he published (1720) his Poems

by subscription with such success, that he raised a thousand pounds; and called his friends to a consultation, what use might be best made of it. Lewis, the steward of Lord Oxford, advised him to intrust it to the funds, and live upon the interest; Arbuthnot bade him intrust it to Providence, and live upon the principal; Pope directed him, and was seconded by Swift, to purchase an annuity.

Gay in that disastrous year had a present from young Craggs of some South Sea stock, and once supposed himself to be master of 20,000*l*. His friends persuaded him to sell his share; but he dreamed of dignity and splendour, and could not bear to obstruct his own fortune. He was then importuned to sell as much as would purchase an hundred a year for life, "which," says Fenton, "will make you sure of a clean shirt and a shoulder of mutton every day." This counsel was rejected: the profit and principal were lost, and Gay sunk under the calamity so low that his life became in danger.

By the care of his friends, among whom Pope appears to have shown particular tenderness, his health was restored; and, returning to his studies, he wrote a tragedy called *The Captives*, which he was invited to read before the Princess of Wales. When the hour came, he saw the Princess and her ladies all in expectation, and advancing with reverence, too great for any other attention, stumbled at a stool, and falling forwards threw down a weighty Japan screen. The Princess started, the ladies screamed, and poor Gay, after all the disturbance, was still to read his play.

The fate of *The Captives*, which was acted at Drury-lane in 1723-4, I know not; but he now thought himself in favour, and undertook (1726) to write a volume of Fables for the improvement of the young Duke of Cumberland. For this he is said to have been promised a reward, which he had doubtless magnified with all the wild expectations of indigence and vanity.

Next year [1727] the Prince and Princess became King and Queen, and Gay was to be great and happy; but on the settlement of the household he found himself appointed gentleman usher to the Princess Louisa. By this offer he thought himself insulted, and sent a message to the Queen, that he was too old for the place. There seem to have been many machinations employed afterwards in his favour; and diligent court was paid to Mrs. Howard, afterwards Countess of Suffolk, who was much beloved by the King and Queen, to engage her interest for his promotion; but solicitations, verses, and flatteries were thrown away; the lady heard them, and did nothing.

All the pain which he suffered from neglect, or, as he perhaps termed it, the ingratitude of the Court, may be supposed to have been driven away by the unexampled success of the *Beggar's Opera*. This play, written in ridicule of the musical Italian Drama, was first offered to Cibber and his brethren at Drury-lane, and rejected; it being then carried to Rich, had the effect, as was ludicrously said, of *making* Gay *rich*, and Rich *gay*.

Of this lucky piece, as the reader cannot but wish to know the original and progress, I have inserted the relation which Spence has given in Pope's words:

"Dr. Swift had been observing once to Mr. Gay, what an odd pretty sort of a thing a Newgate Pastoral might make. Gay was inclined to try at such a thing for some time; but afterwards thought it would be better to write a comedy on the same plan. This was what gave rise to the *Beggar's Opera*. He began on it; and when first he mentioned it to Swift, the Doctor did not much like the project. As he carried it on, he showed what he wrote to both of us, and we now and then gave a correction, or a word or two of advice; but it was wholly of his own writing. When it was done, neither of us thought it would succeed. We showed it to Congreve; who, after reading it over, said, 'It would either take greatly, or be damned confoundedly.' We were all, at the first night of it, in great uncertainty of the event; till we were very much encouraged by overhearing the Duke of Argyle, who sat in the next box to us, say, 'It will do—it must do! I see it in the eyes of them.' This was a good while before the first act was over, and so gave us ease soon; for that Duke (besides his own good taste) has a more particular knack than anyone now living in discovering the taste of the public. He was quite right in this, as usual; the good nature of the audience appeared stronger and stronger every act, and ended in a clamour of applause."

Its reception is thus recorded in the notes to the *Dunciad*:

"The vast success of it was unprecedented and almost incredible. . . . It was acted in London sixty-three days uninterrupted, and renewed the next season with equal applauses. It spread into all the great towns of England; was played in many places to the thirtieth and fortieth time; at Bath and Bristol fifty, etc. It made its progress into Wales, Scotland, and Ireland, where it was performed twenty-four days together.

It was at last acted in Minorca. The fame of it was not confined to the author only; the ladies carried about with them
the favourite songs of it in fans, and houses were furnished with
it in screens. The person who acted Polly, till then obscure,
became all at once the favourite of the town; her pictures
were engraved, and sold in great numbers; her Life written,
books of letters and verses to her published, and pamphlets
made even of her sayings and jests. Furthermore, it drove
out of England (for that season) the Italian Opera, which
had carried all before it for ten years."

Of this performance, when it was printed, the reception
was different according to the different opinion of its readers.
Swift commended it for the excellence of its morality, as a
piece that "placed vices of all kinds in the strongest and
most odious light"; but others, and among them Dr. Herring,
afterwards Archbishop of Canterbury, censured it as giving
encouragement not only to vice but to crimes, by making a
highwayman the hero, and dismissing him at last unpunished.
It has been even said, that, after the exhibition of the *Beggar's
Opera*, the gangs of robbers were evidently multiplied.

Both these decisions are surely exaggerated. The play, like
many others, was plainly written only to divert, without any
moral purpose, and is therefore not likely to do good; nor can
it be conceived, without more speculation than life requires or
admits, to be productive of much evil. Highwaymen and house-
breakers seldom frequent the playhouse, or mingle in any
elegant diversion; nor is it possible for anyone to imagine that
he may rob with safety, because he sees Macheath reprieved
upon the stage.

This objection, however, or some other rather political than
moral, obtained such prevalence, that when Gay produced a
second part under the name of *Polly*, it was prohibited by
the Lord Chamberlain; and he was forced to recompense his
repulse by a subscription, which is said to have been so liberally
bestowed, that what he called oppression ended in profit. The
publication was so much favoured, that though the first part
gained him 400*l.*, near thrice as much was the profit of
the second.

He received yet another recompense for this supposed hardship, in the affectionate attention of the Duke and Duchess of
Queensberry, into whose house he was taken, and with whom
he passed the remaining part of his life. The Duke, considering
his want of economy, undertook the management of his money,

and gave it to him as he wanted it. But it is supposed that the discountenance of the Court sunk deep into his heart, and gave him more discontent than the applauses or tenderness of his friends could overpower. He soon fell into his old distemper, an habitual colic, and languished, though with many intervals of ease and cheerfulness, till a violent fit at last seized him, and carried him to the grave, as Arbuthnot reported, with more precipitance than he had ever known. He died on the 4th of December, 1732, and was buried in Westminster Abbey. The letter which brought an account of his death to Swift was laid by for some days unopened, because when he received it he was impressed with the preconception of some misfortune.

After his death was published a second volume of Fables, more political than the former. His opera of *Achilles* was acted, and the profits were given to two widow sisters, who inherited what he left, as his lawful heirs; for he died without a will, though he had gathered 3000*l.* There have appeared likewise under his name a comedy called the *Distrest Wife*, and the *Rehearsal at Gotham*, a piece of humour.

The character given him by Pope is this: that "he was a natural man, without design, who spoke what he thought, and just as he thought it"; and that "he was of a timid temper, and fearful of giving offence to the great"; which caution, however, says Pope, was of no avail.

As a poet he cannot be rated very high. He was, as I once heard a female critic remark, "of a lower order." He had not in any great degree the *mens divinior*, the dignity of genius. Much however must be allowed to the author of a new species of composition, though it be not of the highest kind. We owe to Gay the Ballad Opera; a mode of comedy which at first was supposed to delight only by its novelty, but has now by the experience of half a century been found so well accommodated to the disposition of a popular audience, that it is likely to keep long possession of the stage. Whether this new drama was the product of judgment or of luck, the praise of it must be given to the inventor; and there are many writers read with more reverence, to whom such merit of originality cannot be attributed.

His first performance, the *Rural Sports*, is such as was easily planned and executed; it is never contemptible, nor ever excellent. The *Fan* [1714] is one of those mythological fictions which antiquity delivers ready to the hand, but which, like other things that lie open to everyone's use, are of little value.

The attention naturally retires from a new tale of Venus,
Diana, and Minerva.

His Fables seem to have been a favourite work; for having
published one volume, he left another behind him. Of this kind
of Fables, the authors do not appear to have formed any distinct or settled notion. Phædrus evidently confounds them with
Tales, and Gay both with *Tales* and *Allegorical Prosopopœias*.
A *Fable*, or *Apologue*, such as is now under consideration,
seems to be, in its genuine state, a narrative in which beings
irrational, and sometimes inanimate, *arbores loquuntur, non
tantum feræ*, are, for the purpose of moral instruction, feigned
to act and speak with human interests and passions. To this
description the compositions of Gay do not always conform.
For a Fable he gives now and then a Tale, or an abstracted
Allegory; and from some, by whatever name they may be
called, it will be difficult to extract any moral principle. They
are, however, told with liveliness; the versification is smooth;
and the diction, though now and then a little constrained by
the measure or the rhyme, is generally happy.

To *Trivia* [1716] may be allowed all that it claims; it is
sprightly, various, and pleasant. The subject is of that kind
which Gay was by nature qualified to adorn; yet some of his
decorations may be justly wished away. An honest blacksmith
might have done for Patty what is performed by Vulcan. The
appearance of Cloacina is nauseous and superfluous; a shoe-boy
could have been produced by the casual cohabitation of mere
mortals. Horace's rule is broken in both cases; there is no
dignus vindice nodus, no difficulty that required any supernatural interposition. A pattern may be made by the hammer
of a mortal; and a bastard may be dropped by a human strumpet.
On great occasions, and on small, the mind is repelled by
useless and apparent falsehood.

Of his little poems the public judgment seems to be right;
they are neither much esteemed, nor totally despised. The
story of the Apparition is borrowed from one of the tales of
Poggio. Those that please least are the pieces to which *Gulliver*
gave occasion; for who can much delight in the echo of an
unnatural fiction?

Dione is a counterpart to *Amynta* and *Pastor Fido*, and
other trifles of the same kind, easily imitated, and unworthy
of imitation. What the Italians call comedies from a happy
conclusion, Gay calls a tragedy from a mournful event; but
the style of the Italians and of Gay is equally tragical. There

is something in the poetical Arcadia so remote from known reality and speculative possibility, that we can never support its representation through a long work. A Pastoral of an hundred lines may be endured; but who will hear of sheep and goats, and myrtle-bowers and purling rivulets, through five acts? Such scenes please barbarians in the dawn of literature, and children in the dawn of life; but will be for the most part thrown away, as men grow wise, and nations grow learned.

GEORGE GRANVILLE
LORD LANSDOWN
1665 — 1734-35

Birth—Educated at Cambridge—Is commended by Waller—His Dramatic Pieces—His *Mira*—Made Secretary of War and a Peer—Encourages Pope—Death and Burial in St. Clement's Danes—Works and Character.

OF George Granville, or, as others write, *Greenville*, or *Grenville*, afterwards Lord Lansdown, of Bideford, in the county of Devon, less is known than his name and rank might give reason to expect. He was born about 1665, the son of Bernard Greenville, who was entrusted by Monk with the most private transactions of the Restoration, and the grandson of Sir Bevil Greenville, who died in the King's cause at the battle of Lansdown.

His early education was superintended by Sir William Ellis; and his progress was such that before the age of twelve he was sent to Cambridge, where he pronounced a copy of his own verses to the Princess Mary d'Este of Modena, then Duchess of York, when she visited the university.

At the accession of King James, being now at eighteen, he again exerted his poetical powers, and addressed the new monarch in three short pieces, of which the first is profane, and the two others such as a boy might be expected to produce; but he was commended by old Waller, who perhaps was pleased to find himself imitated in six lines, which, though they begin with nonsense and end with dullness, excited in the young author a rapture of acknowledgment:

In numbers such as Waller's self might use.

It was probably about this time that he wrote the poem to the Earl of Peterborough, upon his *accomplishment* of the Duke of York's marriage with the Princess of Modena, whose charms appear to have gained a strong prevalence over his imagination, and upon whom nothing ever has been charged

45

but imprudent piety, an intemperate and misguided zeal for the propagation of popery.

However faithful Granville might have been to the King, or however enamoured of the Queen, he has left no reason for supposing that he approved either the artifices or the violence with which the King's religion was insinuated or obtruded. He endeavoured to be true at once to the King and to the Church.

Of this regulated loyalty he has transmitted to posterity a sufficient proof in the letter which he wrote to his father about a month before the Prince of Orange landed.

To the Hon. Mr. Bernard Granville, at the Earl of Bathe's, St. James's

MAR, near DONCASTER, *Oct.* 6, 1688.

SIR,—Your having no prospect of obtaining a commission for me can no way alter or cool my desire at this important juncture to venture my life, in some manner or other, for my King and my country.

I cannot bear living under the reproach of lying obscure and idle in a country retirement, when every man who has the least sense of honour should be preparing for the field.

You may remember, Sir, with what reluctance I submitted to your commands upon Monmouth's rebellion, when no importunity could prevail with you to permit me to leave the Academy: I was too young to be hazarded; but, give me leave to say, it is glorious at any age to die for one's country, and the sooner the nobler the sacrifice.

I am now older by three years. My uncle Bathe was not so old when he was left among the slain at the battle of Newbury; nor you yourself, Sir, when you made your escape from your tutor's, to join your brother at the defence of Scilly.

The same cause is now come round about again. The King has been misled; let those who have misled him be answerable for it. Nobody can deny but he is sacred in his own person; and it is every honest man's duty to defend it.

You are pleased to say, it is yet doubtful if the Hollanders are rash enough to make such an attempt; but, be that as it will, I beg leave to insist upon it, that I may be presented to his Majesty, as one whose utmost ambition is to devote his life to his service, and my country's, after the example of all my ancestors.

The gentry assembled at York, to agree upon the choice of representatives for the county, have prepared an address, to assure his Majesty they are ready to sacrifice their lives and fortunes for him upon this and all other occasions; but at the same time they humbly beseech him to give them such magistrates as may be agreeable to the laws of the land; for, at present, there is no authority to which they can legally submit.

They have been beating up for volunteers at York, and the towns adjacent, to supply the regiments at Hull; but nobody will list.

By what I can hear, everybody wishes well to the King; but they would be glad his ministers were hanged.

The winds continue so contrary, that no landing can be so soon as was apprehended; therefore I may hope, with your leave and assistance, to be in readiness before any action can begin. I beseech you, Sir, most humbly and most earnestly, to add this one act of indulgence more to so many other testimonies which I have constantly received of your goodness; and be pleased to believe me always, with the utmost duty and submission, Sir,

Your most dutiful son,
And most obedient servant,
GEO. GRANVILLE.

Through the whole reign of King William he is supposed to have lived in literary retirement, and indeed had for some time few other pleasures but those of study in his power. He was, as the biographers observe, the younger son of a younger brother; a denomination by which our ancestors proverbially expressed the lowest state of penury and dependence. He is said, however, to have preserved himself at this time from disgrace and difficulties by economy, which he forgot or neglected in life more advanced, and in better fortune.

About this time he became enamoured of the Countess of Newburgh, whom he has celebrated with so much ardour by the name of Mira. He wrote verses to her before he was three-and-twenty, and may be forgiven if he regarded the face more than the mind. Poets are sometimes in too much haste to praise.

In the time of his retirement it is probable that he composed his dramatic pieces, the *She-Gallants* (acted 1696), which he revised, and called *Once a Lover, and always a Lover*; *The Jew of Venice*, altered from Shakespeare's *Merchant of Venice* (1698); *Heroic Love*, a tragedy (1698); *The British Enchanters* (1706), a dramatic poem; and *Peleus and Thetis*, a masque, written to accompany *The Jew of Venice*.

The comedies, which he has not printed in his own edition of his works, I never saw: *Once a Lover, and always a Lover* is said to be in a great degree indecent and gross. Granville could not admire without bigotry; he copied the wrong as well as the right from his masters, and may be supposed to have learned obscenity from Wycherley, as he learned mythology from Waller.

In his *Jew of Venice*, as Rowe remarks, the character of Shylock is made comic, and we are prompted to laughter instead of detestation.

It is evident that *Heroic Love* was written and presented on the stage before the death of Dryden. It is a mythological tragedy, upon the love of Agamemnon and Chryseis, and therefore easily sunk into neglect, though praised in verse by Dryden, and in prose by Pope.

It is concluded by the wise Ulysses with this speech:

> Fate holds the strings, and men like children move
> But as they're led; success is from above.

At the accession of Queen Anne, having his fortune improved by bequests from his father and his uncle, the Earl of Bath, he was chosen into Parliament for Fowey. He soon after engaged in a joint translation of the *Invectives against Philip*, with a design, surely weak and puerile, of turning the thunder of Demosthenes upon the head of Louis.

He afterwards (in 1706) had his estate again augmented by an inheritance from his elder brother, Sir Bevil Granville, who, as he returned from the government of Barbadoes, died at sea He continued to serve in parliament; and in the ninth year of Queen Anne was chosen knight of the shire for Cornwall.

At the memorable change of the ministry (1710) he was made Secretary at War, in the place of Mr. Robert Walpole.

Next year, when the violence of party made twelve peers in a day, Mr. Granville became [31st Dec., 1711] Baron Lansdown of Bideford, by a promotion justly remarked to be not invidious, because he was the heir of a family in which two peerages, that of the Earl of Bath and Lord Granville of Potheridge, had lately become extinct. Being now high in the Queen's favour, he (1712) was appointed Comptroller of the Household, and a privy councillor; and to his other honours were added the Dedication of Pope's *Windsor Forest*. He was advanced next year to be Treasurer of the Household.

Of these favours he soon lost all but his title; for, at the accession [1st Aug., 1714] of King George, his place was given to the Earl Cholmondeley, and he was persecuted with the rest of his party. Having protested against the bill for attainting Ormond and Bolingbroke, he was, after the insurrection in Scotland, seized Sept. 26, 1715, as a suspected man, and confined in the Tower till Feb. 8, 1716–17, when he was at last released and restored to his seat in parliament, where (1719) he made a very ardent and animated speech against the repeal of the bill to prevent Occasional Conformity, which, however, though it was then printed, he has not inserted into his works.

Some time afterwards (about 1722), being perhaps embarrassed by his profusion, he went into foreign countries, with the usual pretence of recovering his health. In this state of leisure and retirement he received the first volume of Burnet's *History*, of which he cannot be supposed to have approved the general tendency, and where he thought himself able to detect some particular falsehoods. He therefore undertook the vindication of General Monk from some calumnies of Dr. Burnet, and some misrepresentations of Mr. Echard. This was answered civilly by Mr. Thomas Burnet and Oldmixon, and more roughly by Dr. Colbatch.

His other historical performance is a defence of his relation Sir Richard Greenville, whom Lord Clarendon has shown in a form very unamiable. So much is urged in this apology to justify many actions that have been represented as culpable, and to palliate the rest, that the reader is reconciled for the greater part; and it is made very probable that Clarendon was by personal enmity disposed to think the worst of Greenville, as Greenville was also very willing to think the worst of Clarendon. These pieces were published at his return to England.

Being now desirous to conclude his labours and enjoy his reputation, he published (1732) a very beautiful and splendid edition of his works, in which he omitted what he disapproved, and enlarged what seemed deficient.

He now went to Court, and was kindly received by Queen Caroline, to whom and to the Princess Anne he presented his works, with verses on the blank leaves, with which he concluded his poetical labours.

He died in Hanover-square, Jan. 30, 1734-5, having a few days before buried his wife, the Lady Mary Villiers, widow to Mr. Thynne, by whom he had four daughters, but no son.

Writers commonly derive their reputation from their works; but there are works which owe their reputation to the character of the writer. The public sometimes has its favourites, whom it rewards for one species of excellence with the honours due to another. From him whom we reverence for his beneficence we do not willingly withhold the praise of genius; a man of exalted merit becomes at once an accomplished writer, as a beauty finds no great difficulty in passing for a wit.

Granville was a man illustrious by his birth, and therefore attracted notice: since he is by Pope styled "the polite," he must be supposed elegant in his manners, and generally loved·

he was in times of contests and turbulence steady to his party, and obtained that esteem which is always conferred upon firmness and consistency. With those advantages, having learned the art of versifying, he declared himself a poet; and his claim to the laurel was allowed.

But by a critic of a later generation, who takes up his book without any favourable prejudices, the praise already received will be thought sufficient; for his works do not show him to have had much comprehension from nature, or illumination from learning. He seems to have had no ambition above the imitation of Waller, of whom he has copied the faults, and very little more. He is for ever amusing himself with the puerilities of mythology; his King is Jupiter, who, if the Queen brings no children, has a barren Juno. The Queen is compounded of Juno, Venus, and Minerva. His poem on the Duchess of Grafton's law-suit, after having rattled a while with Juno and Pallas, Mars and Alcides, Cassiope, Niobe, and the Propetides, Hercules, Minos, and Rhadamanthus, at last concludes its folly with profaneness.

His verses to Mira, which are most frequently mentioned, have little in them of either art or nature, of the sentiments of a lover, or the language of a poet: there may be found, now and then, a happier effort; but they are commonly feeble and unaffecting, or forced and extravagant.

His little pieces are seldom either sprightly or elegant, either keen or weighty. They are trifles written by idleness, and published by vanity. But his Prologues and Epilogues have a just claim to praise.

The *Progress of Beauty* seems one of his most elaborate pieces, and is not deficient in splendour and gaiety; but the merit of original thought is wanting. Its highest praise is the spirit with which he celebrates King James's consort when she was a queen no longer.

The *Essay on Unnatural Flights in Poetry* is not inelegant nor injudicious, and has something of vigour beyond most of his other performances: his precepts are just, and his cautions proper; they are indeed not new, but in a didactic poem novelty is to be expected only in the ornaments and illustrations. His poetical precepts are accompanied with agreeable and instructive notes.

The masque of *Peleus and Thetis* has here and there a pretty line; but it is not always melodious, and the conclusion is wretched.

In his *British Enchanters* he has bidden defiance to all chronology by confounding the inconsistent manners of different ages; but the dialogue has often the air of Dryden's rhyming plays; and the songs are lively, though not very correct. This is, I think, far the best of his works; for if it has many faults, it has likewise passages which are at least pretty, though they do not rise to any high degree of excellence.

THOMAS YALDEN

1671–1736

Born and Educated at Oxford—His earliest Poetry—Made Preacher at Bridewell—Taken into custody about Atterbury's Plot—Death and Burial in Bridewell Precinct—Character and Works.

THOMAS YALDEN, the sixth son of Mr. John Yalden of Sussex, was born in the city of Exeter in 1671. Having been educated in the grammar-school belonging to Magdalen College in Oxford, he was in 1690, at the age of nineteen, admitted commoner of Magdalen Hall, under the tuition of Josiah Pullen, a man whose name is still remembered in the university. He became next year one of the scholars of Magdalen College, where he was distinguished by a lucky accident.

It was his turn, one day, to pronounce a declamation; and Dr. Hough, the president, happening to attend, thought the composition too good to be the speaker's. Some time after, the Doctor finding him a little irregularly busy in the library, set him an exercise for punishment; and, that he might not be deceived by any artifice, locked the door. Yalden, as it happened, had been lately reading on the subject given, and produced with little difficulty a composition which so pleased the president, that he told him his former suspicions, and promised to favour him.

Among his contemporaries in the college were Addison and Sacheverell, men who were in those times friends, and who both adopted Yalden to their intimacy. Yalden continued, throughout his life, to think as probably he thought at first, yet did not lose the friendship of Addison.

When Namur was taken by King William, Yalden made an ode. There was never any reign more celebrated by the poets than that of William, who had very little regard for song himself, but happened to employ ministers who pleased themselves with the praise of patronage.

Of this ode mention is made in an humorous poem of that time, called *The Oxford Laureat*; in which, after many claims had been made and rejected, Yalden is represented as demanding

the laurel, and as being called to his trial, instead of receiving a reward.

> His crime was for being a felon in verse,
>   And presenting his theft to the king;
> The first was a trick not uncommon or scarce,
>   But the last was an impudent thing:
> Yet what he had stol'n was so little worth stealing,
>   They forgave him the damage and cost:
> Had he ta'en the whole ode, as he took it piece-mealing,
>   They had fin'd him but ten-pence at most.

The poet whom he was charged with robbing was Congreve.

He wrote another poem on the death of the Duke of Gloucester.

In 1710 he became Fellow of the college; and next year,
entering into orders, was presented by the society with a living
in Warwickshire, consistent with the fellowship, and chosen
lecturer of moral philosophy—a very honourable office.

On the accession of Queen Anne [1702–3] he wrote another
poem; and is said, by the author of the *Biographia*, to have
declared himself of the party who had the honourable distinction
of high-churchmen.

In 1706 he was received into the family of the Duke of Beau-
fort. Next year [1st July, 1707] he became Doctor in Divinity,
and soon after [1713] resigned his fellowship and lecture; and
as a token of his gratitude, gave the college a picture of their
founder.

He was made rector of Chalton and Cleanville, two adjoining
towns and benefices in Hampshire; and had the prebends, or
sinecures, of Deans, Hains, and Pendles, in Devonshire. He
had before been chosen, in 1698, preacher of Bridewell Hospital,
upon the resignation of Dr. Atterbury.

From this time he seems to have led a quiet and inoffensive
life, till the clamour was raised about Atterbury's plot. Every
loyal eye was on the watch for abettors or partakers of the
horrid conspiracy; and Dr. Yalden, having some acquaintance
with the Bishop, and being familiarly conversant with Kelly his
secretary, fell under suspicion, and was taken into custody.

Upon his examination he was charged with a dangerous
correspondence with Kelly. The correspondence he acknowledged; but maintained that it had no treasonable tendency.
His papers were seized; but nothing was found that could fix
a crime upon him, except two words in his pocket-book, *thorough-
paced doctrine*. This expression the imagination of his examiners
had impregnated with treason, and the Doctor was enjoined
to explain them. Thus pressed, he told them that the words

had lain unheeded in his pocket-book from the time of Queen Anne, and that he was ashamed to give an account of them; but the truth was, that he had gratified his curiosity one day by hearing Daniel Burgess in the pulpit, and those words were a memorial hint of a remarkable sentence by which he warned his congregation to "beware of" thorough-paced doctrine, "that doctrine which, coming in at one ear, paces through the head, and goes out at the other."

Nothing worse than this appearing in his papers, and no evidence arising against him, he was set at liberty.

It will not be supposed that a man of this character attained high dignities in the Church; but he still retained the friendship, and frequented the conversation, of a very numerous and splendid set of acquaintance. He died July 16, 1736, in the sixty-sixth year of his age.

Of his poems, many are of that irregular kind which, when he formed his poetical character, was supposed to be Pindaric. Having fixed his attention on Cowley as a model, he has attempted in some sort to rival him, and has written a *Hymn to Darkness,* evidently as a counterpart to Cowley's *Hymn to Light.*

This hymn seems to be his best performance, and is, for the most part, imagined with great vigour, and expressed with great propriety. I will not transcribe it. The seven first stanzas are good; but the third, fourth, and seventh are the best; the eighth seems to involve a contradiction; the tenth is exquisitely beautiful; the thirteenth, fourteenth, and fifteenth are partly mythological, and partly religious, and therefore not suitable to each other; he might better have made the whole merely philosophical.

There are two stanzas in this poem where Yalden may be suspected, though hardly convicted, of having consulted the *Hymnus ad Umbram* of Wowerus, in the sixth stanza, which answers in some sort to these lines:

> Illa suo præest nocturnis numine sacris—
> Perque vias errare novis dat spectra figuris,
> Manesque excitos medios ululare per agros
> Sub noctem, et questu notos complere penates.

And again, at the conclusion:

> Illa suo senium secludit corpore toto
> Haud numerans jugi fugientia secula lapsu,
> Ergo ubi postremum mundi compage solutâ
> Hanc rerum molem suprema absumpserit hora
> Ipsa leves cineres nube amplectetur opacâ,
> Et prisco imperio rursus dominabitur umbra.

His *Hymn to Light* is not equal to the other. He seems to think that there is an East absolute and positive where the Morning rises.

In the last stanza, having mentioned the sudden eruption of new created Light, he says:

> A while th' Almighty wondering viewed.

He ought to have remembered that Infinite Knowledge can never wonder. All wonder is the effect of novelty upon ignorance.

Of his other poems it is sufficient to say that they deserve perusal, though they are not always exactly polished, though the rhymes are sometimes very ill sorted, and though his faults seem rather the omissions of idleness than the negligences of enthusiasm.

THOMAS TICKELL
1686-1740

Born at Bridekirk, in Cumberland—Educated at Oxford—Marries—
Acquires the Friendship of Addison—His first Poems—His Translation of
the First Book of the Iliad—Made Under-Secretary—Addison leaves him
the charge of Publishing his Works—His Elegy on Addison—Made
Secretary to the Lords Justices—Death at Bath—Works and Character.

THOMAS TICKELL, the son of the Reverend Richard Tickell,
was born in 1686 at Bridekirk in Cumberland; and in April
1701 became a member of Queen's College in Oxford; in 1708
he was made Master of Arts, and two years afterwards [9th
Nov., 1710] was chosen Fellow; for which, as he did not comply
with the statutes by taking orders, he obtained [25th Oct.,
1717] a dispensation from the Crown. He held his Fellowship till 1726, and then vacated it, by marrying, in that year,
at Dublin.

Tickell was not one of those scholars who wear away their
lives in closets; he entered early into the world, and was long
busy in public affairs; in which he was initiated under the
patronage of Addison, whose notice he is said to have gained
by his verses in praise of *Rosamond*.

To those verses it would not have been just to deny regard;
for they contain some of the most elegant encomiastic strains;
and, among the innumerable poems of the same kind, it will
be hard to find one with which they need to fear a comparison.
It may deserve observation, that when Pope wrote long afterwards in praise of Addison, he has copied, at least has
resembled, Tickell,

> Let joy transport fair Rosamonda's shade,
> And wreaths of myrtle crown the lovely maid.
> While now perhaps with Dido's ghost she roves,
> And hears and tells the story of their loves,
> Alike they mourn, alike they bless their fate,
> Since Love, which made them wretched, makes them great.
> Nor longer that relentless doom bemoan
> Which gain'd a Virgil and an Addison.
>
> TICKELL [1709].

> Then future ages with delight shall see
> How Plato's, Bacon's, Newton's looks agree;
> Or in fair series laurell'd bards be shown,
> A Virgil there, and here an Addison.
>
> POPE [1721].

57

He produced another piece of the same kind at the appearance of *Cato*, with equal skill, but not equal happiness.

When the ministers of Queen Anne were negotiating with France, Tickell published [1713] *The Prospect of Peace*, a poem, of which the tendency was to reclaim the nation from the pride of conquest to the pleasures of tranquillity. How far Tickell, whom Swift afterwards mentioned as *Whiggissimus*, had then connected himself with any party, I know not; this poem certainly did not flatter the practices, or promote the opinions, of the men by whom he was afterwards befriended.

Mr. Addison, however he hated the men then in power, suffered his friendship to prevail over his public spirit, and gave in *The Spectator* such praises of Tickell's poem, that when, after having long wished to peruse it, I laid hold on it at last, I thought it unequal to the honours which it had received, and found it a piece to be approved rather than admired. But the hope excited by a work of genius, being general and indefinite, is rarely gratified. It was read at that time with so much favour, that six editions were sold.

At the arrival of King George he sung *The Royal Progress*; which being inserted in *The Spectator* is well known, and of which it is just to say, that it is neither high nor low.

The poetical incident of most importance in Tickell's life was his publication [June 1715] of the first book of the Iliad, as translated by himself, in apparent opposition to Pope's Homer, of which the first part made its entrance into the world at the same time.

Addison declared that the rival versions were both good; but that Tickell's was the best that ever was made; and with Addison the wits, his adherents and followers, were certain to concur. Pope does not appear to have been much dismayed; "for," says he, "I have the town, that is, the mob on my side." But he remarks, "that it is common for the smaller party to make up in diligence what they want in numbers; he appeals to the people as his proper judges; and if they are not inclined to condemn him, he is in little care about the high-flyers at Button's."

Pope did not long think Addison an impartial judge; for he considered him as the writer of Tickell's version. The reasons for his suspicion I will literally transcribe from Mr. Spence's *Collections*:

"There had been a coldness (said Mr. Pope) between Mr. Addison and me for some time; and we had not been in company together, for a good while, anywhere but at Button's coffee-house, where I used to see him almost every day. On his meeting me there, one day in particular, he took me aside, and said he should be glad to dine with me, at such a tavern, if I would stay till those people (Budgell and Philips) were gone. We went accordingly; and after dinner Mr. Addison said, 'That he had wanted for some time to talk with me; that his friend Tickell had formerly, whilst at Oxford, translated the first book of the Iliad; that he now designed to print it, and had desired him to look it over; he must therefore beg that I would not desire him to look over my first book, because, if he did, it would have the air of double-dealing.' I assured him that I did not at all take it ill of Mr. Tickell that he was going to publish his translation; that he certainly had as much right to translate any author as myself; and that publishing both was entering on a fair stage. I then added, that I would not desire him to look over my first book of the Iliad, because he had looked over Mr. Tickell's; but could wish to have the benefit of his observations on my second, which I had then finished, and which Mr. Tickell had not touched upon. Accordingly I sent him the second book the next morning; and in a few days he returned it, with very high commendation. Soon after it was generally known that Mr. Tickell was publishing the first book of the Iliad, I met Dr. Young in the street; and, upon our falling into that subject, the Doctor expressed a great deal of surprise at Tickell's having such a translation by him so long. He said, that it was inconceivable to him, and that there must be some mistake in the matter; that he and Tickell were so intimately acquainted at Oxford, that each used to communicate to the other whatever verses they wrote, even to the least things; that Tickell could not have been busied in so long a work there without his knowing something of the matter; and that he had never heard a single word of it till on this occasion. This surprise of Dr. Young, together with what Steele has said against Tickell in relation to this affair, make it highly probable that there was some underhand dealing in that business; and indeed Tickell himself, who is a very fair, worthy man, has since, in a manner, as good as owned it to me. [To which Spence adds:] When it was introduced in conversation between Mr. Tickell and Mr. Pope, by a third person, Tickell did not deny it; which, considering his honour and zeal for his departed friend, was the same as owning it."

Upon these suspicions, with which Dr. Warburton hints

that other circumstances concurred, Pope always in his *Art of Sinking* quotes this book as the work of Addison.

To compare the two translations would be tedious; the palm is now given universally to Pope; but I think the first lines of Tickell's were rather to be preferred, and Pope seems to have since borrowed something from them in the correction of his own.

When the Hanover succession was disputed, Tickell gave what assistance his pen would supply. His *Letter to Avignon* stands high among party-poems; it expresses contempt without coarseness, and superiority without insolence. It had the success which it deserved, being five times printed.

He was now intimately united to Mr. Addison, who, when he went into Ireland as Secretary to the Lord Sunderland, took him thither, and employed him in public business; and when (1717) afterwards he rose to be Secretary of State, made him Under-Secretary. Their friendship seems to have continued without abatement; for when Addison died, he left him the charge of publishing his works, with a solemn recommendation to the patronage of Craggs.

To these works he prefixed [1721] an elegy on the author, which could owe none of its beauties to the assistance which might be suspected to have strengthened or embellished his earlier compositions; but neither he nor Addison ever produced nobler lines than are contained in the third and fourth paragraphs; nor is a more sublime or more elegant funeral-poem to be found in the whole compass of English literature.

He was afterwards (4th May, 1724) made Secretary to the Lords Justices of Ireland, a place of great honour; in which he continued till 1740, when he died on the 23rd of April at Bath.

Of the poems yet unmentioned the longest is *Kensington Gardens*, of which the versification is smooth and elegant, but the fiction unskilfully compounded of Grecian deities and Gothic fairies. Neither species of those exploded beings could have done much; and when they are brought together, they only make each other contemptible. To Tickell, however, cannot be refused a high place among the minor poets; nor should it be forgotten that he was one of the contributors to *The Spectator*. With respect to his personal character, he is said to have been a man of gay conversation, at least a temperate lover of wine and company, and in his domestic relations without censure.

JAMES HAMMOND

1710–1742

Birth—Educated at Westminster School—Equerry to Frederick Prince of Wales—His Elegies—Death and Character.

Of Mr. Hammond, though he be well remembered as a man esteemed and caressed by the elegant and the great, I was at first able to obtain no other memorials than such as are supplied by a book called *Cibber's Lives of the Poets*; of which I take this opportunity to testify that it was not written, nor, I believe, ever seen, by either of the Cibbers; but was the work of Robert Shiels, a native of Scotland, a man of very acute understanding, though with little scholastic education, who, not long after the publication of his work, died in London of a consumption. His life was virtuous, and his end was pious. Theophilus Cibber, then a prisoner for debt, imparted, as I was told, his name for ten guineas. The manuscript of Shiels is now in my possession.

I have since found that Mr. Shiels, though he was no negligent inquirer, had been misled by false accounts; for he relates that James Hammond, the author of the Elegies, was the son of a Turkey merchant, and had some office at the Prince of Wales's court, till love of a lady, whose name was Dashwood, for a time disordered his understanding. He was unextinguishably amorous, and his mistress inexorably cruel.

Of this narrative, part is true, and part false. He was the second son of Anthony Hammond, a man of note among the wits, poets, and parliamentary orators, in the beginning of this century, who was allied to Sir Robert Walpole by marrying his sister. He was born about 1710, and educated at Westminster-school; but it does not appear that he was of any university. He was equerry to the Prince of Wales, and seems to have come very early into public notice, and to have been distinguished by those whose friendship prejudiced mankind at that time in favour of the man on whom they were bestowed; for he was the companion of Cobham, Lyttelton, and Chesterfield. He is said to have divided his life between pleasure and

books; in his retirement forgetting the town, and in his gaiety
losing the student. Of his literary hours all the effects are here
exhibited, of which the Elegies were written very early, and
the Prologue not long before his death.

In 1741 he was chosen into Parliament for Truro in Cornwall, probably one of those who were elected by the Prince's
influence; and died next year in June [7th June, 1742] at
Stowe, the famous seat of the Lord Cobham. His mistress
long outlived him, and in 1779 died unmarried. The character
which her lover bequeathed her was, indeed, not likely to
attract courtship.

The Elegies were published after his death; and while the
writer's name was remembered with fondness, they were read
with a resolution to admire them. The recommendatory Preface of the editor, who was then believed, and is now affirmed
by Dr. Maty, to be the Earl of Chesterfield, raised strong
prejudices in their favour.

But of the prefacer, whoever he was, it may be reasonably
suspected that he never read the poems; for he professes to
value them for a very high species of excellence, and recom-
mends them as the genuine effusions of the mind, which
expresses a real passion in the language of nature. But the
truth is, these Elegies have neither passion, nature, nor manners.
Where there is fiction, there is no passion; he that describes
himself as a shepherd, and his Neæra or Delia as a shep-
herdess, and talks of goats and lambs, feels no passion. He
that courts his mistress with Roman imagery deserves to lose
her; for she may with good reason suspect his sincerity.
Hammond has few sentiments drawn from nature, and few
images from modern life. He produces nothing but frigid
pedantry. It would be hard to find in all his productions three
stanzas that deserve to be remembered.

Like other lovers, he threatens the lady with dying; and
what then shall follow?

> Wilt thou in tears thy lover's corse attend;
>   With eyes averted light the solemn pyre,
> Till all around the doleful flames ascend,
>   Then slowly sinking, by degrees expire?
> To soothe the hovering soul be thine the care,
>   With plaintive cries to lead the mournful band;
> In sable weeds the golden vase to bear,
>   And cull my ashes with thy trembling hand:
> Panchaia's odours be their costly feast,
>   And all the pride of Asia's fragrant year,
> Give them the treasures of the farthest East,
>   And what is still more precious, give thy tear.

Surely no blame can fall upon a nymph who rejected a swain of so little meaning?

His verses are not rugged, but they have no sweetness; they never glide in a stream of melody. Why Hammond or other writers have thought the quatrain of ten syllables elegiac, it is difficult to tell. The character of the Elegy is gentleness and tenuity; but this stanza has been pronounced by Dryden, whose knowledge of English metre was not inconsiderable, to be the most magnificent of all the measures which our language affords.

WILLIAM SOMERVILE

1692–1742

Born at Edston, in Warwickshire—Educated at Winchester and Oxford—His *Chace* and other Poems—Death and Burial at Wotton, in Warwickshire—Works and Character.

OF Mr. Somervile's life I am not able to say anything that can satisfy curiosity.

He was a gentleman whose estate was in Warwickshire; his house, where he was born in 1692, is called Edston, a seat inherited from a long line of ancestors; for he was said to be of the first family in his county. He tells of himself, that he was born near the Avon's banks. He was bred at Winchester-school, and was elected Fellow of New College. It does not appear that in the places of his education he exhibited any uncommon proofs of genius or literature. His powers were first displayed in the country, where he was distinguished as a poet, a gentleman, and a skilful and useful justice of the peace.

Of the close of his life, those whom his poems have delighted will read with pain the following account, copied from the Letters of his friend Shenstone, by whom he was too much resembled:

"Our old friend Somervile is dead! I did not imagine I could have been so sorry as I find myself on this occasion.— *Sublatum quærimus.* I can now excuse all his foibles; impute them to age, and to distress of circumstances: the last of these considerations wrings my very soul to think on. For a man of high spirit, conscious of having (at least in one production) generally pleased the world, to be plagued and threatened by wretches that are low in every sense; to be forced to drink himself into pains of the body, in order to get rid of the pains of the mind, is a misery," etc.—He died July 19, 1742, and was buried at Wotton, near Henley in Arden.

His distresses need not be much pitied: his estate is said to have been fifteen hundred a year, which by his death devolved to Lord Somerville of Scotland. His mother indeed, who lived till ninety, had a jointure of six hundred.

It is with regret that I find myself not better enabled to

exhibit memorials of a writer who at least must be allowed to have set a good example to men of his own class, by devoting part of his time to elegant knowledge; and who has shown, by the subjects which his poetry has adorned, that it is practicable to be at once a skilful sportsman and a man of letters.

Somervile has tried many modes of poetry; and though perhaps he has not in any reached such excellence as to raise much envy, it may commonly be said at least, that "he writes very well for a gentleman." His serious pieces are sometimes elevated, and his trifles are sometimes elegant. In his verses to Addison, the couplet which mentions Clio is written with the most exquisite delicacy of praise; it exhibits one of those happy strokes that are seldom attained. In his Odes to Marlborough there are beautiful lines; but in the second Ode he shows that he knew little of his hero, when he talks of his private virtues. His subjects are commonly such as require no great depth of thought or energy of expression. His Fables are generally stale, and therefore excite no curiosity. Of his favourite, *The Two Springs*, the fiction is unnatural, and the moral inconsequential. In his Tales there is too much coarseness, with too little care of language, and not sufficient rapidity of narration.

His great work is his *Chace*, which he undertook in his maturer age when his ear was improved to the approbation of blank verse, of which however his two first lines give a bad specimen. To this poem praise cannot be totally denied. He is allowed by sportsmen to write with great intelligence of his subject, which is the first requisite to excellence; and though it is impossible to interest the common readers of verse in the dangers or pleasures of the chace, he has done all that transition and variety could easily effect; and has with great propriety enlarged his plan by the modes of hunting used in other countries.

With still less judgment did he choose blank verse as the vehicle of *Rural Sports*. If blank verse be not tumid and gorgeous, it is crippled prose; and familiar images in laboured language have nothing to recommend them but absurd novelty, which, wanting the attractions of Nature, cannot please long. One excellence of *The Splendid Shilling* is, that it is short. Disguise can gratify no longer than it deceives.

RICHARD SAVAGE

1697-98 — 1743

The Natural Son of Earl Rivers by the Countess of Macclesfield—
Cruelty of his Mother—His Father's Death—His Godmother's Death—
His Early Misfortunes—Lady Mason's Kindness—Is placed with a Shoe-
maker—Becomes an Author by Profession—Sir Richard Steele interests
himself in his behalf—His Two Comedies—Mrs. Oldfield's Kindness—
His Tragedy of *Sir Thomas Overbury*—Aaron Hill's kindness—Publishes
a Miscellany—Is tried for killing Mr. James Sinclair—Obtains a Pardon
—Received into Lord Tyrconnel's Family—Publishes *The Wanderer*, a
Poem—His Poem of *The Bastard*—Assumes the Office of Volunteer Laureat
—Obtains a Pension from Queen Caroline—Loses his Pension on the
Death of the Queen—Fruitless Endeavours of Pope and others to serve
him—His Irregular Life—His Retirement to Swansea—Death in a Prison
at Bristol—Burial in the Churchyard of St. Peter's, Bristol—Works
and Character.

IT has been observed in all ages that the advantages of nature
or of fortune have contributed very little to the promotion of
happiness; and that those whom the splendour of their rank, or
the extent of their capacity, have placed upon the summit of
human life have not often given any just occasion to envy in
those who look up to them from a lower station; whether it
be that apparent superiority incites great designs, and great
designs are naturally liable to fatal miscarriages; or that the
general lot of mankind is misery, and the misfortunes of those
whose eminence drew upon them an universal attention have
been more carefully recorded because they were more generally
observed, and have in reality been only more conspicuous than
those of others, not more frequent, or more severe.

That affluence and power, advantages extrinsic and adventitious, and therefore easily separable from those by whom they
are possessed, should very often flatter the mind with expectations of felicity which they cannot give, raises no astonishment;
but it seems rational to hope that intellectual greatness should
produce better effects; that minds qualified for great attainments should first endeavour their own benefit; and that they
who are most able to teach others the way to happiness should
with most certainty follow it themselves.

But this expectation, however plausible, has been very frequently disappointed. The heroes of literary as well as civil

history have been very often no less remarkable for what they have suffered than for what they have achieved; and volumes have been written only to enumerate the miseries of the learned, and relate their unhappy lives and untimely deaths.

To these mournful narratives I am about to add the Life of Richard Savage, a man whose writings entitle him to an eminent rank in the classes of learning, and whose misfortunes claim a degree of compassion not always due to the unhappy, as they were often the consequences of the crimes of others rather than his own.

In the year 1697, Anne Countess of Macclesfield, having lived some time upon very uneasy terms with her husband, thought a public confession of adultery the most obvious and expeditious method of obtaining her liberty; and therefore declared that the child with which she was then great was begotten by the Earl Rivers. This, as may be imagined, made her husband no less desirous of a separation than herself, and he prosecuted his design in the most effectual manner; for he applied not to the ecclesiastical courts for a divorce, but to the parliament for an act by which his marriage might be dissolved, the nuptial contract annulled, and the children of his wife illegitimated. This act, after the usual deliberation, he obtained, though without the approbation of some, who considered marriage as an affair only cognisable by ecclesiastical judges; and, on March 3rd, was separated from his wife, whose fortune, which was very great, was repaid her, and who having, as well as her husband, the liberty of making another choice, was in a short time married to Colonel Brett.

While the Earl of Macclesfield was prosecuting this affair, his wife was, on the 10th of January, 1697-8, delivered of a son; and the Earl Rivers, by appearing to consider him as his own, left none any reason to doubt of the sincerity of her declaration; for he was his godfather and gave him his own name, which was by his direction inserted in the register of St. Andrew's parish in Holborn; but, unfortunately, left him to the care of his mother, whom, as she was now set free from her husband, he probably imagined likely to treat with great tenderness the child that had contributed to so pleasing an event. It is not indeed easy to discover what motives could be found to overbalance that natural affection of a parent, or what interest could be promoted by neglect or cruelty. The dread of shame or of poverty, by which some wretches have been incited to abandon or to murder their children, cannot be supposed to have affected a woman who had proclaimed her crimes and solicited reproach, and on whom the clemency of the legislature had undeservedly bestowed a fortune, which would have been very little diminished by the expenses which the care of her child could have brought upon her. It was therefore not likely that she would be wicked without temptation; that she would look upon her son from his birth with a kind of resentment and abhorrence; and, instead of supporting, assisting, and defending him, delight to see him struggling with misery, or that she would take every opportunity of aggravating his misfortunes and obstructing his resources, and with an implacable and restless cruelty continue her persecution from the first hour of his life to the last.

But, whatever were her motives, no sooner was her son born than she discovered a resolution of disowning him; and in a very short time removed him from her sight by committing him to the care of a poor woman, whom she directed to educate him as her own, and enjoined never to inform him of his true parents.

Such was the beginning of the life of Richard Savage. Born with a legal claim to honour and to affluence, he was in two months illegitimated by the parliament, and disowned by his mother, doomed to poverty and obscurity, and launched upon the ocean of life only that he might be swallowed by its quicksands or dashed upon its rocks.

His mother could not indeed infect others with the same cruelty. As it was impossible to avoid the inquiries which the curiosity or tenderness of her relations made after her child, she was obliged to give some account of the measures she had taken; and her mother, the Lady Mason, whether in approbation of her design or to prevent more criminal contrivances, engaged to transact with the nurse, to pay her for her care, and to superintend the education of the child.

In this charitable office she was assisted by his godmother, Mrs. Lloyd, who while she lived always looked upon him with that tenderness which the barbarity of his mother made peculiarly necessary; but her death, which happened in his tenth year, was another of the misfortunes of his childhood; for though she kindly endeavoured to alleviate his loss by a legacy of 300*l.*, yet, as he had none to prosecute his claim, to shelter him from oppression, or call in law to the assistance of justice, her will was eluded by the executors, and no part of the money was ever paid.

He was, however, not yet wholly abandoned. The Lady
Mason still continued her care and directed him to be placed at
a small grammar-school near St. Alban's, where he was called
by the name of his nurse, without the least intimation that he
had a claim to any other.

Here he was initiated in literature, and passed through
several of the classes, with what rapidity or with what applause
cannot now be known. As he always spoke with respect of his
master, it is probable that the mean rank in which he then
appeared did not hinder his genius from being distinguished, or
his industry from being rewarded; and if in so low a state he
obtained distinction and rewards, it is not likely that they were
gained but by genius and industry.

It is very reasonable to conjecture that his application was
equal to his abilities, because his improvement was more than
proportioned to the opportunities which he enjoyed; nor can
it be doubted that, if his earliest productions had been preserved like those of happier students, we might in some have
found vigorous sallies of that sprightly humour which distinguishes *The Author to be Let*, and in others strong touches
of that imagination which painted the solemn scenes of *The
Wanderer*.

While he was thus cultivating his genius, his father, the Earl
Rivers, was seized with a distemper which in a short time
put an end to his life. He had frequently inquired after his
son, and had always been amused with fallacious and evasive
answers; but, being now in his own opinion on his death-bed,
he thought it his duty to provide for him among his other
natural children, and therefore demanded a positive account of
him, with an importunity not to be diverted or denied. His
mother, who could no longer refuse an answer, determined at
least to give such as should cut him off for ever from that
happiness which competence affords, and therefore declared
that he was dead; which is perhaps the first instance of a lie
invented by a mother to deprive her son of a provision which
was designed him by another, and which she could not expect
herself though he should lose it.

This was therefore an act of wickedness which could not be
defeated, because it could not be suspected; the Earl did not
imagine there could exist in a human form a mother that
would ruin her son without enriching herself, and therefore
bestowed upon some other person 6000*l*. which he had in his
will bequeathed to Savage.

The same cruelty which incited his mother to intercept this provision which had been intended him prompted her in a short time to another project, a project worthy of such a disposition. She endeavoured to rid herself from the danger of being at any time made known to him, by sending him secretly to the American Plantations.

By whose kindness this scheme was counteracted, or by whose interposition she was induced to lay aside her design, I know not: it is not improbable that the Lady Mason might persuade or compel her to desist; or perhaps she could not easily find accomplices wicked enough to concur in so cruel an action; for it may be conceived that those who had by a long gradation of guilt hardened their hearts against the sense of common wickedness would yet be shocked at the design of a mother to expose her son to slavery and want, to expose him without interest and without provocation; and Savage might on this occasion find protectors and advocates among those who had long traded in crimes, and whom compassion had never touched before.

Being hindered, by whatever means, from banishing him into another country, she formed soon after a scheme for burying him in poverty and obscurity in his own; and, that his station of life, if not the place of his residence, might keep him for ever at a distance from her, she ordered him to be placed with a shoemaker in Holborn, that, after the usual time of trial, he might become his apprentice.

It is generally reported that this project was for some time successful, and that Savage was employed at the awl longer than he was willing to confess; nor was it perhaps any great advantage to him that an unexpected discovery determined him to quit his occupation.

About this time his nurse, who had always treated him as her own son, died; and it was natural for him to take care of those effects which by her death were, as he imagined, become his own: he therefore went to her house, opened her boxes, and examined her papers, among which he found some letters written to her by the Lady Mason, which informed him of his birth, and the reasons for which it was concealed.

He was no longer satisfied with the employment which had been allotted him, but thought he had a right to share the affluence of his mother; and therefore, without scruple, applied to her as her son, and made use of every art to awaken her tenderness and attract her regard. But neither his letters nor the interposition of those friends which his merit or his distress procured him made any impression upon her mind. She still resolved to neglect, though she could no longer disown him.

It was to no purpose that he frequently solicited her to admit him to see her; she avoided him with the most vigilant precaution, and ordered him to be excluded from her house, by whomsoever he might be introduced, and what reason soever he might give for entering it.

Savage was at the same time so touched with the discovery of his real mother that it was his frequent practice to walk in the dark evenings for several hours before her door, in hopes of seeing her as she might come by accident to the window or cross her apartment with a candle in her hand.

But all his assiduity and tenderness were without effect, for he could neither soften her heart nor open her hand, and was reduced to the utmost miseries of want while he was endeavouring to awaken the affection of a mother. He was therefore obliged to seek some other means of support; and, having no profession, became by necessity an author.

At this time the attention of the literary world was engrossed by the Bangorian controversy, which filled the press with pamphlets, and the coffee-houses with disputants. Of this subject, as most popular, he made choice for his first attempt, and, without any other knowledge of the question than he had casually collected from conversation, published [1717] a poem against the Bishop.

What was the success or merit of this performance I know not; it was probably lost among the innumerable pamphlets to which that dispute gave occasion. Mr. Savage was himself in a little time ashamed of it, and endeavoured to suppress it by destroying all the copies that he could collect.

He then attempted a more gainful kind of writing, and in his eighteenth year offered to the stage a comedy borrowed from a Spanish plot, which was refused by the players, and was therefore given by him to Mr. Bullock, who, having more interest, made some slight alterations, and brought it upon the stage under the title of *Woman's a Riddle*, but allowed the unhappy author no part of the profit.

Not discouraged, however, at his repulse, he wrote, two years afterwards, *Love in a Veil*, another comedy, borrowed likewise from the Spanish, but with little better success than before; for though it was received and acted, yet it appeared so late in the year that the author obtained no other advantage from it than the acquaintance of Sir Richard Steele and Mr. Wilks, by whom he was pitied, caressed, and relieved.

Sir Richard Steele, having declared in his favour with all the ardour of benevolence which constituted his character, promoted his interest with the utmost zeal, related his misfortunes, applauded his merit, took all the opportunities of recommending him, and asserted that "the inhumanity of his mother had given him a right to find every good man his father."

Nor was Mr. Savage admitted to his acquaintance only, but to his confidence, of which he sometimes related an instance too extraordinary to be omitted, as it affords a very just idea of his patron's character.

He was once desired by Sir Richard, with an air of the utmost importance, to come very early to his house the next morning. Mr. Savage came as he had promised, found the chariot at the door, and Sir Richard waiting for him and ready to go out. What was intended, and whither they were to go, Savage could not conjecture, and was not willing to inquire; but immediately seated himself with Sir Richard. The coachman was ordered to drive, and they hurried with the utmost expedition to Hyde Park Corner, where they stopped at a petty tavern and retired to a private room. Sir Richard then informed him that he intended to publish a pamphlet, and that he had desired him to come thither that he might write for him. He soon sat down to the work. Sir Richard dictated, and Savage wrote, till the dinner that had been ordered was put upon the table. Savage was surprised at the meanness of the entertainment, and after some hesitation ventured to ask for wine, which Sir Richard, not without reluctance, ordered to be brought. They then finished their dinner, and proceeded in their pamphlet, which they concluded in the afternoon.

Mr. Savage then imagined his task over, and expected that Sir Richard would call for the reckoning and return home; but his expectations deceived him, for Sir Richard told him that he was without money, and that the pamphlet must be sold before the dinner could be paid for; and Savage was therefore obliged to go and offer their new production to sale for two guineas, which with some difficulty he obtained. Sir Richard then returned home, having retired that day only to avoid his creditors, and composed the pamphlet only to discharge his reckoning.

Mr. Savage related another fact equally uncommon, which, though it has no relation to his life, ought to be preserved. Sir

Richard Steele having one day invited to his house a great number of persons of the first quality, they were surprised at the number of liveries which surrounded the table; and, after dinner, when wine and mirth had set them free from the observation of a rigid ceremony, one of them inquired of Sir Richard how such an expensive train of domestics could be consistent with his fortune. Sir Richard very frankly confessed that they were fellows of whom he would very willingly be rid. And being then asked why he did not discharge them, declared that they were bailiffs, who had introduced themselves with an execution, and whom, since he could not send them away, he had thought it convenient to embellish with liveries, that they might do him credit while they stayed.

His friends were diverted with the expedient, and by paying the debt discharged their attendants, having obliged Sir Richard to promise that they should never again find him graced with a retinue of the same kind.

Under such a tutor, Mr. Savage was not likely to learn prudence or frugality; and perhaps many of the misfortunes which the want of those virtues brought upon him in the following parts of his life might be justly imputed to so unimproving an example.

Nor did the kindness of Sir Richard end in common favours. He proposed to have established him in some settled scheme of life, and to have contracted a kind of alliance with him by marrying him to a natural daughter, on whom he intended to bestow a thousand pounds. But though he was always lavish of future bounties, he conducted his affairs in such a manner that he was very seldom able to keep his promises or execute his own intentions; and, as he was never able to raise the sum which he had offered, the marriage was delayed. In the meantime he was officiously informed that Mr. Savage had ridiculed him; by which he was so much exasperated that he withdrew the allowance which he had paid him, and never afterwards admitted him to his house.

It is not indeed unlikely that Savage might, by his imprudence, expose himself to the malice of a tale-bearer; for his patron had many follies, which, as his discernment easily discovered, his imagination might sometimes incite him to mention too ludicrously. A little knowledge of the world is sufficient to discover that such weakness is very common, and that there are few who do not sometimes, in the wantonness of thoughtless mirth, or the heat of transient resentment, speak of their friends and benefactors with levity and contempt, though in their cooler moments they want neither sense of their kindness nor reverence for their virtue. The fault therefore of Mr. Savage was rather negligence than ingratitude: but Sir Richard must likewise be acquitted of severity; for who is there that can patiently bear contempt from one whom he has relieved and supported, whose establishment he has laboured, and whose interest he has promoted?

He was now again abandoned to fortune without any other friend than Mr. Wilks; a man who, whatever were his abilities or skill as an actor, deserves at least to be remembered for his virtues, which are not often to be found in the world, and perhaps less often in his profession than in others. To be humane, generous, and candid, is a very high degree of merit in any case; but those qualities deserve still greater praise when they are found in that condition which makes almost every other man, for whatever reason, contemptuous, insolent, petulant, selfish, and brutal.

As Mr. Wilks was one of those to whom calamity seldom complained without relief, he naturally took an unfortunate wit into his protection, and not only assisted him in any casual distresses, but continued an equal and steady kindness to the time of his death.

By his interposition Mr. Savage once obtained from his mother 50l., and a promise of 150l. more; but it was the fate of this unhappy man that few promises of any advantage to him were performed. His mother was infected, among others, with the general madness of the South Sea traffic; and, having been disappointed in her expectations, refused to pay what perhaps nothing but the prospect of sudden affluence prompted her to promise.

Being thus obliged to depend upon the friendship of Mr. Wilks, he was consequently an assiduous frequenter of the theatres; and in a short time the amusements of the stage took such possession of his mind that he never was absent from a play in several years.

This constant attendance naturally procured him the acquaintance of the players, and, among others, of Mrs. Oldfield, who was so much pleased with his conversation, and touched with his misfortunes, that she allowed him a settled pension of 50l. a year, which was during her life regularly paid.

That this act of generosity may receive its due praise, and that the good actions of Mrs. Oldfield may not be sullied by her general character, it is proper to mention that Mr. Savage often declared in the strongest terms, that he never saw her alone, or in any other place than behind the scenes.

At her death [23rd Oct., 1730] he endeavoured to show his gratitude in the most decent manner, by wearing mourning as for a mother; but did not celebrate her in elegies; because he knew that too great profusion of praise would only have revived those faults which his natural equity did not allow him to think less because they were committed by one who favoured him; but of which, though his virtue would not endeavour to palliate them, his gratitude would not suffer him to prolong the memory or diffuse the censure.

In his *Wanderer* he has indeed taken an opportunity of mentioning her; but celebrates her not for her virtue, but her beauty, an excellence which none ever denied her: this is the only encomium with which he has rewarded her liberality, and perhaps he has even in this been too lavish of his praise. He seems to have thought, that never to mention his benefactress would have an appearance of ingratitude, though to have dedicated any particular performance to her memory would have only betrayed an officious partiality, that, without exalting her character, would have depressed his own.

He had sometimes, by the kindness of Mr. Wilks, the advantage of a benefit, on which occasions he often received uncommon marks of regard and compassion; and was once told by the Duke of Dorset that it was just to consider him as an injured nobleman, and that in his opinion the nobility ought to think themselves obliged, without solicitation, to take every opportunity of supporting him by their countenance and patronage. But he had generally the mortification to hear that the whole interest of his mother was employed to frustrate his applications, and that she never left any expedient untried by which he might be cut off from the possibility of supporting life. The same disposition she endeavoured to diffuse among all those over whom nature or fortune gave her any influence, and indeed succeeded too well in her design, but could not always propagate her effrontery with her cruelty, for some of those whom she incited against him were ashamed of their own conduct, and boasted of that relief which they never gave him.

In this censure I do not indiscriminately involve all his relations; for he has mentioned with gratitude the humanity of one lady whose name I am now unable to recollect, and to whom therefore I cannot pay the praises which she deserves for having acted well in opposition to influence, precept, and example.

The punishment which our laws inflict upon those parents who murder their infants is well known, nor has its justice ever been contested; but if they deserve death who destroy a child in its birth; what pains can be severe enough for her who forbears to destroy him only to inflict sharper miseries upon him; who prolongs his life only to make him miserable; and who exposes him, without care and without pity, to the malice of oppression, the caprices of chance, and the temptations of poverty; who rejoices to see him overwhelmed with calamities; and, when his own industry, or the charity of others, has enabled him to rise for a short time above his miseries, plunges him again into his former distress?

The kindness of his friends not affording him any constant supply, and the prospect of improving his fortune by enlarging his acquaintance necessarily leading him to places of expense, he found it necessary to endeavour once more at dramatic poetry, for which he was now better qualified by a more extensive knowledge and longer observation. But having been unsuccessful in comedy, though rather for want of opportunities than genius, he resolved now to try whether he should not be more fortunate in exhibiting a tragedy.

The story which he chose for the subject was that of Sir Thomas Overbury, a story well adapted to the stage, though perhaps not far enough removed from the present age to admit properly the fictions necessary to complete the plan: for the mind, which naturally loves truth, is always most offended with the violation of those truths of which we are most certain; and we of course conceive those facts most certain which approach nearest to our own time.

Out of this story he formed a tragedy, which, if the circumstances in which he wrote it be considered, will afford at once an uncommon proof of strength of genius and evenness of mind, of a serenity not to be ruffled and an imagination not to be suppressed.

During a considerable part of the time in which he was employed upon this performance he was without lodging, and often without meat; nor had he any other conveniences for study than the fields or the streets allowed him; there he used to walk and form his speeches, and afterwards step into a shop, beg for a few moments the use of the pen and ink, and write

down what he had composed upon paper which he had picked
up by accident.

If the performance of a writer thus distressed is not perfect, its
faults ought surely to be imputed to a cause very different from
want of genius, and must rather excite pity than provoke censure.

But when under these discouragements the tragedy was
finished, there yet remained the labour of introducing it on
the stage—an undertaking which, to an ingenuous mind, was
in a very high degree vexatious and disgusting; for, having
little interest or reputation, he was obliged to submit himself
wholly to the players, and admit, with whatever reluctance,
the emendations of Mr. Cibber, which he always considered as
the disgrace of his performance.

He had indeed in Mr. Hill another critic of a very different
class, from whose friendship he received great assistance on
many occasions, and whom he never mentioned but with the
utmost tenderness and regard. He had been for some time
distinguished by him with very particular kindness, and on
this occasion it was natural to apply to him as an author of an
established character. He therefore sent this tragedy to him,
with a short copy of verses, in which he desired his correction.
Mr. Hill, whose humanity and politeness are generally known,
readily complied with his request; but as he is remarkable for
singularity of sentiment, and bold experiments in language,
Mr. Savage did not think his play much improved by his
innovation, and had even at that time the courage to reject
several passages which he could not approve; and, what is still
more laudable, Mr. Hill had the generosity not to resent the
neglect of his alterations, but wrote the Prologue and Epilogue,
in which he touches on the circumstances of the author with
great tenderness.

After all these obstructions and compliances he was only
able to bring his play upon the stage in the summer, when
the chief actors had retired, and the rest were in possession
of the house for their own advantage. Among these Mr. Savage
was admitted to play the part of Sir Thomas Overbury, by
which he gained no great reputation, the theatre being a
province for which nature seemed not to have designed him;
for neither his voice, look, nor gesture were such as were
expected on the stage; and he was so much ashamed of having
been reduced to appear as a player, that he always blotted out
his name from the list when a copy of his tragedy was to be
shown to his friends.

In the publication of his performance he was more successful, for the rays of genius that glimmered in it, that glimmered through all the mists which poverty and Cibber had been able to spread over it, procured him the notice and esteem of many persons eminent for their rank, their virtue, and their wit.

Of this play, acted, printed, and dedicated, the accumulated profits arose to 100*l.*, which he thought at that time a very large sum, having been never master of so much before.

In the Dedication, for which he received ten guineas, there is nothing remarkable. The Preface contains a very liberal encomium on the blooming excellence of Mr. Theophilus Cibber, which Mr. Savage could not in the latter part of his life see his friends about to read without snatching the play out of their hands. The generosity of Mr. Hill did not end on this occasion; for afterwards, when Mr. Savage's necessities returned, he encouraged a subscription to a *Miscellany of Poems* in a very extraordinary manner, by publishing his story in *The Plain Dealer*, with some affecting lines, which he asserts to have been written by Mr. Savage upon the treatment received by him from his mother, but of which he was himself the author, as Mr. Savage afterwards declared. These lines, and the paper in which they were inserted, had a very powerful effect upon all but his mother, whom, by making her cruelty more public, they only hardened in her aversion.

Mr. Hill not only promoted the subscription to the *Miscellany*, but furnished likewise the greatest part of the poems of which it is composed, and particularly *The Happy Man*, which he published as a specimen.

The subscriptions of those whom these papers should influence to patronise merit in distress, without any other solicitation, were directed to be left at Button's coffee-house; and Mr. Savage going thither a few days afterwards, without expectation of any effect from his proposal, found to his surprise seventy guineas, which had been sent him in consequence of the compassion excited by Mr. Hill's pathetic representation.

To this *Miscellany* he wrote a Preface, in which he gives an account of his mother's cruelty in a very uncommon strain of humour, and with a gaiety of imagination which the success of his subscription probably produced.

The Dedication is addressed to the Lady Mary Wortley Montagu, whom he flatters without reserve, and to confess the truth, with very little art. The same observation may be extended to all his dedications: his compliments are constrained and violent, heaped together without the grace of order, or the decency of introduction: he seems to have written his panegyrics for the perusal only of his patrons, and to imagine that he had no other task than to pamper them with praises however gross, and that flattery would make its way to the heart without the assistance of elegance or invention.

Soon afterwards [11th June, 1727] the death of the King furnished a general subject for a poetical contest, in which Mr. Savage engaged, and is allowed to have carried the prize of honour from his competitors: but I know not whether he gained by his performance any other advantage than the increase of his reputation; though it must certainly have been with farther views that he prevailed upon himself to attempt a species of writing of which all the topics had been long before exhausted, and which was made at once difficult by the multitudes that had failed in it, and those that had succeeded.

He was now advancing in reputation, and though frequently involved in very distressful perplexities, appeared however to be gaining upon mankind, when both his fame and his life were endangered by an event, of which it is not yet determined whether it ought to be mentioned as a crime or a calamity.

On the 20th of November, 1727, Mr. Savage came from Richmond, where he then lodged, that he might pursue his studies with less interruption, with an intent to discharge another lodging which he had in Westminster; and accidentally meeting two gentlemen, his acquaintances, whose names were Merchant and Gregory, he went in with them to a neighbouring coffee-house, and sat drinking till it was late, it being in no time of Mr. Savage's life any part of his character to be the first of the company that desired to separate. He would willingly have gone to bed in the same house; but there was not room for the whole company, and therefore they agreed to ramble about the streets, and divert themselves with such amusements as should offer themselves till morning.

In this walk they happened unluckily to discover a light in Robinson's coffee-house, near Charing-Cross, and therefore went in. Merchant with some rudeness demanded a room, and was told that there was a good fire in the next parlour, which the company were about to leave, being then paying their reckoning. Merchant, not satisfied with this answer, rushed into the room, and was followed by his companions. He then petulantly placed himself between the company and the fire, and soon after kicked down the table. This produced a quarrel, swords were drawn on both sides, and one Mr. James Sinclair was killed. Savage having likewise wounded a maid that held him, forced his way with Merchant out of the house, but being intimidated and confused, without resolution either to fly or stay, they were taken in a back court by one of the company and some soldiers, whom he had called to his assistance.

Being secured and guarded that night, they were in the morning carried before three justices, who committed them to the Gatehouse [at Westminster], from whence, upon the death of Mr. Sinclair, which happened the same day, they were removed in the night to Newgate, where they were however treated with some distinction, exempted from the ignominy of chains, and confined, not among the common criminals, but in the Press-yard.

When the day of trial came the court was crowded in a very unusual manner, and the public appeared to interest itself as in a cause of general concern. The witnesses against Mr. Savage and his friends were the woman who kept the house, which was a house of ill fame, and her maid, the men who were in the room with Mr. Sinclair, and a woman of the town, who had been drinking with them, and with whom one of them had been seen in bed. They swore in general that Merchant gave the provocation, which Savage and Gregory drew their swords to justify; that Savage drew first, and that he stabbed Sinclair when he was not in a posture of defence, or while Gregory commanded his sword; that after he had given the thrust he turned pale, and would have retired, but the maid clung round him, and one of the company endeavoured to detain him, from whom he broke, by cutting the maid on the head, but was afterwards taken in a court.

There was some difference in their depositions: one did not see Savage give the wound, another saw it given when Sinclair held his point towards the ground; and the woman of the town asserted that she did not see Sinclair's sword at all: this difference however was very far from amounting to inconsistency; but it was sufficient to show that the hurry of the dispute was such, that it was not easy to discover the truth with relation to particular circumstances, and that therefore some deductions were to be made from the credibility of the testimonies.

Sinclair had declared several times before his death that he received his wound from Savage; nor did Savage at his trial deny the fact, but endeavoured partly to extenuate it, by urging the suddenness of the whole action, and the impossibility of any ill design or premeditated malice; and partly to justify it by

the necessity of self-defence, and the hazard of his own life, if
he had lost that opportunity of giving the thrust: he observed
that neither reason nor law obliged a man to wait for the blow
which was threatened, and which, if he should suffer it, he
might never be able to return; that it was always allowable
to prevent an assault, and to preserve life by taking away that
of the adversary by whom it was endangered.

With regard to the violence with which he endeavoured to
escape, he declared that it was not his design to fly from justice,
or decline a trial, but to avoid the expenses and severities of
a prison; and that he intended to have appeared at the bar
without compulsion.

This defence, which took up more than an hour, was heard
by the multitude that thronged the court with the most attentive and respectful silence: those who thought he ought not to
be acquitted, owned that applause could not be refused him;
and those who before pitied his misfortunes, now reverenced
his abilities.

The witnesses which appeared against him were proved to
be persons of characters which did not entitle them to much
credit; a common strumpet, a woman by whom strumpets were
entertained, and a man by whom they were supported; and
the character of Savage was by several persons of distinction
asserted to be that of a modest, inoffensive man, not inclined
to broils or to insolence, and who had, to that time, been only
known for his misfortunes and his wit.

Had his audience been his judges, he had undoubtedly been
acquitted; but Mr. Page, who was then upon the bench, treated
him with his usual insolence and severity, and when he had
summed up the evidence, endeavoured to exasperate the jury, as
Mr. Savage used to relate it, with this eloquent harangue:

"Gentlemen of the jury, you are to consider that Mr. Savage
is a very great man, a much greater man than you or I, gentlemen of the jury; that he wears very fine clothes, much finer
clothes than you or I, gentlemen of the jury; that he has
abundance of money in his pocket, much more money than
you or I, gentlemen of the jury; but, gentlemen of the jury, is
it not a very hard case, gentlemen of the jury, that Mr. Savage
should therefore kill you or me, gentlemen of the jury?"

Mr. Savage hearing his defence thus misrepresented, and
the men who were to decide his fate incited against him by
invidious comparisons, resolutely asserted that his cause was
not candidly explained, and began to recapitulate what he had

before said with regard to his condition, and the necessity of endeavouring to escape the expenses of imprisonment; but the judge having ordered him to be silent, and repeated his orders without effect, commanded that he should be taken from the bar by force.

The jury then heard the opinion of the judge that good characters were of no weight against positive evidence, though they might turn the scale where it was doubtful; and that though, when two men attack each other, the death of either is only manslaughter; but where one is the aggressor, as in the case before them, and, in pursuance of his first attack, kills the other, the law supposes the action, however sudden, to be malicious. They then deliberated upon their verdict, and determined that Mr. Savage and Mr. Gregory were guilty of murder; and Mr. Merchant, who had no sword, only of manslaughter.

Thus ended this memorable trial, which lasted eight hours. Mr. Savage and Mr. Gregory were conducted back to prison, where they were more closely confined, and loaded with irons of fifty pounds weight: four days afterwards they were sent back to the court to receive sentence; on which occasion Mr. Savage made, as far as it could be retained in memory, the following speech:

"It is now, my Lord, too late to offer anything by way of defence or vindication; nor can we expect aught from your Lordships in this court but the sentence which the law requires you, as judges, to pronounce against men of our calamitous condition. But we are also persuaded, that as mere men, and out of this seat of rigorous justice, you are susceptive of the tender passions, and too humane not to commiserate the unhappy situation of those whom the law sometimes, perhaps, exacts from you to pronounce upon. No doubt you distinguish between offences which arise out of premeditation and a disposition habituated to vice or immorality, and transgressions which are the unhappy and unforeseen effects of a casual absence of reason and sudden impulse of passion: we therefore hope you will contribute all you can to an extension of that mercy which the gentlemen of the jury have been pleased to show Mr. Merchant, who (allowing facts as sworn against us by the evidence) has led us into this our calamity. I hope this will not be construed as if we meant to reflect upon that gentleman, or remove anything from us upon him, or that we repine the more at our fate because he has no participation of it: No, my Lord! For my part I declare nothing could more soften my grief than to be without any companion in so great a misfortune."

Mr. Savage had now no hopes of life but from the mercy of the Crown, which was very earnestly solicited by his friends, and which, with whatever difficulty the story may obtain belief, was obstructed only by his mother.

To prejudice the Queen [Caroline, Queen of George II.] against him, she made use of an incident which was omitted in the order of time, that it might be mentioned together with the purpose which it was made to serve. Mr. Savage, when he had discovered his birth, had an incessant desire to speak to his mother, who always avoided him in public, and refused him admission into her house. One evening walking, as it was his custom, in the street that she inhabited, he saw the door of her house by accident open, he entered it, and, finding no person in the passage to hinder him, went up stairs to salute her. She discovered him before he entered her chamber, alarmed the family with the most distressful outcries, and when she had by her screams gathered them about her, ordered them to drive out of the house that villain who had forced himself in upon her and endeavoured to murder her. Savage, who had attempted with the most submissive tenderness to soften her rage, hearing her utter so detestable an accusation, thought it prudent to retire, and, I believe, never attempted afterwards to speak to her.

But, shocked as he was with her falsehood and her cruelty, he imagined that she intended no other use of her lie than to set herself free from his embraces and solicitations, and was very far from suspecting that she would treasure it in her memory as an instrument of future wickedness, or that she would endeavour for this fictitious assault to deprive him of his life.

But when the Queen was solicited for his pardon, and informed of the severe treatment which he had suffered from his judge, she answered, that however unjustifiable might be the manner of his trial, or whatever extenuation the action for which he was condemned might admit, she could not think that man a proper object of the King's mercy who had been capable of entering his mother's house in the night with an intent to murder her.

By whom this atrocious calumny had been transmitted to the Queen; whether she that invented had the front to relate it; whether she found anyone weak enough to credit it, or corrupt enough to concur with her in her hateful design, I know not; but methods had been taken to persuade the Queen so strongly of the truth of it, that she for a long time refused to hear anyone of those who petitioned for his life.

Thus had Savage perished by the evidence of a bawd, a strumpet, and his mother, had not justice and compassion procured him an advocate of rank too great to be rejected unheard, and of virtue too eminent to be heard without being believed. His merit and his calamities happened to reach the ear of the Countess of Hertford, who engaged in his support with all the tenderness that is excited by pity, and all the zeal which is kindled by generosity; and, demanding an audience of the Queen, laid before her the whole series of his mother's cruelty, exposed the improbability of an accusation by which he was charged with an intent to commit a murder that could produce no advantage, and soon convinced her how little his former conduct could deserve to be mentioned as a reason for extraordinary severity.

The interposition of this lady was so successful that he was soon after admitted to bail, and, on the 9th of March, 1728, pleaded the King's pardon.

It is natural to inquire upon what motives his mother could persecute him in a manner so outrageous and implacable; for what reason she could employ all the arts of malice, and all the snares of calumny, to take away the life of her own son, of a son who never injured her, who was never supported by her expense, nor obstructed any prospect of pleasure or advantage; why she should endeavour to destroy him by a lie—a lie which could not gain credit, but must vanish of itself at the first moment of examination, and of which only this can be said to make it probable, that it may be observed from her conduct that the most execrable crimes are sometimes committed without apparent temptation.

This mother is still alive, and may perhaps even yet, though her malice was so often defeated, enjoy the pleasure of reflecting that the life which she often endeavoured to destroy was at last shortened by her maternal offices; that though she could not transport her son to the plantations, bury him in the shop of a mechanic, or hasten the hand of the public executioner, she has yet had the satisfaction of embittering all his hours, and forcing him into exigences that hurried on his death.

It is by no means necessary to aggravate the enormity of this woman's conduct by placing it in opposition to that of the

Countess of Hertford; no one can fail to observe how much more amiable it is to relieve than to oppress, and to rescue innocence from destruction than to destroy without an injury.

Mr. Savage, during his imprisonment, his trial, and the time in which he lay under sentence of death, behaved with great firmness and equality of mind, and confirmed by his fortitude the esteem of those who before admired him for his abilities. The peculiar circumstances of his life were made more generally known by a short account, which was then published, and of which several thousands were in a few weeks dispersed over the nation: and the compassion of mankind operated so powerfully in his favour, that he was enabled by frequent presents not only to support himself, but to assist Mr. Gregory in prison; and when he was pardoned and released, he found the number of his friends not lessened.

The nature of the act for which he had been tried was in itself doubtful; of the evidences which appeared against him, the character of the man was not unexceptionable, that of the women notoriously infamous; she whose testimony chiefly influenced the jury to condemn him, afterwards retracted her assertions. He always himself denied that he was drunk, as had been generally reported. Mr. Gregory, who is now (1744) Collector of Antigua, is said to declare him far less criminal than he was imagined, even by some who favoured him; and Page himself afterwards confessed that he had treated him with uncommon rigour. When all these particulars are rated together, perhaps the memory of Savage may not be much sullied by his trial.

Some time after he obtained his liberty, he met in the street the woman that had sworn with so much malignity against him. She informed him that she was in distress, and, with a degree of confidence not easily attainable, desired him to relieve her. He, instead of insulting her misery, and taking pleasure in the calamities of one who had brought his life into danger, reproved her gently for her perjury; and changing the only guinea that he had, divided it equally between her and himself.

This is an action which in some ages would have made a saint, and perhaps in others a hero, and which, without any hyperbolical encomiums, must be allowed to be an instance of uncommon generosity, an act of complicated virtue; by which he at once relieved the poor, corrected the vicious, and forgave an enemy; by which he at once remitted the strongest provocations, and exercised the most ardent charity.

Compassion was indeed the distinguishing quality of Savage; he never appeared inclined to take advantage of weakness, to attack the defenceless, or to press upon the falling: whoever was distressed, was certain at least of his good wishes; and when he could give no assistance to extricate them from misfortunes, he endeavoured to soothe them by sympathy and tenderness.

But when his heart was not softened by the sight of misery, he was sometimes obstinate in his resentment, and did not quickly lose the remembrance of an injury. He always continued to speak with anger of the insolence and partiality of Page, and a short time before his death revenged it by a satire.

It is natural to inquire in what terms Mr. Savage spoke of this fatal action when the danger was over, and he was under no necessity of using any art to set his conduct in the fairest light. He was not willing to dwell upon it; and, if he transiently mentioned it, appeared neither to consider himself as a murderer, nor as a man wholly free from the guilt of blood. How much and how long he regretted it, appeared in a poem which he published many years afterwards. On occasion of a copy of verses, in which the failings of good men were recounted, and in which the author had endeavoured to illustrate his position, that "the best may sometimes deviate from virtue," by an instance of murder committed by Savage in the heat of wine, Savage remarked, that it was no very just representation of a good man, to suppose him liable to drunkenness, and disposed in his riots to cut throats.

He was now indeed at liberty, but was, as before, without any other support than accidental favours and uncertain patronage afforded him; sources by which he was sometimes very liberally supplied, and which at other times were suddenly stopped; so that he spent his life between want and plenty; or, what was yet worse, between beggary and extravagance; for, as whatever he received was the gift of chance, which might as well favour him at one time as another, he was tempted to squander what he had, because he always hoped to be immediately supplied.

Another cause of his profusion was the absurd kindness of his friends, who at once rewarded and enjoyed his abilities by treating him at taverns, and habituating him to pleasures which he could not afford to enjoy, and which he was not able to deny himself, though he purchased the luxury of a single night by the anguish of cold and hunger for a week.

The experience of these inconveniences determined him to endeavour after some settled income, which, having long found submission and entreaties fruitless, he attempted to extort from his mother by rougher methods. He had now, as he acknowledged, lost that tenderness for her which the whole series of her cruelty had not been able wholly to repress, till he found, by the efforts which she made for his destruction, that she was not content with refusing to assist him, and being neutral in his struggles with poverty, but was as ready to snatch every opportunity of adding to his misfortunes; and that she was now to be considered as an enemy implacably malicious, whom nothing but his blood could satisfy. He therefore threatened to harass her with lampoons, and to publish a copious narrative of her conduct, unless she consented to purchase an exemption from infamy by allowing him a pension.

This expedient proved successful. Whether shame still survived, though virtue was extinct, or whether her relations had more delicacy than herself, and imagined that some of the darts which satire might point at her would glance upon them, Lord Tyrconnel, whatever were his motives, upon his promise to lay aside his design of exposing the cruelty of his mother, received him into his family, treated him as his equal, and engaged to allow him a pension of 200*l.* a year.

This was the golden part of Mr. Savage's life, and for some time he had no reason to complain of fortune; his appearance was splendid, his expenses large, and his acquaintance extensive. He was courted by all who endeavoured to be thought men of genius, and caressed by all who valued themselves upon a refined taste. To admire Mr. Savage was a proof of discernment, and to be acquainted with him was a title to poetical reputation. His presence was sufficient to make any place of public entertainment popular, and his approbation and example constituted the fashion. So powerful is genius when it is invested with the glitter of affluence! Men willingly pay to fortune that regard which they owe to merit, and are pleased when they have an opportunity at once of gratifying their vanity and practising their duty.

This interval of prosperity furnished him with opportunities of enlarging his knowledge of human nature, by contemplating life from its highest gradations to its lowest; and, had he afterwards applied to dramatic poetry, he would perhaps not have had many superiors; for as he never suffered any scene to pass before his eyes without notice, he had treasured in his mind all the different combinations of passions, and the innumerable mixtures of vice and virtue, which distinguish one character from another; and, as his conception was strong, his expressions were clear, he easily received impressions from objects, and very forcibly transmitted them to others.

Of his exact observations on human life he has left a proof, which would do honour to the greatest names, in a small pamphlet, called *The Author to be Let*, where he introduces Iscariot Hackney, a prostitute scribbler, giving an account of his birth, his education, his disposition and morals, habits of life, and maxims of conduct. In the Introduction are related many secret histories of the petty writers of that time, but sometimes mixed with ungenerous reflections on their birth, their circumstances, or those of their relations; nor can it be denied that some passages are such as Iscariot Hackney might himself have produced.

He was accused likewise of living in an appearance of friendship with some whom he satirised, and of making use of the confidence which he gained by a seeming kindness, to discover failings and expose them: it must be confessed that Mr. Savage's esteem was no very certain possession, and that he would lampoon at one time those whom he had praised at another.

It may be alleged, that the same man may change his principles; and that he who was once deservedly commended, may be afterwards satirised with equal justice; or that the poet was dazzled with the appearance of virtue, and found the man whom he had celebrated, when he had an opportunity of examining him more narrowly, unworthy of the panegyric which he had too hastily bestowed; and that, as a false satire ought to be recanted for the sake of him whose reputation may be injured, false praise ought likewise to be obviated, lest the distinction between vice and virtue should be lost, lest a bad man should be trusted upon the credit of his encomiast, or lest others should endeavour to obtain the like praises by the same means.

But though these excuses may be often plausible, and sometimes just, they are very seldom satisfactory to mankind; and the writer who is not constant to his subject quickly sinks into contempt, his satire loses its force, and his panegyric its value, and he is only considered at one time as a flatterer, and as a calumniator at another.

To avoid these imputations, it is only necessary to follow the rules of virtue, and to preserve an unvaried regard to truth.

For though it is undoubtedly possible that a man, however cautious, may be sometimes deceived by an artful appearance of virtue, or by false evidences of guilt, such errors will not be frequent; and it will be allowed, that the name of an author would never have been made contemptible, had no man ever said what he did not think, or misled others but when he was himself deceived.

The Author to be Let was first published in a single pamphlet, and afterwards inserted in a collection of pieces relating to the *Dunciad*, which were addressed by Mr. Savage to the Earl of Middlesex, in a Dedication which he was prevailed upon to sign, though he did not write it, and in which there are some positions that the true author would perhaps not have published under his own name, and on which Mr. Savage afterwards reflected with no great satisfaction. The enumeration of the bad effects of the "uncontrolled freedom of the press," and the assertion that the "liberties taken by the writers of journals with their superiors were exorbitant and unjustifiable," very ill became men who have themselves not always shown the exactest regard to the laws of subordination in their writings, and who have often satirised those that at least thought themselves their superiors, as they were eminent for their hereditary rank, and employed in the highest offices of the kingdom. But this is only an instance of that partiality which almost every man indulges with regard to himself: the liberty of the press is a blessing when we are inclined to write against others, and a calamity when we find ourselves overborne by the multitude of our assailants; as the power of the Crown is always thought too great by those who suffer by its influence, and too little by those in whose favour it is exerted; and a standing army is generally accounted necessary by those who command, and dangerous and oppressive by those who support it.

Mr. Savage was likewise very far from believing that the letters annexed to each species of bad poets in the Bathos were, as he was directed to assert, "set down at random"; for when he was charged by one of his friends with putting his name to such an improbability, he had no other answer to make, than that "he did not think of it"; and his friend had too much tenderness to reply, that next to the crime of writing contrary to what he thought, was that of writing without thinking.

After having remarked what is false in this Dedication, it is proper that I observe the impartiality which I recommend, by declaring what Savage asserted; that the account of the circumstances which attended the publication of the *Dunciad*, however strange and improbable, was exactly true.

The publication of this piece at this time raised Mr. Savage a great number of enemies among those that were attacked by Mr. Pope, with whom he was considered as a kind of confederate, and whom he was suspected of supplying with private intelligence and secret incidents: so that the ignominy of an informer was added to the terror of a satirist.

That he was not altogether free from literary hypocrisy, and that he sometimes spoke one thing, and wrote another, cannot be denied; because he himself confessed, that, when he lived with great familiarity with Dennis, he wrote an epigram against him.

Mr. Savage, however, set all the malice of all the pigmy writers at defiance, and thought the friendship of Mr. Pope cheaply purchased by being exposed to their censure and their hatred; nor had he any reason to repent of the preference, for he found Mr. Pope a steady and unalienable friend almost to the end of his life.

About this time, notwithstanding his avowed neutrality with regard to party, he published (1732) a panegyric on Sir Robert Walpole, for which he was rewarded by him with twenty guineas, a sum not very large, if either the excellence of the performance, or the affluence of the patron, be considered; but greater than he afterwards obtained from a person of yet higher rank [Frederick Prince of Wales], and more desirous in appearance of being distinguished as a patron of literature.

As he was very far from approving the conduct of Sir Robert Walpole, and in conversation mentioned him sometimes with acrimony, and generally with contempt; as he was one of those who were always zealous in their assertions of the justice of the late opposition, jealous of the rights of the people, and alarmed by the long-continued triumph of the Court, it was natural to ask him what could induce him to employ his poetry in praise of that man who was, in his opinion, an enemy to liberty, and an oppressor of his country? He alleged, that he was then dependent upon the Lord Tyrconnel, who was an implicit follower of the ministry; and that being enjoined by him, not without menaces, to write in praise of his leader, he had not resolution sufficient to sacrifice the pleasure of affluence to that of integrity.

On this, and on many other occasions, he was ready to lament the misery of living at the tables of other men, which was his fate from the beginning to the end of his life; for I know not whether he ever had, for three months together, a settled habitation, in which he could claim a right of residence.

To this unhappy state it is just to impute much of the inconstancy of his conduct; for though a readiness to comply with the inclination of others was no part of his natural character, yet he was sometimes obliged to relax his obstinacy, and submit his own judgment, and even his virtue, to the government of those by whom he was supported: so that, if his miseries were sometimes the consequences of his faults, he ought not yet to be wholly excluded from compassion, because his faults were very often the effects of his misfortunes.

In this gay period (1729) of his life, while he was surrounded by affluence and pleasure, he published *The Wanderer*, a moral poem, of which the design is comprised in these lines:

> I fly all public care, all venal strife,
> To try the still, compar'd with active, life;
> To prove, by these, the sons of men may owe
> The fruits of bliss to bursting clouds of woe;
> That ev'n calamity, by thought refin'd,
> Inspirits and adorns the thinking mind.

And more distinctly in the following passage:

> By woe, the soul to daring action swells;
> By woe, in plaintless patience it excels;
> From patience, prudent clear experience springs,
> And traces knowledge thro' the course of things!
> Thence hope is form'd, thence fortitude, success,
> Renown:—whate'er men covet and caress.

This performance was always considered by himself as his masterpiece; and Mr. Pope, when he asked his opinion of it, told him, that he read it once over, and was not displeased with it; that it gave him more pleasure at the second perusal, and delighted him still more at the third.

It has been generally objected to *The Wanderer*, that the disposition of the parts is irregular; that the design is obscure, and the plan perplexed; that the images, however beautiful, succeed each other without order; and that the whole performance is not so much a regular fabric, as a heap of shining materials thrown together by accident, which strikes rather with the solemn magnificence of a stupendous ruin, than the elegant grandeur of a finished pile.

This criticism is universal, and therefore it is reasonable to believe it at least in a great degree just; but Mr. Savage was always of a contrary opinion, and thought his drift could only be missed by negligence or stupidity, and that the whole plan was regular, and the parts distinct.

It was never denied to abound with strong representations of nature, and just observations upon life; and it may easily be observed, that most of his pictures have an evident tendency to illustrate his first great position, "that good is the consequence of evil." The sun that burns up the mountains, fructifies the vales; the deluge that rushes down the broken rocks with dreadful impetuosity, is separated into purling brooks; and the rage of the hurricane purifies the air.

Even in this poem he has not been able to forbear one touch upon the cruelty of his mother, which, though remarkably delicate and tender, is a proof how deep an impression it had upon his mind.

This must be at least acknowledged, which ought to be thought equivalent to many other excellences, that this poem can promote no other purposes than those of virtue, and that it is written with a very strong sense of the efficacy of religion.

But my province is rather to give the history of Mr. Savage's performances than to display their beauties, or to obviate the criticisms which they have occasioned; and therefore I shall not dwell upon the particular passages which deserve applause: I shall neither show the excellence of his descriptions, nor expatiate on the terrific portrait of suicide, nor point out the artful touches by which he has distinguished the intellectual features of the rebels, who suffer death in his last canto. It is, however, proper to observe, that Mr. Savage always declared the characters wholly fictitious, and without the least allusion to any real persons or actions.

From a poem so diligently laboured, and so successfully finished, it might be reasonably expected that he should have gained considerable advantage; nor can it, without some degree of indignation and concern, be told, that he sold the copy for ten guineas, of which he afterwards returned two, that the two last sheets of the work might be reprinted, of which he had in his absence intrusted the correction to a friend, who was too indolent to perform it with accuracy.

A superstitious regard to the correction of his sheets was one of Mr. Savage's peculiarities: he often altered, revised, recurred to his first reading or punctuation, and again adopted the alteration; he was dubious and irresolute without end, as on a question of the last importance, and at last was seldom satisfied: the intrusion or omission of a comma was sufficient to

discompose him, and he would lament an error of a single
letter as a heavy calamity. In one of his letters relating to
an impression of some verses, he remarks, that he had, with
regard to the correction of the proof, "a spell upon him"; and
indeed the anxiety with which he dwelt upon the minutest
and most trifling niceties deserved no other name than that
of fascination.

That he sold so valuable a performance for so small a price,
was not to be imputed either to necessity, by which the learned
and ingenious are often obliged to submit to very hard conditions; or to avarice, by which the booksellers are frequently
incited to oppress that genius by which they are supported;
but to that intemperate desire of pleasure, and habitual slavery
to his passions, which involved him in many perplexities. He
happened at that time to be engaged in the pursuit of some
trifling gratification, and, being without money for the present
occasion, sold his poem to the first bidder, and perhaps for the
first price that was proposed, and would probably have been
content with less if less had been offered him.

This poem was addressed to the Lord Tyrconnel, not only
in the first lines, but in a formal Dedication filled with the
highest strains of panegyric, and the warmest professions of
gratitude, but by no means remarkable for delicacy of connexion
or elegance of style.

These praises in a short time he found himself inclined to
retract, being discarded by the man on whom he had bestowed
them, and whom he then immediately discovered not to have
deserved them. Of this quarrel, which every day made more
bitter, Lord Tyrconnel and Mr. Savage assigned very different
reasons, which might perhaps all in reality concur, though they
were not all convenient to be alleged by either party. Lord
Tyrconnel affirmed that it was the constant practice of Mr.
Savage to enter a tavern with any company that proposed it,
drink the most expensive wines with great profusion, and when
the reckoning was demanded, to be without money: if, as it
often happened, his company were willing to defray his part,
the affair ended, without any ill consequences; but if they were
refractory, and expected that the wine should be paid for by
him that drank it, his method of composition was, to take them
with him to his own apartment, assume the government of the
house, and order the butler in an imperious manner to set the
best wine in the cellar before his company, who often drank till
they forgot the respect due to the house in which they were

entertained, indulged themselves in the utmost extravagance of merriment, practised the most licentious frolics, and committed all the outrages of drunkenness.

Nor was this the only charge which Lord Tyrconnel brought against him. Having given him a collection of valuable books, stamped with his own arms, he had the mortification to see them in a short time exposed to sale upon the stalls, it being usual with Mr. Savage, when he wanted a small sum, to take his books to the pawnbroker.

Whoever was acquainted with Mr. Savage easily credited both these accusations; for having been obliged, from his first entrance into the world, to subsist upon expedients, affluence was not able to exalt him above them; and so much was he delighted with wine and conversation, and so long had he been accustomed to live by chance, that he would at any time go to the tavern without scruple, and trust for the reckoning to the liberality of his company, and frequently of company to whom he was very little known. This conduct indeed very seldom drew upon him those inconveniences that might be feared by any other person; for his conversation was so entertaining, and his address so pleasing, that few thought the pleasure which they received from him dearly purchased by paying for his wine. It was his peculiar happiness that he scarcely ever found a stranger whom he did not leave a friend; but it must likewise be added, that he had not often a friend long without obliging him to become a stranger.

Mr. Savage, on the other hand, declared that Lord Tyrconnel quarrelled with him because he would not subtract from his own luxury and extravagance what he had promised to allow him, and that his resentment was only a plea for the violation of his promise. He asserted that he had done nothing that ought to exclude him from that subsistence which he thought not so much a favour as a debt, since it was offered him upon conditions which he had never broken; and that his only fault was, that he could not be supported with nothing.

He acknowledged that Lord Tyrconnel often exhorted him to regulate his method of life, and not to spend all his nights in taverns, and that he appeared desirous that he would pass those hours with him which he so freely bestowed upon others. This demand Mr. Savage considered as a censure of his conduct, which he could never patiently bear, and which, in the latter and cooler parts of his life, was so offensive to him that he declared it as his resolution "to spurn that friend who should presume to dictate to him"; and it is not likely that in his earlier years he received admonitions with more calmness.

He was likewise inclined to resent such expectations, as tending to infringe his liberty, of which he was very jealous, when it was necessary to the gratification of his passions; and declared that the request was still more unreasonable, as the company to which he was to have been confined was insupportably disagreeable. This assertion affords another instance of that inconsistency of his writings with his conversation which was so often to be observed. He forgot how lavishly he had, in his Dedication to *The Wanderer*, extolled the delicacy and penetration, the humanity and generosity, the candour and politeness of the man whom, when he no longer loved him, he declared to be a wretch without understanding, without good nature, and without justice, of whose name he thought himself obliged to leave no trace in any future edition of his writings, and accordingly blotted it out of that copy of *The Wanderer* which was in his hands.

During his continuance with the Lord Tyrconnel, he wrote [1730] *The Triumph of Health and Mirth*, on the recovery of Lady Tyrconnel from a languishing illness. This performance is remarkable, not only for the gaiety of the ideas and the melody of the numbers, but for the agreeable fiction upon which it is formed. Mirth, overwhelmed with sorrow for the sickness of her favourite, takes a flight in quest of her sister Health, whom she finds reclined upon the brow of a lofty mountain, amidst the fragrance of perpetual spring, with the breezes of the morning sporting about her. Being solicited by her sister Mirth, she readily promises her assistance, flies away in a cloud, and impregnates the waters of Bath with new virtues, by which the sickness of Belinda is relieved.

As the reputation of his abilities, the particular circumstances of his birth and life, the splendour of his appearance, and the distinction which was for some time paid him by Lord Tyrconnel, entitled him to familiarity with persons of higher rank than those to whose conversation he had been before admitted, he did not fail to gratify that curiosity, which induced him to take a nearer view of those whom their birth, their employments, or their fortunes necessarily place at a distance from the greatest part of mankind, and to examine whether their merit was magnified or diminished by the medium through which it was contemplated; whether the splendour with which they dazzled their admirers was inherent in themselves, or only reflected on them by the objects that surrounded them; and whether great men were selected for high stations, or high stations made great men.

For this purpose he took all opportunities of conversing familiarly with those who were most conspicuous at that time for their power or their influence; he watched their looser moments, and examined their domestic behaviour with that acuteness which nature had given him, and which the uncommon variety of his life had contributed to increase, and that inquisitiveness which must always be produced in a vigorous mind by an absolute freedom from all pressing or domestic engagements.

His discernment was quick, and therefore he soon found in every person, and in every affair, something that deserved attention; he was supported by others, without any care for himself, and was therefore at leisure to pursue his observations.

More circumstances to constitute a critic on human life could not easily concur; nor indeed could any man, who assumed from accidental advantages more praise than he could justly claim from his real merit, admit any acquaintance more dangerous than that of Savage; of whom likewise it must be confessed, that abilities really exalted above the common level, or virtue refined from passion, or proof against corruption, could not easily find an abler judge, or a warmer advocate.

What was the result of Mr. Savage's inquiry, though he was not much accustomed to conceal his discoveries, it may not be entirely safe to relate, because the persons whose characters he criticised are powerful, and power and resentment are seldom strangers; nor would it perhaps be wholly just, because what he asserted in conversation might, though true in general, be heightened by some momentary ardour of imagination, and, as it can be delivered only from memory, may be imperfectly represented; so that the picture, at first aggravated, and then unskilfully copied, may be justly suspected to retain no great resemblance of the original.

It may, however, be observed that he did not appear to have formed very elevated ideas of those to whom the administration of affairs, or the conduct of parties, has been entrusted—who have been considered as the advocates of the Crown, or the guardians of the people, and who have obtained the most implicit confidence, and the loudest applauses. Of one particular person, who has been at one time so popular as to be generally esteemed, and at another so formidable as to be universally detested, he observed, that his acquisitions had been small, or that his capacity was narrow, and that the whole range of his mind was from obscenity to politics, and from politics to obscenity.

But the opportunity of indulging his speculations on great characters was now at an end. He was banished from the table of Lord Tyrconnel, and turned again adrift upon the world, without prospect of finding quickly any other harbour. As prudence was not one of the virtues by which he was distinguished, he had made no provision against a misfortune like this. And though it is not to be imagined but that the separation must for some time have been preceded by coldness, peevishness, or neglect, though it was undoubtedly the consequence of accumulated provocations on both sides, yet everyone that knew Savage will readily believe that to him it was sudden as a stroke of thunder—that though he might have transiently suspected it, he had never suffered any thought so unpleasing to sink into his mind, but that he had driven it away by amusements, or dreams of future felicity and affluence, and had never taken any measures by which he might prevent a precipitation from plenty to indigence.

This quarrel and separation, and the difficulties to which Mr. Savage was exposed by them, were soon known both to his friends and enemies; nor was it long before he perceived, from the behaviour of both, how much is added to the lustre of genius by the ornaments of wealth.

His condition did not appear to excite much compassion; for he had not always been careful to use the advantages he enjoyed with that moderation which ought to have been with more than usual caution preserved by him, who knew, if he had reflected, that he was only a dependant on the bounty of another, whom he could expect to support him no longer than he endeavoured to preserve his favour by complying with his inclinations, and whom he nevertheless set at defiance, and was continually irritating by negligence or encroachments.

Examples need not be sought at any great distance to prove that superiority of fortune has a natural tendency to kindle pride, and that pride seldom fails to exert itself in contempt and insult; and if this is often the effect of hereditary wealth, and of honours enjoyed only by the merits of others, it is some extenuation of any indecent triumphs to which this unhappy man may have been betrayed, that his prosperity was heightened by the force of novelty, and made more intoxicating by a sense of the misery in which he had so long languished, and perhaps of the insults which he had formerly borne, and which he might now think himself entitled to revenge. It is too common for those who have unjustly suffered pain to inflict it likewise in their turn with the same injustice, and to imagine that they have a right to treat others as they have themselves been treated.

That Mr. Savage was too much elevated by any good fortune is generally known; and some passages of his Introduction to *The Author to be Let* sufficiently show that he did not wholly refrain from such satire as he afterwards thought very unjust when he was exposed to it himself; for, when he was afterwards ridiculed in the character of a distressed poet, he very easily discovered that distress was not a proper subject for merriment, or topic of invective. He was then able to discern that if misery be the effect of virtue, it ought to be reverenced; if of ill fortune, to be pitied; and if of vice, not to be insulted, because it is perhaps itself a punishment adequate to the crime by which it was produced. And the humanity of that man can deserve no panegyric who is capable of reproaching a criminal in the hands of the executioner.

But these reflections, though they readily occurred to him in the first and last parts of his life, were, I am afraid, for a long time forgotten—at least they were, like many other maxims, treasured up in his mind, rather for show than use, and operated very little upon his conduct, however elegantly he might sometimes explain, or however forcibly he might inculcate, them.

His degradation, therefore, from the condition which he had enjoyed with such wanton thoughtlessness was considered by many as an occasion of triumph. Those who had before paid their court to him without success soon returned the contempt which they had suffered; and they who had received favours from him—for of such favours as he could bestow he was very liberal—did not always remember them. So much more certain are the effects of resentment than of gratitude: it is not only to many more pleasing to recollect those faults which place others below them than those virtues by which they are themselves comparatively depressed, but it is likewise more easy to neglect than to recompense; and though there are few who will practise a laborious virtue, there will never be wanting multitudes that will indulge in easy vice.

Savage, however, was very little disturbed at the marks of contempt which his ill fortune brought upon him from those whom he never esteemed, and with whom he never considered himself as levelled by any calamities: and though it was not without some uneasiness that he saw some, whose friendship he valued, change their behaviour, he yet observed their coldness without much emotion, considered them as the slaves of fortune and the worshippers of prosperity, and was more inclined to despise them than to lament himself.

It does not appear that, after this return of his wants, he found mankind equally favourable to him as at his first appearance in the world. His story, though in reality not less melancholy, was less affecting because it was no longer new; it therefore procured him no new friends, and those that had formerly relieved him thought they might now consign him to others. He was now likewise considered by many rather as criminal than as unhappy; for the friends of Lord Tyrconnel, and of his mother, were sufficiently industrious to publish his weaknesses, which were indeed very numerous; and nothing was forgotten that might make him either hateful or ridiculous.

It cannot but be imagined that such representations of his faults must make great numbers less sensible of his distress; many, who had only an opportunity to hear one part, made no scruple to propagate the account which they received; many assisted their circulation from malice or revenge; and perhaps many pretended to credit them that they might with a better grace withdraw their regard, or withhold their assistance.

Savage, however, was not one of those who suffered himself to be injured without resistance, nor was less diligent in exposing the faults of Lord Tyrconnel, over whom he obtained at least this advantage, that he drove him first to the practice of outrage and violence; for he was so much provoked by the wit and virulence of Savage, that he came with a number of attendants, that did no honour to his courage, to beat him at a coffee-house. But it happened that he had left the place a few minutes; and his Lordship had, without danger, the pleasure of boasting how he would have treated him. Mr. Savage went next day to repay his visit at his own house, but was prevailed on by his domestics to retire without insisting upon seeing him.

Lord Tyrconnel was accused by Mr. Savage of some actions which scarcely any provocations will be thought sufficient to justify, such as seizing what he had in his lodgings, and other instances of wanton cruelty, by which he increased the distress of Savage without any advantage to himself.

These mutual accusations were retorted on both sides for

many years with the utmost degree of virulence and rage, and time seemed rather to augment than diminish their resentment. That the anger of Mr. Savage should be kept alive is not strange, because he felt every day the consequences of the quarrel; but it might reasonably have been hoped that Lord Tyrconnel might have relented, and at length have forgot those provocations which, however they might have once inflamed him, had not in reality much hurt him.

The spirit of Mr. Savage indeed never suffered him to solicit a reconciliation; he returned reproach for reproach, and insult for insult; his superiority of wit supplied the disadvantages of his fortune, and enabled him to form a party, and prejudice great numbers in his favour.

But though this might be some gratification of his vanity, it afforded very little relief to his necessities; and he was very frequently reduced to uncommon hardships, of which, however, he never made any mean or importunate complaints, being formed rather to bear misery with fortitude than enjoy prosperity with moderation.

He now thought himself again at liberty to expose the cruelty of his mother; and therefore, I believe, about this time published The Bastard, a poem remarkable for the vivacious sallies of thought in the beginning, where he makes a pompous enumeration of the imaginary advantages of base birth, and the pathetic sentiments at the end, where he recounts the real calamities which he suffered by the crime of his parents.

The vigour and spirit of the verses, the peculiar circumstances of the author, the novelty of the subject, and the notoriety of the story to which the allusions are made, procured this performance a very favourable reception; great numbers were immediately dispersed, and editions were multiplied with unusual rapidity.

One circumstance attended the publication which Savage used to relate with great satisfaction. His mother, to whom the poem was with "due reverence" inscribed, happened then to be at Bath, where she could not conveniently retire from censure, or conceal herself from observation; and no sooner did the reputation of the poem begin to spread, than she heard it repeated in all places of concourse, nor could she enter the assembly-rooms, or cross the walks, without being saluted with some lines from The Bastard.

This was perhaps the first time that ever she discovered a sense of shame, and on this occasion the power of wit was very conspicuous: the wretch who had, without scruple, proclaimed herself an adulteress, and who had first endeavoured to starve her son, then to transport him, and afterwards to hang him, was not able to bear the representation of her own conduct; but fled from reproach, though she felt no pain from guilt, and left Bath with the utmost haste, to shelter herself among the crowds of London.

Thus Savage had the satisfaction of finding, that, though he could not reform his mother, he could punish her, and that he did not always suffer alone.

The pleasure which he received from this increase of his poetical reputation was sufficient for some time to overbalance the miseries of want, which this performance did not much alleviate; for it was sold for a very trivial sum to a bookseller [T. Worrall], who, though the success was so uncommon that five impressions were sold, of which many were undoubtedly very numerous, had not generosity sufficient to admit the unhappy writer to any part of the profit.

The sale of this poem was always mentioned by Mr. Savage with the utmost elevation of heart, and referred to by him as an incontestable proof of a general acknowledgment of his abilities. It was indeed the only production of which he could justly boast a general reception.

But though he did not lose the opportunity which success gave him of setting a high rate on his abilities, but paid due deference to the suffrages of mankind when they were given in his favour, he did not suffer his esteem of himself to depend upon others, nor found anything sacred in the voice of the people when they were inclined to censure him; he then readily showed the folly of expecting that the public should judge right, observed how slowly poetical merit had often forced its way into the world; he contented himself with the applause of men of judgment, and was somewhat disposed to exclude all those from the character of men of judgment who did not applaud him.

But he was at other times more favourable to mankind than to think them blind to the beauties of his works, and imputed the slowness of their sale to other causes: either they were published at a time when the town was empty, or when the attention of the public was engrossed by some struggle in the parliament, or some other object of general concern; or they were by the neglect of the publisher not diligently dispersed, or by his avarice not advertised with sufficient frequency. Address, or industry, or liberality was always wanting; and the blame was laid rather on any person than the author.

By arts like these, arts which every man practises in some degree, and to which too much of the little tranquillity of life is to be ascribed, Savage was always able to live at peace with himself. Had he indeed only made use of these expedients to alleviate the loss or want of fortune or reputation, or any other advantages which it is not in man's power to bestow upon himself, they might have been justly mentioned as instances of a philosophical mind, and very properly proposed to the imitation of multitudes, who, for want of diverting their imaginations with the same dexterity, languish under afflictions which might be easily removed.

It were doubtless to be wished that truth and reason were universally prevalent; that everything were esteemed according to its real value, and that men would secure themselves from being disappointed in their endeavours after happiness, by placing it only in virtue, which is always to be obtained; but if adventitious and foreign pleasures must be pursued, it would be perhaps of some benefit, since that pursuit must frequently be fruitless, if the practice of Savage could be taught, that folly might be an antidote to folly, and one fallacy be obviated by another.

But the danger of this pleasing intoxication must not be concealed; nor indeed can anyone, after having observed the life of Savage, need to be cautioned against it. By imputing none of his miseries to himself, he continued to act upon the same principles, and to follow the same path; was never made wiser by his sufferings, nor preserved by one misfortune from falling into another. He proceeded throughout his life to tread the same steps on the same circle; always applauding his past conduct, or at least forgetting it, to amuse himself with phantoms of happiness which were dancing before him; and willingly turned his eyes from the light of reason, when it would have discovered the illusion, and shown him, what he never wished to see, his real state.

He is even accused, after having lulled his imagination with those ideal opiates, of having tried the same experiment upon his conscience; and, having accustomed himself to impute all deviations from the right to foreign causes, it is certain that he was upon every occasion too easily reconciled to himself; and that he appeared very little to regret those practices which had impaired his reputation. The reigning error of his life was, that he mistook the love for the practice of virtue, and was indeed not so much a good man, as the friend of goodness.

This at least must be allowed him, that he always preserved a strong sense of the dignity, the beauty, and the necessity of virtue; and that he never contributed deliberately to spread corruption amongst mankind. His actions, which were generally precipitate, were often blameable; but his writings, being the productions of study, uniformly tended to the exaltation of the mind, and the propagation of morality and piety.

These writings may improve mankind when his failings shall be forgotten; and therefore he must be considered, upon the whole, as a benefactor to the world; nor can his personal example do any hurt, since, whoever hears of his faults, will hear of the miseries which they brought upon him, and which would deserve less pity, had not his condition been such as made his faults pardonable. He may be considered as a child exposed to all the temptations of indigence, at an age when resolution was not yet strengthened by conviction, nor virtue confirmed by habit; a circumstance which, in his *Bastard*, he laments in a very affecting manner:

> ——No Mother's care
> Shielded my infant innocence with prayer:
> No Father's guardian-hand my youth maintain'd,
> Call'd forth my virtues, or from vice restrain'd.

The Bastard, however it might provoke or mortify his mother, could not be expected to melt her to compassion, so that he was still under the same want of the necessaries of life; and he therefore exerted all the interest which his wit, or his birth, or his misfortunes could procure, to obtain, upon the death of Eusden, the place of poet-laureat, and prosecuted his application with so much diligence, that the King publicly declared it his intention to bestow it upon him; but such was the fate of Savage, that even the King, when he intended his advantage, was disappointed in his schemes; for the Lord Chamberlain, who has the disposal of the laurel, as one of the appendages of his office, either did not know the King's design, or did not approve it, or thought the nomination of the laureat an encroachment upon his rights, and therefore bestowed the laurel upon Colley Cibber.

Mr. Savage, thus disappointed, took a resolution of applying to the Queen, that, having once given him life, she would enable him to support it, and therefore published a short poem on her birthday, to which he gave the odd title of *Volunteer Laureat*.

The event of this essay he has himself related in the following letter, which he prefixed to the poem, when he afterwards reprinted it in *The Gentleman's Magazine*, from whence I have copied it entire, as this was one of the few attempts in which Mr. Savage succeeded.

[1738].

MR. URBAN,—In your Magazine for February you published the last *Volunteer Laureat*, written on a very melancholy occasion, viz. the death of the royal patroness of arts and literature in general, and of the author of that poem in particular; I now send you the first that Mr. Savage wrote under that title.—This gentleman, notwithstanding a very considerable interest, being, on the death of Mr. Eusden, disappointed of the Laureat's place, wrote the following verses; which were no sooner published but the late Queen sent to a bookseller for them. The author had not at that time a friend either to get him introduced, or his poem presented at Court; yet such was the unspeakable goodness of that Princess, that, notwithstanding this act of ceremony was wanting, in a few days after publication Mr. Savage received a bank-bill of fifty pounds, and a gracious message from her Majesty, by the Lord North and Guildford, to this effect: "That her Majesty was highly pleased with the verses; that she took particularly kind his lines there relating to the King; that he had permission to write annually on the same subject; and that he should yearly receive the like present till something better (which was her Majesty's intention) could be done for him." After this, he was permitted to present one of his annual poems to her Majesty, had the honour of kissing her hand, and met with the most gracious reception.

Yours, T. B.

THE VOLUNTEER LAUREAT—No. 1

A Poem on the Queen's Birth-Day, 1731-2

Humbly addressed to her MAJESTY, by Richard Savage, Esq.

> Twice twenty tedious moons have roll'd away
> Since Hope, kind flatt'rer! tun'd my pensive lay,
> Whisp'ring that you, who rais'd me from despair,
> Meant, by your smiles, to make life worth my care;
> With pitying hand an orphan's tears to screen,
> And o'er the motherless extend the Queen.
> 'Twill be—the prophet guides the poet's strain!
> Grief never touch'd a heart like yours in vain:
> Heav'n gave you power, because you love to bless,
> And pity, when you feel it, is redress.
>   Two fathers join'd to rob my claim of one!
> My mother too thought fit to have no son!
> The senate next, whose aid the helpless own,
> Forgot my infant wrongs, and mine alone!
> Yet parents pitiless, nor peers unkind,
> Nor titles lost, nor woes mysterious join'd,
> Strip me of Hope—by Heav'n thus lowly laid,
> To find a *Pharaoh's* daughter in the shade.
>   You cannot hear unmov'd, when wrongs implore;

Your heart is woman, though your mind be more;
Kind, like the Pow'r who gave you to our pray'rs,
You would not lengthen life to sharpen cares:
They who a barren leave to live bestow,
Snatch but from Death to sacrifice to Woe.
Hated by her from whom my life I drew,
Whence should I hope, if not from heav'n and you?
Nor dare I groan beneath affliction's rod,
My Queen, my Mother; and my Father, God.
    The pitying Muses saw me wit pursue,
A *Bastard Son*, alas! On that side too
Did not your eyes exalt the poet's fire,
And what the Muse denies, the Queen inspire?
While rising thus your heavenly soul to view,
I learn, how angels think, by copying you.
    Great Princess! 'tis decreed—once ev'ry year
I march uncall'd your Laureat Volunteer;
Thus shall your poet his low genius raise,
And charm the world with truths too vast for praise.
Nor need I dwell on glories all your own,
Since surer means to tempt your smiles are known;
Your poet shall allot your Lord his part,
And paint him in his noblest throne, your heart.
    Is there a greatness that adorns him best,
A rising wish that ripens in his breast?
Has he fore-meant some distant age to bless,
Disarm oppression, or expel distress?
Plans he some scheme to reconcile mankind,
People the seas, and busy every wind?
Would he, by pity, the deceiv'd reclaim,
And smile contending factions into shame?
Would his example lend his laws a weight,
And breathe his own soft morals o'er his state?
The Muse shall find it all, shall make it seem,
And teach the world his praise, to charm his Queen.
    Such be the annual truths my verse imparts,
Nor frown, fair *fav'rite* of a people's hearts!
Happy, if plac'd, perchance, beneath your eye,
My Muse unpension'd might her pinions try
Fearless to fail, while you indulge her flame,
And bid me proudly boast your Laureat's name.
Renobled thus by wreaths my Queen bestows,
I lose all memory of wrongs and woes.

Such was the performance, and such its reception; a reception which, though by no means unkind, was yet not in the highest degree generous: to chain down the genius of a writer to an annual panegyric, showed in the Queen too much desire of hearing her own praises, and a greater regard to herself than to him on whom her bounty was conferred. It was a kind of avaricious generosity, by which flattery was rather purchased than genius rewarded.

Mrs. Oldfield had formerly given him the same allowance with much more heroic intention: she had no other view than to enable him to prosecute his studies, and to set himself above the want of assistance, and was contented with doing good without stipulating for encomiums.

Mr. Savage, however, was not at liberty to make exceptions, but was ravished with the favours which he had received, and probably yet more with those which he was promised: he considered himself now as a favourite of the Queen, and did not doubt but a few annual poems would establish him in some profitable employment.

He therefore assumed the title of "Volunteer Laureat," not without some reprehensions from Cibber, who informed him that the title of "Laureat" was a mark of honour conferred by the King, from whom all honour is derived, and which therefore no man has a right to bestow upon himself; and added, that he might, with equal propriety, style himself a Volunteer Lord, or Volunteer Baronet. It cannot be denied that the remark was just; but Savage did not think any title which was conferred upon Mr. Cibber so honourable as that the usurpation of it could be imputed to him as an instance of very exorbitant vanity, and therefore continued to write under the same title, and received every year the same reward.

He did not appear to consider these encomiums as tests of his abilities, or as anything more than annual hints to the Queen of her promise, or acts of ceremony, by the performance of which he was entitled to his pension, and therefore did not labour them with great diligence, or print more than fifty each year, except that for some of the last years he regularly inserted them in *The Gentleman's Magazine*, by which they were dispersed over the kingdom.

Of some of them he had himself so low an opinion, that he intended to omit them in the collection of poems for which he printed proposals, and solicited subscriptions; nor can it seem strange that, being confined to the same subject, he should be at some times indolent, and at others unsuccessful; that he should sometimes delay a disagreeable task till it was too late to perform it well; or that he should sometimes repeat the same sentiment on the same occasion, or at others be misled by an attempt after novelty to forced conceptions and far-fetched images.

He wrote indeed with a double intention, which supplied him with some variety; for his business was to praise the Queen for the favours which he had received, and to complain to her of the delay of those which she had promised: in some of his pieces, therefore, gratitude is predominant, and in some discontent; in some, he represents himself as happy in her patronage; and in others, as disconsolate to find himself neglected.

Her promise, like other promises made to this unfortunate man, was never performed, though he took sufficient care that it should not be forgotten. The publication of his *Volunteer Laureat* procured him no other reward than a regular remittance of 50*l*.

He was not so depressed by his disappointments as to neglect any opportunity that was offered of advancing his interest. When [14th March, 1734] the Princess Anne was married, he wrote a poem upon her departure, only, as he declared, "because it was expected from him," and he was not willing to bar his own prospects by any appearance of neglect.

He never mentioned any advantage gained by this poem, or any regard that was paid to it; and therefore it is likely that it was considered at court as an act of duty, to which he was obliged by his dependence, and which it was therefore not necessary to reward by any new favour: or perhaps the Queen really intended his advancement, and therefore thought it superfluous to lavish presents upon a man whom she intended to establish for life.

About this time [1735] not only his hopes were in danger of being frustrated, but his pension likewise of being obstructed, by an accidental calumny. The writer of *The Daily Courant*, a paper then published under the direction of the ministry, charged him with a crime, which, though very great in itself, would have been remarkably invidious in him, and might very justly have incensed the Queen against him. He was accused by name of influencing elections against the court, by appearing at the head of a Tory mob; nor did the accuser fail to aggravate his crime, by representing it as the effect of the most atrocious ingratitude, and a kind of rebellion against the Queen, who had first preserved him from an infamous death, and afterwards distinguished him by her favour, and supported him by her charity. The charge, as it was open and confident, was likewise by good fortune very particular. The place of the transaction was mentioned, and the whole series of the rioter's conduct related. This exactness made Mr. Savage's vindication easy; for he never had in his life seen the place which was declared to be the scene of his wickedness, nor ever had been present in any town when its representatives were chosen. This answer he therefore made haste to publish, with all the circumstances necessary to make it credible; and very reasonably demanded that the accusation should be retracted in the same paper, that he might no longer suffer the imputation of sedition and ingratitude. This demand was likewise pressed by him in a private letter to the author of the paper, who, either trusting to the protection of those whose defence he had undertaken, or having entertained some personal malice against Mr. Savage, or fearing lest, by retracting so confident an assertion, he should impair the credit of his paper, refused to give him that satisfaction.

Mr. Savage therefore thought it necessary, to his own vindication, to prosecute him in the King's Bench; but as he did not find any ill effects from the accusation, having sufficiently cleared his innocence, he thought any further procedure would have the appearance of revenge, and therefore willingly dropped it.

He saw soon afterwards a process commenced in the same court against himself, on an information in which he was accused of writing and publishing an obscene pamphlet.

It was always Mr. Savage's desire to be distinguished; and, when any controversy became popular, he never wanted some reason for engaging in it with great ardour, and appearing at the head of the party which he had chosen. As he was never celebrated for his prudence, he had no sooner taken his side, and informed himself of the chief topics of the dispute, than he took all opportunities of asserting and propagating his principles, without much regard to his own interest, or any other visible design than that of drawing upon himself the attention of mankind

The dispute between the Bishop of London and the Chancellor is well known to have been for some time the chief topic of political conversation; and therefore Mr. Savage, in pursuance of his character, endeavoured to become conspicuous among the controvertists with which every coffee-house was filled on that occasion. He was an indefatigable opposer of all the claims of ecclesiastical power, though he did not know on what they were founded; and was therefore no friend to the Bishop of London. But he had another reason for appearing as a warm advocate for Dr. Rundle; for he was the friend of Mr. Foster and Mr. Thomson, who were the friends of Mr. Savage.

Thus remote was his interest in the question, which, however, as he imagined, concerned him so nearly, that it was not sufficient to harangue and dispute, but necessary likewise to write upon it.

He therefore engaged with great ardour in a new poem,

called by him *The Progress of a Divine*; in which he conducts a profligate priest by all the gradations of wickedness from a poor curacy in the country to the highest preferments of the Church, and describes with that humour which was natural to him, and that knowledge which was extended to all the diversities of human life, his behaviour in every station; and insinuates that this priest, thus accomplished, found at last a patron in the Bishop of London.

When he was asked by one of his friends, on what pretence he could charge the Bishop with such an action? he had no more to say, than that he had only inverted the accusation, and that he thought it reasonable to believe, that he who obstructed the rise of a good man without reason, would for bad reasons promote the exaltation of a villain.

The clergy were universally provoked by this satire; and Savage, who, as was his constant practice, had set his name to his performance, was censured in *The Weekly Miscellany* with severity, which he did not seem inclined to forget.

But return of invective was not thought a sufficient punishment. The Court of King's Bench was therefore moved against him, and he was obliged to return an answer to a charge of obscenity. It was urged, in his defence, that obscenity was criminal when it was intended to promote the practice of vice; but that Mr. Savage had only introduced obscene ideas with the view of exposing them to detestation, and of amending the age by showing the deformity of wickedness. This plea was admitted; and Sir Philip Yorke, who then presided in that Court, dismissed the information, with encomiums upon the purity and excellence of Mr. Savage's writings. The prosecution, however, answered in some measure the purpose of those by whom it was set on foot; for Mr. Savage was so far intimidated by it, that, when the edition of his poem was sold, he did not venture to reprint it; so that it was in a short time forgotten, or forgotten by all but those whom it offended.

It is said that some endeavours were used to incense the Queen against him: but he found advocates to obviate at least part of their effect; for though he was never advanced, he still continued to receive his pension.

This poem drew more infamy upon him than any incident of his life; and, as his conduct cannot be vindicated, it is proper to secure his memory from reproach, by informing those whom he made his enemies, that he never intended to repeat the provocation; and that, though, whenever he thought he had any reason to complain of the clergy, he used to threaten them with a new edition of *The Progress of a Divine*, it was his calm and settled resolution to suppress it for ever.

He once intended to have made a better reparation for the folly or injustice with which he might be charged, by writing another poem, called *The Progress of the Freethinker*, whom he intended to lead through all the stages of vice and folly, to convert him from virtue to wickedness, and from religion to infidelity, by all the modish sophistry used for that purpose; and at last to dismiss him by his own hand into the other world.

That he did not execute this design is a real loss to mankind, for he was too well acquainted with all the scenes of debauchery to have failed in his representations of them, and too zealous for virtue not to have represented them in such a manner as should expose them either to ridicule or detestation.

But this plan was, like others, formed and laid aside, till the vigour of his imagination was spent, and the effervescence of invention had subsided; but soon gave way to some other design, which pleased by its novelty for a while, and then was neglected like the former.

He was still in his usual exigences, having no certain support but the pension allowed him by the Queen, which, though it might have kept an exact economist from want, was very far from being sufficient for Mr. Savage, who had never been accustomed to dismiss any of his appetites without the gratification which they solicited, and whom nothing but want of money withheld from partaking of every pleasure that fell within his view.

His conduct with regard to his pension was very particular. No sooner had he changed the bill, than he vanished from the sight of all his acquaintance, and lay for some time out of the reach of all the inquiries that friendship or curiosity could make after him; at length he appeared again penniless as before, but never informed even those whom he seemed to regard most, where he had been; nor was his retreat ever discovered.

This was his constant practice during the whole time that he received the pension from the Queen; he regularly disappeared and returned. He indeed affirmed that he retired to study, and that the money supported him in solitude for many months; but his friends declared that the short time in which it was spent sufficiently confuted his own account of his conduct.

His politeness and his wit still raised him friends, who were desirous of setting him at length free from that indigence by

which he had been hitherto oppressed; and therefore solicited
Sir Robert Walpole in his favour with so much earnestness, that
they obtained a promise of the next place that should become
vacant, not exceeding 200*l.* a year. This promise was made with
an uncommon declaration, "that it was not the promise of a
minister to a petitioner, but of a friend to his friend."

Mr. Savage now concluded himself set at ease for ever, and,
as he observes in a poem written on that incident of his life,
trusted and was trusted; but soon found that his confidence
was ill-grounded, and this friendly promise was not inviolable.
He spent a long time in solicitations, and at last despaired
and desisted.

He did not indeed deny that he had given the minister some
reason to believe that he should not strengthen his own interest
by advancing him, for he had taken care to distinguish himself
in coffee-houses as an advocate for the ministry of the last years
of Queen Anne, and was always ready to justify the conduct
and exalt the character of Lord Bolingbroke, whom he mentions with great regard in an Epistle upon Authors, which he
wrote about that time; but was too wise to publish, and of which
only some fragments have appeared, inserted by him in the
Magazine after his retirement.

To despair was not, however, the character of Savage; when
one patronage failed, he had recourse to another. The Prince
was now extremely popular, and had very liberally rewarded
the merit of some writers whom Mr. Savage did not think
superior to himself, and therefore he resolved to address a poem
to him.

For this purpose he made choice of a subject which could
regard only persons of the highest rank and greatest affluence,
and which was therefore proper for a poem intended to procure
the patronage of a prince; and having retired for some time to
Richmond, that he might prosecute his design in full tranquillity, without the temptations of pleasure, or the solicitations
of creditors, by which his meditations were in equal danger of
being disconcerted, he produced [June 1737] a poem *On Public
Spirit, with regard to Public Works.*

The plan of this poem is very extensive, and comprises a
multitude of topics, each of which might furnish matter sufficient
for a long performance, and of which some have already employed more eminent writers; but as he was perhaps not fully
acquainted with the whole extent of his own design, and was
writing to obtain a supply of wants too pressing to admit of

long or accurate inquiries, he passes negligently over many
public works, which, even in his own opinion, deserved to be
more elaborately treated.

But though he may sometimes disappoint his reader by transient touches upon these subjects, which have often been considered, and therefore naturally raise expectations, he must be
allowed amply to compensate his omissions, by expatiating, in
the conclusion of his work, upon a kind of beneficence not yet
celebrated by any eminent poet, though it now appears more
susceptible of embellishments, more adapted to exalt the ideas,
and affect the passions, than many of those which have hitherto
been thought most worthy of the ornaments of verse. The
settlement of colonies in uninhabited countries, the establishment of those in security whose misfortunes have made their
own country no longer pleasing or safe, the acquisition of property without injury to any, the appropriation of the waste and
luxuriant bounties of nature, and the enjoyment of those gifts
which Heaven has scattered upon regions uncultivated and un-
occupied, cannot be considered without giving rise to a great
number of pleasing ideas, and bewildering the imagination in
delightful prospects; and, therefore, whatever speculations they
may produce in those who have confined themselves to political
studies, naturally fixed the attention, and excited the applause,
of a poet. The politician, when he considers men driven into
other countries for shelter, and obliged to retire to forests and
deserts, and pass their lives and fix their posterity in the
remotest corners of the world, to avoid those hardships which
they suffer or fear in their native place, may very properly
inquire why the legislature does not provide a remedy for these
miseries, rather than encourage an escape from them. He may
conclude, that the flight of every honest man is a loss to the
community; that those who are unhappy without guilt ought to
be relieved; and the life, which is overburthened by accidental
calamities, set at ease by the care of the public; and that those
who have by misconduct forfeited their claim to favour, ought
rather to be made useful to the society which they have injured,
than be driven from it. But the poet is employed in a more
pleasing undertaking than that of proposing laws which, however just or expedient, will never be made, or endeavouring
to reduce to rational schemes of government societies which
were formed by chance, and are conducted by the private
passions of those who preside in them. He guides the unhappy fugitive from want and persecution to plenty, quiet,

and security, and seats him in scenes of peaceful solitude, and undisturbed repose.

Savage has not forgotten, amidst the pleasing sentiments which this prospect of retirement suggested to him, to censure those crimes which have been generally committed by the discoverers of new regions, and to expose the enormous wickedness of making war upon barbarous nations because they cannot resist, and of invading countries because they are fruitful; of extending navigation only to propagate vice, and of visiting distant lands only to lay them waste. He has asserted the natural equality of mankind, and endeavoured to suppress that pride which inclines men to imagine that right is the consequence of power.

His description of the various miseries which force men to seek for refuge in distant countries, affords another instance of his proficiency in the important and extensive study of human life; and the tenderness with which he recounts them, another proof of his humanity and benevolence.

It is observable that the close of this poem discovers a change which experience has made in Mr. Savage's opinions. In a poem written by him in his youth, and published in his *Miscellanies*, he declares his contempt of the contracted views and narrow prospects of the middle state of life, and declares his resolution either to tower like the cedar, or be trampled like the shrub; but in this poem, though addressed to a prince, he mentions this state of life as comprising those who ought most to attract reward, those who merit most confidence of power, and the familiarity of greatness; and, accidentally mentioning this passage to one of his friends, declared, that in his opinion all the virtue of mankind was comprehended in that state.

In describing villas and gardens, he did not omit to condemn that absurd custom which prevails among the English, of permitting servants to receive money from strangers for the entertainment that they receive, and therefore inserted in his poem these lines:

> But what the flowering pride of gardens rare,
> However royal, or however fair,
> If gates, which to access should still give way,
> Ope but, like Peter's paradise, for pay?
> If perquisited varlets frequent stand,
> And each new walk must a new tax demand?
> What foreign eye but with contempt surveys?
> What Muse shall from oblivion snatch their praise?

But before the publication of his performance he recollected that the Queen allowed her garden and cave at Richmond to be shown for money, and that she so openly countenanced the practice, that she had bestowed the privilege of showing them as a place of profit on a man whose merit she valued herself upon rewarding, though she gave him only the liberty of disgracing his country.

He therefore thought, with more prudence than was often exerted by him, that the publication of these lines might be officiously represented as an insult upon the Queen, to whom he owed his life and his subsistence; and that the propriety of his observation would be no security against the censures which the unseasonableness of it might draw upon him; he therefore suppressed the passage in the first edition, but after the Queen's death thought the same caution no longer necessary, and restored it to the proper place.

The poem was, therefore, published without any political faults, and inscribed to the Prince; but Mr. Savage, having no friend upon whom he could prevail to present it to him, had no other method of attracting his observation than the publication of frequent advertisements, and therefore received no reward from his patron, however generous on other occasions.

This disappointment he never mentioned without indignation, being by some means or other confident that the Prince was not ignorant of his address to him; and insinuated that, if any advances in popularity could have been made by distinguishing him, he had not written without notice, or without reward.

He was once inclined to have presented his poem in person, and sent to the printer for a copy with that design; but either his opinion changed, or his resolution deserted him, and he continued to resent neglect without attempting to force himself into regard.

Nor was the public much more favourable than his patron, for only seventy-two were sold, though the performance was much commended by some whose judgment in that kind of writing is generally allowed. But Savage easily reconciled himself to mankind without imputing any defect to his work, by observing that his poem was unluckily published two days after the prorogation of the Parliament, and by consequence at a time when all those who could be expected to regard it were in the hurry of preparing for their departure, or engaged in taking leave of others upon their dismission from public affairs.

It must be however allowed, in justification of the public, that this performance is not the most excellent of Mr. Savage's works; and that, though it cannot be denied to contain many striking sentiments, majestic lines, and just observations, it is in general not sufficiently polished in the language, or enlivened in the imagery, or digested in the plan.

Thus his poem contributed nothing to the alleviation of his poverty, which was such as very few could have supported with equal patience; but to which, it must likewise be confessed, that few would have been exposed who received punctually 50*l.* a year: a salary which, though by no means equal to the demands of vanity and luxury, is yet found sufficient to support families above want, and was undoubtedly more than the necessities of life require.

But no sooner had he received his pension than he withdrew to his darling privacy, from which he returned in a short time to his former distress, and for some part of the year generally lived by chance, eating only when he was invited to the tables of his acquaintances, from which the meanness of his dress often excluded him, when the politeness and variety of his conversation would have been thought a sufficient recompense for his entertainment.

He lodged as much by accident as he dined, and passed the night sometimes in mean houses, which are set open at night to any casual wanderers, sometimes in cellars, among the riot and filth of the meanest and most profligate of the rabble; and sometimes, when he had not money to support even the expenses of these receptacles, walked about the streets till he was weary, and lay down in the summer upon a bulk, or in the winter, with his associates in poverty, among the ashes of a glass-house.

In this manner were passed those days and those nights which nature had enabled him to have employed in elevated speculations, useful studies, or pleasing conversations. On a bulk, in a cellar, or in a glass-house, among thieves and beggars, was to be found the author of *The Wanderer*, the man of exalted sentiments, extensive views, and curious observations; the man whose remarks on life might have assisted the statesman, whose ideas of virtue might have enlightened the moralist, whose eloquence might have influenced senates, and whose delicacy might have polished courts.

It cannot but be imagined that such necessities might sometimes force him upon disreputable practices; and it is probable that these lines in *The Wanderer* were occasioned by his reflections on his own conduct:

Though misery leads to happiness, and truth,
Unequal to the load, this languid youth,
(O, let none censure, if, untried by grief,
If, amidst woes, untempted by relief,)
He stoop'd reluctant to mean acts of shame,
Which then, ev'n then, he scorn'd, and blush'd to name.

Whoever was acquainted with him was certain to be solicited
for small sums, which the frequency of the request made in time
considerable, and he was therefore quickly shunned by those
who were become familiar enough to be trusted with his necessities; but his rambling manner of life, and constant appearance
at houses of public resort, always procured him a new succession
of friends, whose kindness had not been exhausted by repeated
requests; so that he was seldom absolutely without resources,
but had in his utmost exigences this comfort, that he always
imagined himself sure of speedy relief.

It was observed, that he always asked favours of this kind
without the least submission or apparent consciousness of dependence, and that he did not seem to look upon a compliance
with his request as an obligation that deserved any extraordinary acknowledgments; but a refusal was resented by him
as an affront, or complained of as an injury; nor did he readily
reconcile himself to those who either denied to lend, or gave him
afterwards any intimation that they expected to be repaid.

He was sometimes so far compassionated by those who knew
both his merit and distresses that they received him into their
families, but they soon discovered him to be a very incom-
modious inmate; for, being always accustomed to an irregular
manner of life, he could not confine himself to any stated hours,
or pay any regard to the rules of a family, but would prolong
his conversation till midnight, without considering that business
might require his friend's application in the morning; and,
when he had persuaded himself to retire to bed, was not, without
equal difficulty, called up to dinner: it was therefore impossible
to pay him any distinction without the entire subversion of all
economy, a kind of establishment which, wherever he went, he
always appeared ambitious to overthrow.

It must therefore be acknowledged, in justification of mankind, that it was not always by the negligence or coldness of his
friends that Savage was distressed, but because it was in reality
very difficult to preserve him long in a state of ease. To supply
him with money was a hopeless attempt; for no sooner did he see
himself master of a sum sufficient to set him free from care for a
day than he became profuse and luxurious. When once he had

entered a tavern, or engaged in a scheme of pleasure, he never retired till want of money obliged him to some new expedient. If he was entertained in a family, nothing was any longer to be regarded there but amusements and jollity; wherever Savage entered he immediately expected that order and business should fly before him, that all should thenceforward be left to hazard, and that no dull principle of domestic management should be opposed to his inclination or intrude upon his gaiety.

His distresses, however afflictive, never dejected him· in his lowest state he wanted not spirit to assert the natural dignity of wit, and was always ready to repress that insolence which the superiority of fortune incited, and to trample on that reputation which rose upon any other basis than that of merit: he never admitted any gross familiarities, or submitted to be treated otherwise than as an equal. Once, when he was without lodging, meat, or clothes, one of his friends, a man indeed not remarkable for moderation in his prosperity, left a message that he desired to see him about nine in the morning. Savage knew that his intention was to assist him; but was very much disgusted that he should presume to prescribe the hour of his attendance, and, I believe, refused to visit him, and rejected his kindness.

The same invincible temper, whether firmness or obstinacy, appeared in his conduct to the Lord Tyrconnel, from whom he very frequently demanded that the allowance which was once paid him should be restored; but with whom he never appeared to entertain for a moment the thought of soliciting a reconciliation, and whom he treated at once with all the haughtiness of superiority and all the bitterness of resentment. He wrote to him not in a style of supplication or respect, but of reproach, menace, and contempt; and appeared determined, if he ever regained his allowance, to hold it only by the right of conquest.

As many more can discover that a man is richer than that he is wiser than themselves, superiority of understanding is not so readily acknowledged as that of fortune; nor is that haughtiness which the consciousness of great abilities incites borne with the same submission as the tyranny of affluence; and therefore Savage, by asserting his claim to deference and regard, and by treating those with contempt whom better fortune animated to rebel against him, did not fail to raise a great number of enemies in the different classes of mankind. Those who thought themselves raised above him by the advantages of riches hated him because they found no protection from the petulance of his wit. Those who were esteemed for their writings feared him as a critic and maligned him as a rival; and almost all the smaller wits were his professed enemies.

Among these Mr. Miller so far indulged his resentment as to introduce him in a farce, and direct him to be personated on the stage in a dress like that which he then wore; a mean insult, which only insinuated that Savage had but one coat, and which was therefore despised by him rather than resented; for though he wrote a lampoon against Miller, he never printed it: and as no other person ought to prosecute that revenge from which the person who was injured desisted, I shall not preserve what Mr. Savage suppressed; of which the publication would indeed have been a punishment too severe for so impotent an assault.

The great hardships of poverty were to Savage not the want of lodging or of food, but the neglect and contempt which it drew upon him. He complained that as his affairs grew desperate, he found his reputation for capacity visibly decline; that his opinion in questions of criticism was no longer regarded when his coat was out of fashion; and that those who, in the interval of his prosperity, were always encouraging him to great undertakings by encomiums on his genius and assurances of success, now received any mention of his designs with coldness—thought that the subjects on which he proposed to write were very difficult; and were ready to inform him that the event of a poem was uncertain; that an author ought to employ much time in the consideration of his plan, and not presume to sit down to write in consequence of a few cursory ideas and a superficial knowledge: difficulties were started on all sides, and he was no longer qualified for any performance but "The Volunteer Laureat."

Yet even this kind of contempt never depressed him; for he always preserved a steady confidence in his own capacity, and believed nothing above his reach which he should at any time earnestly endeavour to attain. He formed schemes of the same kind with regard to knowledge and to fortune, and flattered himself with advances to be made in science, as with riches, to be enjoyed in some distant period of his life. For the acquisition of knowledge he was indeed far better qualified than for that of riches; for he was naturally inquisitive and desirous of the conversation of those from whom any information was to be obtained, but by no means solicitous to improve those opportunities that were sometimes offered of raising his fortune; and he was remarkably retentive of his ideas, which, when once

he was in possession of them, rarely forsook him; a quality
which could never be communicated to his money.

While he was thus wearing out his life in expectation that
the Queen would some time recollect her promise, he had
recourse to the usual practice of writers, and published proposals for printing his works by subscription, to which he was
encouraged by the success of many who had not a better right
to the favour of the public; but, whatever was the reason, he
did not find the world equally inclined to favour him; and he
observed, with some discontent, that though he offered his
works at half a guinea, he was able to procure but a small
number in comparison with those who subscribed twice as
much to Duck.

Nor was it without indignation that he saw his proposals
neglected by the Queen, who patronised Mr. Duck's with
uncommon ardour, and incited a competition among those
who attended the court who should most promote his interest,
and who should first offer a subscription. This was a distinction
to which Mr. Savage made no scruple of asserting that his
birth, his misfortunes, and his genius gave a fairer title than
could be pleaded by him on whom it was conferred.

Savage's applications were, however, not universally unsuccessful; for some of the nobility countenanced his design,
encouraged his proposals, and subscribed with great liberality.
He related of the Duke of Chandos particularly, that upon
receiving his proposals he sent him ten guineas.

But the money which his subscriptions afforded him was not
less volatile than that which he received from his other schemes;
whenever a subscription was paid him he went to a tavern;
and, as money so collected is necessarily received in small sums,
he never was able to send his poems to the press, but for many
years continued his solicitation and squandered whatever
he obtained.

This project of printing his works was frequently revived;
and, as his proposals grew obsolete, new ones were printed
with fresher dates. To form schemes for the publication was
one of his favourite amusements; nor was he ever more at ease
than when, with any friend who readily fell in with his schemes,
he was adjusting the print, forming the advertisements, and
regulating the dispersion of his new edition, which he really
intended some time to publish, and which, as long as experience had shown him the impossibility of printing the volume
together, he at last determined to divide into weekly or monthly

numbers, that the profits of the first might supply the expenses of the next.

Thus he spent his time in mean expedients and tormenting suspense, living for the greatest part in fear of prosecutions from his creditors, and consequently skulking in obscure parts of the town, of which he was no stranger to the remotest corners. But, wherever he came, his address secured him friends, whom his necessities soon alienated; so that he had, perhaps, a more numerous acquaintance than any man ever before attained, there being scarcely any person eminent on any account to whom he was not known, or whose character he was not in some degree able to delineate.

To the acquisition of this extensive acquaintance every circumstance of his life contributed. He excelled in the arts of conversation, and therefore willingly practised them. He had seldom any home, or even a lodging in which he could be private; and therefore was driven into public-houses for the common conveniences of life and supports of nature. He was always ready to comply with every invitation, having no employment to withhold him, and often no money to provide for himself; and by dining with one company he never failed of obtaining an introduction into another.

Thus dissipated was his life, and thus casual his subsistence; yet did not the distraction of his views hinder him from reflection, nor the uncertainty of his condition depress his gaiety. When he had wandered about without any fortunate adventure by which he was led into a tavern, he sometimes retired into the fields, and was able to employ his mind in study, to amuse it with pleasing imaginations; and seldom appeared to be melancholy but when some sudden misfortune had just fallen upon him, and even then in a few moments he would disentangle himself from his perplexity, adopt the subject of conversation, and apply his mind wholly to the objects that others presented to it.

This life, unhappy as it may be already imagined, was yet embittered, in 1738, with new calamities. The death of the Queen [20th Nov. 1737] deprived him of all the prospects of preferment with which he so long entertained his imagination; and, as Sir Robert Walpole had before given him reason to believe that he never intended the performance of his promise, he was now abandoned again to fortune.

He was, however, at that time supported by a friend; and as it was not his custom to look out for distant calamities, or to feel any other pain than that which forced itself upon his senses, he was not much afflicted at his loss, and perhaps comforted himself that his pension would be now continued without the annual tribute of a panegyric.

Another expectation contributed likewise to support him: he had taken a resolution to write a second tragedy upon the story of Sir Thomas Overbury, in which he preserved a few lines of his former play, but made a total alteration of the plan, added new incidents, and introduced new characters; so that it was a new tragedy, not a revival of the former.

Many of his friends blamed him for not making choice of another subject; but, in vindication of himself, he asserted that it was not easy to find a better; and that he thought it his interest to extinguish the memory of the first tragedy, which he could only do by writing one less defective upon the same story; by which he should entirely defeat the artifice of the booksellers, who, after the death of any author of reputation, are always industrious to swell his works by uniting his worst productions with his best.

In the execution of this scheme, however, he proceeded but slowly, and probably only employed himself upon it when he could find no other amusement; but he pleased himself with counting the profits, and perhaps imagined that the theatrical reputation which he was about to acquire would be equivalent to all that he had lost by the death of his patroness.

He did not, in confidence of his approaching riches, neglect the measures proper to secure the continuance of his pension, though some of his favourers thought him culpable for omitting to write on her death; but on her birthday next year [1st March, 1737–8] he gave a proof of the solidity of his judgment and the power of his genius. He knew that the track of elegy had been so long beaten that it was impossible to travel in it without treading in the footsteps of those who had gone before him; and that therefore it was necessary, that he might distinguish himself from the herd of encomiasts, to find out some new walk of funeral panegyric.

This difficult task he performed in such a manner that his poem may be justly ranked among the best pieces that the death of princes has produced. By transferring the mention of her death to her birthday he has formed a happy combination of topics, which any other man would have thought it very difficult to connect in one view, but which he has united in such a manner that the relation between them appears natural; and it may be justly said, that what no other man would have thought on, it now appears scarcely possible for any man to miss.

The beauty of this peculiar combination of images is so masterly that it is sufficient to set this poem above censure; and therefore it is not necessary to mention many other delicate touches which may be found in it, and which would deservedly be admired in any other performance.

To these proofs of his genius may be added, from the same poem, an instance of his prudence, an excellence for which he was not so often distinguished; he does not forget to remind the King, in the most delicate and artful manner, of continuing his pension.

With regard to the success of this address he was for some time in suspense, but was in no great degree solicitous about it, and continued his labour upon his new tragedy with great tranquillity, till the friend who had for a considerable time supported him, removing his family to another place, took occasion to dismiss him. It then became necessary to inquire more diligently what was determined in his affair, having reason to suspect that no great favour was intended him, because he had not received his pension at the usual time.

It is said that he did not take those methods of retrieving his interest which were most likely to succeed; and some of those who were employed in the Exchequer cautioned him against too much violence in his proceedings: but Mr. Savage, who seldom regulated his conduct by the advice of others, gave way to his passion, and demanded of Sir Robert Walpole, at his levee, the reason of the distinction that was made between him and the other pensioners of the Queen, with a degree of roughness which perhaps determined him to withdraw what had been only delayed.

Whatever was the crime of which he was accused or suspected, and whatever influence was employed against him, he received soon after an account that took from him all hopes of regaining his pension; and he had now no prospect of subsistence but from his play, and he knew no way of living for the time required to finish it.

So peculiar were the misfortunes of this man, deprived of an estate and title by a particular law, exposed and abandoned by a mother, defrauded by a mother of a fortune which his father had allotted him, he entered the world without a friend; and though his abilities forced themselves into esteem and reputation, he was never able to obtain any real advantage, and whatever prospects arose were always intercepted as he

began to approach them. The King's intentions in his favour
were frustrated; his Dedication to the Prince, whose generosity
on every other occasion was eminent, procured him no reward;
Sir Robert Walpole, who valued himself upon keeping his
promise to others, broke it to him without regret; and the
bounty of the Queen was, after her death, withdrawn from
him, and from him only.

Such were his misfortunes, which yet he bore not only with
decency, but with cheerfulness; nor was his gaiety clouded even
by his last disappointments, though he was in a short time
reduced to the lowest degree of distress, and often wanted both
lodging and food. At this time he gave another instance of
the insurmountable obstinacy of his spirit: his clothes were
worn out, and he received notice that at a coffee-house some
clothes and linen were left for him; the person who sent them
did not, I believe, inform him to whom he was to be obliged,
that he might spare the perplexity of acknowledging the benefit;
but though the offer was so far generous, it was made with some
neglect of ceremonies, which Mr. Savage so much resented that
he refused the present, and declined to enter the house till the
clothes that had been designed for him were taken away.

His distress was now publicly known, and his friends, therefore, thought it proper to concert some measures for his relief;
and one of them [Pope] wrote a letter to him, in which he
expressed his concern "for the miserable withdrawing of his
pension," and gave him hopes that in a short time he should find
himself supplied with a competence, "without any dependence
on those little creatures which we are pleased to call the great."

The scheme proposed for this happy and independent subsistence was, that he should retire into Wales, and receive
an allowance of 50l. a year, to be raised by a subscription,
on which he was to live privately in a cheap place, without
aspiring any more to affluence, or having any further care
of reputation.

This offer Mr. Savage gladly accepted, though with intentions
very different from those of his friends; for they proposed that
he should continue an exile from London for ever, and spend
all the remaining part of his life at Swansea; but he designed
only to take the opportunity which their scheme offered him
of retreating for a short time that he might prepare his play
for the stage, and his other works for the press, and then to
return to London to exhibit his tragedy, and live upon the
profits of his own labour.

With regard to his works, he proposed very great improvements, which would have required much time or great application; and when he had finished them, he designed to do justice to his subscribers by publishing them according to his proposals.

As he was ready to entertain himself with future pleasures, he had planned out a scheme of life for the country, of which he had no knowledge but from pastorals and songs. He imagined that he should be transported to scenes of flowery felicity, like those which one poet has reflected to another; and had projected a perpetual round of innocent pleasures, of which he suspected no interruption from pride, or ignorance, or brutality.

With these expectations he was so enchanted, that when he was once gently reproached by a friend for submitting to live upon a subscription, and advised rather by a resolute exertion of his abilities to support himself, he could not bear to debar himself from the happiness which was to be found in the calm of a cottage, or lose the opportunity of listening without intermission to the melody of the nightingale, which he believed was to be heard from every bramble, and which he did not fail to mention as a very important part of the happiness of a country life.

While this scheme was ripening, his friends directed him to take a lodging in the liberties of the Fleet, that he might be secure from his creditors, and sent him every Monday a guinea, which he commonly spent before the next morning, and trusted, after his usual manner, the remaining part of the week to the bounty of fortune.

He now began very sensibly to feel the miseries of dependence. Those by whom he was to be supported began to prescribe to him with an air of authority, which he knew not how decently to resent, nor patiently to bear; and he soon discovered, from the conduct of most of his subscribers, that he was yet in the hands of "little creatures."

Of the insolence that he was obliged to suffer he gave many instances, of which none appeared to raise his indignation to a greater height than the method which was taken of furnishing him with clothes. Instead of consulting him, and allowing him to send a tailor his orders for what they thought proper to allow him, they proposed to send for a tailor to take his measure, and then to consult how they should equip him.

This treatment was not very delicate, nor was it such as Savage's humanity would have suggested to him on a like occasion; but it had scarcely deserved mention had it not, by affecting him in an uncommon degree, shown the peculiarity of his character. Upon hearing the design that was formed, he came to the lodging of a friend with the most violent agonies of rage; and, being asked what it could be that gave him such disturbance, he replied with the utmost vehemence of indignation, "That they had sent for a tailor to measure him."

How the affair ended was never inquired, for fear of renewing his uneasiness. It is probable that, upon recollection, he submitted with a good grace to what he could not avoid, and that he discovered no resentment where he had no power.

He was, however, not humbled to implicit and universal compliance; for when the gentleman who had first informed him of the design to support him by a subscription attempted to procure a reconciliation with the Lord Tyrconnel, he could by no means be prevailed upon to comply with the measures that were proposed.

A letter was written for him to Sir William Leman, to prevail upon him to interpose his good offices with Lord Tyrconnel, in which he solicited Sir William's assistance "for a man who really needed it as much as any man could well do"; and informed him that he was retiring "for ever to a place where he should no more trouble his relations, friends, or enemies"; he confessed that his passion had betrayed him to some conduct with regard to Lord Tyrconnel for which he could not but heartily ask his pardon; and as he imagined Lord Tyrconnel's passion might be yet so high that he would not "receive a letter from him," begged that Sir William would endeavour to soften him; and expressed his hopes that he would comply with his request, and that "so small a relation would not harden his heart against him."

That any man should presume to dictate a letter to him was not very agreeable to Mr. Savage; and therefore he was, before he had opened it, not much inclined to approve it. But when he read it, he found it contained sentiments entirely opposite to his own, and, as he asserted, to the truth; and, therefore, instead of copying it, wrote his friend a letter full of masculine resentment and warm expostulations. He very justly observed, that the style was too supplicatory, and the representation too abject, and that he ought at least to have made him complain with "the dignity of a gentleman in distress." He declared that he would not write the paragraph in which he was to ask Lord Tyrconnel's pardon, for "he despised his pardon, and therefore could not heartily, and would not hypocritically, ask it." He remarked that his friend made a very unreasonable distinction between himself and him; for, says he, "when you mention men of high rank in your own character," they are "those little creatures whom we are pleased to call the great"; but when you address them "in mine," no servility is sufficiently humble. He then with great propriety explained the ill consequences which might be expected from such a letter, which his relations would print in their own defence, and which would for ever be produced as a full answer to all that he should allege against them; for he always intended to publish a minute account of the treatment which he had received. It is to be remembered, to the honour of the gentleman by whom this letter was drawn up, that he yielded to Mr. Savage's reasons, and agreed that it ought to be suppressed.

After many alterations and delays a subscription was at length raised, which did not amount to 50*l*. a year, though twenty were paid by one gentleman: such was the generosity of mankind, that what had been done by a player without solicitation could not now be effected by application and interest; and Savage had a great number to court and to obey for a pension less than that which Mrs. Oldfield paid him without exacting any servilities.

Mr. Savage, however, was satisfied, and willing to retire, and was convinced that the allowance, though scanty, would be more than sufficient for him, being now determined to commence a rigid economist, and to live according to the exact rules of frugality; for nothing was in his opinion more contemptible than a man who, when he knew his income, exceeded it; and yet he confessed that instances of such folly were too common, and lamented that some men were not to be trusted with their own money.

Full of these salutary resolutions, he left London in July 1739, having taken leave with great tenderness of his friends, and parted from the author of this narrative with tears in his eyes. He was furnished with fifteen guineas, and informed that they would be sufficient, not only for the expense of his journey, but for his support in Wales for some time; and that there remained but little more of the first collection. He promised a strict adherence to his maxims of parsimony, and went away in the stage-coach; nor did his friends expect to hear from him till he informed them of his arrival at Swansea.

But when they least expected, arrived a letter dated the fourteenth day after his departure, in which he sent them word that he was yet upon the road, and without money, and that he therefore could not proceed without a remittance. They then sent him the money that was in their hands, with which he was enabled to reach Bristol, from whence he was to go to Swansea by water.

At Bristol he found an embargo laid upon the shipping, so that he could not immediately obtain a passage; and being therefore obliged to stay there some time, he with his usual felicity ingratiated himself with many of the principal inhabitants, was invited to their houses, distinguished at their public feasts, and treated with a regard that gratified his vanity, and therefore easily engaged his affection.

He began very early after his retirement to complain of the conduct of his friends in London, and irritated many of them so much by his letters that they withdrew, however honourably, their contributions; and it is believed that little more was paid him than the 20l. a year which were allowed him by the gentleman who proposed the subscription.

After some stay at Bristol he retired [Sept. 1742] to Swansea, the place originally proposed for his residence, where he lived about a year, very much dissatisfied with the diminution of his salary; but contracted, as in other places, acquaintance with those who were most distinguished in that country, among whom he has celebrated Mr. Powell and Mrs. Jones, by some verses which he inserted in *The Gentleman's Magazine*.

Here he completed his tragedy, of which two acts were wanting when he left London; and was desirous of coming to town to bring it upon the stage. This design was very warmly opposed; and he was advised, by his chief benefactor [Pope], to put it into the hands of Mr. Thomson and Mr. Mallet that it might be fitted for the stage, and to allow his friends to receive the profits, out of which an annual pension should be paid him.

This proposal he rejected with the utmost contempt. He was by no means convinced that the judgment of those to whom he was required to submit was superior to his own. He was now determined, as he expressed it, to be "no longer kept in leading-strings," and had no elevated idea of "his bounty who proposed to pension him out of the profits of his own labours."

He attempted in Wales to promote a subscription for his works, and had once hopes of success; but in a short time afterwards formed a resolution of leaving that part of the country, to which he thought it not reasonable to be confined for the gratification of those who, having promised him a liberal income, had no sooner banished him to a remote corner than they reduced his allowance to a salary scarcely equal to the necessities of life.

His resentment of this treatment, which, in his own opinion at least, he had not deserved, was such that he broke off all correspondence with most of his contributors, and appeared to consider them as persecutors and oppressors; and in the latter part of his life declared that their conduct towards him since his departure from London "had been perfidiousness improving on perfidiousness, and inhumanity on inhumanity."

It is not to be supposed that the necessities of Mr. Savage did not sometimes incite him to satirical exaggerations of the behaviour of those by whom he thought himself reduced to them. But it must be granted that the diminution of his allowance was a great hardship, and that those who withdrew their subscription from a man who, upon the faith of their promise, had gone into a kind of banishment, and abandoned all those by whom he had been before relieved in his distresses, will find it no easy task to vindicate their conduct.

It may be alleged, and perhaps justly, that he was petulant and contemptuous—that he more frequently reproached his subscribers for not giving him more, than thanked them for what he received; but it is to be remembered that his conduct —and this is the worst charge that can be drawn up against him—did them no real injury; and that it therefore ought rather to have been pitied than resented—at least the resentment it might provoke ought to have been generous and manly; epithets which his conduct will hardly deserve that starves a man whom he has persuaded to put himself into his power.

It might have been reasonably demanded by Savage that they should, before they had taken away what they promised, have replaced him in his former state—that they should have taken no advantages from the situation to which the appearance of their kindness had reduced him—and that he should have been recalled to London before he was abandoned. He might justly represent that he ought to have been considered as a lion in the toils, and demand to be released before the dogs should be loosed upon him.

He endeavoured, indeed, to release himself, and, with an intent to return to London, went to Bristol, where a repetition of the kindness which he had formerly found, invited him to stay. He was not only caressed and treated, but had a collection

made for him of about 30*l.*, with which it had been happy if
he had immediately departed for London; but his negligence
did not suffer him to consider that such proofs of kindness
were not often to be expected, and that this ardour of benevolence was in a great degree the effect of novelty, and might,
probably, be every day less; and therefore he took no care to
improve the happy time, but was encouraged by one favour
to hope for another, till at length generosity was exhausted,
and officiousness wearied.

Another part of his misconduct was the practice of prolonging
his visits to unseasonable hours, and disconcerting all the
families into which he was admitted. This was an error in a
place of commerce, which all the charms of his conversation
could not compensate: for what trader would purchase such airy
satisfaction by the loss of solid gain?—which must be the
consequence of midnight merriment, as those hours which were
gained at night were generally lost in the morning.

Thus Mr. Savage, after the curiosity of the inhabitants was
gratified, found the number of his friends daily decreasing,
perhaps without suspecting for what reason their conduct was
altered; for he still continued to harass, with his nocturnal
intrusions, those that yet countenanced him, and admitted
him to their houses.

But he did not spend all the time of his residence at Bristol
in visits or at taverns, for he sometimes returned to his studies,
and began several considerable designs. When he felt an inclination to write, he always retired from the knowledge of his
friends, and lay hid in an obscure part of the suburbs, till he
found himself again desirous of company, to which it is likely
that intervals of absence made him more welcome.

He was always full of his design of returning to London to
bring his tragedy upon the stage; but having neglected to
depart with the money that was raised for him, he could not
afterwards procure a sum sufficient to defray the expenses of
his journey; nor perhaps would a fresh supply have had any
other effect than, by putting immediate pleasures into his
power, to have driven the thoughts of his journey out of
his mind.

While he was thus spending the day in contriving a scheme
for the morrow, distress stole upon him by imperceptible
degrees. His conduct had already wearied some of those who
were at first enamoured of his conversation; but he might,
perhaps, still have devolved to others, whom he might have

entertained with equal success, had not the decay of his clothes made it no longer consistent with their vanity to admit him to their tables, or to associate with him in public places. He now began to find every man from home at whose house he called, and was therefore no longer able to procure the necessaries of life, but wandered about the town, slighted and neglected, in quest of a dinner, which he did not always obtain.

To complete his misery, he was pursued by the officers for small debts which he had contracted, and was therefore obliged to withdraw from the small number of friends from whom he had still reason to hope for favours. His custom was to lie in bed the greatest part of the day, and to go out in the dark with the utmost privacy, and, after having paid his visit, return again before morning to his lodging, which was in the garret of an obscure inn.

Being thus excluded on one hand, and confined on the other, he suffered the utmost extremities of poverty, and often fasted so long that he was seized with faintness, and had lost his appetite, not being able to bear the smell of meat till the action of his stomach was restored by a cordial.

In this distress he received a remittance of 5*l.* from London, with which he provided himself a decent coat, and determined to go to London, but unhappily spent his money at a favourite tavern. Thus was he again confined to Bristol, where he was every day hunted by bailiffs. In this exigence he once more found a friend, who sheltered him in his house, though at the usual inconveniences with which his company was attended; for he could neither be persuaded to go to bed in the night, nor to rise in the day.

It is observable that in these various scenes of misery he was always disengaged and cheerful: he at some times pursued his studies, and at others continued or enlarged his epistolary correspondence; nor was he ever so far dejected as to endeavour to procure an increase of his allowance by any other methods than accusations and reproaches.

He had now no longer any hopes of assistance from his friends at Bristol, who as merchants, and by consequence sufficiently studious of profit, cannot be supposed to have looked with much compassion upon negligence and extravagance, or to think any excellence equivalent to a fault of such consequence as neglect of economy. It is natural to imagine that many of those who would have relieved his real wants were discouraged from the exertion of their benevolence by observation of the use which was made of their favours, and conviction that relief would only be momentary, and that the same necessity would quickly return.

At last he quitted the house of his friend, and returned to his lodging at the inn, still intending to set out in a few days for London; but on the 10th of January, 1742-3, having been at supper with two of his friends, he was at his return to his lodgings arrested for a debt of about 8*l*., which he owed at a coffee-house, and conducted to the house of a sheriff's officer. The account which he gives of this misfortune, in a letter to one of the gentlemen with whom he had supped, is too remarkable to be omitted.

"It was not a little unfortunate for me that I spent yesterday's evening with you, because the hour hindered me from entering on my new lodging; however, I have now got one, but such an one as I believe nobody would choose.

"I was arrested, at the suit of Mrs. Read, just as I was going upstairs to bed at Mr. Bowyer's, but taken in so private a manner, that I believe nobody at the White Lion is apprised of it: though I let the officers know the strength (or rather weakness) of my pocket, yet they treated me with the utmost civility; and even when they conducted me to confinement, it was in such a manner that I verily believe I could have escaped, which I would rather be ruined than have done, notwithstanding the whole amount of my finances was but threepence-halfpenny.

"In the first place I must insist that you will industriously conceal this from Mrs. S——s, because I would not have her good-nature suffer that pain which, I know, she would be apt to feel on this occasion.

"Next, I conjure you, dear Sir, by all the ties of friendship, by no means to have one uneasy thought on my account, but to have the same pleasantry of countenance and unruffled serenity of mind which (God be praised!) I have in this, and have had in a much severer calamity. Furthermore, I charge you, if you value my friendship as truly as I do yours, not to utter, or even harbour, the least resentment against Mrs. Read. I believe she has ruined me, but I freely forgive her; and (though I will never more have any intimacy with her) I would, at a due distance, rather do her an act of good than ill will. Lastly (pardon the expression), I absolutely command you not to offer me any pecuniary assistance, nor to attempt getting me any from any one of your friends. At another time, or on any other occasion, you may, dear friend, be well assured, I would rather write to you in the submissive style of a request, than that of a peremptory command.

"However, that my truly valuable friend may not think I am too proud to ask a favour, let me entreat you to let me have your boy to attend me for this day, not only for the sake of saving me the expense of porters, but for the delivery of some letters to people whose names I would not have known to strangers.

"The civil treatment I have thus far met from those whose prisoner I am makes me thankful to the Almighty, that though he has thought fit to visit me (on my birth-night) with affliction, yet (such is His great goodness!) my affliction is not without alleviating circumstances. I murmur not, but am all resignation to the Divine will. As to the world, I hope that I shall be endued by Heaven with that presence of mind, that serene dignity in misfortune, that constitutes the character of a true noble-man; a dignity far beyond that of coronets; a nobility arising from the just principles of philosophy, refined and exalted by those of Christianity."

He continued five days at the officer's, in hopes that he should be able to procure bail, and avoid the necessity of going to prison. The state in which he passed his time, and the treatment which he received, are very justly expressed by him in a letter which he wrote to a friend: "The whole day," says he, "has been employed in various people's filling my head with their foolish, chimerical systems, which has obliged me coolly (as far as nature will admit) to digest, and accommodate myself to every different person's way of thinking; hurried from one wild system to another, till it has quite made a chaos of my imagination, and nothing done—promised—disappointed —ordered to send every hour from one part of the town to the other."

When his friends, who had hitherto caressed and applauded, found that to give bail and pay the debt was the same, they all refused to preserve him from a prison at the expense of 8l.; and therefore, after having been for some time at the officer's house, "at an immense expense," as he observes in his letter, he was at length removed to Newgate.

This expense he was enabled to support by the generosity of Mr. Nash, at Bath, who, upon receiving from him an account of his condition, immediately sent him five guineas, and promised to promote his subscription at Bath with all his interest.

By his removal to Newgate he obtained at least a freedom from suspense, and rest from the disturbing vicissitudes of hope and disappointment; he now found that his friends were only companions who were willing to share his gaiety, but not to partake of his misfortunes; and therefore he no longer expected any assistance from them.

It must, however, be observed of one gentleman that he offered to release him by paying the debt, but that Mr. Savage would not consent, I suppose, because he thought he had before been too burthensome to him.

He was offered by some of his friends that a collection should be made for his enlargement, but he "treated the proposal," and declared "he should again treat it, with disdain. As to writing any mendicant letters, he had too high a spirit, and determined only to write to some ministers of State to try to regain his pension."

He continued to complain of those that had sent him into the country, and objected to them that he had "lost the profits of his play, which had been finished three years"; and in another letter declares his resolution to publish a pamphlet, that the world might know how "he had been used."

This pamphlet was never written; for he in a very short time recovered his usual tranquillity, and cheerfully applied himself to more inoffensive studies. He indeed steadily declared that he was promised a yearly allowance of 50*l*., and never received half the sum; but he seemed to resign himself to that as well as to other misfortunes, and lose the remembrance of it in his amusements and employments.

The cheerfulness with which he bore his confinement appears from the following letter which he wrote, January the 30th [1742-3], to one of his friends in London:

"I now write to you from my confinement in Newgate, where I have been ever since Monday last was se'nnight, and where I enjoy myself with much more tranquillity than I have known for upwards of a twelvemonth past, having a room entirely to myself, and pursuing the amusement of my poetical studies uninterrupted and agreeable to my mind. I thank the Almighty I am now all collected in myself, and though my person is in confinement, my mind can expatiate on ample and useful subjects with all the freedom imaginable. I am now more conversant with the Nine than ever, and if, instead of a Newgate bird, I may be allowed to be a bird of the Muses, I assure you, Sir, I sing very freely in my cage; sometimes indeed in the plaintive notes of the nightingale, but, at others, in the cheerful strains of the lark."

In another letter he observes that he ranges from one subject to another without confining himself to any particular task, and that he was employed one week upon one attempt, and the next upon another.

Surely the fortitude of this man deserves at least to be mentioned with applause; and whatever faults may be imputed to him, the virtue of suffering well cannot be denied him. The two powers which, in the opinion of Epictetus, constituted a wise man, are those of bearing and forbearing, which it cannot indeed be affirmed to have been equally possessed by Savage; and indeed the want of one obliged him very frequently to practise the other.

He was treated by Mr. Dagge, the keeper of the prison, with great humanity; was supported by him at his own table without any certainty of recompense; had a room to himself to which he could at any time retire from all disturbance; was allowed to stand at the door of the prison, and sometimes taken out into the fields; so that he suffered fewer hardships in prison than he had been accustomed to undergo in the greatest part of his life.

The keeper did not confine his benevolence to a gentle execution of his office, but made some overtures to the creditor for his release, though without effect; and continued, during the whole time of his imprisonment, to treat him with the utmost tenderness and civility.

Virtue is undoubtedly most laudable in that state which makes it most difficult, and therefore the humanity of a gaoler certainly deserves this public attestation; and the man whose heart has not been hardened by such an employment, may be justly proposed as a pattern of benevolence. If an inscription was once engraved "to the honest toll-gatherer," less honours ought not to be paid "to the tender gaoler."

Mr. Savage very frequently received visits, and sometimes presents, from his acquaintances, but they did not amount to a subsistence, for the greater part of which he was indebted to the generosity of this keeper; but these favours, however they might endear to him the particular persons from whom he received them, were very far from impressing upon his mind any advantageous ideas of the people of Bristol, and therefore he thought he could not more properly employ himself in prison than in writing a poem called *London and Bristol delineated*.

When he had brought this poem to its present state, which, without considering the chasm, is not perfect, he wrote to

London an account of his design, and informed his friend that
he was determined to print it with his name, but enjoined him
not to communicate his intention to his Bristol acquaintance.
The gentleman, surprised at his resolution, endeavoured to
dissuade him from publishing it, at least from prefixing his
name; and declared that he could not reconcile the injunction of
secrecy with his resolution to own it at its first appearance. To
this Mr. Savage returned an answer agreeable to his character
in the following terms:

"I received yours this morning, and not without a little
surprise at the contents. To answer a question with a question,
you ask me concerning London and Bristol, Why will I add
delineated? Why did Mr. Woolaston add the same word to his
RELIGION OF NATURE? I suppose that it was his will and
pleasure to add it in his case; and it is mine to do so in my
own. You are pleased to tell me that you understand not why
secrecy is enjoined, and yet I intend to set my name to it. My
answer is, I have my private reasons, which I am not obliged
to explain to anyone. You doubt my friend Mr. S—— would
not approve of it. And what is it to me whether he does or
not? Do you imagine that Mr. S—— is to dictate to me? If
any man who calls himself my friend should assume such an
air, I would spurn at his friendship with contempt. You say
I seem to think so by not letting him know it. And suppose I do,
what then? Perhaps I can give reasons for that disapprobation,
very foreign from what you would imagine. You go on in saying,
Suppose I should not put my name to it. My answer is, that
I will not suppose any such thing, being determined to the
contrary: neither, Sir, would I have you suppose that I applied
to you for want of another press; nor would I have you imagine
that I owe Mr. S—— obligations which I do not."

Such was his imprudence, and such his obstinate adherence
to his own resolutions, however absurd! A prisoner! supported
by charity! and, whatever insults he might have received during
the latter part of his stay at Bristol, once caressed, esteemed,
and presented with a liberal collection, he could forget on a
sudden his danger and his obligations to gratify the petulance
of his wit or the eagerness of his resentment, and publish a
satire, by which he might reasonably expect that he should
alienate those who then supported him, and provoke those
whom he could neither resist nor escape.

This resolution, from the execution of which it is probable
that only his death could have hindered him, is sufficient to

show how much he disregarded all considerations that opposed his present passions, and how readily he hazarded all future advantages for any immediate gratifications. Whatever was his predominant inclination, neither hope nor fear hindered him from complying with it; nor had opposition any other effect than to heighten his ardour and irritate his vehemence.

This performance was however laid aside while he was employed in soliciting assistance from several great persons; and one interruption succeeding another hindered him from supplying the chasm, and perhaps from retouching the other parts, which he can hardly be imagined to have finished in his own opinion, for it is very unequal, and some of the lines are rather inserted to rhyme to others than to support or improve the sense; but the first and last parts are worked up with great spirit and elegance.

His time was spent in the prison for the most part in study, or in receiving visits; but sometimes he descended to lower amusements, and diverted himself in the kitchen with the conversation of the criminals; for it was not pleasing to him to be much without company; and though he was very capable of a judicious choice, he was often contented with the first that offered; for this he was sometimes reproved by his friends, who found him surrounded with felons; but the reproof was on that, as on other occasions, thrown away; he continued to gratify himself, and to set very little value on the opinion of others.

But here, as in every other scene of his life, he made use of such opportunities as occurred of benefiting those who were more miserable than himself, and was always ready to perform any office of humanity to his fellow-prisoners.

He had now ceased from corresponding with any of his subscribers except one [Pope], who yet continued to remit him the 20*l.* a year which he had promised him, and by whom it was expected that he would have been in a very short time enlarged, because he had directed the keeper to inquire after the state of his debts.

However, he took care to enter his name according to the forms of the court, that the creditor might be obliged to make him some allowance if he was continued a prisoner, and when on that occasion he appeared in the hall, was treated with very unusual respect.

But the resentment of the city was afterwards raised by some accounts that had been spread of the satire; and he was informed that some of the merchants intended to pay the allowance which the law required, and to detain him a prisoner at their own expense. This he treated as an empty menace, and perhaps might have hastened the publication, only to show how much he was superior to their insults, had not all his schemes been suddenly destroyed.

When he had been six months in prison he received from one of his friends [Pope], in whose kindness he had the greatest confidence, and on whose assistance he chiefly depended, a letter that contained a charge of very atrocious ingratitude, drawn up in such terms as sudden resentment dictated. Henley, in one of his advertisements, had mentioned "Pope's treatment of Savage." This was supposed by Pope to be the consequence of a complaint made by Savage to Henley, and was therefore mentioned by him with much resentment. Mr. Savage returned a very solemn protestation of his innocence, but, however, appeared much disturbed at the accusation. Some days afterwards he was seized with a pain in his back and side, which, as it was not violent, was not suspected to be dangerous; but growing daily more languid and dejected, on the 25th of July he confined himself to his room and a fever seized his spirits. The symptoms grew every day more formidable, but his condition did not enable him to procure any assistance. The last time that the keeper saw him was on July the 31st, 1743, when Savage, seeing him at his bedside, said with an uncommon earnestness, "I have something to say to you, Sir," but, after a pause, moved his hand in a melancholy manner, and finding himself unable to recollect what he was going to communicate, said, "'Tis gone!" The keeper soon after left him, and the next morning he died. He was buried in the churchyard of St. Peter [at Bristol], at the expense of the keeper.

Such were the life and death of Richard Savage, a man equally distinguished by his virtues and vices, and at once remarkable for his weaknesses and abilities.

He was of a middle stature, of a thin habit of body, a long visage, coarse features, and melancholy aspect; of a grave and manly deportment, a solemn dignity of mien, but which, upon a nearer acquaintance, softened into an engaging easiness of manners. His walk was slow, and his voice tremulous and mournful. He was easily excited to smiles, but very seldom provoked to laughter.

His mind was in an uncommon degree vigorous and active. His judgment was accurate, his apprehension quick, and his memory so tenacious that he was frequently observed to know what he had learned from others in a short time, better than those by whom he was informed, and could frequently recollect incidents, with all their combination of circumstances, which few would have regarded at the present time, but which the quickness of his apprehension impressed upon him. He had the art of escaping from his own reflections, and accommodating himself to every new scene.

To this quality is to be imputed the extent of his knowledge, compared with the small time which he spent in visible endeavours to acquire it. He mingled in cursory conversation with the same steadiness of attention as others apply to a lecture; and, amidst the appearance of thoughtless gaiety, lost no new idea that was started, nor any hint that could be improved. He had therefore made in coffee-houses the same proficiency as others in their closets; and it is remarkable that the writings of a man of little education and little reading have an air of learning scarcely to be found in any other performances, but which perhaps as often obscures as embellishes them.

His judgment was eminently exact both with regard to writings and to men. The knowledge of life was indeed his chief attainment; and it is not without some satisfaction that I can produce the suffrage of Savage in favour of human nature, of which he never appeared to entertain such odious ideas as some, who perhaps had neither his judgment nor experience, have published either in ostentation of their sagacity, vindication of their crimes, or gratification of their malice.

His method of life particularly qualified him for conversation, of which he knew how to practise all the graces. He was never vehement or loud, but at once modest and easy, open and respectful; his language was vivacious or elegant, and equally happy upon grave and humorous subjects. He was generally censured for not knowing when to retire; but that was not the defect of his judgment, but of his fortune; when he left his company, he was frequently to spend the remaining part of the night in the street, or at least was abandoned to gloomy reflections, which it is not strange that he delayed as long as he could; and sometimes forgot that he gave others pain to avoid it himself.

It cannot be said that he made use of his abilities for the direction of his own conduct: an irregular and dissipated manner of life had made him the slave of every passion that happened to be excited by the presence of its object, and that slavery to his passions reciprocally produced a life irregular and dissipated. He was not master of his own motions, nor could promise anything for the next day.

With regard to his economy, nothing can be added to the relation of his life. He appeared to think himself born to be supported by others, and dispensed from all necessity of providing for himself; he therefore never prosecuted any scheme of advantage, nor endeavoured even to secure the profits which his writings might have afforded him. His temper was, in consequence of the dominion of his passions, uncertain and capricious; he was easily engaged, and easily disgusted; but he is accused of retaining his hatred more tenaciously than his benevolence.

He was compassionate both by nature and principle, and always ready to perform offices of humanity; but when he was provoked (and very small offences were sufficient to provoke him), he would prosecute his revenge with the utmost acrimony till his passion had subsided.

His friendship was therefore of little value; for though he was zealous in the support or vindication of those whom he loved, yet it was always dangerous to trust him, because he considered himself as discharged by the first quarrel from all ties of honour or gratitude, and would betray those secrets which in the warmth of confidence had been imparted to him. This practice drew upon him an universal accusation of ingratitude: nor can it be denied that he was very ready to set himself free from the load of an obligation; for he could not bear to conceive himself in a state of dependence, his pride being equally powerful with his other passions, and appearing in the form of insolence at one time, and of vanity at another. Vanity, the most innocent species of pride, was most frequently predominant: he could not easily leave off when he had once begun to mention himself or his works; nor ever read his verses without stealing his eyes from the page, to discover in the faces of his audience how they were affected with any favourite passage.

A kinder name than that of vanity ought to be given to the delicacy with which he was always careful to separate his own merit from every other man's, and to reject that praise to which he had no claim. He did not forget, in mentioning his performances, to mark every line that had been suggested or amended; and was so accurate as to relate that he owed *three words* in *The Wanderer* to the advice of his friends.

His veracity was questioned, but with little reason; his

accounts, though not indeed always the same, were generally consistent. When he loved any man, he suppressed all his faults; and, when he had been offended by him, concealed all his virtues: but his characters were generally true, so far as he proceeded; though it cannot be denied that his partiality might have sometimes the effect of falsehood.

In cases indifferent, he was zealous for virtue, truth, and justice: he knew very well the necessity of goodness to the present and future happiness of mankind; nor is there perhaps any writer who has less endeavoured to please by flattering the appetites, or perverting the judgment.

As an author, therefore (and he now ceases to influence mankind in any other character), if one piece which he had resolved to suppress be excepted, he has very little to fear from the strictest moral or religious censure. And though he may not be altogether secure against the objections of the critic, it must however be acknowledged that his works are the productions of a genius truly poetical; and, what many writers who have been more lavishly applauded cannot boast, that they have an original air, which has no resemblance of any foregoing writer; that the versification and sentiments have a cast peculiar to themselves, which no man can imitate with success, because what was nature in Savage, would in another be affectation. It must be confessed, that his descriptions are striking, his images animated, his fictions justly imagined, and his allegories artfully pursued; that his diction is elevated, though sometimes forced, and his numbers sonorous and majestic, though frequently sluggish and encumbered. Of his style, the general fault is harshness, and its general excellence is dignity; of his sentiments, the prevailing beauty is simplicity, and uniformity the prevailing defect.

For his life, or for his writings, none, who candidly consider his fortune, will think an apology either necessary or difficult. If he was not always sufficiently instructed in his subject, his knowledge was at least greater than could have been attained by others in the same state. If his works were sometimes unfinished, accuracy cannot reasonably be exacted from a man oppressed with want, which he has no hope of relieving but by a speedy publication. The insolence and resentment of which he is accused were not easily to be avoided by a great mind, irritated by perpetual hardships, and constrained hourly to return the spurns of contempt, and repress the insolence of prosperity; and vanity surely may be readily pardoned in him to whom life afforded no other comforts than barren praises, and the consciousness of deserving them.

Those are no proper judges of his conduct who have slumbered away their time on the down of plenty; nor will any wise man easily presume to say, "Had I been in Savage's condition, I should have lived or written better than Savage."

This relation will not be wholly without its use, if those who languish under any part of his sufferings shall be enabled to fortify their patience by reflecting that they feel only those afflictions from which the abilities of Savage did not exempt him; or those who, in confidence of superior capacities or attainments, disregard the common maxims of life, shall be reminded that nothing will supply the want of prudence; and that negligence and irregularity, long continued, will make knowledge useless, wit ridiculous, and genius contemptible.

ALEXANDER POPE

1688-1744

Born in London—Both Parents Roman Catholics—Educated by
Priests—Early distinguished as a Poet—Lives at Binfield in Berkshire—
Sees Dryden—Becomes acquainted with Wycherley, Walsh, Sir W.
Trumbull, etc.—Writes his *Pastorals*—Publishes his *Pastorals* in Tonson's
Miscellany—Publishes *An Essay on Criticism*—Dennis attacks the *Essay*
—Publishes *The Rape of the Lock* in Lintot's *Miscellany*—His intimacy
with Addison—Publishes *Windsor Forest*—Commences a Translation of
the Iliad—History of the Subscription for the Iliad—Lord Halifax and
Pope—Collects his Poems—*Eloisa to Abelard*—*Verses on an Unfortunate
Lady*—Commences a Translation of the Odyssey—Fenton and Broome—
Publication of his Letters to Cromwell—Curll—Edits Shakespeare—
Theobald's Attack—The *Bathos*—History of *The Dunciad*—Writes his
Moral Epistles and *Epistle to Dr. Arbuthnot*—The *Essay on Man*—Boling-
broke and Warburton—Quarrels with Lord Hervey and Lady Mary
Montagu—His Imitations of Horace—Collects a Second Volume of his
Poems—Publication of his Letters by Curll—Writes his two Dialogues,
"1738"—Quarrels with Cibber—Writes a Fourth Book of *The Dunciad*
—Theobald dethroned—Death and Burial at Twickenham—Personal
Character—Works and Character—Dryden and Pope compared—Criticism
on his Epitaphs.

ALEXANDER POPE was born in London, May 22, 1688, of
parents whose rank or station was never ascertained: we are
informed that they were of "gentle blood"; that his father
was of a family of which the Earl of Downe was the head; and
that his mother was the daughter of William Turner, Esq., of
York, who had likewise three sons, one of whom had the honour
of being killed, and the other of dying, in the service of Charles
the First; the third [the eldest] was made a general officer in
Spain, from whom the sister inherited what sequestrations and
forfeitures had left in the family.

This, and this only, is told by Pope, who is more willing, as I
have heard observed, to show what his father was not, than
what he was. It is allowed that he grew rich by trade, but
whether in a shop or on the Exchange was never discovered
till Mr. Tyers told, on the authority of Mrs. Rackett, that he
was a linen-draper in the Strand. Both parents were Papists.

Pope was from his birth of a constitution tender and delicate,
but is said to have shown remarkable gentleness and sweetness

of disposition. The weakness of his body continued through his life; but the mildness of his mind perhaps ended with his childhood. His voice, when he was young, was so pleasing, that he was called in fondness the "little Nightingale."

Being not sent early to school, he was taught to read by an aunt; and when he was seven or eight years old, became a lover of books. He first learned to write by imitating printed books; a species of penmanship in which he retained great excellence through his whole life, though his ordinary hand was not elegant.

When he was about eight, he was placed in Hampshire under Taverner, a Romish priest, who, by a method very rarely practised, taught him the Greek and Latin rudiments together. He was now first regularly initiated in poetry by the perusal of Ogilby's Homer, and Sandys's Ovid. Ogilby's assistance he never repaid with any praise; but of Sandys he declared in his notes to the Iliad, that English poetry owed much of its beauty to his translations. Sandys very rarely attempted original composition.

From the care of Taverner, under whom his proficiency was considerable, he was removed to a school at Twyford, near Winchester, and again to another school about Hyde Park Corner, from which he used sometimes to stroll to the play-house, and was so delighted with theatrical exhibitions, that he formed a kind of play from Ogilby's Iliad, with some verses of his own intermixed, which he persuaded his school-fellows to act, with the addition of his master's gardener, who personated Ajax.

At the two last schools he used to represent himself as having lost part of what Taverner had taught him; and on his master at Twyford he had already exercised his poetry in a lampoon. Yet under those masters he translated more than a fourth part of the *Metamorphoses*. If he kept the same proportion in his other exercises, it cannot be thought that his loss was great.

He tells of himself, in his poems, that "he lisp'd in numbers"; and used to say that he could not remember the time when he began to make verses. In the style of fiction it might have been said of him as of Pindar, that when he lay in his cradle, "the bees swarmed about his mouth."

About the time of the Revolution his father, who was un-doubtedly disappointed by the sudden blast of Popish prosperity, quitted his trade, and retired to Binfield, in Windsor Forest, with about twenty thousand pounds; for which, being conscientiously determined not to entrust it to the Government, he found no better use than that of locking it up in a chest, and taking from it what his expenses required; and his life was long enough to consume a great part of it before his son came to the inheritance.

To Binfield Pope was called by his father when he was about twelve years old; and there he had for a few months the assistance of one Deane, another priest, of whom he learned only to construe a little of Tully's *Offices*. How Mr. Deane could spend, with a boy who had translated so much of Ovid, some months over a small part of Tully's *Offices*, it is now vain to inquire.

Of a youth so successfully employed, and so conspicuously improved, a minute account must be naturally desired; but curiosity must be contented with confused, imperfect, and sometimes improbable intelligence. Pope, finding little advantage from external help, resolved thenceforward to direct himself, and at twelve formed a plan of study which he completed with little other incitement than the desire of excellence.

His primary and principal purpose was to be a poet, with which his father accidentally concurred by proposing subjects, and obliging him to correct his performances by many revisals; after which the old gentleman, when he was satisfied, would say, "These are good rhymes."

In his perusal of the English poets he soon distinguished the versification of Dryden, which he considered as the model to be studied, and was impressed with such veneration for his instructor, that he persuaded some friends to take him to the coffee-house which Dryden frequented, and pleased himself with having seen him.

Dryden died May 1, 1700, some days before Pope was twelve, so early must he therefore have felt the power of harmony and the zeal of genius. Who does not wish that Dryden could have known the value of the homage that was paid him, and foreseen the greatness of his young admirer?

The earliest of Pope's productions is his *Ode on Solitude*, written before he was twelve, in which there is nothing more than other forward boys have attained, and which is not equal to Cowley's performances at the same age.

His time was now wholly spent in reading and writing. As he read the Classics, he amused himself with translating them; and at fourteen made a version of the first book of the *Thebais*, which, with some revision, he afterwards published. He must have been at this time, if he had no help, a considerable proficient in the Latin tongue.

By Dryden's *Fables*, which had then been not long published, and were much in the hands of poetical readers, he was tempted to try his own skill in giving Chaucer a more fashionable appearance, and put *January and May*, and the *Prologue of the Wife of Bath*, into modern English. He translated likewise the *Epistle of Sappho to Phaon* from Ovid, to complete the version which was before imperfect; and wrote some other small pieces which he afterwards printed.

He sometimes imitated the English poets, and professed to have written at fourteen his poem upon *Silence*, after Rochester's *Nothing*. He had now formed his versification, and the smoothness of his numbers surpassed his original: but this is a small part of his praise; he discovers such acquaintance both with human and public affairs as is not easily conceived to have been attainable by a boy of fourteen in Windsor Forest.

Next year he was desirous of opening to himself new sources of knowledge by making himself acquainted with modern languages, and removed for a time to London, that he might study French and Italian, which, as he desired nothing more than to read them, were by diligent application soon despatched. Of Italian learning he does not appear to have ever made much use in his subsequent studies.

He then returned to Binfield, and delighted himself with his own poetry. He tried all styles and many subjects. He wrote a comedy, a tragedy, an epic poem, with panegyrics on all the princes of Europe; and as he confesses, "thought himself the greatest genius that ever was." Self-confidence is the first requisite to great undertakings. He, indeed, who forms his opinion of himself in solitude, without knowing the powers of other men, is very liable to error; but it was the felicity of Pope to rate himself at his real value.

Most of his puerile productions were, by his maturer judgment, afterwards destroyed: *Alcander*, the epic poem, was burned by the persuasion of Atterbury. The tragedy was founded on the legend of St. Genevieve. Of the comedy there is no account.

Concerning his studies it is related that he translated *Tully on Old Age*; and that, besides his books of poetry and criticism, he read Temple's *Essays* and *Locke on Human Understanding*. His reading, though his favourite authors are not known, appears to have been sufficiently extensive and multifarious;

for his early pieces show, with sufficient evidence, his knowledge of books.

He that is pleased with himself easily imagines that he shall please others. Sir William Trumbull, who had been ambassador at Constantinople, and Secretary of State when he retired from business, fixed his residence in the neighbourhood of Binfield. Pope, not yet sixteen, was introduced to the statesman of sixty, and so distinguished himself, that their interviews ended in friendship and correspondence. Pope was, through his whole life, ambitious of splendid acquaintance; and he seems to have wanted neither diligence nor success in attracting the notice of the great; for from his first entrance into the world (and his entrance was very early) he was admitted to familiarity with those whose rank or station made them most conspicuous.

From the age of sixteen the life of Pope, as an author, may be properly computed. He now [1704] wrote his *Pastorals*, which were shown to the poets and critics of that time: as they well deserved, they were read with admiration, and many praises were bestowed upon them and upon the Preface, which is both elegant and learned in a high degree: they were, however, not published till five years afterwards.

Cowley, Milton, and Pope are distinguished among the English poets by the early exertion of their powers; but the works of Cowley alone were published in his childhood, and therefore of him only can it be certain that his puerile performances received no improvement from his maturer studies.

At this time began his acquaintance with Wycherley, a man who seems to have had among his contemporaries his full share of reputation, to have been esteemed without virtue, and caressed without good humour. Pope was proud of his notice; Wycherley wrote verses in his praise, which he was charged by Dennis with writing to himself; and they agreed for a while to flatter one another. It is pleasant to remark how soon Pope learned the cant of an author, and began to treat critics with contempt, though he had yet suffered nothing from them.

But the fondness of Wycherley was too violent to last. His esteem of Pope was such that he submitted some poems to his revision, and when Pope, perhaps proud of such confidence, was sufficiently bold in his criticisms, and liberal in his alterations, the old scribbler was angry to see his pages defaced, and felt more pain from the detection than content from the amendment of his faults. They parted, but Pope always considered him with kindness, and visited him a little time before he died.

Another of his early correspondents was Mr. Cromwell, of whom I have learned nothing particular but that he used to ride a-hunting in a tye-wig. He was fond, and perhaps vain, of amusing himself with poetry and criticism; and sometimes sent his performances to Pope, who did not forbear such remarks as were now and then unwelcome. Pope, in his turn, put the juvenile version of Statius into his hands for correction.

Their correspondence afforded the public its first knowledge of Pope's epistolary powers; for his letters were given by Cromwell to one Mrs. Thomas, and she many years afterwards sold them to Curll, who inserted them [1727] in a volume of his *Miscellanies*.

Walsh, a name yet preserved among the minor poets, was one of his first encouragers. His regard was gained by the *Pastorals*, and from him Pope received the counsel from which he seems to have regulated his studies. Walsh advised him to correctness, which, as he told him, the English poets had hitherto neglected, and which therefore was left to him as a basis of fame; and being delighted with rural poems, recommended to him to write a pastoral comedy, like those which are read so eagerly in Italy; a design which Pope probably did not approve, as he did not follow it.

Pope had now declared himself a poet; and thinking himself entitled to poetical conversation, began at seventeen to frequent Will's, a coffee-house on the north side of Russell-street, in Covent-garden, where the wits of that time used to assemble, and where Dryden had, when he lived, been accustomed to preside.

During this period of his life he was indefatigably diligent, and insatiably curious: wanting health for violent, and money for expensive pleasures, and having excited in himself very strong desires of intellectual eminence, he spent much of his time over his books; but he read only to store his mind with facts and images, seizing all that his authors presented with undistinguishing voracity, and with an appetite for knowledge too eager to be nice. In a mind like his, however, all the faculties were at once involuntarily improving. Judgment is forced upon us by experience. He that reads many books must compare one opinion or one style with another, and when he compares, must necessarily distinguish, reject, and prefer. But the account given by himself of his studies was, that from fourteen to twenty he read only for amusement, from twenty to twenty-seven for improvement and instruction; that in the first part of this time he desired only to know, and in the second he endeavoured to judge.

The *Pastorals*, which had been for some time handed about among poets and critics, were at last printed (1709) in Tonson's [Sixth] *Miscellany*, in a volume which began with the *Pastorals* of Philips, and ended with those of Pope.

The same year [1709] was written the *Essay on Criticism*; a work which displays such extent of comprehension, such nicety of distinction, such acquaintance with mankind, and such knowledge both of ancient and modern learning, as are not often attained by the maturest age and longest experience. It was published about two years afterwards; and being praised by Addison in *The Spectator*, with sufficient liberality, met with so much favour as enraged Dennis, "who," he says, "found himself attacked without any manner of provocation on his side, and attacked in his person, instead of his writings, by one who was wholly a stranger to him, at a time when all the world knew he was persecuted by fortune; and not only saw that this was attempted in a clandestine manner, with the utmost falsehood and calumny, but found that all this was done by a little affected hypocrite, who had nothing in his mouth at the same time but truth, candour, friendship, good nature, humanity, and magnanimity."

How the attack was clandestine is not easily perceived, nor how his person is depreciated; but he seems to have known something of Pope's character, in whom may be discovered an appetite to talk too frequently of his own virtues.

The pamphlet is such as rage might be expected to dictate. He supposes himself to be asked two questions: whether the *Essay* will succeed, and who or what is the author.

Its success he admits to be secured by the false opinions then prevalent; the author he concludes to be "young and raw."

"First; because he discovers a sufficiency beyond his last ability, and hath rashly undertaken a task infinitely above his force. Secondly; while this little author struts and affects the dictatorian air, he plainly shows that at the same time he is under the rod; and while he pretends to give law to others, is a pedantic slave to authority and opinion. Thirdly; he hath, like schoolboys, borrowed both from living and dead. Fourthly; he knows not his own mind, and frequently contradicts himself. Fifthly; he is almost perpetually in the wrong."

All these positions he attempts to prove by quotations and remarks; but his desire to do mischief is greater than his power. He has, however, justly criticised some passages in these lines:

> There are whom Heaven has bless'd with store of wit,
> Yet want as much again to manage it;
> For wit and judgment ever are at strife—
>
> [First Edition, 4to., 1711, p. 7.]

It is apparent that wit has two meanings, and that what is wanted, though called wit, is truly judgment. So far Dennis is undoubtedly right; but not content with argument, he will have a little mirth, and triumphs over the first couplet in terms too elegant to be forgotten. "By the way, what rare numbers are here! Would not one swear that this youngster had espoused some antiquated muse, who had sued out a divorce on account of impotence from some superannuated sinner; and having been p——xed by her former spouse, has got the gout in her decrepit age, which makes her hobble so damnably." This was the man who would reform a nation sinking into barbarity.

In another place Pope himself allowed that Dennis had detected one of those blunders which are called "bulls." The first edition had this line:

> What is this wit—
> Where wanted, scorned; and envied where acquir'd?

"How," says the critic, "can wit be scorn'd where it is not? Is not this a figure frequently employed in Hibernian land? The person that wants this wit may indeed be scorned, but the scorn shows the honour which the contemner has for wit." Of this remark Pope made the proper use by correcting the passage.

I have preserved, I think, all that is reasonable in Dennis's criticism; it remains that justice be done to his delicacy. "For his acquaintance (says Dennis) he names Mr. Walsh, who had by no means the qualification which this author reckons absolutely necessary to a critic, it being very certain that he was, like this essayer, a very indifferent poet; he loved to be well dressed; and I remember a little young gentleman whom Mr. Walsh used to take into his company, as a double foil to his person and capacity. Inquire between Sunninghill and Oakingham for a young, short, squab gentleman, the very bow of the God of Love, and tell me whether he be a proper author to make personal reflections? He may extol the ancients, but he has reason to thank the gods that he was born a modern; for had he been born of Grecian parents, and his father consequently had by law had the absolute disposal of him, his life had been no longer than that of one of his poems, the life of half a day. Let the person of a gentleman of his parts be never so contemptible, his inward man is ten times more ridiculous; it being impossible that his outward form, though it be that of downright monkey, should differ so much from human shape as his unthinking, immaterial part does from human understanding." Thus began the hostility between Pope and Dennis, which, though it was suspended for a short time, never was appeased. Pope seems, at first, to have attacked him wantonly; but though he always professed to despise him, he discovers, by mentioning him very often, that he felt his force or his venom.

Of this *Essay* Pope declared that he did not expect the sale to be quick, because "not one gentleman in sixty, even of liberal education, could understand it." The gentlemen and the education of that time seem to have been of a lower character than they are of this. He mentioned a thousand copies as a numerous impression.

Dennis was not his only censurer: the zealous Papists thought the monks treated with too much contempt, and Erasmus too studiously praised; but to these objections he had not much regard.

The *Essay* has been translated into French by Hamilton, author of the *Comte de Grammont*, whose version was never printed; by Robotham, secretary to the King for Hanover, and by Resnel; and commented by Dr. Warburton, who has discovered in it such order and connection as was not perceived by Addison, nor, as is said, intended by the author.

Almost every poem consisting of precepts is so far arbitrary and immethodical, that many of the paragraphs may change places with no apparent inconvenience; for of two or more positions, depending upon some remote and general principle, there is seldom any cogent reason why one should precede the other. But for the order in which they stand, whatever it be, a little ingenuity may easily give a reason. "It is possible," says Hooker, "that, by long circumduction from any one truth, all truth may be inferred." Of all homogeneous truths, at least of all truths respecting the same general end, in whatever series they may be produced, a concatenation by intermediate ideas may be formed, such as, when it is once shown, shall appear natural; but if this order be reversed, another mode of connection equally specious may be found or made. Aristotle is praised for naming Fortitude first of the cardinal virtues, as that without which no other virtue can steadily be practised; but he might, with equal propriety, have placed Prudence and Justice before it, since without Prudence Fortitude is mad; without Justice it is mischievous.

As the end of method is perspicuity, that series is sufficiently regular that avoids obscurity; and where there is no obscurity, it will not be difficult to discover method.

In *The Spectator* was published the *Messiah*, which he first submitted to the perusal of Steele, and corrected in compliance with his criticisms.

It is reasonable to infer from his Letters that the verses on the *Unfortunate Lady* were written about the time when his *Essay* was published. The lady's name and adventures I have sought with fruitless inquiry.

I can therefore tell no more than I have learned from Mr. Ruffhead, who writes with the confidence of one who could trust his information. She was a woman of eminent rank and large fortune, the ward of an uncle, who, having given her a proper education, expected like other guardians that she should make at least an equal match; and such he proposed to her, but found it rejected in favour of a young gentleman of inferior condition.

Having discovered the correspondence between the two lovers, and finding the young lady determined to abide by her own choice, he supposed that separation might do what can rarely be done by arguments, and sent her into a foreign country, where she was obliged to converse only with those from whom her uncle had nothing to fear.

Her lover took care to repeat his vows, but his letters were intercepted and carried to her guardian, who directed her to be watched with still greater vigilance, till of this restraint she grew so impatient, that she bribed a woman servant to procure her a sword, which she directed to her heart.

From this account, given with evident intention to raise the lady's character, it does not appear that she had any claim to praise, nor much to compassion. She seems to have been impatient, violent, and ungovernable. Her uncle's power could not have lasted long; the hour of liberty and choice would have come in time. But her desires were too hot for delay, and she liked self-murder better than suspense.

Nor is it discovered that the uncle, whoever he was, is with much justice delivered to posterity as "a false Guardian"; he seems to have done only that for which a guardian is appointed; he endeavoured to direct his niece till she should be able to direct herself. Poetry has not often been worse employed than in dignifying the amorous fury of a raving girl.

Not long after he wrote *The Rape of the Lock*, the most airy, the most ingenious, and the most delightful of all his compositions, occasioned by a frolic of gallantry rather too familiar, in which Lord Petre cut off a lock of Mrs. Arabella Fermor's hair. This, whether stealth or violence, was so much resented, that the commerce of the two families, before very friendly, was interrupted. Mr. Caryl, a gentleman who, being secretary to King James's Queen, had followed his mistress into France, and who, being the author of *Sir Solomon Single*, a comedy, and some translations, was entitled to the notice of a wit, solicited Pope to endeavour a reconciliation by a ludicrous poem, which might bring both the parties to a better temper. In compliance with Caryl's request, though his name was for a long time marked only by the first and last letter, C—l, a poem of two cantos was written (1711), as is said, in a fortnight, and sent to the offended lady, who liked it well enough to show it: and, with the usual process of literary transactions, the author, dreading a surreptitious edition, was forced to publish it.

The event is said to have been such as was desired; the pacification and diversion of all to whom it related, except Sir George Brown, who complained with some bitterness that, in the character of Sir Plume, he was made to talk nonsense. Whether all this be true I have some doubt, for at Paris, a few years ago, a niece of Mrs. Fermor, who presided in an English convent, mentioned Pope's work with very little gratitude, rather as an insult than an honour; and she may be supposed to have inherited the opinion of her family.

At its first appearance it was termed by Addison "merum sal." Pope, however, saw that it was capable of improvement; and having luckily contrived to borrow his machinery from the Rosicrucians, imparted the scheme with which his head was teeming to Addison, who told him that his work, as it stood, was "a delicious little thing," and gave him no encouragement to retouch it.

This has been too hastily considered as an instance of Addison's jealousy; for as he could not guess the conduct of the new design, or the possibilities of pleasure comprised in a fiction of which there had been no examples, he might very reasonably and kindly persuade the author to acquiesce in his own prosperity, and forbear an attempt which he considered as an unnecessary hazard.

Addison's counsel was happily rejected. Pope foresaw the future efflorescence of imagery then budding in his mind, and resolved to spare no art or industry of cultivation. The soft luxuriance of his fancy was already shooting, and all the gay varieties of diction were ready at his hand to colour and embellish it.

His attempt was justified by its success. *The Rape of the Lock* stands forward, in the classes of literature, as the most exquisite example of ludicrous poetry. Berkeley congratulated him upon the display of powers more truly poetical than he had shown before: with elegance of description and justness of precepts he had now exhibited boundless fertility of invention.

He always considered the intermixture of the machinery with the action as his most successful exertion of poetical art. He indeed could never afterwards produce anything of such un-exampled excellence. Those performances which strike with wonder, are combinations of skilful genius with happy casualty; and it is not likely that any felicity, like the discovery of a new race of preternatural agents, should happen twice to the same man.

Of this poem the author was, I think, allowed to enjoy the praise for a long time without disturbance. Many years afterwards [1728] Dennis published some remarks upon it, with very little force and with no effect; for the opinion of the public was already settled, and it was no longer at the mercy of criticism.

About this time he published *The Temple of Fame*, which, as he tells Steele in their correspondence, he had written two years before; that is, when he was only twenty-two years old, an early time of life for so much learning and so much observation as that work exhibits.

On this poem Dennis afterwards published some remarks, of which the most reasonable is, that some of the lines represent Motion as exhibited by Sculpture.

Of the *Epistle from Eloisa to Abelard* I do not know the date. His first inclination to attempt a composition of that tender kind arose, as Mr. Savage told me, from his perusal of Prior's *Nut-brown Maid*. How much he has surpassed Prior's work it is not necessary to mention, when perhaps it may be said with justice that he has excelled every composition of the same kind. The mixture of religious hope and resignation gives an elevation and dignity to disappointed love, which images merely natural cannot bestow. The gloom of a convent strikes the imagination with far greater force than the solitude of a grove.

This piece was, however, not much his favourite in his latter years, though I never heard upon what principle he slighted it.

In the next year (1713) he published *Windsor Forest*; of which part was, as he relates, written at sixteen, about the same time as his *Pastorals*; and the latter part was added afterwards: where the addition begins we are not told. The lines relating to the Peace confess their own date. It is dedicated to Lord Lansdown, who was then high in reputation and influence among the Tories; and it is said that the conclusion of the poem gave great pain to Addison, both as a poet and a politician. Reports like this are often spread with boldness very disproportionate to their evidence. Why should Addison receive any particular disturbance from the last lines of *Windsor Forest*? If contrariety of opinion could poison a politician, he would not live a day; and, as a poet, he must have felt Pope's force of genius much more from many other parts of his works.

The pain that Addison might feel, it is not likely that he would confess; and it is certain that he so well suppressed his discontent that Pope now thought himself his favourite; for, having been consulted in the revisal of *Cato*, he introduced it [14th April, 1713] by a Prologue; and, when Dennis published his *Remarks*, undertook not indeed to vindicate but to revenge his friend, by "Dr. Norris's" *Narrative of the Frenzy of Mr. John Dennis*.

There is reason to believe that Addison gave no encouragement to this disingenuous hostility; for, says Pope, in a letter to him, "indeed your opinion, that 'tis entirely to be neglected, would have been my own had it been my own case; but I felt more warmth here than I did when I first saw his book against myself (though indeed in two minutes it made me heartily merry)." Addison was not a man on whom such cant of sensibility could make much impression. He left the pamphlet to itself, having disowned it to Dennis, and perhaps did not think Pope to have deserved much by his officiousness.

This year [1713] was printed in *The Guardian* the ironical comparison between the *Pastorals* of Philips and Pope; a composition of artifice, criticism, and literature, to which nothing equal will easily be found. The superiority of Pope is so ingeniously dissembled, and the feeble lines of Philips so skilfully preferred, that Steele, being deceived, was unwilling to print the paper lest Pope should be offended. Addison immediately

saw the writer's design; and, as it seems, had malice enough
to conceal his discovery and to permit a publication which,
by making his friend Philips ridiculous, made him for ever an
enemy to Pope.

It appears that about this time Pope had a strong inclination
to unite the art of Painting with that of Poetry, and put himself
under the tuition of Jervas. He was near-sighted, and therefore
not formed by nature for a painter: he tried, however, how far
he could advance, and sometimes persuaded his friends to sit.
A picture of Betterton, supposed to be drawn by him, was in
the possession of Lord Mansfield: if this was taken from life, he
must have begun to paint earlier; for Betterton was now dead.
Pope's ambition of this new art produced some encomiastic
verses to Jervas, which certainly show his power as a poet; but
I have been told that they betray his ignorance of painting.

He appears to have regarded Betterton with kindness and
esteem; and after his death published, under his name, a
version into modern English of Chaucer's Prologues, and one
of his Tales, which, as was related by Mr. Harte, were believed
to have been the performance of Pope himself by Fenton, who
made him a gay offer of 5*l.* if he would show them in the
hand of Betterton.

The next year (1713) produced a bolder attempt, by which
profit was sought as well as praise. The poems which he had
hitherto written, however they might have diffused his name,
had made very little addition to his fortune. The allowance
which his father made him, though, proportioned to what he
had, it might be liberal, could not be large; his religion
hindered him from the occupation of any civil employment;
and he complained that he wanted even money to buy books.

He therefore resolved [October 1713] to try how far the
favour of the public extended, by soliciting a subscription to
a version of the Iliad, with large notes.

To print by subscription was, for some time, a practice
peculiar to the English. The first considerable work for which
this expedient was employed is said to have been Dryden's
Virgil; and it had been tried again with great success when
The Tatlers were collected into volumes.

There was reason to believe that Pope's attempt would be
successful. He was in the full bloom of reputation, and was
personally known to almost all whom dignity of employment
or splendour of reputation had made eminent; he conversed
indifferently with both parties, and never disturbed the public

with his political opinions; and it might be naturally expected, as each faction then boasted its literary zeal, that the great men, who on other occasions practised all the violence of opposition, would emulate each other in their encouragement of a poet who delighted all, and by whom none had been offended.

With those hopes he offered an English Iliad to subscribers, in six volumes in quarto, for six guineas; a sum, according to the value of money at that time, by no means inconsiderable, and greater than I believe to have been ever asked before. His proposal, however, was very favourably received; and the patrons of literature were busy to recommend his undertaking and promote his interest. Lord Oxford, indeed, lamented that such a genius should be wasted upon a work not original; but proposed no means by which he might live without it. Addison recommended caution and moderation, and advised him not to be content with the praise of half the nation, when he might be universally favoured.

The greatness of the design, the popularity of the author, and the attention of the literary world, naturally raised such expectations of the future sale, that the booksellers made their offers with great eagerness; but the highest bidder was Bernard Lintot, who became proprietor on condition of supplying, at his own expense, all the copies which were to be delivered to subscribers, or presented to friends, and paying 200*l.* for every volume.

Of the quartos it was, I believe, stipulated that none should be printed but for the author, that the subscription might not be depreciated; but Lintot impressed the same pages upon a small folio, and paper perhaps a little thinner; and sold exactly at half the price, for half a guinea each volume, books so little inferior to the quartos, that by a fraud of trade those folios, being afterwards shortened by cutting away the top and bottom, were sold as copies printed for the subscribers.

Lintot printed 250 on royal paper in folio, for two guineas a volume; of the small folio, having printed 1750 copies of the first volume, he reduced the number in the other volumes to 1000.

It is unpleasant to relate that the bookseller, after all his hopes and all his liberality, was, by a very unjust and illegal action, defrauded of his profit. An edition of the English Iliad was printed in Holland in duodecimo, and imported clandestinely for the gratification of those who were impatient to read what they could not yet afford to buy. This fraud could only be counteracted by an edition equally cheap and more

commodious; and Lintot was compelled to contract his folio at
once into a duodecimo, and lose the advantage of an intermediate gradation. The notes, which in the Dutch copies were
placed at the end of each book, as they had been in the large
volumes, were now subjoined to the text in the same page
and are therefore more easily consulted. Of this edition 2500
were first printed, and 5000 a few weeks afterwards; but indeed
great numbers were necessary to produce considerable profit.

Pope, having now emitted his proposals, and engaged not
only his own reputation, but in some degree that of his friends
who patronised his subscription, began to be frightened at his
own undertaking; and finding himself at first embarrassed with
difficulties which retarded and oppressed him, he was for a time
timorous and uneasy; had his nights disturbed by dreams of
long journeys through unknown ways, and wished, as he said,
"that somebody would hang him."

This misery, however, was not of long continuance; he grew
by degrees more acquainted with Homer's images and expressions, and practice increased his facility of versification. In a
short time he represents himself as despatching regularly fifty
verses a day, which would show him by an easy computatior
the termination of his labour.

His own diffidence was not his only vexation. He that asks
a subscription soon finds that he has enemies. All who do not
encourage him defame him. He that wants money will rather
be thought angry than poor; and he that wishes to save his
money conceals his avarice by his malice. Addison had hinted
his suspicion that Pope was too much a Tory; and some of the
Tories suspected his principles because he had contributed to
The Guardian, which was carried on by Steele.

To those who censured his politics were added enemies yet
more dangerous, who called in question his knowledge of Greek
and his qualifications for a translator of Homer. To these he
made no public opposition; but in one of his letters escapes
from them as well as he can. At an age like his (for he was
not more than twenty-five), with an irregular education and a
course of life of which much seems to have passed in conversation, it is not very likely that he overflowed with Greek. But
when he felt himself deficient, he sought assistance; and what
man of learning would refuse to help him? Minute inquiries
into the force of words are less necessary in translating Homer
than other poets, because his positions are general and his
representations natural, with very little dependence on local

or temporary customs, on those changeable scenes of artificial life which, by mingling original with accidental notions, and crowding the mind with images which time effaces, produces ambiguity in diction and obscurity in books. To this open display of unadulterated nature it must be ascribed that Homer has fewer passages of doubtful meaning than any other poet either in the learned or in modern languages. I have read of a man, who being, by his ignorance of Greek, compelled to gratify his curiosity with the Latin printed on the opposite page, declared that from the rude simplicity of the lines literally rendered, he formed nobler ideas of the Homeric majesty than from the laboured elegance of polished versions.

Those literal translations were always at hand, and from them he could easily obtain his author's sense with sufficient certainty; and among the readers of Homer the number is very small of those who find much in the Greek more than in the Latin, except the music of the numbers.

If more help was wanting, he had the poetical translation of Eobanus Hessus, an unwearied writer of Latin verses; he had the French Homers of La Valterie and Dacier, and the English of Chapman, Hobbes, and Ogilby. With Chapman, whose work, though now totally neglected, seems to have been popular almost to the end of the last century, he had very frequent consultations, and perhaps never translated any passage till he had read his version, which indeed he has been sometimes suspected of using instead of the original.

Notes were likewise to be provided; for the six volumes would have been very little more than six pamphlets without them. What the mere perusal of the text could suggest, Pope wanted no assistance to collect or methodise; but more was necessary; many pages were to be filled, and learning must supply materials to wit and judgment. Something might be gathered from Dacier; but no man loves to be indebted to his contemporaries, and Dacier was accessible to common readers. Eustathius was therefore necessarily consulted. To read Eustathius, of whose work there was then no Latin version, I suspect Pope, if he had been willing, not to have been able; some other was therefore to be found who had leisure as well as abilities; and he was doubtless most readily employed who would do much work for little money.

The history of the notes has never been traced. Broome, in his Preface to his Poems, declares himself the commentator "in part upon the Iliad"; and it appears from Fenton's letter, preserved in the Museum, that Broome was at first engaged in consulting Eustathius; but that after a time, whatever was the reason, he desisted; another man of Cambridge was then employed, who soon grew weary of the work; and a third, that was recommended by Thirlby, is now discovered to have been Jortin, a man since well known to the learned world, who complained that Pope, having accepted and approved his performance, never testified any curiosity to see him, and who professed to have forgotten the terms on which he worked. The terms which Fenton uses are very mercantile: "I think at first sight that his performance is commendable enough, and have sent word for him to finish the 17th book, and to send it with his demands for his trouble. . . . I have here enclosed the specimen; if the rest come before you return, I will keep them till I receive your orders."

Broome then offered his service a second time, which was probably accepted, as they had afterwards a closer correspondence. Parnell contributed the Life of Homer, which Pope found so harsh that he took great pains in correcting it; and by his own diligence, with such help as kindness or money could procure him, in somewhat more than five years he completed his version of the Iliad, with the notes. He began it in 1712, his twenty-fifth year; and concluded it in 1718, his thirtieth year.

When we find him translating fifty lines a day, it is natural to suppose that he would have brought his work to a more speedy conclusion. The Iliad, containing less than sixteen thousand verses, might have been despatched in less than three hundred and twenty days by fifty verses in a day. The notes, compiled with the assistance of his mercenaries, could not be supposed to require more time than the text. According to this calculation the progress of Pope may seem to have been slow; but the distance is commonly very great between actual performances and speculative possibility. It is natural to suppose that as much as has been done to-day may be done to-morrow; but on the morrow some difficulty emerges, or some external impediment obstructs. Indolence, interruption, business, and pleasure, all take their turns of retardation; and every long work is lengthened by a thousand causes that can, and ten thousand that cannot, be recounted. Perhaps no extensive and multifarious performance was ever effected within the term originally fixed in the undertaker's mind. He that runs against Time has an antagonist not subject to casualties.

The encouragement given to this translation, though report

seems to have overrated it, was such as the world has not often seen. The subscribers were 575. The copies for which subscriptions were given were 654; and only 660 were printed. For those copies Pope had nothing to pay; he therefore received, including the 200*l.* a volume, 5320*l.* 4*s.* without deduction, as the books were supplied by Lintot.

By the success of his subscription Pope was relieved from those pecuniary distresses with which, notwithstanding his popularity, he had hitherto struggled. Lord Oxford had often lamented his disqualification for public employment, but never proposed a pension. While the translation of Homer was in its progress, Mr. Craggs, then Secretary of State, offered to procure him a pension, which, at least during his ministry, might be enjoyed with secrecy. This was not accepted by Pope, who told him, however, that if he should be pressed with want of money he would send to him for occasional supplies. Craggs was not long in power, and was never solicited for money by Pope, who disdained to beg what he did not want.

With the product of this subscription, which he had too much discretion to squander, he secured his future life from want by considerable annuities. The estate of the Duke of Buckingham was found to have been charged with 500*l.* a year, payable to Pope, which doubtless his translation enabled him to purchase.

It cannot be unwelcome to literary curiosity that I deduce thus minutely the history of the English Iliad. It is certainly the noblest version of poetry which the world has ever seen; and its publication must therefore be considered as one of the great events in the annals of learning.

To those who have skill to estimate the excellence and difficulty of this great work, it must be very desirable to know how it was performed and by what gradations it advanced to correctness. Of such an intellectual process the knowledge has very rarely been attainable; but happily there remains the original copy of the Iliad, which, being obtained by Bolingbroke as a curiosity, descended from him to Mallet, and is now by the solicitation of the late Dr. Maty reposited in the Museum.

Between this manuscript, which is written upon accidental fragments of paper, and the printed edition, there must have been an intermediate copy, that was perhaps destroyed as it returned from the press.

From the first copy I have procured a few transcripts, and shall exhibit first the printed lines; then, in a small print, those

of the manuscripts, with all their variations. Those words in
the small print which are given in italics are cancelled in the
copy and the words placed under them adopted in their stead.
The beginning of the *first book* stands thus:

> The wrath of Peleus' son, the direful spring
> Of all the Grecian woes, O Goddess, sing!
> That wrath which hurl'd to Pluto's gloomy reign
> The souls of mighty chiefs untimely slain.

> The stern Pelides' *rage*, O Goddess, sing,
>   wrath
> Of all the woes *of Greece* the fatal spring,
>   Grecian
> That strew'd with *warriors* dead the Phrygian plain,
>   heroes
> And *peopled the dark hell with heroes* slain;
>   fill'd the shady hell with chiefs untimely

> Whose limbs unburied on the naked shore,
> Devouring dogs and hungry vultures tore,
> Since great Achilles and Atrides strove;
> Such was the sovereign doom, and such the will of Jove.

> Whose limbs, unburied on the hostile shore,
> Devouring dogs and greedy vultures tore,
> Since first *Atrides* and *Achilles* strove;
> Such was the sovereign doom, and such the will of Jove.

> Declare, O Muse, in what ill-fated hour
> Sprung the fierce strife, from what offended Power?
> Latona's son a dire contagion spread,
> And heap'd the camp with mountains of the dead;
> The King of men his reverend priest defied,
> And for the King's offence, the people died.

> Declare, O Goddess, what offended Power
> Enflam'd their *rage*, in that *ill omen'd* hour;
>   anger   fatal, hapless
> Phœbus himself the *dire* debate procur'd,
>   fierce
> T' avenge the wrongs his injur'd priest endur'd;
> For this the God a dire infection spread,
> And heap'd the camp with millions of the dead:
> The King of Men the Sacred Sire defied,
> And for the King's offence the people died.

> For Chryses sought with costly gifts to gain
> His captive daughter from the victor's chain;
> Suppliant the venerable Father stands,
> Apollo's awful ensigns grace his hands;
> By these he begs, and, lowly bending down,
> Extends the sceptre and the laurel crown.

> For Chryses sought by *presents to regain*
>   costly gifts to gain
> His captive daughter from the victor's chain;

Suppliant the venerable Father stands,
Apollo's awful ensigns grac'd his hands.
By these he begs, and lowly bending down
The golden sceptre and the laurel crown,
Presents the sceptre
For these as ensigns of his God he bare,
The God that sends his golden shafts afar ;
Then low on earth, the venerable man,
Suppliant before the brother kings began.

He sued to all, but chief implor'd for grace,
The brother-kings of Atreus' royal race;
Ye kings and warriors, may your vows be crown'd,
And Troy's proud walls lie level with the ground;
May Jove restore you, when your toils are o'er,
Safe to the pleasures of your native shore.

To all he sued, but chief implor'd for grace
The brother kings of Atreus' royal race.
Ye *sons of Atreus*, may your vows be crown'd,
  Kings and warriors
Your labours, by the Gods be all your labours crown'd ;
So may the Gods your arms with conquest bless,
And Troy's proud walls lie level with the ground;
Till   laid
And crown your labours with desir'd success ;
May Jove restore you, when your toils are o'er,
Safe to the pleasures of your native shore.

But, oh! relieve a wretched parent's pain,
And give Chryseis to these arms again;
If mercy fail, yet let my presents move,
And dread avenging Phœbus, son of Jove.

But, oh! relieve a hapless parent's pain,
And give my daughter to these arms again;
Receive my gifts ; if mercy fails, yet let my present move.
And fear *the God that deals his darts around,*
              avenging Phœbus, son of Jove.

The Greeks, in shouts, their joint assent declare
The priest to reverence, and release the fair.
Not so Atrides; he, with kingly pride,
Repuls'd the sacred Sire, and thus replied.

He said, the Greeks their joint assent declare,
The father said, the gen'rous Greeks relent,
T' accept the ransom, and release the fair:
Revere the priest, and speak their joint assent :
Not so *the tyrant*; he, with kingly pride,
              Atrides
Repuls'd the sacred Sire, and thus replied.
    [Not so the tyrant. DRYDEN.]

Of these lines, and of the whole first book, I am told that
there was yet a former copy, more varied, and more deformed
with interlineations.

*F 77¹

The beginning of the *second book* varies very little from the printed page, and is therefore set down without any parallel; the few differences do not require to be elaborately displayed.

Now pleasing sleep had seal'd each mortal eye;
Stretch'd in their tents the Grecian leaders lie;
Th' Immortals slumber'd on their thrones above,
All but the ever-watchful eye of Jove.
To honour Thetis' son he bends his care,
And plunge the Greeks in all the woes of war.
Then bids an empty phantom rise to sight,
And thus *commands* the vision of the night:
            directs
Fly hence, delusive dream, and, light as air,
To Agamemnon's royal tent repair;
Bid him in arms draw forth th' embattled train,
March all his legions to the dusty plain.
Now tell the King 'tis given him to destroy
Declare ev'n now
The lofty *walls* of wide-extended Troy;
      tow'rs
For now no more the Gods with Fate contend;
At Juno's suit the heavenly factions end.
Destruction *hovers* o'er yon devoted wall,
      hangs
And nodding Ilion waits th' impending fall.

Invocation to the Catalogue of Ships.—Book **II.**

Say, Virgins, seated round the throne divine,
All-knowing Goddesses! immortal Nine!
Since earth's wide regions, heaven's unmeasur'd height,
And hell's abyss, hide nothing from your sight,
(We, wretched mortals! lost in doubts below,
But guess by rumour, and but boast we know)
Oh say what heroes, fir'd by thirst of fame,
Or urg'd by wrongs, to Troy's destruction came!
To count them all, demands a thousand tongues,
A throat of brass and adamantine lungs.

Now, Virgin Goddesses, immortal Nine!
That round Olympus' heavenly summit shine,
Who see through heaven and earth, and hell profound,
And all things know, and all things can resound;
Relate what armies sought the Trojan land,
What nations follow'd, and what chiefs command;
(For doubtful Fame distracts mankind below,
And nothing can we tell, and nothing know)
Without your aid, to count th' unnumber'd train,
A thousand mouths, a thousand tongues were vain.

Book V., v. **1**

But Pallas now Tydides' soul inspires,
Fills with her force, and warms with all her fires:

Above the Greeks his deathless fame to raise,
And crown her hero with distinguish'd praise,
High on his helm celestial lightnings play,
His beamy shield emits a living ray;
Th' unwearied blaze incessant streams supplies,
Like the red star that fires th' autumnal skies.

But Pallas now Tydides' soul inspires,
Fills with her *rage*, and warms with all her fires;
   force
O'er all the Greeks decrees his fame to raise,
Above the Greeks *her warrior's* fame to raise,
   his deathless
And crown her hero with *immortal* praise:
   distinguish'd
Bright from his beamy *crest* the lightnings play,
 High on   helm
From his broad buckler flash'd the living ray,
High on his helm celestial lightnings play,
His beamy shield emits a living ray.
The Goddess with her breath the flame supplies,
Bright as the star whose fires in Autumn rise;
Her breath divine thick streaming flames supplies,
Bright as the star that fires th' autumnal skies;
Th' unwearied blaze incessant streams supplies,
Like the red star that fires th' autumnal skies:

When fresh he rears his radiant orb to sight,
And bath'd in ocean shoots a keener light,
Such glories Pallas on the chief bestow'd,
Such from his arms the fierce effulgence flow'd;
Onward she drives him, furious to engage,
Where the fight burns, and where the thickest rage.

When fresh he rears his radiant orb to sight,
And gilds old Ocean with a blaze of light,
Bright as the star that fires th' autumnal skies,
Fresh from the deep, and gilds the seas and skies.
Such glories Pallas on her chief bestow'd,
Such sparkling rays from his bright armour flow'd,
Such from his arms the fierce effulgence flow'd;
Onward she drives him *headlong* to engage,
   furious
Where the *war bleeds*, and where the *fiercest* rage.
 fight burns   thickest

The sons of Dares first the combat sought,
A wealthy priest, but rich without a fault;
In Vulcan's fane the father's days were led.
The sons to toils of glorious battle bred;

There liv'd a Trojan—Dares was his name,
The priest of Vulcan, rich, yet void of blame;
The sons of Dares first the combat sought,
A wealthy priest, but rich without a fault.

Conclusion of Book VIII., v. 687

As when the moon, refulgent lamp of night,
O'er heaven's clear azure spreads her sacred light;
When not a breath disturbs the deep serene,
And not a cloud o'ercasts the solemn scene;
Around her throne the vivid planets roll,
And stars unnumber'd gild the glowing pole:
O'er the dark trees a yellower verdure shed,
And tip with silver every mountain's head:
Then shine the vales—the rocks in prospect rise,
A flood of glory bursts from all the skies;
The conscious swains, rejoicing in the sight,
Eye the blue vault, and bless the useful light.
So many flames before proud Ilion blaze,
And lighten glimmering Xanthus with their rays;
The long reflections of the distant fires
Gleam on the walls, and tremble on the spires:
A thousand piles the dusky horrors gild,
And shoot a shady lustre o'er the field;
Full fifty guards each flaming pile attend,
Whose umber'd arms by fits thick flashes send;
Loud neigh the coursers o'er their heaps of corn,
And ardent warriors wait the rising morn.

    As when in stillness of the silent night,
    As when the moon in all her lustre bright,
    As when the moon, refulgent lamp of night,
    O'er heaven's *clear* azure *sheds* her *silver* light;
            pure   spreads   sacred
    As still in air the trembling lustre stood,
    And o'er its golden border shoots a flood;
    When *no loose gale* disturbs the deep serene,
         not a breath
    And *no dim* cloud o'ercasts the solemn scene;
        not a
    Around her silver throne the planets glow,
    And stars unnumber'd trembling beams bestow;
    Around her throne the vivid planets roll,
    And stars unnumber'd gild the glowing pole:
    Clear gleams of light o'er the dark trees are seen,
              o'er the dark trees a yellow sheds,
    O'er the dark trees a yellower *green* they shed,
                  gleam
                  verdure
    And tip with silver all the *mountain* heads
                    forest
    And tip with silver every mountain's head.
    The valleys open, and the forests rise,
    The vales appear, the rocks in prospect rise,
    Then shine the vales, the rocks in prospect rise,
    All nature stands reveal'd before our eyes;
    A flood of glory bursts from all the skies.
    The conscious shepherd, joyful at the sight,
    Eyes the blue vault, and numbers every light.
    The conscious *swains rejoicing at the sight*
              shepherds gazing with delight

Eye the blue vault, and bless the *vivid* light,
             glorious
             useful
So many flames before *the navy* blaze,
          proud Ilion
And lighten glimmering Xanthus with their rays,
Wide o'er the fields to Troy extend the gleams,
And tip the distant spires with fainter beams;
The long reflexions of the distant fires
Gild the high walls, and tremble on the spires;
Gleam on the walls, and tremble on the spires;
A thousand fires at distant stations bright,
Gild the dark prospect, and dispel the night.

Of these specimens every man who has cultivated poetry, or who delights to trace the mind from the rudeness of its first conceptions to the elegance of its last, will naturally desire a greater number; but most other readers are already tired, and I am not writing only to poets and philosophers.

The Iliad was published volume by volume, as the translation proceeded; the four first books appeared in [June] 1715. The expectation of this work was undoubtedly high, and every man who had connected his name with criticism or poetry was desirous of such intelligence as might enable him to talk upon the popular topic. Halifax, who, by having been first a poet and then a patron of poetry, had acquired the right of being a judge, was willing to hear some books while they were yet unpublished. Of this rehearsal Pope afterwards gave the following account:

"The famous Lord Halifax was rather a pretender to taste than really possessed of it.—When I had finished the two or three first books of my translation of the Iliad, that Lord desired to have the pleasure of hearing them read at his house. Addison, Congreve, and Garth were there at the reading. In four or five places Lord Halifax stopt me very civilly, and with a speech each time much of the same kind, 'I beg your pardon, Mr. Pope, but there is something in that passage that does not quite please me. Be so good as to mark the place, and consider it a little at your leisure. I am sure you can give it a better turn.' I returned from Lord Halifax's with Dr. Garth, in his chariot; and, as we were going along, was saying to the Doctor, that my Lord had laid me under a good deal of difficulty by such loose and general observations; that I had been thinking over the passages almost ever since, and could not guess at what it was that offended his Lordship in either of them. Garth laughed heartily at my embarrassment; said I had not been long enough acquainted with Lord Halifax to know his way yet; that I need not puzzle myself about looking those places over and over when I got home. ' All you need do (said he) is to leave them just as they are; call on Lord Halifax two or three months hence, thank him for his kind observations on those passages, and then read them to him as altered. I have known him much longer than you have, and will be answerable for the event.' I followed his advice; waited on Lord Halifax some time after; said, I hoped he would find his objections to those passages removed; read them to him exactly as they were at first: and his Lordship was extremely pleased with them, and cried out, 'Ay, now, Mr. Pope, they are perfectly right; nothing can be better.'"

It is seldom that the great or the wise suspect that they are despised or cheated. Halifax, thinking this a lucky opportunity of securing immortality, made some advances of favour and some overtures of advantage to Pope, which he seems to have received with sullen coldness. All our knowledge of this transaction is derived from a single letter (Dec. 1, 1714), in which Pope says, "I am obliged to you, both for the favours you have done me, and for those you intend me. I distrust neither your will nor your memory when it is to do good; and if I ever become troublesome or solicitous, it must not be out of expectation, but out of gratitude. Your Lordship may either cause me to live agreeably in the town, or contentedly in the country, which is really all the difference I set between an easy fortune and a small one. It is, indeed, a high strain of generosity in you to think of making me easy all my life, only because I have been so happy as to divert you some few hours: but, if I may have leave to add it is because you think me no enemy to my native Country, there will appear a better reason; for I must of consequence be very much (as I sincerely am) yours," etc.

These voluntary offers, and this faint acceptance, ended without effect. The patron was not accustomed to such frigid gratitude, and the poet fed his own pride with the dignity of independence. They probably were suspicious of each other. Pope would not dedicate till he saw at what rate his praise was valued; he would be "troublesome out of gratitude, not expectation." Halifax thought himself entitled to confidence; and would give nothing, unless he knew what he should receive. Their commerce had its beginning in hope of praise on one side, and of money on the other, and ended because Pope was less eager of money than Halifax of praise. It is not likely that

Halifax had any personal benevolence to Pope; it is evident that Pope looked on Halifax with scorn and hatred.

The reputation of this great work failed of gaining him a patron; but it deprived him of a friend. Addison and he were now [1715] at the head of poetry and criticism; and both in such a state of elevation, that, like the two rivals in the Roman state, one could no longer bear an equal, nor the other a superior. Of the gradual abatement of kindness between friends the beginning is often scarcely discernible by themselves, and the process is continued by petty provocations, and incivilities sometimes peevishly returned, and sometimes contemptuously neglected, which would escape all attention but that of pride, and drop from any memory but that of resentment. That the quarrel of these two wits should be minutely deduced is not to be expected from a writer to whom, as Homer says, "nothing but rumour has reached, and who has no personal knowledge."

Pope doubtless approached Addison, when the reputation of their wit first brought them together, with the respect due to a man whose abilities were acknowledged, and who having attained that eminence to which he was himself aspiring, had in his hands the distribution of literary fame. He paid court [1713] with sufficient diligence by his Prologue to *Cato*, by his abuse of Dennis [1713], and with praise yet more direct by his poem on the *Dialogues on Medals*, of which the immediate publication was then intended. In all this there was no hypocrisy; for he confessed that he found in Addison something more pleasing than in any other man.

It may be supposed that as Pope saw himself favoured by the world, and more frequently compared his own powers with those of others, his confidence increased and his submission lessened; and that Addison felt no delight from the advances of a young wit, who might soon contend with him for the highest place. Every great man, of whatever kind be his greatness, has among his friends those who officiously or insidiously quicken his attention to offences, heighten his disgust, and stimulate his resentment. Of such adherents Addison doubtless had many; and Pope was now too high to be without them.

From the emission and reception of the proposals for the Iliad, the kindness of Addison seems to have abated. Jervas the painter once pleased himself (Aug. 20, 1714) with imagining that he had re-established their friendship; and wrote to Pope that Addison once suspected him of too close a confederacy with Swift, but was now satisfied with his conduct. To this Pope answered, a week after, that his engagements to Swift were such as his services in regard to the subscription demanded, and that the Tories never put him under the necessity of asking leave to be grateful. "But," says he, "as Mr. Addison must be the judge in what regards himself, and has seemed to be no very just one to me, so I must own to you I expect nothing but civility from him." In the same letter he mentions Philips as having been busy to kindle animosity between them; but in a letter to Addison he expresses some consciousness of behaviour inattentively deficient in respect.

Of Swift's industry in promoting the subscription there remains the testimony of Kennet, no friend to either him or Pope:

"Nov. 2, 1713, Dr. Swift came into the coffee-house and had a bow from everybody but me, who, I confess, could not but despise him. When I came to the ante-chamber to wait, before prayers, Dr. Swift was the principal man of talk and business, and acted as master of requests. Then he instructed a young nobleman that the *best Poet in England* was Mr. Pope (a Papist), who had begun a translation of Homer into English verse, for which *he must have them all subscribe*; for, says he, the author *shall not* begin to print till *I have* a thousand guineas for him."

About this time it is likely that Steele, who was, with all his political fury, good-natured and officious, procured an interview between these angry rivals, which ended in aggravated malevolence. On this occasion, if the reports be true, Pope made his complaint with frankness and spirit, as a man undeservedly neglected or opposed; and Addison affected a contemptuous unconcern, and, in a calm, even voice, reproached Pope with his vanity, and telling him of the improvements which his early works had received from his own remarks and those of Steele, said that he, being now engaged in public business, had no longer any care for his poetical reputation; nor had any other desire with regard to Pope than that he should not, by too much arrogance, alienate the public.

To this Pope is said to have replied with great keenness and severity, upbraiding Addison with perpetual dependence, and with the abuse of those qualifications which he had obtained at the public cost, and charging him with mean endeavours to obstruct the progress of rising merit. The contest rose so high, that they parted at last without any interchange of civility.

The first volume of Homer was (1715) in time published;

and a rival version of the first Iliad, for rivals the time of their appearance inevitably made them, was immediately printed, with the name of Tickell. It was soon perceived that, among the followers of Addison, Tickell had the preference, and the critics and poets divided into factions. "I, like the Tories," says Pope, "have the town in general, that is, the mob, on my side; but 'tis usual with the smaller party to make up in industry what they want in numbers. . . . I appeal to the people as my rightful judges, and while they are not inclined to condemn me, I fear no arbitrary, high-flying proceedings from the small court faction at Button's." This opposition he immediately imputed to Addison, and complained of it in terms sufficiently resentful to Craggs, their common friend.

When Addison's opinion was asked, he declared the versions to be both good, but Tickell's the best that had ever been written; and sometimes said that they were both good, but that Tickell had more of Homer.

Pope was now sufficiently irritated; his reputation and his interest were at hazard. He once intended to print together the four versions of Dryden, Maynwaring, Pope, and Tickell, that they might be readily compared and fairly estimated. This design seems to have been defeated by the refusal of Tonson, who was the proprietor of the other three versions.

Pope intended at another time a rigorous criticism of Tickell's translation, and had marked a copy, which I have seen, in all places that appeared defective. But while he was thus meditating defence or revenge, his adversary sunk before him without a blow; the voice of the public was not long divided, and the preference was universally given to Pope's performance.

He was convinced, by adding one circumstance to another, that the other translation was the work of Addison himself; but if he knew it in Addison's lifetime, it does not appear that he told it. He left his illustrious antagonist to be punished by what has been considered as the most painful of all reflections, the remembrance of a crime perpetrated in vain.

The other circumstances of their quarrel were thus related by Pope:

"Philips seemed to have been encouraged to abuse me in coffee-houses and conversations: Gildon wrote a thing about Wycherley, in which he had abused both me and my relations very grossly. Lord Warwick himself told me one day, that it was in vain for me to endeavour to be well with Mr. Addison; that his jealous temper would never admit of a settled friendship between us: and, to convince me of what he had said, assured me that Addison had encouraged Gildon to publish those scandals, and had given him ten guineas after they were published. The next day, while I was heated with what I had heard, I wrote a letter to Mr. Addison, to let him know that I was not unacquainted with this behaviour of his; that if I was to speak severely of him in return for it, it should be not in such a dirty way; that I should rather tell him, himself, fairly of his faults, and allow his good qualities; and that it should be something in the following manner:—I then subjoined the first sketch of what has been since called my Satire on Addison. He used me very civilly ever after, and never did me any injustice that I know of, from that time to his death, which was about three years after."

The verses on Addison, when they were sent to Atterbury, were considered by him as the most excellent of Pope's performances; and the writer was advised, since he knew where his strength lay, not to suffer it to remain unemployed.

This year (1715) being, by the subscription, enabled to live more by choice, having persuaded his father to sell their estate at Binfield, he purchased, I think only for his life, that house at Twickenham to which his residence afterwards procured so much celebration, and removed thither with his father and mother.

Here he planted the vines and the quincunx which his verses mention; and being under the necessity of making a subterraneous passage to a garden on the other side of the road, he adorned it with fossil bodies, and dignified it with the title of a grotto; a place of silence and retreat, from which he endeavoured to persuade his friends and himself that cares and passions could be excluded.

A grotto is not often the wish or pleasure of an Englishman, who has more frequent need to solicit than exclude the sun; but Pope's excavation was requisite as an entrance to his garden, and, as some men try to be proud of their defects, he extracted an ornament from an inconvenience, and vanity produced a grotto where necessity enforced a passage. It may be frequently remarked of the studious and speculative, that they are proud of trifles, and that their amusements seem frivolous and childish; whether it be that men conscious of great reputation think themselves above the reach of censure, and safe in the admission of negligent indulgences, or that mankind expect from elevated genius an uniformity of greatness, and watch its degradation with malicious wonder; like him who, having followed with his eye an eagle into the clouds, should lament that she ever descended to a perch.

While the volumes of his Homer were annually published, he collected his former works (1717) into one quarto volume, to which he prefixed a Preface, written with great sprightliness and elegance, which was afterwards reprinted, with some passages subjoined that he at first omitted; other marginal additions of the same kind he made in the later editions of his poems. Waller remarks, that poets lose half their praise, because the reader knows not what they have blotted. Pope's voracity of fame taught him the art of obtaining the accumulated honour both of what he had published, and of what he had suppressed.

In this year [1717] his father died suddenly, in his seventy-fifth year, having passed twenty-nine years in privacy. He is not known but by the character which his son has given him. If the money with which he retired was all gotten by himself, he had traded very successfully in times when sudden riches were rarely attainable.

The publication of the Iliad was at last completed in 1720. The splendour and success of this work raised Pope many enemies, that endeavoured to depreciate his abilities. Burnet, who was afterwards a judge of no mean reputation, censured him in a piece called *Homerides* before it was published. Ducket likewise endeavoured to make him ridiculous. Dennis was the perpetual persecutor of all his studies. But, whoever his critics were, their writings are lost; and the names which are preserved, are preserved in *The Dunciad*.

In this disastrous year (1720) of national infatuation, when more riches than Peru can boast were expected from the South Sea, when the contagion of avarice tainted every mind, and even poets panted after wealth, Pope was seized with the universal passion, and ventured some of his money. The stock rose in its price; and for a while he thought himself the lord of thousands. But this dream of happiness did not last long; and he seems to have waked soon enough to get clear with the loss of what he once thought himself to have won, and perhaps not wholly of that.

Next year he published some select poems of his friend Dr. Parnell, with a very elegant Dedication to the Earl of Oxford; who, after all his struggles and dangers, then lived in retirement, still under the frown of a victorious faction, who could take no pleasure in hearing his praise.

He gave the same year (1721) an edition of Shakespeare. His name was now of so much authority, that Tonson thought himself entitled, by annexing it, to demand a subscription of six guineas for Shakespeare's Plays in six quarto volumes; nor did his expectation much deceive him; for of 750 which he printed, he dispersed a great number at the price proposed. The reputation of that edition indeed sunk afterwards so low, that 140 copies were sold at 16s. each.

On this undertaking, to which Pope was induced by a reward of 217l. 12s., he seems never to have reflected afterwards without vexation; for Theobald, a man of heavy diligence, with very slender powers, first [1726] in a book called *Shakespeare Restored*, and then [1733] in a formal edition, detected his deficiencies with all the insolence of victory; and as he was now high enough to be feared and hated, Theobald had from others all the help that could be supplied by the desire of humbling a haughty character.

From this time Pope became an enemy to editors, collators, commentators, and verbal critics; and hoped to persuade the world that he miscarried in this undertaking only by having a mind too great for such minute employment.

Pope in his edition undoubtedly did many things wrong, and left many things undone; but let him not be defrauded of his due praise. He was the first that knew, at least the first that told, by what helps the text might be improved. If he inspected the early editions negligently, he taught others to be more accurate. In his Preface he expanded with great skill and elegance the character which had been given of Shakespeare by Dryden; and he drew the public attention upon his works, which, though often mentioned, had been little read.

Soon after the appearance of the Iliad, resolving not to let the general kindness cool, he published proposals for a translation of the Odyssey, in five volumes, for five guineas. He was willing, however, now to have associates in his labour, being either weary with toiling upon another's thoughts, or having heard, as Ruffhead relates, that Fenton and Broome had already begun the work, and liking better to have them confederates than rivals.

In the patent, instead of saying that he had "translated" the Odyssey, as he had said of the Iliad, he says that he had "undertaken" a translation; and in the proposals, the subscription is said to be not solely for his own use, but for that of "two of his friends who have assisted him in this work."

In 1723, while he was engaged in this new version, he appeared before the Lords at the memorable trial of Bishop Atterbury, with whom he had lived in great familiarity, and frequent correspondence. Atterbury had honestly recommended to him the study of the Popish controversy, in hope of his conversion; to which Pope answered in a manner that cannot much recommend his principles or his judgment. In questions and projects of learning they agreed better. He was called at the trial to give an account of Atterbury's domestic life, and private employment, that it might appear how little time he had left for plots. Pope had but few words to utter, and in those few he made several blunders.

His Letters to Atterbury express the utmost esteem, tenderness, and gratitude: "perhaps," says he, "it is not only in this world that I may have cause to remember the Bishop of Rochester." At their last interview in the Tower, Atterbury presented him with a Bible.

Of the Odyssey Pope translated only twelve books; the rest were the work of Broome and Fenton: the notes were written wholly by Broome, who was not over-liberally rewarded. The public was carefully kept ignorant of the several shares; and an account was subjoined at the conclusion, which is now known not to be true.

The first copy of Pope's books, with those of Fenton, are to be seen in the Museum. The parts of Pope are less interlined than the Iliad; and the latter books of the Iliad less than the former. He grew dexterous by practice, and every sheet enabled him to write the next with more facility. The books of Fenton have very few alterations by the hand of Pope. Those of Broome have not been found; but Pope complained, as it is reported, that he had much trouble in correcting them.

His contract with Lintot was the same as for the Iliad, except that only 100*l*. were to be paid him for each volume. The number of subscribers were 574, and of copies 819; so that his profit, when he paid his assistants, was still very considerable. The work was finished in 1725; and from that time he resolved to make no more translations.

The sale did not answer Lintot's expectation; and he then pretended to discover something of fraud in Pope, and commenced or threatened a suit in Chancery.

On the English Odyssey a criticism was published [1727] by Spence, at that time Prelector of Poetry at Oxford; a man whose learning was not very great, and whose mind was not very powerful. His criticism, however, was commonly just; what he thought, he thought rightly; and his remarks were recommended by his coolness and candour. In him Pope had the first experience of a critic without malevolence, who thought it as much his duty to display beauties as expose faults; who censured with respect, and praised with alacrity.

With this criticism Pope was so little offended that he sought the acquaintance of the writer, who lived with him from that time in great familiarity, attended him in his last hours, and compiled memorials of his conversation. The regard of Pope recommended him to the great and powerful; and he obtained very valuable preferments in the Church.

Not long after [Sept. 1726] Pope was returning home from a visit in a friend's coach, which, in passing a bridge, was overturned into the water; the windows were closed, and being unable to force them open, he was in danger of immediate death, when the postilion snatched him out by breaking the glass, of which the fragments cut two of his fingers in such a manner that he lost their use.

Voltaire, who was then in England, sent him a letter of consolation. He had been entertained by Pope at his table, where he talked with so much grossness that Mrs. Pope was driven from the room. Pope discovered by a trick that he was a spy for the Court, and never considered him as a man worthy of confidence.

He soon afterwards (1727) joined with Swift, who was then in England, to publish three volumes of *Miscellanies*, in which amongst other things he inserted the *Memoirs of a Parish Clerk*, in ridicule of Burnet's importance in his own *History*, and a *Debate upon Black and White Horses*, written in all the formalities of a legal process by the assistance, as is said, of Mr. Fortescue, afterwards Master of the Rolls. Before these *Miscellanies* is a Preface signed by Swift and Pope, but apparently written by Pope; in which he makes a ridiculous and romantic complaint of the robberies committed upon authors by the clandestine seizure and sale of their papers. He tells in tragic strains how "the cabinets of the sick and the closets of the dead have been broken open and ransacked"; as if those violences were often committed for papers of uncertain and accidental value, which are rarely provoked by real treasures; as if epigrams and essays were in danger where gold and diamonds are safe. A cat hunted for his musk is, according to Pope's account, but the emblem of a wit winded by booksellers.

His complaint, however, received some attestation; for the same year the letters written by him to Mr. Cromwell, in his youth, were sold by Mrs. Thomas to Curll, who printed them.

In these *Miscellanies* was first published the *Art of Sinking in Poetry*, which, by such a train of consequences as usually passes in literary quarrels, gave in a short time, according to Pope's account, occasion to *The Dunciad*.

In the following year (1728) he began to put Atterbury's advice in practice, and showed his satirical powers by publishing *The Dunciad*, one of his greatest and most elaborate perform-ances, in which he endeavoured to sink into contempt all the writers by whom he had been attacked, and some others whom he thought unable to defend themselves.

At the head of the Dunces he placed poor Theobald, whom he accused of ingratitude, but whose real crime was supposed to be that of having revised Shakespeare more happily than himself. This satire had the effect which he intended, by blasting the characters which it touched. Ralph, who, unnecessarily inter-posing in the quarrel, got a place in a subsequent edition, complained that for a time he was in danger of starving, as the booksellers had no longer any confidence in his capacity.

The prevalence of this poem was gradual and slow: the plan, if not wholly new, was little understood by common readers. Many of the allusions required illustration; the names were often expressed only by the initial and final letters, and, if they had been printed at length, were such as few had known or recollected. The subject itself had nothing generally interesting, for whom did it concern to know that one or another scribbler was a dunce? If therefore it had been possible for those who were attacked to conceal their pain and their resentment, *The Dunciad* might have made its way very slowly in the world.

This, however, was not to be expected: every man is of importance to himself, and, therefore, in his own opinion, to others; and, supposing the world already acquainted with all his pleasures and his pains, is perhaps the first to publish injuries or misfortunes which had never been known unless related by himself, and at which those that hear them will only laugh, for no man sympathises with the sorrows of vanity.

The history of *The Dunciad* is very minutely related by Pope himself, in a Dedication which he wrote to Lord Middlesex in the name of Savage:

"I will relate the war of the 'Dunces' (for so it has been com-monly called), which began in the year 1727, and ended in 1730.

" When Dr. Swift and Mr. Pope thought it proper, for reasons specified in the Preface to their *Miscellanies*, to publish such little pieces of theirs as had casually got abroad, there was added to them the *Treatise of the Bathos*, or the *Art of Sinking in Poetry*. It happened that in one chapter of this piece the several species of bad poets were ranged in classes, to which were prefixed almost all the letters of the alphabet (the greatest part of them at random); but such was the number of poets eminent in that art, that some one or other took every letter to himself: all fell into so violent a fury, that, for half a year or more, the common newspapers (in most of which they had some property, as being hired writers) were filled with the most abusive falsehoods and scurrilities they could possibly devise; a liberty no way to be wondered at in those people, and in those papers, that for many years, during the uncontrolled licence of the press, had aspersed almost all the great characters of the age; and this with impunity, their own persons and names being utterly secret and obscure.

" This gave Mr. Pope the thought that he had now some opportunity of doing good, by detecting and dragging into light these common enemies of mankind; since, to invalidate this universal slander, it sufficed to show what contemptible men were the authors of it. He was not without hopes, that by manifesting the dullness of those who had only malice to recommend them, either the booksellers would not find their account in employing them, or the men themselves, when discovered, want courage to proceed in so unlawful an occupation. This it was that gave birth to *The Dunciad*; and he thought it an happiness, that, by the late flood of slander on himself, he had acquired such a peculiar right over their names as was necessary to this design.

" On the 12th of March, 1728-9, at St. James's, that poem was presented to the King and Queen (who had before been pleased to read it) by the Right Honourable Sir Robert Walpole; and some days after the whole impression was taken and dispersed by several noblemen and persons of the first distinction.

" It is certainly a true observation, that no people are so impatient of censure as those who are the greatest slanderers, which was wonderfully exemplified on this occasion. On the day the book was first vended, a crowd of authors besieged the shop; entreaties, advices, threats of law and battery, nay cries of treason, were all employed to hinder the coming out of *The*

Dunciad; on the other side the booksellers and hawkers made as great efforts to procure it. What could a few poor authors do against so great a majority as the public? There was no stopping a torrent with a finger; so out it came.

"Many ludicrous circumstances attended it. The 'Dunces' (for by this name they were called) held weekly clubs to consult of hostilities against the author: one wrote a letter to a great minister, assuring him Mr. Pope was the greatest enemy the Government had; and another brought his image in clay to execute him in effigy; with which sad sort of satisfaction the gentlemen were a little comforted.

"Some false editions of the book having an owl in their frontispiece, the true one, to distinguish it, fixed in his stead an ass laden with authors. Then another surreptitious one being printed with the same ass, the new edition in octavo returned for distinction to the owl again. Hence arose a great contest of booksellers against booksellers, and advertisements against advertisements; some recommending the edition of the owl, and others the edition of the ass; by which names they came to be distinguished, to the great honour also of the gentlemen of *The Dunciad*."

Pope appears by this narrative to have contemplated his victory over the "Dunces" with great exultation; and such was his delight in the tumult which he had raised, that for a while his natural sensibility was suspended, and he read reproaches and invectives without emotion, considering them only as the necessary effects of that pain which he rejoiced in having given.

It cannot, however, be concealed that, by his own confession, he was the aggressor; for nobody believes that the letters in the *Bathos* were placed at random; and it may be discovered that, when he thinks himself concealed, he indulges the common vanity of common men, and triumphs in those distinctions which he had affected to despise. He is proud that his book was presented to the King and Queen by the Right Honourable Sir Robert Walpole; he is proud that they had read it before; he is proud that the edition was taken off by the nobility and persons of the first distinction.

The edition of which he speaks was, I believe, that which, by telling in the text the names, and in the notes the characters of those whom he had satirised, was made intelligible and diverting. The critics had now declared their approbation of the plan, and the common reader began to like it without fear; those who were strangers to petty literature, and therefore unable to decipher initials and blanks, had now names and persons brought within their view; and delighted in the visible effect of those shafts of malice which they had hitherto contemplated as shot into the air.

Dennis, upon the fresh provocation now given him, renewed the enmity which had for a time been appeased by mutual civilities; and published [1728] remarks, which he had till then suppressed, upon *The Rape of the Lock.* Many more grumbled in secret, or vented their resentment in the newspapers by epigrams or invectives.

Ducket, indeed, being mentioned as loving Burnet with "pious passion," pretended that his moral character was injured, and for some time declared his resolution to take vengeance with a cudgel. But Pope appeased him by changing "pious passion" to "cordial friendship," and by a note, in which he vehemently disclaims the malignity of meaning imputed to the first expression.

Aaron Hill, who was represented as diving for the prize, expostulated with Pope, in a manner so much superior to all mean solicitation, that Pope was reduced to sneak and shuffle, sometimes to deny, and sometimes to apologise; he first endeavours to wound, and then is afraid to own that he meant a blow.

The Dunciad, in the complete edition, is addressed to Dr. Swift: of the notes, part were written by Dr. Arbuthnot, and an apologetical letter was prefixed, signed by Cleland, but supposed to have been written by Pope.

After this general war upon Dullness, he seems to have indulged himself awhile in tranquillity; but his subsequent productions prove that he was not idle. He published (1731) a poem on *Taste*, in which he very particularly and severely criticises the house, the furniture, the gardens, and the entertainments of Timon, a man of great wealth and little taste. By Timon he was universally supposed, and by the Earl of Burlington, to whom the poem is addressed, was privately said, to mean the Duke of Chandos; a man perhaps too much delighted with pomp and show, but of a temper kind and beneficent, and who had consequently the voice of the public in his favour.

A violent outcry was therefore raised against the ingratitude and treachery of Pope, who was said to have been indebted to the patronage of Chandos for a present of a thousand pounds, and who gained the opportunity of insulting him by the kindness of his invitation.

The receipt of a thousand pounds Pope publicly denied; but from the reproach which the attack on a character so amiable brought upon him, he tried all means of escaping. The name of Cleland was again employed in an apology, by which no man was satisfied; and he was at last reduced to shelter his temerity behind dissimulation, and endeavour to make that disbelieved which he never had confidence openly to deny. He wrote an exculpatory letter to the Duke, which was answered with great magnanimity, as by a man who accepted his excuse without believing his professions. He said, that to have ridiculed his taste, or his buildings, had been an indifferent action in another man; but that in Pope, after the reciprocal kindness that had been exchanged between them, it had been less easily excused.

Pope, in one of his letters, complaining of the treatment which his poem had found, "owns that such critics can intimidate him, nay, almost persuade him to write no more, which is a compliment this age deserves." The man who threatens the world is always ridiculous; for the world can easily go on without him, and in a short time will cease to miss him. I have heard of an idiot who used to revenge his vexations by lying all night upon the bridge. "There is nothing," says Juvenal, "that a man will not believe in his own favour." Pope had been flattered till he thought himself one of the moving powers in the system of life. When he talked of laying down his pen, those who sat round him intreated and implored; and self-love did not suffer him to suspect that they went away and laughed.

The following year [4th Dec., 1732] deprived him of Gay, a man whom he had known early, and whom he seemed to love with more tenderness than any other of his literary friends. Pope was now forty-four years old; an age at which the mind begins less easily to admit new confidence, and the will to grow less flexible, and when, therefore, the departure of an old friend is very acutely felt.

In the next year [7th June, 1733] he lost his mother, not by an unexpected death, for she had lasted to the age of ninety-three; but she did not die unlamented. The filial piety of Pope was in the highest degree amiable and exemplary; his parents had the happiness of living till he was at the summit of poetical reputation, till he was at ease in his fortune, and without a rival in his fame, and found no diminution of his respect or tenderness. Whatever was his pride, to them he was obedient; and whatever was his irritability, to them he was gentle. Life has, among its soothing and quiet comforts, few things better to give than such a son.

One of the passages of Pope's life which seems to deserve some inquiry was a publication of Letters between him and many of his friends, which falling into the hands of Curll, a rapacious bookseller of no good fame, were by him [May 1735] printed and sold. This volume containing some letters from noblemen, Pope incited a prosecution against him in the House of Lords for breach of privilege, and attended himself to stimulate the resentment of his friends. Curll appeared at the bar, and, knowing himself in no great danger, spoke of Pope with very little reverence. "He has," said Curll, "a knack at versifying, but in prose I think myself a match for him." When the orders of the House were examined, none of them appeared to have been infringed; Curll went away triumphant; and Pope was left to seek some other remedy.

Curll's account was, that one evening a man in a clergyman's gown, but with a lawyer's band, brought and offered for sale a number of printed volumes, which he found to be Pope's epistolary correspondence; that he asked no name, and was told none, but gave the price demanded, and thought himself authorised to use his purchase to his own advantage.

That Curll gave a true account of the transaction, it is reasonable to believe, because no falsehood was ever detected; and when some years afterwards I mentioned it to Lintot, the son of Bernard, he declared his opinion to be, that Pope knew better than anybody else how Curll obtained the copies, because another parcel was at the same time sent to himself, for which no price had ever been demanded, and he made known his resolution not to pay a porter, and consequently not to deal with a nameless agent.

Such care had been taken to make them public, that they were sent at once to two booksellers: to Curll, who was likely to seize them as prey; and to Lintot, who might be expected to give Pope information of the seeming injury. Lintot, I believe, did nothing, and Curll did what was expected. That to make them public was the only purpose may be reasonably supposed, because the numbers offered to sale by the private messengers showed that hope of gain could not have been the motive of the impression.

It seems that Pope, being desirous of printing his letters, and not knowing how to do, without imputation of vanity, what has in this country been done very rarely, contrived an appearance of compulsion; that when he could complain that his letters were surreptitiously published, he might decently and defensively publish them himself.

Pope's private correspondence, thus promulgated, filled the nation with praises of his candour, tenderness, and benevolence, the purity of his purposes, and the fidelity of his friendship. There were some letters which a very good or a very wise man would wish suppressed, but, as they had been already exposed, it was impracticable now to retract them.

From the perusal of those Letters, Mr. Allen first conceived the desire of knowing him; and with so much zeal did he cultivate the friendship which he had newly formed, that when Pope told his purpose of vindicating his own property by a genuine edition, he offered to pay the cost.

This, however, Pope did not accept; but in time solicited a subscription for a quarto volume, which appeared (1737), I believe, with sufficient profit. In the Preface he tells that his Letters were reposited in a friend's library, said to be the Earl of Oxford's, and that the copy thence stolen was sent to the press. The story was doubtless received with different degrees of credit. It may be suspected that the Preface to the *Miscellanies* was written to prepare the public for such an incident; and, to strengthen this opinion, James Worsdale, a painter, who was employed in clandestine negotiations, but whose veracity was very doubtful, declared that he was the messenger who carried, by Pope's direction, the books to Curll.

When they were thus published and avowed, as they had relation to recent facts and persons either then living or not yet forgotten, they may be supposed to have found readers; but, as the facts were minute, and the characters, being either private or literary, were little known or little regarded, they awaked no popular kindness or resentment; the book never became much the subject of conversation; some read it as a contemporary history, and some perhaps as a model of epistolary language; but those who read it did not talk of it. Not much therefore was added by it to fame or envy; nor do I remember that it produced either public praise or public censure.

It had, however, in some degree the recommendation of novelty. Our language has few Letters, except those of statesmen. Howel, indeed, about a century ago, published his Letters, which are commended by Morhoff, and which alone of his hundred volumes continue his memory. Loveday's Letters were printed only once; those of Herbert and Suckling are hardly known. Mrs. Phillips's [Orinda's] are equally neglected; and those of Walsh seem written as exercises, and were never sent to any living mistress or friend. Pope's epistolary excellence had an open field; he had no English rival, living or dead.

Pope is seen in this collection as connected with the other contemporary wits, and certainly suffers no disgrace in the comparison: but it must be remembered that he had the power of favouring himself; he might have originally had publication in his mind, and have written with care, or have afterwards selected those which he had most happily conceived, or most diligently laboured: and I know not whether there does not appear something more studied and artificial in his productions than the rest, except one long letter by Bolingbroke, composed with all the skill and industry of a professed author. It is indeed not easy to distinguish affectation from habit; he that has once studiously formed a style, rarely writes afterwards with complete ease. Pope may be said to write always with his reputation in his head; Swift perhaps like a man who remembered that he was writing to Pope; but Arbuthnot like one who lets thoughts drop from his pen as they rise into his mind.

Before these Letters appeared, he published the first part of what he persuaded himself to think a system of ethics, under the title of an *Essay on Man*; which, if his Letter to Swift (of Sept. 14, 1725) be rightly explained by the commentator, had been eight years under his consideration, and of which he seems to have desired the success with great solicitude. He had now many open and doubtless many secret enemies. The " Dunces " were yet smarting with the war; and the superiority which he publicly arrogated disposed the world to wish his humiliation.

All this he knew, and against all this he provided. His own name, and that of his friend to whom the work is inscribed [Lord Bolingbroke], were in the first editions carefully suppressed; and the poem, being of a new kind, was ascribed to one or another, as favour determined or conjecture wandered: it was given, says Warburton, to every man except him only who could write it. Those who like only when they like the author, and who are under the dominion of a name, condemned it; and those admired it who are willing to scatter praise at random, which while it is unappropriated excites no envy. Those friends of Pope that were trusted with the secret went about lavishing honours on the new-born poet, and hinting that Pope was never so much in danger from any former rival.

To those authors whom he had personally offended, and to

those whose opinion the world considered as decisive, and whom he suspected of envy or malevolence, he sent his *Essay* as a present before publication, that they might defeat their own enmity by praises which they could not afterwards decently retract.

With these precautions, in 1732 was published the first part of the *Essay on Man*. There had been for some time a report that Pope was busy upon a System of Morality; but this design was not discovered in the new poem, which had a form and a title with which its readers were unacquainted. Its reception was not uniform: some thought it a very imperfect piece, though not without good lines. While the author was unknown, some, as will always happen, favoured him as an adventurer, and some censured him as an intruder; but all thought him above neglect; the sale increased, and editions were multiplied.

The subsequent editions of the first Epistle exhibited two memorable corrections. At first, the poet and his friend

> Expatiate freely o'er this scene of man,
> A mighty maze *of walks without a plan.*

For which he wrote afterwards:

> A mighty maze, *but not without a plan:*

for, if there was no plan, it was in vain to describe or to trace the maze.

The other alteration was of these lines:

> And spite of pride, *and in thy reason's spite,*
> One truth is clear, whatever is, is right:

but having afterwards discovered, or been shown, that the "truth" which subsisted "in spite of reason" could not be very "clear," he substituted:

> And spite of pride, *in erring reason's spite.*

To such oversights will the most vigorous mind be liable when it is employed at once upon argument and poetry.

The second and third Epistles were published; and Pope was, I believe, more and more suspected of writing them: at last, in 1734, he avowed the fourth, and claimed the honour of a moral poet.

In the conclusion it is sufficiently acknowledged that the doctrine of the *Essay on Man* was received from Bolingbroke, who is said to have ridiculed Pope, among those who enjoyed his confidence, as having adopted and advanced principles of which he did not perceive the consequence, and as blindly propagating opinions contrary to his own. That those communications had been consolidated into a scheme regularly drawn, and delivered to Pope, from whom it returned only transformed from prose to verse, has been reported, but hardly can be true. The *Essay* plainly appears the fabric of a poet: what Bolingbroke supplied could be only the first principles; the order, illustration, and embellishments must all be Pope's.

These principles it is not my business to clear from obscurity, dogmatism, or falsehood; but they were not immediately examined; philosophy and poetry have not often the same readers; and the *Essay* abounded in splendid amplifications and sparkling sentences, which were read and admired with no great attention to their ultimate purpose; its flowers caught the eye which did not see what the gay foliage concealed, and for a time flourished in the sunshine of universal approbation. So little was any evil tendency discovered, that, as innocence is unsuspicious, many read it for a manual of piety.

Its reputation soon invited a translator. It was first turned into French prose, and afterwards by Resnel into verse. Both translations fell into the hands of Crousaz, who first, when he had the version in prose, wrote a general censure, and afterwards reprinted Resnel's version, with particular remarks upon every paragraph.

Crousaz was a professor of Switzerland, eminent for his treatise of Logic, and his *Examen de Pyrrhonisme*, and, however little known or regarded here, was no mean antagonist. His mind was one of those in which philosophy and piety are happily united. He was accustomed to argument and disquisition, and perhaps was grown too desirous of detecting faults; but his intentions were always right, his opinions were solid, and his religion pure.

His incessant vigilance for the promotion of piety disposed him to look with distrust upon all metaphysical systems of theology, and all schemes of virtue and happiness purely rational; and therefore it was not long before he was persuaded that the positions of Pope, as they terminated for the most part in natural religion, were intended to draw mankind away from revelation, and to represent the whole course of things as a necessary concatenation of indissoluble fatality: and it is undeniable that, in many passages, a religious eye may easily discover expressions not very favourable to morals or to liberty.

About this time Warburton began to make his appearance in

the first ranks of learning. He was a man of vigorous faculties, a mind fervid and vehement, supplied by incessant and unlimited inquiry, with wonderful extent and variety of knowledge, which yet had not oppressed his imagination nor clouded his perspicacity. To every work he brought a memory full fraught, together with a fancy fertile of original combinations, and at once exerted the powers of the scholar, the reasoner, and the wit. But his knowledge was too multifarious to be always exact, and his pursuits too eager to be always cautious. His abilities gave him a haughty confidence, which he disdained to conceal or mollify; and his impatience of opposition disposed him to treat his adversaries with such contemptuous superiority as made his readers commonly his enemies, and excited against the advocate the wishes of some who favoured the cause. He seems to have adopted the Roman emperor's determination, *oderint dum metuant*; he used no allurements of gentle language, but wished to compel rather than persuade.

His style is copious without selection, and forcible without neatness; he took the words that presented themselves; his diction is coarse and impure, and his sentences are unmeasured.

He had in the early part of his life pleased himself with the notice of inferior wits, and corresponded with the enemies of Pope. A letter was produced, when he had perhaps himself forgotten it, in which he tells Concanen, "Dryden, I observe, borrows for want of leisure, and Pope for want of genius; Milton out of pride, and Addison out of modesty." And when [1733] Theobald published Shakespeare, in opposition to Pope, the best notes were supplied by Warburton.

But the time was now come when Warburton was to change his opinion; and Pope was to find a defender in him who had contributed so much to the exaltation of his rival.

The arrogance of Warburton excited against him every artifice of offence, and therefore it may be supposed that his union with Pope was censured as hypocritical inconstancy; but surely to think differently at different times of poetical merit may be easily allowed. Such opinions are often admitted, and dismissed, without nice examination. Who is there that has not found reason for changing his mind about questions of greater importance?

Warburton, whatever was his motive, undertook, without solicitation, to rescue Pope from the talons of Crousaz, by freeing him from the imputation of favouring fatality, or rejecting revelation; and from month to month continued a vindication of the *Essay on Man* in the literary journal of that time called *The Republic of Letters*.

Pope, who probably began to doubt the tendency of his own work, was glad that the positions, of which he perceived himself not to know the full meaning, could by any mode of interpretation be made to mean well. How much he was pleased with his gratuitous defender the following letter evidently shows:

April 11, 1739.

SIR,—I have just received from Mr. R. two more of your letters. It is in the greatest hurry imaginable that I write this; but I cannot help thanking you in particular for your third letter, which is so extremely clear, short, and full, that I think Mr. Crousaz ought never to have another answerer, and deserved not so good an one. I can only say, you do him too much honour, and me too much right, so odd as the expression seems; for you have made my system as clear as I ought to have done, and could not. It is indeed the same system as mine, but illustrated with a ray of your own, as they say our natural body is the same still when it is glorified. I am sure I like it better than I did before, and so will every man else. I know I meant just what you explain; but I did not explain my own meaning so well as you. You understand me as well as I do myself; but you express me better than I could express myself. Pray accept the sincerest acknowledgments. I cannot but wish these letters were put together in one book, and intend (with your leave) to procure a translation of part, at least, or of all of them into French; but I shall not proceed a step without your consent and opinion, &c.

By this fond and eager acceptance of an exculpatory comment, Pope testified that, whatever might be the seeming or real import of the principles which he had received from Bolingbroke, he had not intentionally attacked religion; and Bolingbroke, if he meant to make him, without his own consent, an instrument of mischief, found him now engaged, with his eyes open, on the side of truth.

It is known that Bolingbroke concealed from Pope his real opinions. He once discovered them to Mr. Hooke, who related them again to Pope, and was told by him that he must have mistaken the meaning of what he heard; and Bolingbroke, when Pope's uneasiness incited him to desire an explanation, declared that Hooke had misunderstood him.

Bolingbroke hated Warburton, who had drawn his pupil from him; and a little before Pope's death they had a dispute, from which they parted with mutual aversion.

From this time Pope lived in the closest intimacy with his commentator, and amply rewarded his kindness and his zeal; for he introduced him to Mr. Murray, by whose interest he became preacher at Lincoln's Inn, and to Mr. Allen, who gave him his niece and his estate, and by consequence a bishopric. When he died, he left him the property of his works, a legacy which may be reasonably estimated at 4000*l.*

Pope's fondness for the *Essay on Man* appeared by his desire of its propagation. Dobson, who had gained reputation by his version of Prior's *Solomon*, was employed by him to translate it into Latin verse, and was for that purpose some time at Twickenham; but he left his work, whatever was the reason, unfinished, and, by Benson's invitation, undertook the longer task of *Paradise Lost.* Pope then desired his friend to find a scholar who should turn his *Essay* into Latin prose, but no such performance has ever appeared.

Pope lived at this time *among the great*, with that reception and respect to which his works entitled him, and which he had not impaired by any private misconduct or factitious partiality. Though Bolingbroke was his friend, Walpole was not his enemy, but treated him with so much consideration as, at his request, to solicit and obtain [1728] from the French Minister an abbey for Mr. Southcott, whom he considered himself as obliged to reward, by this exertion of his interest, for the benefit which he had received from his attendance in a long illness.

It was said that, when the Court was at Richmond, Queen Caroline had declared her intention to visit him. This may have been only a careless effusion, thought on no more: the report of such notice, however, was soon in many mouths, and if I do not forget or misapprehend Savage's account, Pope, pretending to decline what was not yet offered, left his house for a time, not, I suppose, for any other reason than lest he should be thought to stay at home in expectation of an honour which would not be conferred. He was therefore angry at Swift, who represents him as "refusing the visits of a Queen," because he knew that what had never been offered had never been refused.

Beside the general system of morality, supposed to be contained in the *Essay on Man*, it was his intention to write distinct poems upon the different duties or conditions of life; one of which is the Epistle to Lord Bathurst (1732) on the *Use of Riches*, a piece on which he declared great labour to have been bestowed.

Into this poem some hints are historically thrown, and some known characters are introduced, with others of which it is difficult to say how far they are real or fictitious: but the praise of Kyrle, the Man of Ross, deserves particular examination, who, after a long and pompous enumeration of his public works and private charities, is said to have diffused all those blessings from *five hundred a year*. Wonders are willingly told, and willingly heard. The truth is, that Kyrle was a man of known integrity and active benevolence, by whose solicitation the wealthy were persuaded to pay contributions to his charitable schemes; this influence he obtained by an example of liberality exerted to the utmost extent of his power, and was thus enabled to give more than he had. This account Mr. Victor received from the minister of the place, and I have preserved it, that the praise of a good man, being made more credible, may be more solid. Narrations of romantic and impracticable virtue will be read with wonder, but that which is unattainable is recommended in vain: that good may be endeavoured, it must be shown to be possible.

This is the only piece in which the author has given a hint of his religion by ridiculing the ceremony of burning the Pope, and by mentioning with some indignation the inscription on the Monument.

When this poem was first published, the dialogue, having no letters of direction, was perplexed and obscure. Pope seems to have written with no very distinct idea, for he calls that an *Epistle to Bathurst,* in which Bathurst is introduced as speaking.

He afterwards (1733) inscribed to Lord Cobham his *Characters of Men,* written with close attention to the operations of the mind and modifications of life. In this poem he has endeavoured to establish and exemplify his favourite theory of the *ruling passion,* by which he means an original direction of desire to some particular object, an innate affection which gives all action a determinate and invariable tendency, and operates upon the whole system of life, either openly, or more secretly by the intervention of some accidental or subordinate propension.

Of any passion, thus innate and irresistible, the existence may reasonably be doubted. Human characters are by no means constant; men change by change of place, of fortune, of acquaintance; he who is at one time a lover of pleasure, is at another a lover of money. Those indeed who attain any excellence commonly spend life in one pursuit; for excellence is not often gained upon easier terms. But to the particular species of excellence men are directed, not by an ascendant planet or predominating humour, but by the first book which they read, some early conversation which they heard, or some accident which excited ardour and emulation.

It must be at least allowed that this *ruling passion*, antecedent to reason and observation, must have an object independent of human contrivance, for there can be no natural desire of artificial good. No man therefore can be born, in the strict acceptation, a lover of money, for he may be born where money does not exist: nor can he be born, in a moral sense, a lover of his country; for society, politically regulated, is a state contradistinguished from a state of nature, and any attention to that coalition of interests which makes the happiness of a country, is possible only to those whom inquiry and reflection have enabled to comprehend it.

This doctrine is in itself pernicious as well as false: its tendency is to produce the belief of a kind of moral predestination, or overruling principle which cannot be resisted; he that admits it, is prepared to comply with every desire that caprice or opportunity shall excite, and to flatter himself that he submits only to the lawful dominion of Nature, in obeying the resistless authority of his *ruling passion*.

Pope has formed his theory with so little skill, that, in the examples by which he illustrates and confirms it, he has confounded passions, appetites, and habits.

To the *Characters of Men* he added soon after [1735], in an Epistle supposed to have been addressed to Martha Blount, but which the last edition has taken from her, the *Characters of Women*. This poem, which was laboured with great diligence, and in the author's opinion with great success, was neglected at its first publication, as the commentator supposes, because the public was informed, by an advertisement, that it contained *no character drawn from the life*: an assertion which Pope probably did not expect or wish to have been believed, and which he soon gave his readers sufficient reason to distrust by telling them in a note that the work was imperfect, because part of his subject was *vice too high* to be yet exposed.

The time, however, soon came in which it was safe to display the Duchess of Marlborough under the name of *Atossa*; and her character was inserted with no great honour to the writer's gratitude.

He published from time to time (between 1733 and 1738) imitations of different poems of Horace, generally with his name, and once, as was suspected, without it. What he was upon moral principles ashamed to own, he ought to have suppressed. Of these pieces it is useless to settle the dates, as they had seldom much relation to the times, and perhaps had been long in his hands.

This mode of imitation, in which the ancients are familiar-ised, by adapting their sentiments to modern topics, by making Horace say of Shakespeare what he originally said of Ennius, and accommodating his satires on Pantolabus and Nomentanus to the flatterers and prodigals of our own time, was first practised in the reign of Charles the Second by Oldham and Rochester; at least I remember no instances more ancient. It is a kind of middle composition between translation and original design, which pleases when the thoughts are unexpectedly appli-cable, and the parallels lucky. It seems to have been Pope's favourite amusement, for he has carried it farther than any former poet.

He published likewise a revival, in smoother numbers, of Dr. Donne's *Satires*, which was recommended to him by the Duke of Shrewsbury and the Earl of Oxford. They made no great impression on the public. Pope seems to have known their imbecility, and therefore suppressed them while he was yet contending to rise in reputation, but ventured them when he thought their deficiencies more likely to be imputed to Donne than to himself.

The *Epistle to Dr. Arbuthnot*, which seems to be derived in its first design from Boileau's Address *à son Esprit*, was published in January 1734-5, about a month before the death of him to whom it is inscribed. It is to be regretted that either honour or pleasure should have been missed by Arbuthnot,— a man estimable for his learning, amiable for his life, and venerable for his piety.

Arbuthnot was a man of great comprehension, skilful in his profession, versed in the sciences, acquainted with ancient literature, and able to animate his mass of knowledge by a bright and active imagination; a scholar with great brilliance of wit; a wit who, in the crowd of life, retained and discovered a noble ardour of religious zeal.

In this poem Pope seems to reckon with the public. He vindicates himself from censures, and with dignity, rather than arrogance, enforces his own claims to kindness and respect.

Into this poem are interwoven several paragraphs which had been before printed as a fragment, and among them the satirical lines upon Addison, of which the last couplet has been twice corrected. It was at first:

> Who would not smile if such a man there be?
> Who would not laugh if Addison were he?

Then:

> Who would not grieve if such a man there be?
> Who would not laugh if Addison were he?

At last it is:

> Who but must laugh if such a man there be?
> Who would not weep if Atticus were he?

He was at this time at open war with Lord Hervey, who had distinguished himself as a steady adherent to the Ministry, and being offended with a contemptuous answer to one of his pamphlets, had summoned Pulteney to a duel. Whether he or Pope made the first attack perhaps cannot now be easily known; he had written an invective against Pope, whom he calls, "Hard as thy heart, and as thy birth obscure," and hints that his father was a *hatter*. To this Pope wrote a reply in verse and prose; the verses are in this poem, and the prose, though it was never sent, is printed among his Letters, but to a cool reader of the present time exhibits nothing but tedious malignity.

His last Satires, of the general kind, were two Dialogues, named, from the year in which they were published, *Seventeen Hundred and Thirty-eight*. In these poems many are praised and many are reproached. Pope was then entangled in the Opposition; a follower of the Prince of Wales, who dined at his house, and the friend of many who obstructed and censured the conduct of the Ministers. His political partiality was too plainly shown; he forgot the prudence with which he passed, in his earlier years, uninjured and unoffending, through much more violent conflicts of faction.

In the first Dialogue, having an opportunity of praising Allen of Bath, he asked his leave to mention him as a man not illustrious by any merit of his ancestors, and called him in his verses "low-born Allen." Men are seldom satisfied with praise introduced or followed by any mention of defect. Allen seems not to have taken any pleasure in his epithet, which was afterwards softened into "humble Allen."

In the second Dialogue he took some liberty with one of the Foxes, among others; which Fox, in a reply to Lyttelton, took an opportunity of repaying, by reproaching him with the friendship of a lampooner, who scattered his ink without fear or decency, and against whom he hoped the resentment of the Legislature would quickly be discharged.

About this time [1739] Paul Whitehead, a small poet, was

summoned before the Lords for a poem called *Manners*, together
with Dodsley, his publisher. Whitehead, who hung loose upon
society, sculked and escaped; but Dodsley's shop and family
made his appearance necessary. He was, however, soon dismissed; and the whole process was probably intended rather
to intimidate Pope than to punish Whitehead.

Pope never afterwards attempted to join the patriot with
the poet, nor drew his pen upon statesmen. That he desisted
from his attempts of reformation is imputed by his commentator
to his despair of prevailing over the corruption of the time.
He was not likely to have been ever of opinion that the dread
of his satire would countervail the love of power or of money;
he pleased himself with being important and formidable, and
gratified sometimes his pride, and sometimes his resentment;
till at last he began to think he should be more safe if he were
less busy.

The *Memoirs of Scriblerus*, published about this time, extend
only to the first book of a work projected in concert by Pope,
Swift, and Arbuthnot, who used to meet in the time of Queen
Anne, and denominated themselves the "Scriblerus Club."
Their purpose was to censure the abuses of learning by a fictitious
Life of an infatuated Scholar. They were dispersed; the design
was never completed; and Warburton laments its miscarriage
as an event very disastrous to polite letters.

If the whole may be estimated by this specimen, which seems
to be the production of Arbuthnot, with a few touches perhaps
by Pope, the want of more will not be much lamented; for the
follies which the writer ridicules are so little practised, that
they are not known: nor can the satire be understood but by
the learned; he raises phantoms of absurdity, and then drives
them away. He cures diseases that were never felt.

For this reason this joint production of three great writers
has never obtained any notice from mankind; it has been little
read, or when read has been forgotten, as no man could be
wiser, better, or merrier by remembering it.

The design cannot boast of much originality; for besides its
general resemblance to Don Quixote, there will be found in it
particular imitations of the History of Mr. Ouffle.

Swift carried so much of it into Ireland as supplied him with
hints for his travels; and with those the world might have been
contented, though the rest had been suppressed.

Pope had sought for images and sentiments in a region not
known to have been explored by many other of the English

writers; he had consulted the modern writers of Latin poetry, a class of authors whom Boileau endeavoured to bring into contempt, and who are too generally neglected. Pope, however, was not ashamed of their acquaintance, nor ungrateful for the advantages which he might have derived from it. A small selection from the Italians who wrote in Latin had been published at London, about the latter end of the last century, by a man who concealed his name, but whom his Preface shows to have been well qualified for his undertaking. This collection Pope amplified by more than half, and (1740) published it in two volumes, but injuriously omitted his predecessor's Preface. To these books, which had nothing but the mere text, no regard was paid, the authors were still neglected, and the editor was neither praised nor censured.

He did not sink into idleness; he had planned a work, which he considered as subsequent to his *Essay on Man*, of which he has given this account to Dr. Swift:

March 25, 1736.

If ever I write more Epistles in verse, one of them shall be addressed to you. I have long concerted it, and begun it; but I would make what bears your name as finished as my last work ought to be, that is to say, more finished than any of the rest. The subject is large, and will divide into four Epistles, which naturally follow the *Essay on Man*, viz.—1. Of the Extent and Limits of Human Reason and Science. 2. A View of the Useful and therefore Attainable, and of the Unuseful and therefore Unattainable Arts. 3. Of the Nature, Ends, Application, and Use of different Capacities. 4. Of the Use of Learning, of the Science, of the World, and of Wit. It will conclude with a Satire against the misapplication of all these, exemplified by Pictures, Characters, and Examples.

This work, in its full extent, being now afflicted with an asthma, and finding the powers of life gradually declining, he had no longer courage to undertake; but, from the materials which he had provided, he added, at Warburton's request, another book to *The Dunciad*, of which the design is to ridicule such studies as are either hopeless or useless, as either pursue what is unattainable, or what, if it be attained, is of no use.

When this book was printed (March 1742) the laurel had been for some time upon the head of Cibber; a man whom it cannot be supposed that Pope could regard with much kindness or esteem, though in one of the *Imitations of Horace* he has liberally enough praised "The Careless Husband." In *The Dunciad*, among other worthless scribblers, he had mentioned Cibber; who, in his *Apology*, complains of the great poet's unkindness as more injurious, "because," says he, "I never have offended him."

It might have been expected that Pope should have been, in some degree, mollified by this submissive gentleness, but no such consequence appeared. Though he condescended to commend Cibber once, he mentioned him afterwards contemptuously in one of his satires, and again in his *Epistle to Arbuthnot*; and in the fourth book of *The Dunciad* attacked him with acrimony, to which the provocation is not easily discoverable. Perhaps he imagined that, in ridiculing the laureat, he satirised those by whom the laurel had been given, and gratified that ambitious petulance with which he affected to insult the great.

The severity of this satire left Cibber no longer any patience. He had confidence enough in his own powers to believe that he could disturb the quiet of his adversary, and doubtless did not want instigators, who, without any care about the victory, desired to amuse themselves by looking on the contest. He therefore gave the town a pamphlet, in which he declares his resolution from that time never to bear another blow without returning it, and to tire out his adversary by perseverance, if he cannot conquer him by strength.

The incessant and unappeasable malignity of Pope he imputes to a very distant cause. After the *Three Hours after Marriage* had been driven off the stage by the offence which the mummy and crocodile gave the audience, while the exploded scene was yet fresh in memory, it happened that Cibber played Bayes in *The Rehearsal*; and, as it had been usual to enliven the part by the mention of any recent theatrical transactions, he said that he once thought to have introduced his lovers disguised in a mummy and a crocodile. "This," says he, "was received with loud claps, which indicated contempt of the play." Pope, who was behind the scenes, meeting him as he left the stage, attacked him, as he says, with all the virulence of a "wit out of his senses"; to which he replied, "that he would take no other notice of what was said by so particular a man, than to declare, that, as often as he played that part, he would repeat the same provocation."

He shows his opinion to be, that Pope was one of the authors of the play which he so zealously defended; and adds an idle story of Pope's behaviour at a tavern.

The pamphlet was written with little power of thought or language, and, if suffered to remain without notice, would have been very soon forgotten. Pope had now been enough acquainted with human life to know, if his passion had not been too powerful for his understanding, that, from a contention like his with Cibber, the world seeks nothing but diversion, which is given at the expense of the higher character. When Cibber lampooned Pope, curiosity was excited; what Pope would say of Cibber nobody inquired, but in hope that Pope's asperity might betray his pain and lessen his dignity.

He should therefore have suffered the pamphlet to flutter and die, without confessing that it stung him. The dishonour of being shown as Cibber's antagonist could never be compensated by the victory. Cibber had nothing to lose: when Pope had exhausted all his malignity upon him, he would rise in the esteem both of his friends and his enemies. Silence only could have made him despicable; the blow which did not appear to be felt would have been struck in vain.

But Pope's irascibility prevailed, and he resolved to tell the whole English world that he was at war with Cibber; and to show that he thought him no common adversary, he prepared no common vengeance; he published [October 1743] a new edition of The Dunciad, in which he degraded Theobald from his painful pre-eminence, and enthroned Cibber in his stead. Unhappily the two heroes were of opposite characters, and Pope was unwilling to lose what he had already written; he has therefore depraved his poem by giving to Cibber the old books, the cold pedantry, and sluggish pertinacity of Theobald.

Pope was ignorant enough of his own interest to make another change, and introduced Osborne contending for the prize among the booksellers. Osborne was a man entirely destitute of shame, without sense of any disgrace but that of poverty. He told me, when he was doing that which raised Pope's resentment, that he should be put into The Dunciad; but he had the fate of Cassandra. I gave no credit to his prediction, till in time I saw it accomplished. The shafts of satire were directed equally in vain against Cibber and Osborne; being repelled by the impenetrable impudence of one, and deadened by the impassive dullness of the other. Pope confessed his own pain by his anger; but he gave no pain to those who had provoked him. He was able to hurt none but himself; by transferring the same ridicule from one to another he destroyed its efficacy; for by showing that what he had said of one he was ready to say of another, he reduced himself to the insignificance of his own magpie, who from his cage calls cuckold at a venture.

Cibber, according to his engagement, repaid *The Dunciad* with another pamphlet, which, Pope said, "would be as good as a dose of hartshorn to him"; but his tongue and his heart were at variance. I have heard Mr. Richardson relate, that he attended his father the painter on a visit, when one of Cibber's pamphlets came into the hands of Pope, who said, "These things are my diversion." They sat by him while he perused it, and saw his features written with anguish; and young Richardson said to his father, when they returned, that he hoped to be preserved from such diversion as had been that day the lot of Pope.

From this time, finding his diseases more oppressive, and his vital powers gradually declining, he no longer strained his faculties with any original composition, nor proposed any other employment for his remaining life than the revisal and correction of his former works; in which he received advice and assistance from Warburton, whom he appears to have trusted and honoured in the highest degree.

He laid aside his epic poem, perhaps without much loss to mankind; for his hero was Brutus the Trojan, who, according to a ridiculous fiction, established a colony in Britain. The subject therefore was of the fabulous age; the actors were a race upon whom imagination has been exhausted and attention wearied, and to whom the mind will not easily be recalled when it is invited in blank verse, which Pope had adopted with great imprudence, and I think without due consideration of the nature of our language. The sketch is, at least in part, preserved by Ruffhead; by which it appears that Pope was thoughtless enough to model the names of his heroes with terminations not consistent with the time or country in which he places them.

He lingered through the next year; but perceived himself, as he expresses it, "going down the hill." He had for at least five years been afflicted with an asthma, and other disorders, which his physicians were unable to relieve. Towards the end of his life he consulted Dr. Thomson, a man who had, by large promises and free censures of the common practice of physic, forced himself up into sudden reputation. Thomson declared his distemper to be a dropsy, and evacuated part of the water by tincture of jalap, but confessed that his belly did not subside. Thomson had many enemies, and Pope was persuaded to dismiss him.

While he was yet capable of amusement and conversation,

as he was one day sitting in the air with Lord Bolingbroke and Lord Marchmont, he saw his favourite Martha Blount at the bottom of the terrace, and asked Lord Bolingbroke to go and hand her up. Bolingbroke, not liking his errand, crossed his legs and sat still; but Lord Marchmont, who was younger and less captious, waited on the lady; who, when he came to her, asked, "What, is he not dead yet?" She is said to have neglected him, with shameful unkindness, in the latter time of his decay; yet, of the little which he had to leave, she had a very great part. Their acquaintance began early; the life of each was pictured on the other's mind; their conversation therefore was endearing, for when they met, there was an immediate coalition of congenial notions. Perhaps he considered her unwillingness to approach the chamber of sickness as female weakness or human frailty; perhaps he was conscious to himself of peevishness and impatience, or, though he was offended by her inattention, might yet consider her merit as overbalancing her fault; and if he had suffered his heart to be alienated from her, he could have found nothing that might fill her place; he could have only shrunk within himself; it was too late to transfer his confidence or fondness.

In May 1744 his death was approaching; on the 6th, he was all day delirious, which he mentioned four days afterwards as a sufficient humiliation of the vanity of man; he afterwards complained of seeing things as through a curtain and in false colours, and one day, in the presence of Dodsley, asked what arm it was that came out from the wall. He said that his greatest inconvenience was inability to think.

Bolingbroke sometimes wept over him in this state of helpless decay; and being told by Spence that Pope, at the intermission of his deliriousness, was always saying something kind either of his present or absent friends, and that his humanity seemed to have survived his understanding, answered, "It has so." And added, "I never in my life knew a man that had so tender a heart for his particular friends, or a more general friendship for mankind." At another time he said, "I have known Pope these thirty years, and value myself more in his friendship than"—his grief then suppressed his voice.

Pope expressed undoubting confidence of a future state. Being asked by his friend Mr. Hooke, a Papist, whether he would not die like his father and mother, and whether a priest should not be called, he answered, "I do not think it essential, but it will be very right; and I thank you for putting me in mind of it."

In the morning, after the priest had given him the last sacraments, he said, "There is nothing that is meritorious but virtue and friendship; and indeed friendship itself is only a part of virtue."

He died in the evening of the 30th day of May, 1744, so placidly, that the attendants did not discern the exact time of his expiration. He was buried at Twickenham, near his father and mother, where a monument has been erected to him by his commentator, the Bishop of Gloucester.

He left the care of his papers to his executors; first to Lord Bolingbroke, and if he should not be living, to the Earl of Marchmont; undoubtedly expecting them to be proud of the trust, and eager to extend his fame. But let no man dream of influence beyond his life. After a decent time, Dodsley the bookseller went to solicit preference as the publisher, and was told that the parcel had not been yet inspected; and whatever was the reason, the world has been disappointed of what was "reserved for the next age."

He lost, indeed, the favour of Bolingbroke by a kind of posthumous offence. The political pamphlet called *The Patriot King* had been put into his hands that he might procure the impression of a very few copies, to be distributed, according to the author's direction, among his friends, and Pope assured him that no more had been printed than were allowed; but, soon after his death, the printer brought and resigned a complete edition of fifteen hundred copies, which Pope had ordered him to print, and to retain in secret. He kept, as was observed, his engagement to Pope better than Pope had kept it to his friend; and nothing was known of the transaction till, upon the death of his employer, he thought himself obliged to deliver the books to the right owner, who, with great indignation, made a fire in his yard, and delivered the whole impression to the flames.

Hitherto nothing had been done which was not naturally dictated by resentment of violated faith; resentment more acrimonious, as the violator had been more loved or more trusted. But here the anger might have stopped; the injury was private, and there was little danger from the example.

Bolingbroke, however, was not yet satisfied; his thirst of vengeance excited him to blast the memory of the man over whom he had wept in his last struggles; and he employed Mallet, another friend of Pope, to tell the tale to the public, with all its aggravations. Warburton, whose heart was warm with his legacy, and tender by the recent separation, thought it proper for him to interpose; and undertook, not indeed to vindicate the action, for breach of trust has always something criminal, but to extenuate it by an apology. Having advanced what cannot be denied, that moral obliquity is made more or less excusable by the motives that produce it, he inquires what evil purpose could have induced Pope to break his promise. He could not delight his vanity by usurping the work, which, though not sold in shops, had been shown to a number more than sufficient to preserve the author's claim; he could not gratify his avarice, for he could not sell his plunder till Bolingbroke was dead; and even then, if the copy was left to another, his fraud would be defeated, and if left to himself, would be useless.

Warburton therefore supposes, with great appearance of reason, that the irregularity of his conduct proceeded wholly from his zeal for Bolingbroke, who might perhaps have destroyed the pamphlet, which Pope thought it his duty to preserve, even without its author's approbation. To this apology an answer was written in *A Letter to the most impudent Man living.*

He brought some reproach upon his own memory by the petulant and contemptuous mention made in his will of Mr. Allen, and an affected repayment of his benefactions. Mrs. Blount, as the known friend and favourite of Pope, had been invited to the house of Allen, where she comported herself with such indecent arrogance, that she parted from Mrs. Allen in a state of irreconcileable dislike, and the door was for ever barred against her. This exclusion she resented with so much bitterness as to refuse any legacy from Pope, unless he left the world with a disavowal of obligation to Allen. Having been long under her dominion, now tottering in the decline of life, and unable to resist the violence of her temper, or perhaps, with the prejudice of a lover, persuaded that she had suffered improper treatment, he complied with her demand, and polluted his will with female resentment. Allen accepted the legacy, which he gave to the hospital at Bath, observing that Pope was always a bad accountant, and that if to 150*l.* he had put a cypher more, he had come nearer to the truth.

The person of Pope is well known not to have been formed by the nicest model. He has, in his account of the " Little Club," compared himself to a spider, and by another is described as protuberant behind and before. He is said to have been beautiful in his infancy; but he was of a constitution originally feeble and weak; and as bodies of a tender frame are easily distorted, his deformity was probably in part the effect of his application. His stature was so low, that, to bring him to a level with common tables, it was necessary to raise his seat. But his face was not displeasing, and his eyes were animated and vivid.

By natural deformity, or accidental distortion, his vital functions were so much disordered, that his life was a "long disease." His most frequent assailant was the headache, which he used to relieve by inhaling the steam of coffee, which he very frequently required.

Most of what can be told concerning his petty peculiarities was communicated by a female domestic of the Earl of Oxford, who knew him perhaps after the middle of life. He was then so weak as to stand in perpetual need of female attendance; extremely sensible of cold, so that he wore a kind of fur doublet under a shirt of a very coarse warm linen with fine sleeves. When he rose, he was invested in bodice made of stiff canvas, being scarce able to hold himself erect till they were laced, and he then put on a flannel waistcoat. One side was contracted. His legs were so slender, that he enlarged their bulk with three pair of stockings, which were drawn on and off by the maid; for he was not able to dress or undress himself, and neither went to bed nor rose without help. His weakness made it very difficult for him to be clean.

His hair had fallen almost all away; and he used to dine sometimes with Lord Oxford, privately, in a velvet cap. His dress of ceremony was black, with a tye-wig and a little sword.

The indulgence and accommodation which his sickness required had taught him all the unpleasing and unsocial qualities of a valetudinary man. He expected that everything should give way to his ease or humour, as a child whose parents will not hear her cry, has an unresisted dominion in the nursery.

> *C'est que l'enfant toujours est homme,*
> *C'est que l'homme est toujours enfant.*

When he wanted to sleep, he "nodded in company"; and once slumbered at his own table while the Prince of Wales was talking of poetry.

The reputation which his friendship gave procured him many invitations; but he was a very troublesome inmate. He brought no servant, and had so many wants that a numerous attendance was scarcely able to supply them. Wherever he was, he left no room for another, because he exacted the attention and employed the activity of the whole family. His errands were so frequent and frivolous that the footmen in time avoided and neglected him; and the Earl of Oxford discharged some of the servants for their resolute refusal of his messages. The maids, when they had neglected their business, alleged that they had been employed by Mr. Pope. One of his constant demands was of coffee in the night, and to the woman that waited on him in his chamber he was very burthensome: but he was careful to recompense her want of sleep; and Lord Oxford's servant declared, that in a house where her business was to answer his call she would not ask for wages.

He had another fault, easily incident to those who, suffering much pain, think themselves entitled to what pleasures they can snatch. He was too indulgent to his appetite; he loved meat highly seasoned and of strong taste; and, at the intervals of the table, amused himself with biscuits and dry conserves. If he sat down to a variety of dishes, he would oppress his stomach with repletion; and though he seemed angry when a dram was offered him, did not forbear to drink it. His friends, who knew the avenues to his heart, pampered him with presents of luxury, which he did not suffer to stand neglected. The death of great men is not always proportioned to the lustre of their lives. Hannibal, says Juvenal, did not perish by a javelin or a sword; the slaughters of Cannæ were revenged by a ring. The death of Pope was imputed by some of his friends to a silver saucepan, in which it was his delight to heat potted lampreys.

That he loved too well to eat is certain; but that his sensuality shortened his life will not be hastily concluded, when it is remembered that a conformation so irregular lasted six and fifty years, notwithstanding such pertinacious diligence of study and meditation.

In all his intercourse with mankind he had great delight in artifice, and endeavoured to attain all his purposes by indirect and unsuspected methods. "He hardly drank tea without a stratagem." If, at the house of his friends, he wanted any accommodation, he was not willing to ask for it in plain terms, but would mention it remotely as something convenient; though, when it was procured, he soon made it appear for whose sake it had been recommended. Thus he teased Lord Orrery till he obtained a screen. He practised his arts on such small occasions, that Lady Bolingbroke used to say, in a French phrase, that "he played the politician about cabbages and turnips." His unjustifiable impression of *The Patriot King*, as it can be imputed to no particular motive, must have proceeded from his general habit of secrecy and cunning; he caught an opportunity of a sly trick, and pleased himself with the thought of outwitting Bolingbroke.

In familiar or convivial conversation it does not appear that he excelled. He may be said to have resembled Dryden as being not one that was distinguished by vivacity in company. It is remarkable that, so near his time, so much should be known of what he has written and so little of what he has said: traditional memory retains no sallies of raillery nor sentences of observation; nothing either pointed or solid, either wise or merry. One apophthegm only stands upon record. When an objection raised against his inscription for Shakespeare was defended by the authority of Patrick, he replied—"horresco referens"—that "he would allow the publisher of a Dictionary to know the meaning of a single word, but not of two words put together."

He was fretful and easily displeased, and allowed himself to be capriciously resentful. He would sometimes leave Lord Oxford silently, no one could tell why, and was to be courted back by more letters and messages than the footmen were willing to carry. The table was indeed infested by Lady Mary Wortley, who was the friend of Lady Oxford, and who, knowing his peevishness, could by no intreaties be restrained from contradicting him, till their disputes were sharpened to such asperity that one or the other quitted the house.

He sometimes condescended to be jocular with servants or inferiors; but by no merriment, either of others or his own, was he ever seen excited to laughter.

Of his domestic character frugality was a part eminently remarkable. Having determined not to be dependent, he determined not to be in want, and therefore wisely and magnanimously rejected all temptations to expense unsuitable to his fortune. This general care must be universally approved; but it sometimes appeared in petty artifices of parsimony, such as the practice of writing his compositions on the back of letters, as may be seen in the remaining copy of the Iliad, by which perhaps in five years five shillings were saved; or in a niggardly reception of his friends and scantiness of entertainment, as, when he had two guests in his house, he would set at supper a single pint upon the table; and, having himself taken two small glasses, would retire and say, "Gentlemen, I leave you to your wine." Yet he tells his friends that "he has a heart for all, a house for all, and, whatever they may think, a fortune for all."

He sometimes, however, made a splendid dinner, and is said to have wanted no part of the skill or elegance which such performances require. That this magnificence should be often displayed, that obstinate prudence with which he conducted his affairs would not permit; for his revenue, certain and casual, amounted only to about eight hundred pounds a year, of which however he declares himself able to assign one hundred to charity.

Of this fortune, which, as it arose from public approbation, was very honourably obtained, his imagination seems to have been too full: it would be hard to find a man, so well entitled to notice by his wit, that ever delighted so much in talking of his money. In his letters and in his poems, his garden and his grotto, his quincunx and his vines, or some hints of his opulence, are always to be found. The great topic of his ridicule is poverty; the crimes with which he reproaches his antagonists are their debts, their habitation in the Mint, and their want of a dinner. He seems to be of an opinion not very uncommon in the world, that to want money is to want everything.

Next to the pleasure of contemplating his possessions seems to be that of enumerating the men of high rank with whom he was acquainted, and whose notice he loudly proclaims not to have been obtained by any practices of meanness or servility, a boast which was never denied to be true, and to which very few poets have ever aspired. Pope never set genius to sale; he never flattered those whom he did not love, or praised those whom he did not esteem. Savage however remarked, that he began a little to relax his dignity when he wrote a distich for "his Highness's dog."

His admiration of the great seems to have increased in the advance of life. He passed over peers and statesmen to inscribe his Iliad to Congreve, with a magnanimity of which the praise had been complete, had his friend's virtue been equal to his wit. Why he was chosen for so great an honour it is not now possible to know; there is no trace in literary history of any particular intimacy between them. The name of Congreve appears in the letters among those of his other friends, but without any observable distinction or consequence.

To his latter works, however, he took care to annex names dignified with titles, but was not very happy in his choice; for, except Lord Bathurst, none of his noble friends were such as that a good man would wish to have his intimacy with them known to posterity: he can derive little honour from the notice of Cobham, Burlington, or Bolingbroke.

Of his social qualities, if an estimate be made from his Letters, an opinion too favourable cannot easily be formed; they exhibit a perpetual and unclouded effulgence of general benevolence and particular fondness. There is nothing but liberality, gratitude, constancy, and tenderness. It has been so long said as to be commonly believed, that the true characters of men may be found in their letters, and that he who writes to his friend lays his heart open before him. But the truth is, that such were the simple friendships of the "Golden Age," and are now the friendships only of children. Very few can boast of hearts which they dare lay open to themselves, and of which, by whatever accident exposed, they do not shun a distinct and continued view; and, certainly, what we hide from ourselves we do not show to our friends. There is, indeed, no transaction which offers stronger temptations to fallacy and sophistication than epistolary intercourse. In the eagerness of conversation the first emotions of the mind often burst out before they are considered; in the tumult of business, interest and passion have their genuine effect; but a friendly letter is a calm and deliberate performance, in the cool of leisure, in the stillness of solitude, and surely no man sits down to depreciate by design his own character.

Friendship has no tendency to secure veracity; for by whom can a man so much wish to be thought better than he is, as by him whose kindness he desires to gain or keep? Even in writing to the world there is less constraint; the author is not confronted with his reader, and takes his chance of approbation among the different dispositions of mankind; but a letter is addressed to a single mind, of which the prejudices and partialities are known, and must therefore please, if not by favouring them, by forbearing to oppose them.

To charge those favourable representations which men give of their own minds with the guilt of hypocritical falsehood, would show more severity than knowledge. The writer commonly believes himself. Almost every man's thoughts, while they are general, are right; and most hearts are pure while temptation is away. It is easy to awaken generous sentiments in privacy; to despise death when there is no danger; to glow with benevolence when there is nothing to be given. While such ideas are formed they are felt, and self-love does not suspect the gleam of virtue to be the meteor of fancy.

If the Letters of Pope are considered merely as compositions, they seem to be premeditated and artificial. It is one thing to write, because there is something which the mind wishes to discharge; and another to solicit the imagination, because ceremony or vanity requires something to be written. Pope confesses his early letters to be vitiated with *affectation and ambition*: to know whether he disentangled himself from these perverters of epistolary integrity his book and his life must be set in comparison.

One of his favourite topics is contempt of his own poetry. For this, if it had been real, he would deserve no commendation; and in this he was certainly not sincere, for his high value of himself was sufficiently observed; and of what could he be proud but of his poetry? He writes, he says, when "he has just nothing else to do"; yet Swift complains that he was never at leisure for conversation, because he "had always some poetical scheme in his head." It was punctually required that his writing-box should be set upon his bed before he rose; and Lord Oxford's domestic related, that in the dreadful winter of Forty [1740] she was called from her bed by him four times in one night to supply him with paper lest he should lose a thought.

He pretends insensibility to censure and criticism, though it was observed by all who knew him that every pamphlet disturbed his quiet, and that his extreme irritability laid him open to perpetual vexation; but he wished to despise his critics, and therefore hoped that he did despise them.

As he happened to live in two reigns when the Court paid little attention to poetry, he nursed in his mind a foolish disesteem of Kings, and proclaims that "he never sees Courts." Yet a little regard shown him by the Prince of Wales melted his obduracy; and he had not much to say when he was asked by his Royal Highness, "How he could love a Prince while he disliked Kings?"

He very frequently professes contempt of the world, and represents himself as looking on mankind, sometimes with gay indifference, as on emmets of a hillock, below his serious attention; and sometimes with gloomy indignation, as on monsters more worthy of hatred than of pity. These were dispositions apparently counterfeited. How could he despise those whom he lived by pleasing, and on whose approbation his esteem of himself was superstructed? Why should he hate those to whose

favour he owed his honour and his ease? Of things that termi-
nate in human life, the world is the proper judge; to despise
its sentence, if it were possible, is not just; and if it were just,
is not possible. Pope was far enough from this unreasonable
temper; he was sufficiently *a fool to Fame*, and his fault was,
that he pretended to neglect it. His levity and his sullenness
were only in his Letters; he passed through common life, sometimes vexed, and sometimes pleased, with the natural emotions
of common men.

His scorn of the Great is repeated too often to be real; no
man thinks much of that which he despises; and as falsehood
is always in danger of inconsistency, he makes it his boast at
another time that he lives among them.

It is evident that his own importance swells often in his
mind. He is afraid of writing, lest the clerks of the Post-office
should know his secrets; he has many enemies; he considers
himself as surrounded by universal jealousy; "after many
deaths, and many dispersions, two or three of us," says he,
"may still be brought together, not to plot, but to divert ourselves, and the world too, if it pleases"; and they can live
together, and "show what friends wits may be, in spite of all
the fools in the world." All this while it was likely that the
clerks did not know his hand; he certainly had no more enemies
than a public character like his inevitably excites; and with
what degree of friendship the wits might live, very few were
so much fools as ever to inquire.

Some part of this pretended discontent he learned from Swift,
and expresses it, I think, most frequently in his correspondence
with him. Swift's resentment was unreasonable, but it was
sincere; Pope's was the mere mimicry of his friend, a fictitious
part which he began to play before it became him. When he
was only twenty-five years old, he related that "a glut of study
and retirement had thrown him on the world," and that there
was danger lest "a glut of the world should throw him back
upon study and retirement." To this Swift answered with great
propriety, that Pope had not yet either acted or suffered enough
in the world to have become weary of it. And, indeed, it must
be some very powerful reason that can drive back to solitude
him who has once enjoyed the pleasures of society.

In the Letters both of Swift and Pope there appears such
narrowness of mind as makes them insensible of any excellence
that has not some affinity with their own, and confines their
esteem and approbation to so small a number, that whoever

should form his opinion of the age from their representation, would suppose them to have lived amidst ignorance and barbarity, unable to find among their contemporaries either virtue or intelligence, and persecuted by those that could not understand them.

When Pope murmurs at the world, when he professes contempt of fame, when he speaks of riches and poverty, of success and disappointment, with negligent indifference, he certainly does not express his habitual and settled sentiments, but either wilfully disguises his own character, or, what is more likely, invests himself with temporary qualities, and sallies out in the colours of the present moment. His hopes and fears, his joys and sorrows, acted strongly upon his mind; and if he differed from others, it was not by carelessness; he was irritable and resentful; his malignity to Philips, whom he had first made ridiculous, and then hated for being angry, continued too long. Of his vain desire to make Bentley contemptible, I never heard any adequate reason. He was sometimes wanton in his attacks; and, before Chandos, Lady Wortley, and Hill, was mean in his retreat.

The virtues which seem to have had most of his affection were liberality and fidelity of friendship, in which it does not appear that he was other than he describes himself. His fortune did not suffer his charity to be splendid and conspicuous; but he assisted Dodsley with a hundred pounds, that he might open a shop; and of the subscription of forty pounds a year that he raised for Savage, twenty were paid by himself. He was accused of loving money, but his love was eagerness to gain, not solicitude to keep it.

In the duties of friendship he was zealous and constant; his early maturity of mind commonly united him with men older than himself; and therefore, without attaining any considerable length of life, he saw many companions of his youth sink into the grave; but it does not appear that he lost a single friend by coldness or by injury; those who loved him once, continued their kindness. His ungrateful mention of Allen in his will was the effect of his adherence to one whom he had known much longer, and whom he naturally loved with greater fondness. His violation of the trust reposed in him by Bolingbroke could have no motive inconsistent with the warmest affection; he either thought the action so near to indifferent that he forgot it, or so laudable that he expected his friend to approve it.

It was reported, with such confidence as almost to enforce

belief, that in the papers intrusted to his executors was found a defamatory Life of Swift, which he had prepared as an instrument of vengeance, to be used if any provocation should be ever given. About this I inquired of the Earl of Marchmont, who assured me that no such piece was among his remains.

The religion in which he lived and died was that of the Church of Rome, to which in his correspondence with Racine he professes himself a sincere adherent. That he was not scrupulously pious in some part of his life, is known by many idle and indecent applications of sentences taken from the Scriptures; a mode of merriment which a good man dreads for its profaneness, and a witty man disdains for its easiness and vulgarity. But to whatever levities he has been betrayed, it does not appear that his principles were ever corrupted, or that he ever lost his belief of Revelation. The positions which he transmitted from Bolingbroke he seems not to have understood, and was pleased with an interpretation that made them orthodox.

A man of such exalted superiority, and so little moderation, would naturally have all his delinquencies observed and aggravated: those who could not deny that he was excellent, would rejoice to find that he was not perfect.

Perhaps it may be imputed to the unwillingness with which the same man is allowed to possess many advantages, that his learning has been depreciated. He certainly was, in his early life, a man of great literary curiosity; and when he wrote his *Essay on Criticism* had, for his age, a very wide acquaintance with books. When he entered into the living world, it seems to have happened to him as to many others, that he was less attentive to dead masters; he studied in the academy of Paracelsus, and made the universe his favourite volume. He gathered his notions fresh from reality, not from the copies of authors, but the originals of Nature. Yet there is no reason to believe that literature ever lost his esteem; he always professed to love reading; and Dobson, who spent some time at his house translating his *Essay on Man*, when I asked him what learning he found him to possess, answered, "More than I expected." His frequent references to history, his allusions to various kinds of knowledge, and his images selected from art and nature, with his observations on the operations of the mind and the modes of life, show an intelligence perpetually on the wing, excursive, vigorous, and diligent, eager to pursue knowledge, and attentive to retain it.

From this curiosity arose the desire of travelling, to which he alludes in his verses to Jervas, and which, though he never found an opportunity to gratify it, did not leave him till his life declined.

Of his intellectual character, the constituent and fundamental principle was good sense, a prompt and intuitive perception of consonance and propriety. He saw immediately, of his own conceptions, what was to be chosen, and what to be rejected; and, in the works of others, what was to be shunned, and what was to be copied.

But good sense alone is a sedate and quiescent quality, which manages its possessions well, but does not increase them; it collects few materials for its own operations, and preserves safety, but never gains supremacy. Pope had likewise genius; a mind active, ambitious, and adventurous, always investigating, always aspiring; in its widest searches still longing to go forward, in its highest flights still wishing to be higher; always imagining something greater than it knows, always endeavouring more than it can do.

To assist these powers, he is said to have had great strength and exactness of memory. That which he had heard or read was not easily lost; and he had before him not only what his own meditations suggested, but what he had found in other writers, that might be accommodated to his present purpose.

These benefits of nature he improved by incessant and unwearied diligence; he had recourse to every source of intelligence, and lost no opportunity of information; he consulted the living as well as the dead; he read his compositions to his friends, and was never content with mediocrity when excellence could be attained. He considered poetry as the business of his life; and, however he might seem to lament his occupation, he followed it with constancy; to make verses was his first labour, and to mend them was his last.

From his attention to poetry he was never diverted. If conversation offered anything that could be improved, he committed it to paper; if a thought, or perhaps an expression more happy than was common, rose to his mind, he was careful to write it; an independent distich was preserved for an opportunity of insertion; and some little fragments have been found containing lines, or parts of lines, to be wrought upon at some other time.

He was one of those few whose labour is their pleasure: he was never elevated to negligence, nor wearied to impatience; he never passed a fault unamended by indifference, nor quitted it by despair. He laboured his works first to gain reputation and afterwards to keep it.

Of composition there are different methods. Some employ at once memory and invention, and, with little intermediate use of the pen, form and polish large masses by continued meditation, and write their productions only when, in their own opinion, they have completed them. It is related of Virgil, that his custom was to pour out a great number of verses in the morning, and pass the day in retrenching exuberances and correcting inaccuracies. The method of Pope, as may be collected from his translation, was to write his first thoughts in his first words, and gradually to amplify, decorate, rectify, and refine them.

With such faculties, and such dispositions, he excelled every other writer in poetical prudence; he wrote in such a manner as might expose him to few hazards. He used almost always the same fabric of verse; and, indeed, by those few essays which he made of any other, he did not enlarge his reputation. Of this uniformity the certain consequence was readiness and dexterity. By perpetual practice, language had, in his mind, a systematical arrangement; having always the same use for words, he had words so selected and combined as to be ready at his call. This increase of facility he confessed himself to have perceived in the progress of his translation.

But what was yet of more importance, his effusions were always voluntary, and his subjects chosen by himself. His independence secured him from drudging at a task, and labouring upon a barren topic: he never exchanged praise for money, nor opened a shop of condolence or congratulation. His poems, therefore, were scarce ever temporary. He suffered coronations and royal marriages to pass without a song, and derived no opportunities from recent events, nor any popularity from the accidental disposition of his readers. He was never reduced to the necessity of soliciting the sun to shine upon a birthday, of calling the Graces and Virtues to a wedding, or of saying what multitudes have said before him. When he could produce nothing new, he was at liberty to be silent.

His publications were for the same reason never hasty. He is said to have sent nothing to the press till it had lain two years under his inspection: it is at least certain that he ventured nothing without nice examination. He suffered the tumult of imagination to subside, and the novelties of invention to grow familiar. He knew that the mind is always enamoured of its own productions, and did not trust his first fondness. He consulted his friends, and listened with great willingness to criticism; and, what was of more importance, he consulted himself, and let nothing pass against his own judgment.

He professed to have learned his poetry from Dryden, whom, whenever an opportunity was presented, he praised through his whole life with unvaried liberality; and perhaps his character may receive some illustration, if he be compared with his master.

Integrity of understanding and nicety of discernment were not allotted in a less proportion to Dryden than to Pope. The rectitude of Dryden's mind was sufficiently shown by the dismission of his poetical prejudices, and the rejection of unnatural thoughts and rugged numbers. But Dryden never desired to apply all the judgment that he had. He wrote, and professed to write, merely for the people; and when he pleased others, he contented himself. He spent no time in struggles to rouse latent powers; he never attempted to make that better which was already good, nor often to mend what he must have known to be faulty. He wrote, as he tells us, with very little consideration; when occasion or necessity called upon him, he poured out what the present moment happened to supply, and, when once it had passed the press, ejected it from his mind; for when he had no pecuniary interest, he had no further solicitude.

Pope was not content to satisfy; he desired to excel, and therefore always endeavoured to do his best: he did not court the candour, but dared the judgment of his reader, and, expecting no indulgence from others, he showed none to himself. He examined lines and words with minute and punctilious observation, and retouched every part with indefatigable diligence, till he had left nothing to be forgiven.

For this reason he kept his pieces very long in his hands, while he considered and reconsidered them. The only poems which can be supposed to have been written with such regard to the times as might hasten their publication were the two satires of *Thirty-eight*; of which Dodsley told me that they were brought to him by the author, that they might be fairly copied. "Almost every line," he said, "was then written twice over; I gave him a clean transcript, which he sent some time afterwards to me for the press, with almost every line written twice over a second time."

His declaration that his care for his works ceased at their publication was not strictly true. His parental attention never abandoned them; what he found amiss in the first edition, he silently corrected in those that followed. He appears to have revised the Iliad, and freed it from some of its imperfections; and the *Essay on Criticism* received many improvements after its first appearance. It will seldom be found that he altered without adding clearness, elegance, or vigour. Pope had perhaps the judgment of Dryden; but Dryden certainly wanted the diligence of Pope.

In acquired knowledge, the superiority must be allowed to Dryden, whose education was more scholastic, and who before he became an author had been allowed more time for study, with better means of information. His mind has a larger range, and he collects his images and illustrations from a more extensive circumference of science. Dryden knew more of man in his general nature, and Pope in his local manners. The notions of Dryden were formed by comprehensive speculation, and those of Pope by minute attention. There is more dignity in the knowledge of Dryden, and more certainty in that of Pope.

Poetry was not the sole praise of either; for both excelled likewise in prose; but Pope did not borrow his prose from his predecessor. The style of Dryden is capricious and varied; that of Pope is cautious and uniform. Dryden observes the motions of his own mind; Pope constrains his mind to his own rules of composition. Dryden is sometimes vehement and rapid; Pope is always smooth, uniform, and gentle. Dryden's page is a natural field, rising into inequalities, and diversified by the varied exuberance of abundant vegetation; Pope's is a velvet lawn, shaven by the scythe, and levelled by the roller.

Of genius, that power which constitutes a poet; that quality without which judgment is cold, and knowledge is inert; that energy which collects, combines, amplifies, and animates; the superiority must, with some hesitation, be allowed to Dryden. It is not to be inferred that of this poetical vigour Pope had only a little, because Dryden had more; for every other writer since Milton must give place to Pope; and even of Dryden it must be said, that, if he has brighter paragraphs, he has not better poems. Dryden's performances were always hasty, either excited by some external occasion, or extorted by domestic necessity; he composed without consideration, and published without correction. What his mind could supply at call, or gather in one excursion, was all that he sought, and all that he gave. The dilatory caution of Pope enabled him to condense his sentiments, to multiply his images, and to accumulate all that study might produce or chance might supply. If the flights of Dryden therefore are higher, Pope continues longer on the wing. If of Dryden's fire the blaze is brighter, of Pope's the heat is more regular and constant. Dryden often surpasses expectation, and Pope never falls below it. Dryden is read with frequent astonishment, and Pope with perpetual delight.

This parallel will, I hope, when it is well considered, be found just; and if the reader should suspect me, as I suspect myself, of some partial fondness for the memory of Dryden, let him not too hastily condemn me; for meditation and inquiry may, perhaps, show him the reasonableness of my determination.

The Works of Pope are now to be distinctly examined, not so much with attention to slight faults or petty beauties, as to the general character and effect of each performance.

It seems natural for a young poet to initiate himself by pastorals, which, not professing to imitate real life, require no experience; and, exhibiting only the simple operation of unmingled passions, admit no subtle reasoning or deep inquiry. Pope's *Pastorals* are not, however, composed but with close thought; they have reference to the time of the day, the seasons of the year, and the periods of human life. The last, that which turns the attention upon age and death, was the author's favourite. To tell of disappointment and misery, to thicken the darkness of futurity, and perplex the labyrinth of uncertainty, has been always a delicious employment of the poets. His preference was probably just. I wish, however, that his fondness had not overlooked a line in which the *Zephyrs* are made *to lament in silence*.

To charge these *Pastorals* with want of invention, is to require what was never intended. The imitations are so ambitiously frequent, that the writer evidently means rather to show his literature than his wit. It is surely sufficient for an author of sixteen, not only to be able to copy the poems of antiquity with judicious selection, but to have obtained sufficient power of language and skill in metre to exhibit a series of versification which had in English poetry no precedent, nor has since had an imitation.

The design of *Windsor Forest* is evidently derived from *Cooper's Hill*, with some attention to Waller's poem on *The Park*; but Pope cannot be denied to excel his masters in variety and elegance, and the art of interchanging description, narrative, and morality. The objection made by Dennis is the want of plan, of a regular subordination of parts terminating in the principal and original design. There is this want in most descriptive poems, because as the scenes, which they must exhibit successively, are all subsisting at the same time, the order in which they are shown must by necessity be arbitrary, and more is not to be expected from the last part than from the first. The attention, therefore, which cannot be detained by suspense, must be excited by diversity, such as his poem offers to its reader.

But the desire of diversity may be too much indulged; the parts of *Windsor Forest* which deserve least praise, are those which were added to enliven the stillness of the scene, the appearance of Father Thames, and the transformation of Lodona. Addison had in his *Campaign* derided the rivers that "rise from their oozy beds" to tell stories of heroes; and it is therefore strange that Pope should adopt a fiction not only unnatural, but lately censured. The story of Lodona is told with sweetness; but a new metamorphosis is a ready and puerile expedient: nothing is easier than to tell how a flower was once a blooming virgin, or a rock an obdurate tyrant.

The *Temple of Fame* has, as Steele warmly declared, "a thousand beauties." Every part is splendid; there is great luxuriance of ornaments; the original vision of Chaucer was never denied to be much improved; the allegory is very skilfully continued, the imagery is properly selected, and learnedly displayed: yet, with all this comprehension of excellence, as its scene is laid in remote ages, and its sentiments, if the concluding paragraph be excepted, have little relation to general manners or common life, it never obtained much notice, but is turned silently over, and seldom quoted or mentioned with either praise or blame.

That the *Messiah* excels the *Pollio* is no great praise, if it be considered from what original the improvements are derived.

The *Verses on the Unfortunate Lady* have drawn much attention by the illaudable singularity of treating suicide with respect; and they must be allowed to be written in some parts with vigorous animation, and in others with gentle tenderness; nor has Pope produced any poem in which the sense predominates more over the diction. But the tale is not skilfully told; it is not easy to discover the character of either the Lady or her Guardian. History relates that she was about to disparage herself by a marriage with an inferior; Pope praises her for the dignity of ambition, and yet condemns the uncle to detestation for his pride; the ambitious love of a niece may be opposed by the interest, malice, or envy of an uncle, but never by his pride. On such an occasion a poet may be allowed to be obscure, but inconsistency never can be right.

The *Ode for St. Cecilia's Day* was undertaken at the desire of Steele: in this the author is generally confessed to have miscarried, yet he has miscarried only as compared with Dryden; for he has far outgone other competitors. Dryden's plan is better chosen; history will always take stronger hold of the attention than fable: the passions excited by Dryden are the pleasures and pains of real life, the scene of Pope is laid in imaginary existence; Pope is read with calm acquiescence, Dryden with turbulent delight; Pope hangs upon the ear, and Dryden finds the passes of the mind.

Both the odes want the essential constituent of metrical compositions, the stated recurrence of settled numbers. It may be alleged, that Pindar is said by Horace to have written *numeris lege solutis*: but as no such lax performances have been transmitted to us, the meaning of that expression cannot be fixed; and perhaps the like return might properly be made to a modern Pindarist, as Mr. Cobb received from Bentley, who, when he found his criticisms upon a Greek Exercise, which Cobb had presented, refuted one after another by Pindar's authority, cried out at last, "Pindar was a bold fellow, but thou art an impudent one."

If Pope's ode be particularly inspected, it will be found that the first stanza consists of sounds well chosen indeed, but only sounds.

The second consists of hyperbolical common-places, easily to be found, and perhaps without much difficulty to be as well expressed.

In the third, however, there are numbers, images, harmony, and vigour, not unworthy the antagonist of Dryden. Had all been like this—but every part cannot be the best.

The next stanzas place and detain us in the dark and dismal regions of mythology, where neither hope nor fear, neither joy nor sorrow, can be found: the poet, however, faithfully attends us; we have all that can be performed by elegance of diction or sweetness of versification; but what can form avail without better matter?

The last stanza recurs again to common-places. The conclusion is too evidently modelled by that of Dryden; and it may be remarked that both end with the same fault; the comparison of each is literal on one side, and metaphorical on the other.

Poets do not always express their own thoughts: Pope, with all this labour in the praise of music, was ignorant of its principles, and insensible of its effects.

One of his greatest, though of his earliest works, is the *Essay on Criticism*, which, if he had written nothing else, would have placed him among the first critics and the first poets, as it exhibits every mode of excellence that can embellish or dignify didactic composition—selection of matter, novelty of arrangement, justness of precept, splendour of illustration, and propriety of digression. I know not whether it be pleasing to consider that he produced this piece at twenty, and never afterwards excelled it: he that delights himself with observing that such powers may be soon attained, cannot but grieve to think that life was ever after at a stand.

To mention the particular beauties of the *Essay* would be unprofitably tedious; but I cannot forbear to observe, that the comparison of a student's progress in the sciences with the journey of a traveller in the Alps, is perhaps the best that English poetry can show. A simile, to be perfect, must both illustrate and ennoble the subject; must show it to the understanding in a clearer view, and display it to the fancy with greater dignity; but either of these qualities may be sufficient to recommend it. In didactic poetry, of which the great purpose is instruction, a simile may be praised which illustrates, though it does not ennoble; in heroics, that may be admitted which ennobles, though it does not illustrate. That it may be complete, it is required to exhibit, independently of its references, a pleasing image; for a simile is said to be a short episode. To this antiquity was so attentive, that circumstances were sometimes added, which, having no parallels, served only to fill the imagination, and produced what Perrault ludicrously called "comparisons with a long tail." In their similes the greatest writers have sometimes failed: the ship-race, compared with the chariot-race, is neither illustrated nor aggrandised; land and water make all the difference: when Apollo, running after Daphne, is likened to a greyhound chasing a hare, there is nothing gained; the ideas of pursuit and flight are too plain to be made plainer; and a god and the daughter of a god are not represented much to their advantage by a hare and dog. The simile of the Alps has no useless parts, yet affords a striking picture by itself; it makes the foregoing position better understood, and enables it to take faster hold on the attention; it assists the apprehension and elevates the fancy.

Let me likewise dwell a little on the celebrated paragraph in which it is directed that "the sound should seem an echo to the sense"; a precept which Pope is allowed to have observed beyond any other English poet.

This notion of representative metre, and the desire of discovering frequent adaptations of the sound to the sense, have produced, in my opinion, many wild conceits and imaginary beauties. All that can furnish this representation are the sounds of the words considered singly, and the time in which they are pronounced. Every language has some words framed to exhibit the noises which they express, as *thump, rattle, growl, hiss*. These, however, are but few; and the poet cannot make them more, nor can they be of any use but when sound is to be mentioned. The time of pronunciation was in the dactylic measures of the learned languages capable of considerable variety; but that variety could be accommodated only to motion or duration, and different degrees of motion were perhaps expressed by verses rapid or slow, without much attention of the writer, when the image had full possession of his fancy; but our language having little flexibility, our verses can differ very little in their cadence. The fancied resemblances, I fear, arise sometimes merely from the ambiguity of words; there is supposed to be some relation between a *soft* line and *soft* couch, or between *hard* syllables and *hard* fortune.

Motion, however, may be in some sort exemplified; and yet it may be suspected that in such resemblances the mind often governs the ear, and the sounds are estimated by their meaning. One of their most successful attempts has been to describe the labour of Sisyphus:

> With many a weary step, and many a groan,
> Up the high hill he heaves a huge round stone;
> The huge round stone, resulting with a bound,
> Thunders impetuous down, and smokes along the ground.

Who does not perceive the stone to move slowly upward, and roll violently back? But set the same numbers to another sense:

> While many a merry tale, and many a song,
> Cheer'd the rough road, we wish'd the rough road long;
> The rough road then, returning in a round,
> Mock'd our impatient steps, for all was fairy ground.

We have now surely lost much of the delay, and much of the rapidity.

But, to show how little the greatest master of numbers can fix the principles of representative harmony, it will be sufficient to remark that the poet who tells us that

> When Ajax strives some rock's vast weight to throw,
> The line too labours, and the words move slow;
> Not so when swift Camilla scours the plain,
> Flies o'er th' unbending corn, and skims along the main;

when he had enjoyed for about thirty years the praise of Camilla's lightness of foot, he tried another experiment upon *sound* and *time*, and produced this memorable triplet:

> Waller was smooth; but Dryden taught to join ⎫
> The varying verse, the full resounding line, ⎬
> The long majestic march, and energy divine. ⎭

Here are the swiftness of the rapid race, and the march of slow-paced majesty, exhibited by the same poet in the same sequence of syllables, except that the exact prosodist will find the line of *swiftness* by one time longer than that of *tardiness*.

Beauties of this kind are commonly fancied; and, when real, are technical and nugatory, not to be rejected, and not to be solicited.

To the praises which have been accumulated on *The Rape of the Lock* by readers of every class, from the critic to the waiting-maid, it is difficult to make any addition. Of that which is universally allowed to be the most attractive of all ludicrous compositions, let it rather be now inquired from what sources the power of pleasing is derived.

Dr. Warburton, who excelled in critical perspicacity, has remarked that the preternatural agents are very happily adapted to the purposes of the poem. The heathen deities can no longer gain attention: we should have turned away from a contest between Venus and Diana. The employment of allegorical persons always excites conviction of its own absurdity; they may produce effects, but cannot conduct actions: when the phantom is put in motion, it dissolves: thus *Discord* may raise a mutiny; but *Discord* cannot conduct a march, nor besiege a town. Pope brought in view a new race of beings, with powers and passions proportionate to their operation. The sylphs and gnomes act at the toilet and the tea-table, what more terrific and more powerful phantoms perform on the stormy ocean or the field of battle; they give their proper help, and do their proper mischief.

Pope is said, by an objector, not to have been the inventor of this petty nation; a charge which might with more justice

have been brought against the author of the Iliad, who doubtless adopted the religious system of his country; for what is
there but the names of his agents which Pope has not invented?
Has he not assigned them characters and operations never
heard of before? Has he not, at least, given them their first
poetical existence? If this is not sufficient to denominate his
work original, nothing original ever can be written.

In this work are exhibited, in a very high degree, the two
most engaging powers of an author. New things are made
familiar, and familiar things are made new. A race of aerial
people, never heard of before, is presented to us in a manner so
clear and easy, that the reader seeks for no further information,
but immediately mingles with his new acquaintance, adopts
their interests, and attends their pursuits, loves a sylph, and
detests a gnome.

That familiar things are made new, every paragraph will
prove. The subject of the poem is an event below the common
incidents of common life; nothing real is introduced that is
not seen so often as to be no longer regarded; yet the whole
detail of a female-day is here brought before us, invested
with so much art of decoration, that, though nothing is disguised, everything is striking, and we feel all the appetite of
curiosity for that from which we have a thousand times
turned fastidiously away.

The purpose of the poet is, as he tells us, to laugh at "the
little unguarded follies of the female sex." It is therefore without
justice that Dennis charges *The Rape of the Lock* with the want
of a moral, and for that reason sets it below the *Lutrin*, which
exposes the pride and discord of the clergy. Perhaps neither
Pope nor Boileau has made the world much better than he
found it; but, if they had both succeeded, it were easy to tell
who would have deserved most from public gratitude. The
freaks, and humours, and spleen, and vanity of women, as they
embroil families in discord, and fill houses with disquiet, do
more to obstruct the happiness of life in a year than the ambition
of the clergy in many centuries. It has been well observed, that
the misery of man proceeds not from any single crush of overwhelming evil, but from small vexations continually repeated.

It is remarked by Dennis likewise that the machinery is
superfluous; that, by all the bustle of preternatural operation,
the main event is neither hastened nor retarded. To this charge
an efficacious answer is not easily made. The Sylphs cannot
be said to help or to oppose, and it must be allowed to imply

some want of art, that their power has not been sufficiently intermingled with the action. Other parts may likewise be charged with want of connection; the game at *ombre* might be spared; but if the Lady had lost her hair while she was intent upon her cards, it might have been inferred that those who are too fond of play will be in danger of neglecting more important interests. Those perhaps are faults; but what are such faults to so much excellence?

The *Epistle of Eloisa to Abelard* is one of the most happy productions of human wit; the subject is so judiciously chosen, that it would be difficult, in turning over the annals of the world, to find another which so many circumstances concur to recommend. We regularly interest ourselves most in the fortune of those who most deserve our notice. Abelard and Eloisa were conspicuous in their days for eminence of merit. The heart naturally loves truth. The adventures and misfortunes of this illustrious pair are known from undisputed history. Their fate does not leave the mind in hopeless dejection, for they both found quiet and consolation in retirement and piety. So new and so affecting is their story, that it supersedes invention, and imagination ranges at full liberty without straggling into scenes of fable.

The story, thus skilfully adopted, has been diligently improved. Pope has left nothing behind him which seems more the effect of studious perseverance and laborious revisal. Here is particularly observable the *curiosa felicitas*, a fruitful soil and careful cultivation. Here is no crudeness of sense, nor asperity of language.

The sources from which sentiments which have so much vigour and efficacy have been drawn, are shown to be the mystic writers by the learned author of the *Essay on the Life and Writings of Pope*; a book which teaches how the brow of Criticism may be smoothed, and how she may be enabled, with all her severity, to attract and to delight.

The train of my disquisition has now conducted me to that poetical wonder, the translation of the Iliad, a performance which no age or nation can pretend to equal. To the Greeks translation was almost unknown; it was totally unknown to the inhabitants of Greece. They had no recourse to the Barbarians for poetical beauties, but sought for everything in Homer, where indeed there is but little which they might not find.

The Italians have been very diligent translators, but I can hear of no version, unless perhaps Anguillara's Ovid may be excepted, which is read with eagerness. The Iliad of Salvini every reader may discover to be punctiliously exact; but it seems to be the work of a linguist skilfully pedantic, and his countrymen, the proper judges of its power to please, reject it with disgust.

Their predecessors the Romans have left some specimens of translation behind them, and that employment must have had some credit in which Tully and Germanicus engaged; but unless we suppose, what is perhaps true, that the plays of Terence were versions of Menander, nothing translated seems ever to have risen to high reputation. The French, in the meridian hour of their learning, were very laudably industrious to enrich their own language with the wisdom of the ancients; but found themselves reduced, by whatever necessity, to turn the Greek and Roman poetry into prose. Whoever could read an author could translate him. From such rivals little can be feared.

The chief help of Pope in this arduous undertaking was drawn from the versions of Dryden. Virgil had borrowed much of his imagery from Homer, and part of the debt was now paid by his translator. Pope searched the pages of Dryden for happy combinations of heroic diction; but it will not be denied that he added much to what he found. He cultivated our language with so much diligence and art that he has left in his Homer a treasure of poetical elegances to posterity. His version may be said to have tuned the English tongue; for since its appearance no writer, however deficient in other powers, has wanted melody. Such a series of lines, so elaborately corrected and so sweetly modulated, took possession of the public ear; the vulgar was enamoured of the poem, and the learned wondered at the translation.

But in the most general applause discordant voices will always be heard. It has been objected by some, who wish to be numbered among the sons of learning, that Pope's version of Homer is not Homerical; that it exhibits no resemblance of the original and characteristic manner of the father of poetry, as it wants his awful simplicity, his artless grandeur, his unaffected majesty. This cannot be totally denied; but it must be remembered that *necessitas quod cogit defendit*; that may be lawfully done which cannot be forborne. Time and place will always enforce regard. In estimating this translation, consideration must be had of the nature of our language, the form of our metre, and above all of the change which two thousand years have made in the modes of life and the habits of thought. Virgil wrote in a language of the same general fabric with that of Homer, in verses of the same measure, and in an age nearer to Homer's time by eighteen hundred years, yet he found, even then, the state of the world so much altered, and the demand for elegance so much increased, that mere nature would be endured no longer; and perhaps, in the multitude of borrowed passages, very few can be shown which he has not embellished.

There is a time when nations emerging from barbarity, and falling into regular subordination, gain leisure to grow wise, and feel the shame of ignorance and the craving pain of un- satisfied curiosity. To this hunger of the mind plain sense is grateful; that which fills the void removes uneasiness, and to be free from pain for a while is pleasure; but repletion generates fastidiousness; a saturated intellect soon becomes luxurious, and knowledge finds no willing reception till it is recommended by artificial diction. Thus it will be found, in the progress of learning, that in all nations the first writers are simple, and that every age improves in elegance. One refinement always makes way for another; and what was expedient to Virgil was necessary to Pope.

I suppose many readers of the English Iliad, when they have been touched with some unexpected beauty of the lighter kind, have tried to enjoy it in the original, where, alas! it was not to be found. Homer doubtless owes to his translator many Ovidian graces not exactly suitable to his character; but to have added can be no great crime, if nothing be taken away. Elegance is surely to be desired, if it be not gained at the expense of dignity. A hero would wish to be loved as well as to be reverenced.

To a thousand cavils one answer is sufficient: the purpose of a writer is to be read, and the criticism which would destroy the power of pleasing must be blown aside. Pope wrote for his own age and his own nation; he knew that it was necessary to colour the images and point the sentiments of his author; he therefore made him graceful, but lost him some of his sublimity.

The copious notes with which the version is accompanied, and by which it is recommended to many readers, though they were undoubtedly written to swell the volumes, ought not to pass without praise: commentaries which attract the reader by the pleasure of perusal have not often appeared; the notes of others are read to clear difficulties, those of Pope to vary entertainment.

It has, however, been objected, with sufficient reason, that there is in the commentary too much of unseasonable levity and affected gaiety; that too many appeals are made to the ladies, and the ease which is so carefully preserved is sometimes the ease of a trifler. Every art has its terms, and every kind of instruction its proper style; the gravity of common critics may be tedious, but is less despicable than childish merriment.

Of the Odyssey nothing remains to be observed: the same general praise may be given to both translations, and a particular examination of either would require a large volume. The notes were written by Broome, who endeavoured, not unsuccessfully, to imitate his master.

Of *The Dunciad* the hint is confessedly taken from Dryden's *Mac Flecknoe*; but the plan is so enlarged and diversified as justly to claim the praise of an original, and affords perhaps the best specimen that has yet appeared of personal satire ludicrously pompous.

That the design was moral, whatever the author might tell either his readers or himself, I am not convinced. The first motive was the desire of revenging the contempt with which Theobald had treated his Shakespeare, and regaining the honour which he had lost, by crushing his opponent. Theobald was not of bulk enough to fill a poem, and therefore it was necessary to find other enemies with other names, at whose expense he might divert the public.

In this design there was petulance and malignity enough; but I cannot think it very criminal. An author places himself uncalled before the tribunal of criticism, and solicits fame at the hazard of disgrace. Dullness or deformity are not culpable in themselves, but may be very justly reproached when they pretend to the honour of wit or the influence of beauty. If bad writers were to pass without reprehension, what should restrain them? *impune diem consumpserit ingens Telephus* ; and upon bad writers only will censure have much effect. The satire which brought Theobald and Moore into contempt, dropped impotent from Bentley like the javelin of Priam.

All truth is valuable, and satirical criticism may be considered as useful when it rectifies error and improves judgment; he that refines the public taste is a public benefactor.

The beauties of this poem are well known; its chief fault is the grossness of its images. Pope and Swift had an unnatural delight in ideas physically impure, such as every other tongue utters with unwillingness, and of which every ear shrinks from the mention.

made up for in excellence of other passages.

But even this fault, offensive as it is, may be forgiven for the excellence of other passages—such as the formation and dissolution of Moore, the account of the Traveller, the misfortune of the Florist, and the crowded thoughts and stately numbers which dignify the concluding paragraph.

The alterations which have been made in *The Dunciad*, not always for the better, require that it should be published, as in the present collection, with all its variations.

The *Essay on Man* was a work of great labour and long consideration, but certainly not the happiest of Pope's performances. The subject is perhaps not very proper for poetry, and the poet was not sufficiently master of his subject; metaphysical morality was to him a new study, he was proud of his acquisitions, and, supposing himself master of great secrets, was in haste to teach what he had not learned. Thus he tells us, in the first epistle, that from the nature of the Supreme Being may be deduced an order of beings such as mankind, because Infinite Excellence can do only what is best. He finds out that these beings must be "somewhere," and that "all the question is whether man be in a wrong place." Surely if, according to the poet's Leibnitian reasoning, we may infer that man ought to be, only because he is, we may allow that his place is the right place because he has it. Supreme Wisdom is not less infallible in disposing than in creating. But what is meant by *somewhere* and *place*, and *wrong place*, it had been vain to ask Pope, who probably had never asked himself.

Having exalted himself into the chair of wisdom, he tells us much that every man knows, and much that he does not know himself: that we see but little, and that the order of the universe is beyond our comprehension—an opinion not very uncommon; and that there is a chain of subordinate beings "from infinite to nothing," of which himself and his readers are equally ignorant. But he gives us one comfort which, without his help, he supposes unattainable, in the position "that though we are fools, yet God is wise."

This essay affords an egregious instance of the predominance of genius, the dazzling splendour of imagery, and the seductive powers of eloquence. Never was penury of knowledge and vulgarity of sentiment so happily disguised. The reader feels his mind full, though he learns nothing; and when he meets it in its new array, no longer knows the talk of his mother and his nurse. When these wonder-working sounds sink into sense, and the doctrine of the *Essay*, disrobed of its ornaments, is left to the powers of its naked excellence, what shall we discover? That we are, in comparison with our Creator, very weak and ignorant—that we do not uphold the chain of existence—and that we could not make one another with more skill than we are made. We may learn yet more—that the arts of human life were copied from the instinctive operations of other animals —that if the world be made for man, it may be said that man was made for geese. To these profound principles of natural knowledge are added some moral instructions equally new: that self-interest, well understood, will produce social concord— that men are mutual gainers by mutual benefits—that evil is sometimes balanced by good—that human advantages are unstable and fallacious, of uncertain duration and doubtful effect —that our true honour is, not to have a great part, but to act it well—that virtue only is our own—and that happiness is always in our power.

Surely a man of no very comprehensive search may venture to say that he has heard all this before; but it was never till now recommended by such a blaze of embellishments, or such sweetness of melody. The vigorous contraction of some thoughts, the luxuriant amplification of others, the incidental illustrations, and sometimes the dignity, sometimes the softness of the verses, enchain philosophy, suspend criticism, and oppress judgment by overpowering pleasure.

This is true of many paragraphs; yet if I had undertaken to exemplify Pope's felicity of composition before a rigid critic, I should not select the *Essay on Man*; for it contains more lines unsuccessfully laboured, more harshness of diction, more thoughts imperfectly expressed, more levity without elegance, and more heaviness without strength, than will easily be found in all his other works.

The *Characters of Men and Women* are the product of diligent speculation upon human life; much labour has been bestowed upon them, and Pope very seldom laboured in vain. That his excellence may be properly estimated, I recommend a comparison of his *Characters of Women* with Boileau's Satire; it will then be seen with how much more perspicacity female nature is investigated, and female excellence selected; and he surely is no mean writer to whom Boileau shall be found inferior. The *Characters of Men*, however, are written with more, if not with deeper thought, and exhibit many passages exquisitely beautiful. The " Gem and the Flower " will not easily be equalled. In the women's part are some defects: the character of Atossa is not so

neatly finished as that of Clodio; and some of the female
characters may be found perhaps more frequently among men;
what is said of Philomede was true of Prior.

In the Epistles to Lord Bathurst and Lord Burlington, Dr.
Warburton has endeavoured to find a train of thought which
was never in the writer's head, and, to support his hypothesis,
has printed that first which was published last. In one, the most
valuable passage is perhaps the Elegy on " Good Sense"; and the
other, the " End of the Duke of Buckingham."

The *Epistle to Arbuthnot*, now arbitrarily called the *Prologue
to the Satires*, is a performance consisting, as it seems, of many
fragments wrought into one design, which by this union of
scattered beauties contains more striking paragraphs than could
probably have been brought together into an occasional work.
As there is no stronger motive to exertion than self-defence,
no part has more elegance, spirit, or dignity than the poet's
vindication of his own character. The meanest passage is the
satire upon Sporus.

Of the two poems which derived their names from the year,
and which are called the *Epilogue to the Satires*, it was very
justly remarked by Savage, that the second was in the whole
more strongly conceived, and more equally supported, but
that it had no single passages equal to the contention in the
first for the dignity of Vice, and the celebration of the triumph
of Corruption.

The *Imitations of Horace* seem to have been written as re-
laxations of his genius. This employment became his favourite
by its facility; the plan was ready to his hand, and nothing
was required but to accommodate as he could the sentiments
of an old author to recent facts or familiar images; but what
is easy is seldom excellent; such imitations cannot give pleasure
to common readers; the man of learning may be sometimes
surprised and delighted by an unexpected parallel; but the
comparison requires knowledge of the original, which will
likewise often detect strained applications. Between Roman
images and English manners there will be an irreconcileable
dissimilitude, and the works will be generally uncouth and
party-coloured; neither original nor translated, neither ancient
nor modern.

Pope had, in proportions very nicely adjusted to each other,
all the qualities that constitute genius. He had *Invention*, by
which new trains of events are formed, and new scenes of
imagery displayed, as in *The Rape of the Lock*; and by which

extrinsic and adventitious embellishments and illustrations are connected with a known subject, as in the *Essay on Criticism*. He had *Imagination*, which strongly impresses on the writer's mind, and enables him to convey to the reader, the various forms of nature, incidents of life, and energies of passion, as in his *Eloisa, Windsor Forest*, and the *Ethic Epistles*. He had *Judgment*, which selects from life or nature what the present purpose requires, and by separating the essence of things from its concomitants, often makes the representation more powerful than the reality: and he had colours of language always before him, ready to decorate his matter with every grace of elegant expression, as when he accommodates his diction to the wonderful multiplicity of Homer's sentiments and descriptions.

Poetical expression includes sound as well as meaning. "Music," says Dryden, "is inarticulate poetry"; among the excellences of Pope, therefore, must be mentioned the melody of his metre. By perusing the works of Dryden, he discovered the most perfect fabric of English verse, and habituated himself to that only which he found the best; in consequence of which restraint, his poetry has been censured as too uniformly musical, and as glutting the ear with unvaried sweetness. I suspect this objection to be the cant of those who judge by principles rather than perception; and who would even themselves have less pleasure in his works, if he had tried to relieve attention by studied discords, or affected to break his lines and vary his pauses.

But though he was thus careful of his versification, he did not oppress his powers with superfluous rigour. He seems to have thought with Boileau, that the practice of writing might be refined till the difficulty should overbalance the advantage. The construction of his language is not always strictly grammatical; with those rhymes which prescription had conjoined he contented himself, without regard to Swift's remonstrances, though there was no striking consonance; nor was he very careful to vary his terminations, or to refuse admission, at a small distance, to the same rhymes.

To Swift's edict for the exclusion of alexandrines and triplets he paid little regard; he admitted them, but, in the opinion of Fenton, too rarely; he uses them more liberally in his translation than his poems.

He has a few double rhymes; and always, I think, unsuccessfully, except once in *The Rape of the Lock*.

Expletives he very early ejected from his verses; but he now and then admits an epithet rather commodious than important.

Each of the six first lines of the Iliad might lose two syllables with very little diminution of the meaning; and sometimes, after all his art and labour, one verse seems to be made for the sake of another. In his latter productions the diction is sometimes vitiated by French idioms, with which Bolingbroke had perhaps infected him.

I have been told that the couplet by which he declared his own ear to be most gratified was this:

> Lo, where Mæotis sleeps, and hardly flows
> The freezing Tanais through a waste of snows.

But the reason of this preference I cannot discover.

It is remarked by Watts, that there is scarcely a happy combination of words, or a phrase poetically elegant in the English language, which Pope has not inserted into his version of Homer. How he obtained possession of so many beauties of speech, it were desirable to know. That he gleaned from authors, obscure as well as eminent, what he thought brilliant or useful, and preserved it all in a regular collection, is not unlikely. When, in his last years, Hall's Satires were shown him, he wished that he had seen them sooner.

New sentiments and new images others may produce; but to attempt any further improvement of versification will be dangerous. Art and diligence have now done their best, and what shall be added will be the effort of tedious toil and needless curiosity.

After all this, it is surely superfluous to answer the question that has once been asked, Whether Pope was a poet? otherwise than by asking in return, If Pope be not a poet, where is poetry to be found? To circumscribe poetry by a definition will only show the narrowness of the definer, though a definition which shall exclude Pope will not easily be made. Let us look round upon the present time, and back upon the past; let us inquire to whom the voice of mankind has decreed the wreath of poetry; let their productions be examined, and their claim stated, and the pretensions of Pope will be no more disputed. Had he given the world only his version, the name of poet must have been allowed him: if the writer of the Iliad were to class his successors, he would assign a very high place to his translator, without requiring any other evidence of Genius.

The following letter, of which the original is in the hands of

Lord Hardwicke, was communicated to me by the kindness of Mr. Jodrell:

To MR. BRIDGES, *at the Bishop of London's at Fulham*

SIR,—The favour of your letter, with your remarks, can never be enough acknowledged; and the speed with which you discharged so troublesome a task doubles the obligation.

I must own you have pleased me very much by the commendations so ill-bestowed upon me; but, I assure you, much more by the frankness of your censure, which I ought to take the more kindly of the two, as it is more advantageous to a scribbler to be improved in his judgment than to be soothed in his vanity. The greater part of those deviations from the Greek, which you have observed, I was led into by Chapman and Hobbes, who are, it seems, as much celebrated for their knowledge of the original, as they are decried for the badness of their translations. Chapman pretends to have restored the genuine sense of the author, from the mistakes of all former explainers, in several hundred places; and the Cambridge editors of the large Homer, in Greek and Latin, attributed so much to Hobbes, that they confess they have corrected the old Latin interpretation very often by his version. For my part, I generally took the author's meaning to be as you have explained it; yet their authority, joined to the knowledge of my own imperfectness in the language, overruled me. However, Sir, you may be confident I think you in the right, because you happen to be of my opinion (for men—let them say what they will—never approve any other's sense but as it squares with their own). But you have made me much more proud of and positive in my judgment, since it is strengthened by yours. I think your criticisms, which regard the expression, very just, and shall make my profit of them: to give you some proof that I am in earnest, I will alter three verses on your bare objection, though I have Mr. Dryden's example for each of them. And this, I hope, you will account no small piece of obedience, from one who values the authority of one true poet above that of twenty critics or commentators. But though I speak thus of commentators, I will continue to read carefully all I can procure, to make up, that way, for my own want of critical understanding in the original beauties of Homer. Though the greatest of them are certainly those of invention and design, which are not at all confined to the language: for the distinguishing excellences of Homer are (by the consent of the best critics of all nations) first in the manners (which include all the speeches, as being no other than the representations of each person's manners by his words), and then in that rapture and fire which carries you away with him with that wonderful force, that no man who has a true poetical spirit is master of himself while he reads him. Homer makes you interested and concerned before you are aware, all at once, whereas Virgil does it by soft degrees. This, I believe, is what a translator of Homer ought principally to imitate; and it is very hard for any translator to come up to it, because the chief reason why all translations fall short of their originals is, that the very constraint they are obliged to, renders them heavy and dispirited.

The great beauty of Homer's language, as I take it, consists in that noble simplicity which runs through all his works (and yet his diction, contrary to what one would imagine consistent with simplicity, is at the same time very copious). I don't know how I have run into this pedantry in a letter, but I find I have said too much, as well as spoken too inconsiderately; what farther thoughts I have upon this subject I shall be glad to communicate to you (for my own improvement) when we meet, which is a happiness I very earnestly desire, as I do likewise some opportunity of proving how much I think myself obliged to your friendship, and how truly I am, Sir,

> Your most faithful, humble servant,
> A. POPE.

The criticism upon Pope's *Epitaphs*, which was printed in *The Universal Visitor*, is placed here, being too minute and particular to be inserted in the Life.

Every art is best taught by example. Nothing contributes more to the cultivation of propriety than remarks on the works of those who have most excelled. I shall therefore endeavour, at this *visit*, to entertain the young students in poetry with an examination of Pope's *Epitaphs*.

To define an epitaph is useless; everyone knows that it is an inscription on a tomb. An epitaph, therefore, implies no particular character of writing, but may be composed in verse or prose. It is indeed commonly panegyrical, because we are seldom distinguished with a stone but by our friends; but it has no rule to restrain or mollify it, except this, that it ought not to be longer than common beholders may be expected to have leisure and patience to peruse.

I

On CHARLES EARL OF DORSET, *in the Church of Wythiam in Sussex*

> Dorset, the grace of courts, the Muses' pride,
> Patron of arts, and judge of nature, died.
> The scourge of pride, though sanctified or great,
> Of fops in learning, and of knaves in state;
> Yet soft in nature, though severe his lay,
> His anger moral, and his wisdom gay.
> Blest satirist! who touch'd the means so true,
> As show'd Vice had his hate and pity too.
> Blest courtier! who could king and country please,
> Yet sacred kept his friendship and his ease.
> Blest peer! his great forefather's every grace
> Reflecting, and reflected on his race;
> Where other Buckhursts, other Dorsets shine,
> And patriots still, or poets, deck the line.

The first distich of this epitaph contains a kind of information which few would want—that the man for whom the tomb was erected *died*. There are indeed some qualities worthy of praise ascribed to the dead, but none that were likely to exempt him from the lot of man, or incline us much to wonder that he should die. What is meant by "judge of nature," is not easy to say. Nature is not the object of human judgment; for it is in vain to judge where we cannot alter. If by nature is meant, what is commonly called *nature* by the critics, a just representation of things really existing, and actions really performed, nature cannot be properly opposed to *art*; nature being, in this sense, only the best effect of *art*.

The scourge of pride—

Of this couplet the second line is not, what is intended, an illustration of the former. *Pride*, in the *great*, is indeed well enough connected with knaves in state, though *knaves* is a word rather too ludicrous and light; but the mention of *sanctified* pride will not lead the thoughts to *fops in learning*, but rather to some species of tyranny or oppression, something more gloomy and more formidable than foppery.

Yet soft his nature—

This is a high compliment, but was not first bestowed on Dorset by Pope. The next verse is extremely beautiful.

Blest satirist!—

In this distich is another line of which Pope was not the author. I do not mean to blame these imitations with much harshness; in long performances they are scarcely to be avoided, and in shorter they may be indulged, because the train of the composition may naturally involve them, or the scantiness of the subject allow little choice. However, what is borrowed is not to be enjoyed as our own; and it is the business of critical justice to give every bird of the Muses his proper feather.

Blest courtier!—

Whether a courtier can properly be commended for keeping his *ease sacred* may perhaps be disputable. To please king and country, without sacrificing friendship to any change of times, was a very uncommon instance of prudence or felicity, and deserved to be kept separate from so poor a commendation as care of his ease. I wish our poets would attend a little more accurately to the use of the word *sacred*, which surely should never be applied in a serious composition, but where some reference may be made to a higher Being, or where some duty is exacted or implied. A man may keep his friendship sacred, because promises of friendship are very awful ties; but methinks he cannot, but in a burlesque sense, be said to keep his ease *sacred*.

Blest peer!—

The blessing ascribed to the *peer* has no connection with his peerage: they might happen to any other man whose ancestors were remembered, or whose posterity were likely to be regarded.

I know not whether this epitaph be worthy either of the writer or the man entombed.

II

On Sir William Trumbull, *one of the Principal Secretaries of State to King William III., who, having resigned his place, died in his retirement at Easthampstead, in Berkshire,* 1716.

> A pleasing form; a firm, yet cautious mind;
> Sincere, though prudent; constant, yet resigned;
> Honour unchanged, a principle profest,
> Fixed to one side, but moderate to the rest:
> An honest courtier, yet a patriot too,
> Just to his prince, and to his country true.
> Filled with the sense of age, the fire of youth,
> A scorn of wrangling, yet a zeal for truth;
> A generous faith, from superstition free;
> A love to peace, and hate of tyranny:
> Such this man was, who, now from earth removed,
> At length enjoys that liberty he loved.

In this epitaph, as in many others, there appears at the first view a fault which I think scarcely any beauty can compensate. The name is omitted. The end of an epitaph is to convey some account of the dead; and to what purpose is anything told of him whose name is concealed? An epitaph and a history of a nameless hero are equally absurd, since the virtues and qualities so recounted in either are scattered at the mercy of fortune, to be appropriated by guess. The name, it is true, may be read upon the stone, but what obligation has it to the poet, whose verses wander over the earth, and leave their subject behind them, and who is forced, like an unskilful painter, to make his purpose known by adventitious help?

This epitaph is wholly without elevation, and contains nothing striking or particular; but the poet is not to be blamed for the defects of his subject. He said perhaps the best that could be said. There are, however, some defects which were not made necessary by the character in which he was employed. There is no opposition between an *honest courtier* and a *patriot*, for an *honest courtier* cannot but be a *patriot*.

It was unsuitable to the nicety required in short compositions to close his verse with the word *too*: every rhyme should be a word of emphasis, nor can this rule be safely neglected, except where the length of the poem makes slight inaccuracies excusable, or allows room for beauties sufficient to overpower the effects of petty faults.

At the beginning of the seventh line the word *filled* is weak and prosaic, having no particular adaptation to any of the words that follow it.

The thought in the last line is impertinent, having no connection with the foregoing character, nor with the condition of the man described. Had the epitaph been written on the poor conspirator who died lately in prison, after a confinement of more than forty years, without any crime proved against him, the sentiment had been just and pathetical; but why should Trumbull be congratulated upon his liberty, who had never known restraint?

III

On the Hon. Simon Harcourt, only Son of the Lord Chancellor Harcourt,
at the Church of Stanton-Harcourt, in Oxfordshire, 1720.

> To this sad shrine, whoe'er thou art, draw near:
> Here lies the friend most loved, the son most dear;
> Who ne'er knew joy, but friendship might divide,
> Or gave his father grief but when he died.
>   How vain is reason, eloquence how weak,
> If Pope must tell what Harcourt cannot speak!
> Oh, let thy once-loved friend inscribe thy stone,
> And with a father's sorrows mix his own!

This epitaph is principally remarkable for the artful introduction of the name, which is inserted with a peculiar felicity, to which chance must concur with genius, which no man can hope to attain twice, and which cannot be copied but with servile imitation.

I cannot but wish that of this inscription the two last lines had been omitted, as they take away from the energy what they do not add to the sense.

IV

On James Craggs, Esq. In Westminster Abbey

JACOBUS CRAGGS,
REGI MAGNAE BRITANNIAE A SECRETIS
ET CONSILIIS SANCTIORIBVS
PRINCIPIS PARITER AC POPULI AMOR ET DELICIAE:
VIXIT TITULIS ET INVIDIA MAJOR,
ANNOS HEV PAVCOS, XXXV.
OB. FEB. XVI. MDCCXX

> Statesman, yet friend to truth; of soul sincere,
> In action faithful, and in honour clear!

Who broke no promise, served no private end,
Who gained no title, and who lost no friend;
Ennobled by himself, by all approved,
Praised, wept, and honoured by the Muse he loved.

The lines on Craggs were not originally intended for an epitaph, and therefore some faults are to be imputed to the violence with which they are torn from the poem that first contained them. We may, however, observe some defects. There is a redundancy of words in the first couplet: it is superfluous to tell of him who was *sincere, true*, and *faithful*, that he was *in honour clear*.

There seems to be an opposition intended in the fourth line, which is not very obvious: where is the relation between the two positions that he *gained no title* and *lost no friend*?

It may be proper here to remark the absurdity of joining in the same inscription Latin and English, or verse and prose. If either language be preferable to the other, let that only be used, for no reason can be given why part of the information should be given in one tongue, and part in another, on a tomb, more than in any other place, on any other occasion; and to tell all that can be conveniently told in verse, and then to call in the help of prose, has always the appearance of a very artless expedient, or of an attempt unaccomplished. Such an epitaph resembles the conversation of a foreigner, who tells part of his meaning by words, and conveys part by signs.

V

Intended for Mr. Rowe. *In Westminster Abbey*

Thy relics, Rowe, to this fair urn we trust,
And sacred, place by Dryden's awful dust:
Beneath a rude and nameless stone he lies,
To which thy tomb shall guide inquiring eyes.
Peace to thy gentle shade, and endless rest!
Blest in thy genius, in thy love too blest;
One grateful woman to thy fame supplies
What a whole thankless land to his denies.

Of this inscription the chief fault is, that it belongs less to Rowe, for whom it was written, than to Dryden, who was buried near him; and indeed gives very little information concerning either.

To wish *peace to thy shade* is too mythological to be admitted into a Christian temple: the ancient worship has infected almost all our other compositions, and might therefore be contented to spare our epitaphs. Let fiction at least cease with life, and let us be serious over the grave.

VI

On MRS. CORBET, *who died of a cancer in her breast*

Here rests a woman, good without pretence,
Blest with plain reason, and with sober sense;
No conquest she, but o'er herself desir'd;
No arts essay'd, but not to be admir'd.
Passion and pride were to her soul unknown,
Convinc'd that virtue only is our own.
So unaffected, so compos'd a mind,
So firm, yet soft, so strong, yet so refin'd,
Heaven, as its purest gold, by tortures tried;
The saint sustain'd it, but the woman died.

I have always considered this as the most valuable of all
Pope's epitaphs: the subject of it is a character not discriminated
by any shining or eminent peculiarities; yet that which really
makes, though not the splendour, the felicity of life, and that
which every wise man will choose for his final and lasting
companion in the languor of age, in the quiet of privacy, when
he departs weary and disgusted from the ostentatious, the
volatile, and the vain. Of such a character, which the dull
overlook, and the gay despise, it was fit that the value should
be made known and the dignity established. Domestic virtue,
as it is exerted without great occasions, or conspicuous consequences, in an even unnoted tenor, required the genius of
Pope to display it in such a manner as might attract regard
and enforce reverence. Who can forbear to lament that this
amiable woman has no name in the verses?

If the particular lines of this inscription be examined, it
will appear less faulty than the rest. There is scarce one line
taken from commonplaces, unless it be that in which *only virtue*
is said to be *our own*. I once heard a lady of great beauty
and excellence object to the fourth line, that it contained an
unnatural and incredible panegyric. Of this let the ladies judge.

VII

On the Monument of the HON. ROBERT DIGBY, *and of his sister* MARY,
*erected by their Father the Lord Digby, in the Church of Sherborne, in
Dorsetshire*, 1727.

Go! fair example of untainted youth,
Of modest wisdom, and pacific truth:
Composed in sufferings, and in joy sedate,
Good without noise, without pretension great.
Just of thy word, in every thought sincere,
Who knew no wish but what the world might hear:
Of softest manners, unaffected mind,
Lover of peace, and friend of human kind:
Go, live! for heaven's eternal year is thine,
Go, and exalt thy mortal to divine.

And thou, blest maid! attendant on his doom,
Pensive hast follow'd to the silent tomb,
Steered the same course to the same quiet shore,
Not parted long, and now to part no more!
Go, then, where only bliss sincere is known!
Go, where to love and to enjoy are one!
  Yet take these tears, Mortality's relief,
And till we share your joys, forgive our grief:
These little rites, a stone, a verse receive,
'Tis all a father, all a friend can give!

This epitaph contains of the brother only a general, indiscriminate character, and of the sister tells nothing but that she died. The difficulty in writing epitaphs is to give a particular and appropriate praise. This, however, is not always to be performed, whatever be the diligence or ability of the writer; for the greater part of mankind *have no character at all*, have little that distinguishes them from others equally good or bad, and therefore nothing can be said of them which may not be applied with equal propriety to a thousand more. It is indeed no great panegyric that there is inclosed in this tomb one who was born in one year and died in another; yet many useful and amiable lives have been spent, which yet leave little materials for any other memorial. These are, however, not the proper subjects of poetry; and whenever friendship, or any other motive, obliges a poet to write on such subjects, he must be forgiven if he sometimes wanders in generalities and utters the same praises over different tombs.

The scantiness of human praises can scarcely be made more apparent than by remarking how often Pope has, in the few epitaphs which he composed, found it necessary to borrow from himself. The fourteen epitaphs which he has written comprise about a hundred and forty lines, in which there are more repetitions than will easily be found in all the rest of his works. In the eight lines which make the character of Digby, there is scarce any thought, or word, which may not be found in the other epitaphs.

The ninth line, which is far the strongest and most elegant, is borrowed from Dryden. The conclusion is the same with that on Harcourt, but is here more elegant and better connected.

VIII

On SIR GODFREY KNELLER. *In Westminster Abbey*, 1723

Kneller, by Heaven, and not a master taught,
Whose Art was nature, and whose pictures thought;
Now for two ages, having snatched from fate
Whate'er was beauteous, or whate'er was great,

Lies crowned with Princes' honours, Poets' lays,
Due to his merit, and brave thirst of praise.
  Living, great Nature feared he might outvie
Her works; and dying, fears herself may die.

Of this epitaph the first couplet is good, the second not bad,
the third is deformed with a broken metaphor, the word *crowned*
not being applicable to the *honours* or the *lays*, and the fourth
is not only borrowed from the epitaph on Raphael, but of a very
harsh construction.

IX

On GENERAL HENRY WITHERS. *In Westminster Abbey*, 1729

Here, Withers, rest! thou bravest, gentlest mind,
Thy country's friend, but more of human kind.
O! born to arms! O! worth in youth approved!
O! soft humanity in age beloved!
For thee the hardy veteran drops a tear,
And the gay courtier feels the sigh sincere.

Withers, adieu! yet not with thee remove
Thy martial spirit, or thy social love!
Amidst corruption, luxury, and rage,
Still leave some ancient virtues to our age:
Nor let us say (those English glories gone)
The last true Briton lies beneath this stone.

The epitaph on Withers affords another instance of common-
places, though somewhat diversified by mingled qualities and
the peculiarity of a profession.

The second couplet is abrupt, general, and unpleasing; exclamation seldom succeeds in our language; and I think it
may be observed that the particle O! used at the beginning of
a sentence always offends.

The third couplet is more happy: the value expressed for him,
by different sorts of men, raises him to esteem; there is yet
something of the common cant of superficial satirists, who
suppose that the insincerity of a courtier destroys all his
sensations, and that he is equally a dissembler to the living
and the dead.

At the third couplet I should wish the epitaph to close, but
that I should be unwilling to lose the two next lines, which yet
are dearly bought if they cannot be retained without the four
that follow them.

X

On MR. ELIJAH FENTON. *At Easthampstead, in Berkshire*, 1730

This modest stone, what few vain marbles can,
May truly say, Here lies an honest man:
A poet, blest beyond the poet's fate,
Whom Heaven kept sacred from the Proud and Great:

Foe to loud praise, and friend to learned ease,
Content with science in the vale of peace.
Calmly he looked on either life; and here
Saw nothing to regret, or there to fear;
From Nature's temperate feast rose satisfied,
Thanked Heaven that he lived, and that he died.

The first couplet of this epitaph is borrowed from Crashaw.
The four next lines contain a species of praise peculiar, original,
and just. Here, therefore, the inscription should have ended,
the latter part containing nothing but what is common to every
man who is wise and good. The character of Fenton was
so amiable, that I cannot forbear to wish for some poet or
biographer to display it more fully for the advantage of posterity. If he did not stand in the first rank of genius, he may
claim a place in the second; and, whatever criticism may object
to his writings, censure could find very little to blame in his life.

XI

On Mr. Gay. In Westminster Abbey, 1732

Of manners gentle, of affections mild;
In wit, a man; simplicity, a child:
With native humour tempering virtuous rage,
Formed to delight at once and lash the age:
Above temptation, in a low estate,
And uncorrupted, ev'n among the Great:
A safe companion, and an easy friend,
Unblamed through life, lamented in thy end.
These are thy honours! not that here thy bust
Is mixed with heroes, or with kings thy dust;
But that the Worthy and the Good shall say,
Striking their pensive bosoms—Here lies Gay.

As Gay was the favourite of our author, this epitaph was
probably written with an uncommon degree of attention; yet
it is not more successfully executed than the rest, for it will not
always happen that the success of a poet is proportionate to his
labour. The same observation may be extended to all works of
imagination, which are often influenced by causes wholly out of
the performer's power, by hints of which he perceives not the
origin, by sudden elevations of mind which he cannot
produce in himself, and which sometimes rise when he expects
them least.

The two parts of the first line are only echoes of each other;
gentle manners and *mild affections,* if they mean anything, must
mean the same.

That Gay was a *man in wit* is a very frigid commendation;
to have the wit of a man is not much for a poet The *wit of man,*

and the *simplicity of a child*, make a poor and vulgar contrast, and raise no ideas of excellence, either intellectual or moral.

In the next couplet *rage* is less properly introduced after the mention of *mildness* and *gentleness*, which are made the constituents of his character; for a man so *mild* and *gentle* to *temper* his *rage*, was not difficult.

The next line is inharmonious in its sound, and mean in its conception; the opposition is obvious, and the word *lash*, used absolutely and without any modification, is gross and improper.

To be *above temptation* in poverty and *free from corruption among the great*, is indeed such a peculiarity as deserved notice. But to be a *safe companion* is a praise merely negative, arising not from possession of virtue, but the absence of vice, and that one of the most odious.

As little can be added to his character by asserting that he was *lamented in his end*. Every man that dies is, at least by the writer of his epitaph, supposed to be lamented, and therefore this general lamentation does no honour to Gay.

The first eight lines have no grammar; the adjectives are without any substantive, and the epithets without a subject.

The thought in the last line, that Gay is buried in the bosoms of the *worthy* and the *good*, who are distinguished only to lengthen the line, is so dark that few understand it; and so harsh when it is explained, that still fewer approve.

XII

Intended for SIR ISAAC NEWTON. *In Westminster Abbey*

ISAACUS NEWTONIUS:

Quem Immortalem
Testantur, *Tempus, Natura, Cælum*:
Mortalem
Hoc marmor fatetur.

Nature, and Nature's laws, lay hid in night:
God said, *Let Newton be!* and all was light.

Of this epitaph, short as it is, the faults seem not to be very few. Why part should be Latin and part English, it is not easy to discover. In the Latin the opposition of *Immortalis* and *Mortalis* is a mere sound or a mere quibble; he is not *immortal* in any sense contrary to that in which he is *mortal*.

In the verses the thought is obvious, and the words *night* and *light* are too nearly allied.

XIII

On EDMUND DUKE OF BUCKINGHAM, *who died in the* 19*th year of his age,*
1735

> If modest youth, with cool reflection crowned,
> And every opening virtue blooming round,
> Could save a parent's justest pride from fate,
> Or add one patriot to a sinking state;
> This weeping marble had not asked thy tear,
> Or sadly told how many hopes lie here!
> The living virtue now had shone approved,
> The senate heard him, and his country loved.
> Yet softer honours, and less noisy fame,
> Attend the shade of gentle Buckingham:
> In whom a race, for courage famed and art,
> Ends in the milder merit of the heart:
> And, chiefs or sages long to Britain given,
> Pays the last tribute of a saint to heaven.

This epitaph Mr. Warburton prefers to the rest, but I know
not for what reason. To *crown* with *reflection* is surely a mode
of speech approaching to nonsense. *Opening virtues blooming
round* is something like tautology; the six following lines are
poor and prosaic. *Art* is in another couplet used for *arts*, that
a rhyme may be had to *heart*. The last six lines are the best,
but not excellent.

The rest of his sepulchral performances hardly deserve the
notice of criticism. The contemptible *Dialogue* between HE and
SHE should have been suppressed for the author's sake.

In his last epitaph, *On Himself*, in which he attempts to be
jocular upon one of the few things that make wise men serious,
he confounds the living man with the dead:

> Under this stone, or under this sill,
> Or under this turf, etc.

When a man is once buried, the question under what he
is buried is easily decided. He forgot that though he wrote
the epitaph in a state of uncertainty, yet it could not be laid
over him till his grave was made. Such is the folly of wit when
it is ill employed.

The world has but little new; even this wretchedness seems
to have been borrowed from the following tuneless lines:

> Ludovici Ariosti humantur ossa
> Sub hoc marmore, vel sub hac humo, seu
> Sub quicquid voluit benignus hæres
> Sive hærede benignior comes, seu
> Opportunius incidens Viator:
> Nam scire haud potuit futura, sed nec

> Tanti erat vacuum sibi cadaver
> Ut utnam cuperet parare vivens,
> Vivens ista tamen sibi paravit.
> Quæ inscribi voluit suo sepulchro
> Olim siquod haberetis sepulchrum.

Surely Ariosto did not venture to expect that his trifle would have ever had such an illustrious imitator.

JONATHAN SWIFT

1667–1745

Born in Dublin of English Parents—Educated at Dublin and Oxford—
Enters the Service of Sir William Temple—Becomes acquainted with
Stella—Is introduced to William III.—Is left Sir William Temple's
Literary Executor—His unpromising Appearance as a Poet—Dryden's
Criticism on his Odes—Publishes *The Tale of a Tub*—Sides with the
Whigs under Somers and Godolphin—Seeks the Patronage of Halifax—
Introduced to Harley and St. John—Sides with the Tories—His Political
Influence—Is made Dean of St. Patrick's—His Church Prospects ruined
by the Death of Queen Anne—His two Visits to England—Publishes
Gulliver's Travels—Supposed to have been married to Stella—Stella and
Vanessa—His Services to Ireland—Disappointments and Idiotcy—Death
and Burial in St. Patrick's Cathedral—Works and Character.

An account of Dr. Swift has been already collected, with great
diligence and acuteness, by Dr. Hawkesworth, according to a
scheme which I laid before him in the intimacy of our friendship. I cannot therefore be expected to say much of a life
concerning which I had long since communicated my thoughts
to a man capable of dignifying his narrations with so much
elegance of language and force of sentiment.

Jonathan Swift was, according to an account said to be
written by himself, the son of Jonathan Swift, an attorney,
and was born at Dublin on St. Andrew's Day, 1667: according
to his own report, as delivered by Pope to Spence, he was born
at Leicester, the son of a clergyman, who was minister of a
parish in Herefordshire. During his life the place of his birth
was undetermined. He was contented to be called an Irishman
by the Irish; but would occasionally call himself an Englishman.
The question may, without much regret, be left in the obscurity
in which he delighted to involve it.

Whatever was his birth, his education was Irish. He was sent
at the age of six to the school at Kilkenny, and in his fifteenth
year (1682) was admitted into the University of Dublin.

In his academical studies he was either not diligent or not
happy. It must disappoint every reader's expectation, that
when at the usual time he claimed the Bachelorship of Arts,
he was found by the examiners too conspicuously deficient for

regular admission, and obtained his degree at last by *special favour*; a term used in that university to denote want of merit.

Of this disgrace it may be easily supposed that he was much ashamed, and shame had its proper effect in producing reformation. He resolved from that time to study eight hours a day, and continued his industry for seven years, with what improvement is sufficiently known. This part of his story well deserves to be remembered; it may afford useful admonition and powerful encouragement to men whose abilities have been made for a time useless by their passions or pleasures, and who, having lost one part of life in idleness, are tempted to throw away the remainder in despair.

In this course of daily application he continued three years longer at Dublin; and in this time, if the observation of an old companion may be trusted, he drew the first sketch of his *Tale of a Tub*.

When he was about one-and-twenty (1688), being by the death of Godwin Swift, his uncle, who had supported him, left without subsistence, he went to consult his mother, who then lived at Leicester, about the future course of his life, and by her direction solicited the advice and patronage of Sir William Temple, who had married one of Mrs. Swift's relations, and whose father, Sir John Temple, Master of the Rolls in Ireland, had lived in great familiarity of friendship with Godwin Swift, by whom Jonathan had been to that time maintained.

Temple received with sufficient kindness the nephew of his father's friend, with whom he was, when they conversed together, so much pleased, that he detained him two years in his house. Here he became known to King William, who sometimes visited Temple when he was disabled by the gout, and, being attended by Swift in the garden, showed him how to cut asparagus in the Dutch way.

King William's notions were all military; and he expressed his kindness to Swift by offering to make him a captain of horse.

When Temple removed to Moor Park, he took Swift with him; and when he was consulted by the Earl of Portland about the expedience of complying with a bill then depending for making parliaments triennial, against which King William was strongly prejudiced, after having in vain tried to show the Earl that the proposal involved nothing dangerous to royal power, he sent Swift for the same purpose to the King. Swift, who probably was proud of his employment, and went with all the confidence of a young man, found his arguments, and his art of displaying them, made totally ineffectual by the predetermination of the King; and used to mention this disappointment as his first antidote against vanity.

Before he left Ireland he contracted a disorder, as he thought, by eating too much fruit. The original of diseases is commonly obscure. Almost every boy eats as much fruit as he can get, without any great inconvenience. The disease of Swift was giddiness with deafness, which attacked him from time to time, began very early, pursued him through life, and at last sent him to the grave, deprived of reason.

Being much oppressed at Moor Park by this grievous malady, he was advised to try his native air, and went to Ireland; but, finding no benefit, returned to Sir William, at whose house he continued his studies, and is known to have read, among other books, Cyprian and Irenæus. He thought exercise of great necessity, and used to run half a mile up and down a hill every two hours.

It is easy to imagine that the mode in which his first degree was conferred left him no great fondness for the University of Dublin, and therefore he resolved to become a Master of Arts at Oxford. In the testimonial which he produced, the words of disgrace were omitted; and he took his Master's degree (July 5, 1692) with such reception and regard as fully contented him.

While he lived with Temple, he used to pay his mother at Leicester a yearly visit. He travelled on foot, unless some violence of weather drove him into a waggon, and at night he would go to a penny lodging, where he purchased clean sheets for sixpence. This practice Lord Orrery imputes to his innate love of grossness and vulgarity: some may ascribe it to his desire of surveying human life through all its varieties; and others, perhaps with equal probability, to a passion which seems to have been deep fixed in his heart—the love of a shilling.

In time he began to think that his attendance at Moor Park deserved some other recompence than the pleasure, however mingled with improvement, of Temple's conversation; and grew so impatient, that (1694) he went away in discontent.

Temple, conscious of having given reason for complaint, is said to have made him Deputy Master of the Rolls in Ireland; which, according to his kinsman's account, was an office which he knew him not able to discharge. Swift therefore resolved to enter into the Church, in which he had at first no higher hopes than of the chaplainship to the Factory at Lisbon; but being recommended to Lord Capel [then Lord Lieutenant of Ireland], he obtained the prebend of Kilroot in Connor, of about a hundred pounds a year.

But the infirmities of Temple made a companion like Swift so necessary, that he invited him back, with a promise to procure him English preferment in exchange for the prebend, which he desired him to resign. With this request Swift complied, having perhaps equally repented their separation, and they lived on together with mutual satisfaction; and, in the four years that passed between his return and Temple's death, it is probable that he wrote *The Tale of a Tub* and *The Battle of the Books*.

Swift began early to think, or to hope, that he was a poet, and wrote Pindaric Odes to Temple, to the King, and to the Athenian Society, a knot of obscure men, who published a periodical pamphlet of answers to questions sent, or supposed to be sent, by letters. I have been told that Dryden, having perused these verses, said, "Cousin Swift, you will never be a poet"; and that this denunciation was the motive of Swift's perpetual malevolence to Dryden.

In 1699 Temple died and left a legacy with his manuscripts to Swift, for whom he had obtained from King William a promise of the first prebend that should be vacant at Westminster or Canterbury.

That this promise might not be forgotten, Swift dedicated to the King the posthumous works with which he was intrusted; but neither the dedication nor tenderness for the man whom he once had treated with confidence and fondness revived in King William the remembrance of his promise. Swift awhile attended the Court, but soon found his solicitations hopeless.

He was then invited by the Earl of Berkeley to accompany him into Ireland as his private secretary; but after having done the business till their arrival at Dublin, he then found that one Bushe had persuaded the Earl that a clergyman was not a proper secretary, and had obtained the office for himself. In a man like Swift such circumvention and inconstancy must have excited violent indignation.

But he had yet more to suffer. Lord Berkeley had the disposal of the deanery of Derry, and Swift expected to obtain it, but by the secretary's influence, supposed to have been secured by a bribe, it was bestowed on somebody else; and Swift was dismissed with the livings of Laracor and Rathbeggan, in the diocese of Meath, which together did not equal half the value of the deanery.

At Laracor he increased the parochial duty by reading prayers on Wednesdays and Fridays, and performed all the offices of his profession with great decency and exactness.

Soon after his settlement at Laracor he invited to Ireland the unfortunate Stella, a young woman whose name was Johnson, the daughter of the steward of Sir William Temple, who, in consideration of her father's virtues, left her 1000*l*. With her came Mrs. Dingley, whose whole fortune was 27*l*. a year for her life. With these ladies he passed his hours of relaxation, and to them he opened his bosom; but they never resided in the same house, nor did he see either without a witness. They lived at the Parsonage when Swift was away; and when he returned, removed to a lodging or to the house of a neighbouring clergyman.

Swift was not one of those minds which amaze the world with early pregnancy: his first work, except his few poetical Essays, was the *Dissensions in Athens and Rome*, published (1701) in his thirty-fourth year. After its appearance, paying a visit to some bishop, he heard mention made of the new pamphlet that Burnet had written, replete with political knowledge. When he seemed to doubt Burnet's right to the work, he was told by the Bishop that he was "a young man"; and still persisting to doubt, that he was "a very positive young man."

Three years afterwards (1704) was published *The Tale of a Tub*: of this book charity may be persuaded to think that it might be written by a man of a peculiar character, without ill intention; but it is certainly of dangerous example. That Swift was its author, though it be universally believed, was never owned by himself, nor very well proved by any evidence; but no other claimant can be produced, and he did not deny it when Archbishop Sharp and the Duchess of Somerset, by showing it to the Queen, debarred him from a bishopric.

When this wild work first raised the attention of the public, Sacheverell, meeting Smalridge, tried to flatter him, seeming to think him the author; but Smalridge answered with indignation, "Not all that you and I have in the world, nor all that ever we shall have, should hire me to write *The Tale of a Tub*."

The digressions relating to Wotton and Bentley must be confessed to discover want of knowledge, or want of integrity; he did not understand the two controversies, or he willingly misrepresented them. But wit can stand its ground against truth only a little while. The honours due to learning have been justly distributed by the decision of posterity.

The Battle of the Books is so like the *Combat des Livres,* which the same question concerning the ancients and moderns had produced in France, that the improbability of such a coincidence of thoughts without communication is not, in my opinion, balanced by the anonymous protestation prefixed, in which all knowledge of the French book is peremptorily disowned.

For some time after Swift was probably employed in solitary study, gaining the qualifications requisite for future eminence. How often he visited England, and with what diligence he attended his parishes, I know not. It was not till about four years afterwards that he became a professed author; and then one year (1708) produced *The Sentiments of a Church of England Man,* the ridicule of astrology, under the name of "Bickerstaff" the *Argument against Abolishing Christianity,* and the defence of the *Sacramental Test.*

The Sentiments of a Church of England Man is written with great coolness, moderation, ease, and perspicuity. The *Argument against Abolishing Christianity* is a very happy and judicious irony. One passage in it deserves to be selected:

"If Christianity were once abolished, how could the free-thinkers, the strong reasoners, and the men of profound learning be able to find another subject so calculated, in all points, whereon to display their abilities? What wonderful productions of wit should we be deprived of from those whose genius by continual practice has been wholly turned upon raillery and invectives against religion, and would therefore never be able to shine, or distinguish themselves, upon any other subject! We are daily complaining of the great decline of wit among us, and would we take away the greatest, perhaps the only topic we have left? Who would ever have suspected Asgill for a wit, or Toland for a philosopher, if the inexhaustible stock of Christianity had not been at hand to provide them with materials? What other subject, through all art or nature, could have produced Tindal for a profound author, or furnished him with readers? It is the wise choice of the subject that alone adorns and distinguishes the writer; for had a hundred such pens as these been employed on the side of religion, they would have immediately sunk into silence and oblivion."

The reasonableness of a *test* is not hard to be proved; but perhaps it must be allowed that the proper test has not been chosen.

The attention paid to the papers published under the name of "Bickerstaff" induced Steele, when he projected *The Tatler,* to assume an appellation which had already gained possession of the reader's notice.

In the year following [1709] he wrote a *Project for the Advancement of Religion*, addressed to Lady Berkeley, by whose kindness it is not unlikely that he was advanced to his benefices. To this project, which is formed with great purity of intention, and displayed with sprightliness and elegance, it can only be objected that, like many projects, it is, if not generally impracticable, yet evidently hopeless, as it supposes more zeal, concord, and perseverance than a view of mankind gives reason for expecting.

He wrote likewise this year [1709] a *Vindication of Bickerstaff*, and an explanation of an *Ancient Prophecy*, part written after the facts, and the rest never completed, but well planned to excite amazement.

Soon after began the busy and important part of Swift's life. He was employed (1710) by the primate of Ireland to solicit the Queen for a remission of the First Fruits and Twentieth parts to the Irish clergy. With this purpose he had recourse to Mr. Harley, to whom he was mentioned as a man neglected and oppressed by the last ministry because he had refused to co-operate with some of their schemes. What he had refused has never been told; what he had suffered was, I suppose, the exclusion from a bishopric by the remonstrances of Sharp, whom he describes as "the harmless tool of others' hate," and whom he represents as afterwards "suing for pardon."

Harley's designs and situation were such as made him glad of an auxiliary so well qualified for his service; he therefore soon admitted him to familiarity—whether ever to confidence some have made a doubt; but it would have been difficult to excite his zeal without persuading him that he was trusted, and not very easy to delude him by false persuasions.

He was certainly admitted to those meetings in which the first hints and original plan of action are supposed to have been formed, and was one of the sixteen ministers, or agents of the ministry, who met weekly at each other's houses, and were united by the name of "Brother."

Being not immediately considered as an obdurate Tory, he conversed indiscriminately with all the wits, and was yet the friend of Steele, who, in *The Tatler*, which began in April 1709, confesses the advantage of his conversation, and mentions something contributed by him to his paper. But he was now immerging into political controversy; for the year 1710 produced *The Examiner*, of which Swift wrote thirty-three papers. In argument he may be allowed to have the advantage; for where a wide system of conduct, and the whole of a public character, is laid open to inquiry, the accuser, having the choice of facts, must be very unskilful if he does not prevail; but with regard to wit, I am afraid none of Swift's papers will be found equal to those by which Addison opposed him.

He wrote in the year 1711 a *Letter to the October Club*, a number of Tory gentlemen sent from the country to Parliament, who formed themselves into a club to the number of about a hundred, and met to animate the zeal and raise the expectations of each other. They thought, with great reason, that the ministers were losing opportunities; that sufficient use was not made of the ardour of the nation; they called loudly for more changes and stronger efforts; and demanded the punishment of part, and the dismission of the rest, of those whom they considered as public robbers.

Their eagerness was not gratified by the Queen or by Harley. The Queen was probably slow because she was afraid, and Harley was slow because he was doubtful: he was a Tory only by necessity, or for convenience; and, when he had power in his hands, had no settled purpose for which he should employ it; forced to gratify to a certain degree the Tories who supported him, but unwilling to make his reconcilement to the Whigs utterly desperate, he corresponded at once with the two expectants of the Crown, and kept, as has been observed, the succession undetermined. Not knowing what to do, he did nothing; and, with the fate of a double dealer, at last he lost his power, but kept his enemies.

Swift seems to have concurred in opinion with the October Club, but it was not in his power to quicken the tardiness of Harley, whom he stimulated as much as he could, but with little effect. He that knows not whither to go is in no haste to move. Harley, who was perhaps not quick by nature, became yet more slow by irresolution; and was content to hear that dilatoriness lamented as natural, which he applauded in himself as politic.

Without the Tories, however, nothing could be done; and as they were not to be gratified they must be appeased, and the conduct of the minister, if it could not be vindicated, was to be plausibly excused.

Early in the next year [1712] he published a *Proposal for Correcting, Improving, and Ascertaining the English Tongue*, in a letter to the Earl of Oxford, written without much knowledge of the general nature of language, and without any accurate inquiry into the history of other tongues. The certainty and stability which, contrary to all experience, he thinks attainable, he proposes to secure by instituting an academy; the decrees of which every man would have been willing, and many would have been proud to disobey, and which, being renewed by successive elections, would in a short time have differed from itself.

Swift now attained the zenith of his political importance: he published (1712) *The Conduct of the Allies*, ten days before the parliament assembled. The purpose was to persuade the nation to a peace, and never had any writer more success. The people, who had been amused with bonfires and triumphal processions, and looked with idolatry on the General [Marlborough] and his friends, and who, as they thought, had made England the arbitress of nations, were confounded between shame and rage when they found that "mines had been exhausted and millions destroyed" to secure the Dutch or aggrandise the Emperor, without any advantage to ourselves; that we had been bribing our neighbours to fight their own quarrel, and that amongst our enemies we might number our allies.

That is now no longer doubted, of which the nation was then first informed, that the war was unnecessarily protracted to fill the pockets of Marlborough; and that it would have been continued without end if he could have continued his annual plunder. But Swift, I suppose, did not yet know what he has since written, that a commission was drawn which would have appointed him General for life, had it not become ineffectual by the resolution of Lord Cowper, who refused the seal.

"Whatever is received," say the schools, "is received in proportion to the recipient." The power of a political treatise depends much upon the disposition of the people; the nation was then combustible, and a spark set it on fire. It is boasted, that between November and January eleven thousand were sold; a great number at that time, when we were not yet a nation of readers. To its propagation certainly no agency of power or influence was wanting. It furnished arguments for conversation, speeches for debate, and materials for parliamentary resolutions.

Yet surely whoever surveys this wonder-working pamphlet with cool perusal, will confess that its efficacy was supplied by the passions of its readers; that it operates by the mere weight of facts, with very little assistance from the hand that produced them.

This year (1712) he published his *Reflections on the Barrier Treaty*, which carries on the design of his *Conduct of the Allies*, and shows how little regard in that negotiation had been shown to the interest of England, and how much of the conquered country had been demanded by the Dutch.

This was followed by *Remarks on the Bishop of Sarum's Introduction to his Third Volume of the History of the Reformation*; a pamphlet which Burnet published as an alarm, to warn the nation of the approach of Popery. Swift, who seems to have disliked the Bishop with something more than political aversion, treats him like one on whom he is glad of an opportunity to insult.

Swift being now [1712–14] the declared favourite and supposed confidant of the Tory ministry, was treated by all that depended on the Court with the respect which dependents know how to pay. He soon began to feel part of the misery of greatness; he that could say that he knew him, considered himself as having fortune in his power. Commissions, solicitations, remonstrances, crowded about him; he was expected to do every man's business, to procure employment for one, and to retain it for another. In assisting those who addressed him, he represents himself as sufficiently diligent; and desires to have others believe, what he probably believed himself, that by his interposition many Whigs of merit, and among them Addison and Congreve, were continued in their places. But every man of known influence has so many petitions which he cannot grant, that he must necessarily offend more than he gratifies, because the preference given to one affords all the rest reason for complaint. "When I give away a place," said Louis XIV., "I make a hundred discontented, and one ungrateful."

Much has been said of the equality and independence which he preserved in his conversation with the ministers, of the frankness of his remonstrances, and the familiarity of his friendship. In accounts of this kind a few single incidents are set against the general tenor of behaviour. No man, however, can pay a more servile tribute to the great than by suffering his liberty in their presence to aggrandise him in his own esteem. Between different ranks of the community there is necessarily some distance: he who is called by his superior to pass the interval, may properly accept the invitation; but petulance and obtrusion are rarely produced by magnanimity, nor have often any nobler cause than the pride of importance and the malice of inferiority. He who knows himself necessary may set, while that necessity lasts, a high value upon himself; as, in a lower condition, a servant eminently skilful may be saucy; but he is saucy only because he is servile. Swift appears to have preserved the kindness of the great when they wanted him no longer; and therefore it must be allowed that the childish freedom, to which he seems enough inclined, was overpowered by his better qualities.

His disinterestedness has been likewise mentioned; a strain of heroism which would have been in his condition romantic and superfluous. Ecclesiastical benefices, when they become vacant, must be given away; and the friends of power may, if there be no inherent disqualification, reasonably expect them. Swift accepted (April 1713) the deanery of St. Patrick, the best preferment that his friends could venture to give him. That ministry was in a great degree supported by the clergy, who were not yet reconciled to the author of *The Tale of a Tub,* and would not, without much discontent and indignation, have borne to see him installed in an English cathedral.

He refused, indeed, 50l. from Lord Oxford; but he accepted afterwards a draft of 1000l. upon the Exchequer, which was intercepted by the Queen's death, and which he resigned, as he says himself, *"multa gemens,* with many a groan."

In the midst of his power and his politics [1710-13] he kept a Journal of his visits, his walks, his interviews with ministers, and quarrels with his servant, and transmitted it to Mrs. Johnson and Mrs. Dingley, to whom he knew that whatever befel him was interesting, and no accounts could be too minute. Whether these diurnal trifles were properly exposed to eyes which had never received any pleasure from the presence of the Dean, may be reasonably doubted; they have, however, some odd attraction; the reader, finding frequent mention of names which he has been used to consider as important, goes on in hope of information; and, as there is nothing to fatigue attention, if he is disappointed he can hardly complain. It is easy to perceive from every page that though ambition pressed Swift into a life of bustle, the wish for a life of ease was always returning.

He went [June 1713] to take possession of his deanery as soon as he had obtained it; but he was not suffered to stay in Ireland more than a fortnight before he was recalled to England, that he might reconcile Lord Oxford and Lord

Bolingbroke, who began to look on one another with malevolence, which every day increased, and which Bolingbroke appeared to retain in his last years.

Swift contrived an interview, from which they both departed discontented: he procured a second, which only convinced him that the feud was irreconcileable; he told them his opinion, that all was lost. This denunciation was contradicted by Oxford; but Bolingbroke whispered that he was right.

Before this violent dissension had shattered the ministry, Swift had published, in the beginning of the year 1714, *The Public Spirit of the Whigs*, in answer to *The Crisis*, a pamphlet for which Steele was expelled from the House of Commons. Swift was now so far alienated from Steele as to think him no longer entitled to decency, and therefore treats him sometimes with contempt, and sometimes with abhorrence.

In this pamphlet the Scotch were mentioned in terms so provoking to that irritable nation, that, resolving "not to be offended with impunity," the Scotch Lords in a body demanded an audience of the Queen, and solicited reparation. A proclamation was issued, in which 300*l.* was offered for discovery of the author. From this storm he was, as he relates, "secured by a sleight"; of what kind, or by whose prudence, is not known; and such was the increase of his reputation, that the Scottish "Nation applied again that he would be their friend."

He was become so formidable to the Whigs, that his familiarity with the ministers was clamoured at in Parliament, particularly by two men afterwards of great note, Aislabie and Walpole.

But, by the disunion of his great friends, his importance and designs were now at an end; and seeing his services at last useless, he retired about June (1714) into Berkshire, where, in the house of a friend, he wrote what was then suppressed, but has since appeared under the title of *Free Thoughts on the present State of Affairs*.

While he was waiting in his retirement for events which time or chance might bring to pass, the death of the Queen [1st Aug., 1714] broke down at once the whole system of Tory politics; and nothing remained but to withdraw from the implacability of triumphant Whiggism, and shelter himself in unenvied obscurity.

The accounts of his reception in Ireland, given by Lord Orrery and Dr. Delany, are so different, that the credit of the writers, both undoubtedly veracious, cannot be saved but by supposing, what I think is true, that they speak of different times. When Delany says that he was received with respect, he means for the first fortnight, when he came to take legal possession; and when Lord Orrery tells that he was pelted by the populace, he is to be understood of the time when, after the Queen's death, he became a settled resident.

The Archbishop of Dublin gave him at first some disturbance in the exercise of his jurisdiction; but it was soon discovered that between prudence and integrity he was seldom in the wrong; and that, when he was right, his spirit did not easily yield to opposition.

Having so lately quitted the tumults of a party and the intrigues of a court, they still kept his thoughts in agitation, as the sea fluctuates a while when the storm has ceased. He therefore filled his hours with some historical attempts, relating to the "Change of the Ministers," and the "Conduct of the Ministry." He likewise is said to have written a *History of the Four last Years of Queen Anne,* which he began in her lifetime, and afterwards laboured with great attention, but never published. It was after his death in the hands of Lord Orrery and Dr. King. A book under that title was published [1758], with Swift's name, by Dr. Lucas; of which I can only say, that it seemed by no means to correspond with the notions that I had formed of it from a conversation which I once heard between the Earl of Orrery and old Mr. Lewis.

Swift now, much against his will, commenced Irishman for life, and was to contrive how he might be best accommodated in a country where he considered himself as in a state of exile. It seems that his first recourse was to piety. The thoughts of death rushed upon him at this time with such incessant importunity, that they took possession of his mind, when he first waked, for many years together.

He opened his house by a public table two days a week, and found his entertainments gradually frequented by more and more visitants of learning among the men, and of elegance among the women. Mrs. Johnson had left the country and lived in lodgings not far from the deanery. On his public days she regulated the table, but appeared at it as a mere guest, like other ladies.

On other days he often dined, at a stated price, with Mr. Worrall, a clergyman of his cathedral, whose house was recommended by the peculiar neatness and pleasantry of his wife. To this frugal mode of living he was first disposed by care to pay some debts which he had contracted, and he continued it for the pleasure of accumulating money. His avarice, however, was not suffered to obstruct the claims of his dignity;

he was served in plate, and used to say that he was the poorest gentleman in Ireland that eat upon plate, and the richest that lived without a coach.

How he spent the rest of his time, and how he employed his hours of study, has been inquired with hopeless curiosity. For who can give an account of another's studies? Swift was not likely to admit any to his privacies, or to impart a minute account of his business or his leisure.

Soon after (1716), in his forty-ninth year, he was privately married to Mrs. Johnson, by Dr. Ashe, Bishop of Clogher, as Dr. Madden told me, in the garden. The marriage made no change in their mode of life; they lived in different houses, as before; nor did she ever lodge in the deanery but when Swift was seized with a fit of giddiness. "It would be difficult," says Lord Orrery, "to prove that they were ever afterwards together without a third person."

The Dean of St. Patrick's lived in a private manner, known and regarded only by his friends, till, about the year 1720, he, by a pamphlet, recommended to the Irish the use, and consequently the improvement, of their manufacture. For a man to use the productions of his own labour is surely a natural right, and to like best what he makes himself is a natural passion. But to excite this passion, and enforce this right, appeared so criminal to those who had an interest in the English trade, that the printer was imprisoned; and, as Hawkesworth justly observes, the attention of the public being by this outrageous resentment turned upon the proposal, the author was by consequence made popular.

In 1723 died [at Celbridge, near Dublin] Mrs. [Esther] Van Homrigh, a woman made unhappy by her admiration of wit, and ignominiously distinguished by the name of Vanessa, whose conduct has been already sufficiently discussed, and whose history is too well known to be minutely repeated. She was a young woman fond of literature, whom Decanus the Dean, called Cadenus by transposition of the letters, took pleasure in directing and instructing; till, from being proud of his praise, she grew fond of his person. Swift was then about forty-seven, at an age when vanity is strongly excited by the amorous attention of a young woman. If it be said that Swift should have checked a passion which he never meant to gratify, recourse must be had to that extenuation which he so much despised, "men are but men": perhaps, however, he did not at first know his own mind, and, as he represents himself, was undetermined.

For his admission of her courtship, and his indulgence of her hopes after his marriage to Stella, no other honest plea can be found, than that he delayed a disagreeable discovery from time to time, dreading the immediate bursts of distress, and watching for a favourable moment. She thought herself neglected, and died of disappointment; having ordered by her will the poem to be published, in which Cadenus had proclaimed her excellence, and confessed his love. The effect of the publication upon the Dean and Stella is thus related by Delany:

"I have good reason to believe that they both were greatly shocked and distressed (though it may be differently) upon this occasion. The Dean made a tour to the south of Ireland, for about two months, at this time, to dissipate his thoughts, and give place to obloquy; and Stella retired (upon the earnest invitation of the owner) to the house of a cheerful, generous, good-natured friend of the Dean's, whom she also much loved and honoured. There my informer often saw her; and, I have reason to believe, used his utmost endeavours to relieve, support, and amuse her, in this sad situation.

"One little incident he told me of, on that occasion, I think I shall never forget. As her friend was an hospitable, open-hearted man, well-beloved, and largely acquainted, it happened one day that some gentlemen dropt in to dinner, who were strangers to Stella's situation; and as the poem of *Cadenus and Vanessa* was then the general topic of conversation, one of them said, 'Surely that Vanessa must be an extraordinary woman, that could inspire the Dean to write so finely upon her.' Mrs. Johnson smiled, and answered, 'that she thought that point not quite so clear; for it was well known the Dean could write finely upon a broomstick.'"

The great acquisition of esteem and influence was made by the *Drapier's Letters* in 1724. One Wood, of Wolverhampton in Staffordshire, a man enterprising and rapacious, had, as is said, by a present to the Duchess of Munster, obtained a patent, empowering him to coin one hundred and eighty thousand pounds of halfpence and farthings for the kingdom of Ireland, in which there was a very inconvenient and embarrassing scarcity of copper coin; so that it was impossible to run in debt upon the credit of a piece of money; for the cook or keeper of an alehouse could not refuse to supply a man that had silver in his hand, and the buyer would not leave his money without change.

The project was therefore plausible. The scarcity, which

was already great, Wood took care to make greater, by agents who gathered up the old halfpence; and was about to turn his brass into gold, by pouring the treasures of his new mint upon Ireland, when Swift, finding that the metal was debased to an enormous degree, wrote Letters, under the name of "M. B. Drapier," to show the folly of receiving, and the mischief that must ensue by giving, gold and silver for coin worth perhaps not a third part of its nominal value.

The nation was alarmed; the new coin was universally refused; but the governors of Ireland considered resistance to the King's patent as highly criminal; and one Whitshed, then Chief Justice, who had tried the printer of the former pamphlet, and sent out the jury nine times, till by clamour and menaces they were frightened into a special verdict, now presented the *Drapier*, but could not prevail on the grand jury to find the bill.

Lord Carteret and the Privy Council published [1724] a proclamation, offering 300*l.* for discovering the author of the Fourth Letter. Swift had concealed himself from his printers, and trusted only his butler, who transcribed the paper. The man, immediately after the appearance of the proclamation, strolled from the house, and stayed out all night and part of the next day. There was reason enough to fear that he had betrayed his master for the reward; but he came home, and the Dean ordered him to put off his livery and leave the house; "for," says he, "I know that my life is in your power, and I will not bear, out of fear, either your insolence or negligence." The man excused his fault with great submission, and begged that he might be confined in the house while it was in his power to endanger his master; but the Dean resolutely turned him out, without taking farther notice of him, till the term of information had expired, and then received him again. Soon afterwards he ordered him and the rest of the servants into his presence, without telling his intentions, and bade them take notice that their fellow-servant was no longer Robert the butler, but that his integrity had made him Mr. Blakeley, verger of St. Patrick's; an officer whose income was between thirty and forty pounds a year: yet he still continued for some years to serve his old master as his butler.

Swift was known from this time by the appellation of *The Dean*. He was honoured by the populace as the champion, patron, and instructor of Ireland; and gained such power as, considered both in its extent and duration, scarcely any man has ever enjoyed without greater wealth or higher station.

He was from this important year the oracle of the traders, and the idol of the rabble, and by consequence was feared and courted by all to whom the kindness of the traders or the populace were necessary. The *Drapier* was a sign; the *Drapier* was a health; and which way soever the eye or the ear was turned, some tokens were found of the nation's gratitude to the *Drapier*.

The benefit was indeed great: he had rescued Ireland from a very oppressive and predatory invasion; and the popularity which he had gained he was diligent to keep, by appearing forward and zealous on every occasion where the public interest was supposed to be involved. Nor did he much scruple to boast his influence; for when, upon some attempts to regulate the coin, Archbishop Boulter, then one of the justices, accused him of exasperating the people, he exculpated himself by saying, "If I had lifted up my finger, they would have torn you to pieces."

But the pleasure of popularity was soon interrupted by domestic misery. Mrs. Johnson, whose conversation was to him the great softener of the ills of life, began in the year of the *Drapier's* triumph to decline; and two years afterwards [1726] was so wasted with sickness, that her recovery was considered as hopeless.

Swift was then [1726] in England, and had been invited by Lord Bolingbroke to pass the winter with him in France; but this call of calamity hastened him to Ireland, where perhaps his presence contributed to restore her to imperfect and tottering health.

He was now so much at ease, that (1727) he returned to England, where he collected three volumes of *Miscellanies* in conjunction with Pope, who prefixed a querulous and apologetical Preface.

This important year [1727] sent likewise into the world *Gulliver's Travels*, a production so new and strange, that it filled the reader with a mingled emotion of merriment and amazement. It was received with such avidity, that the price of the first edition was raised before the second could be made; it was read by the high and the low, the learned and illiterate. Criticism was for a while lost in wonder; no rules of judgment were applied to a book written in open defiance of truth and regularity. But when distinctions came to be made, the part which gave the least pleasure was that which describes the Flying Island, and that which gave most disgust must be the history of the Houyhnhnms.

While Swift was enjoying the reputation of his new work, the news of the King's death [June 1727] arrived; and he kissed the hands of the new King and Queen [George II. and Queen Caroline] three days after their accession.

By the Queen, when she was Princess, he had been treated with some distinction, and was well received by her in her exaltation; but whether she gave hopes which she never took care to satisfy, or he formed expectations which she never meant to raise, the event was, that he always afterwards thought on her with malevolence, and particularly charged her with breaking her promise of some medals which she engaged to send him.

I know not whether she had not in her turn some reason for complaint. A letter was sent her, not so much entreating as requiring her patronage of Mrs. Barber, an ingenious Irish-woman, who was then begging subscriptions for her poems. To this letter was subscribed the name of Swift, and it has all the appearances of his diction and sentiments; but it was not written in his hand, and had some little improprieties. When he was charged with this letter, he laid hold of the inaccuracies and urged the improbability of the accusation, but never denied it: he shuffles between cowardice and veracity, and talks big when he says nothing.

He seemed desirous enough of recommencing courtier, and endeavoured to gain the kindness of Mrs. Howard, remembering what Mrs. Masham had performed in former times; but his flatteries were, like those of other wits, unsuccessful; the lady either wanted power or had no ambition of poetical immortality.

He was seized not long afterwards by a fit of giddiness, and again heard of the sickness and danger of Mrs. Johnson. He then left [Sept. 1727] the house of Pope, as it seems, with very little ceremony, finding "that two sick friends cannot live together"; and did not write to him till he found himself at Chester.

He returned to a home of sorrow: poor Stella was sinking into the grave, and, after a languishing decay of about two months, died in her forty-fourth year, on January 28, 1727–8. How much he wished her life his papers show; nor can it be doubted that he dreaded the death of her whom he loved most, aggravated by the consciousness that himself had hastened it.

Beauty and the power of pleasing, the greatest external advantages that woman can desire or possess, were fatal to the unfortunate Stella. The man whom she had the misfortune to love was, as Delany observes, fond of singularity and desirous to make a mode of happiness for himself, different from the general course of things and order of Providence. From the time of her arrival in Ireland he seems resolved to keep her in his power, and therefore hindered a match sufficiently advantageous by accumulating unreasonable demands and prescribing conditions that could not be performed. While she was at her own disposal he did not consider his possession as secure; resentment, ambition, or caprice might separate them; he was therefore resolved to make "assurance doubly sure," and to appropriate her by a private marriage, to which he had annexed the expectation of all the pleasures of perfect friendship without the uneasiness of conjugal restraint. But with this state poor Stella was not satisfied; she never was treated as a wife, and to the world she had the appearance of a mistress. She lived sullenly on, in hope that in time he would own and receive her; but the time did not come till the change of his manners and depravation of his mind made her tell him, when he offered to acknowledge her, that "it was too late." She then gave up herself to sorrowful resentment, and died under the tyranny of him by whom she was in the highest degree loved and honoured.

What were her claims to this eccentric tenderness, by which the laws of nature were violated to retain her, curiosity will inquire; but how shall it be gratified? Swift was a lover; his testimony may be suspected. Delany and the Irish saw with Swift's eyes, and therefore add little confirmation. That she was virtuous, beautiful, and elegant, in a very high degree, such admiration from such a lover makes it very probable; but she had not much literature, for she could not spell her own language; and of her wit, so loudly vaunted, the smart sayings which Swift himself has collected afford no splendid specimen.

The reader of Swift's *Letter to a Lady on her Marriage* may be allowed to doubt whether his opinion of female excellence ought implicitly to be admitted; for if his general thoughts on women were such as he exhibits, a very little sense in a lady would enrapture and a very little virtue would astonish him. Stella's supremacy therefore was perhaps only local; she was great because her associates were little.

In some remarks lately published on the Life of Swift, his marriage is mentioned as fabulous or doubtful; but, alas! poor Stella, as Dr. Madden told me, related her melancholy story to Dr. Sheridan when he attended her as a clergyman to prepare her for death; and Delany mentions it not with doubt, but only with regret. Swift never mentioned her without a sigh.

The rest of his life [1728-45] was spent in Ireland—in a country to which not even power almost despotic, nor flattery almost idolatrous, could reconcile him. He sometimes wished to visit England, but always found some reason to delay. He tells Pope, in the decline of life, that he hopes once more to see him; "but if not," says he, "we must part as all human beings have parted."

After the death of Stella his benevolence was contracted and his severity exasperated; he drove his acquaintance from his table and wondered why he was deserted. But he continued his attention to the public, and wrote from time to time such directions, admonitions, or censures, as the exigency of affairs, in his opinion, made proper; and nothing fell from his pen in vain.

In a short poem on the Presbyterians, whom he always regarded with detestation, he bestowed [1733-4] one stricture upon Bettesworth, a lawyer eminent for his insolence to the clergy, which, from very considerable reputation, brought him into immediate and universal contempt. Bettesworth, enraged at his disgrace and loss, went to Swift and demanded whether he was the author of that poem? "Mr. Bettesworth," answered he, "I was in my youth acquainted with great lawyers, who, knowing my disposition to satire, advised me that if any scoundrel or blockhead whom I had lampooned should ask, 'Are you the author of this paper?' I should tell him that I was not the author; and therefore I tell you, Mr. Bettesworth, that I am not the author of these lines."

Bettesworth was so little satisfied with this account that he publicly professed his resolution of a violent and corporal revenge; but the inhabitants of St. Patrick's district embodied themselves in the Dean's defence. Bettesworth declared in Parliament that Swift had deprived him of 1200*l.* a year.

Swift was popular awhile by another mode of beneficence. He set aside some hundreds to be lent in small sums to the poor, from 5*s.*, I think, to 5*l.* He took no interest, and only required that, at repayment, a small fee should be given to the accountant: but he required that the day of promised payment should be exactly kept. A severe and punctilious temper is ill qualified for transactions with the poor; the day was often broken, and the loan was not repaid. This might have been easily foreseen; but for this Swift had made no provision of patience or pity. He ordered his debtors to be sued. A severe creditor has no popular character; what then was likely to be said of him who employs the catchpoll under the appearance of charity? The clamour against him was loud, and the resentment of the populace outrageous; he was therefore forced to drop his scheme and own the folly of expecting punctuality from the poor.

His asperity continually increasing condemned him to solitude; and his resentment of solitude sharpened his asperity. He was not, however, totally deserted; some men of learning and some women of elegance often visited him; and he wrote from time to time either verse or prose; of his verses he willingly gave copies, and is supposed to have felt no discontent when he saw them printed. His favourite maxim was "Vive la bagatelle": he thought trifles a necessary part of life, and perhaps found them necessary to himself. It seems impossible to him to be idle, and his disorders made it difficult or dangerous to be long seriously studious or laboriously diligent. The love of ease is always gaining upon age, and he had one temptation to petty amusements peculiar to himself: whatever he did he was sure to hear applauded; and such was his predominance over all that approached, that all their applauses were probably sincere. He that is much flattered soon learns to flatter himself: we are commonly taught our duty by fear or shame, and how can they act upon the man who hears nothing but his own praises?

As his years increased, his fits of giddiness and deafness grew more frequent, and his deafness made conversation difficult: they grew likewise more severe, till in 1736, as he was writing a poem called *The Legion Club*, he was seized with a fit so painful and so long continued that he never after thought it proper to attempt any work of thought or labour.

He was always careful of his money, and was therefore no liberal entertainer; but was less frugal of his wine than of his meat. When his friends of either sex came to him in expectation of a dinner, his custom was to give every one a shilling that they might please themselves with their provision. At last his avarice grew too powerful for his kindness; he would refuse a bottle of wine, and in Ireland no man visits where he cannot drink.

Having thus excluded conversation and desisted from study, he had neither business nor amusement; for, having by some ridiculous resolution or mad vow determined never to wear spectacles, he could make little use of books in his later years: his ideas therefore, being neither renovated by discourse nor increased by reading, wore gradually away and left his mind vacant to the vexations of the hour, till at last his anger was heightened into madness.

He however permitted one book to be published, which had been the production of former years, *Polite Conversation*, which appeared in 1738. The *Directions for Servants* was printed soon after his death. These two performances show a mind incessantly attentive, and, when it was not employed upon great things, busy with minute occurrences. It is apparent that he must have had the habit of noting whatever he observed; for such a number of particulars could never have been assembled by the power of recollection.

He grew more violent; and his mental powers declined, till (1741) it was found necessary that legal guardians should be appointed of his person and fortune. He now lost distinction. His madness was compounded of rage and fatuity. The last face that he knew was that of Mrs. Whiteway; and her he ceased to know in a little time. His meat was brought him cut into mouthfuls; but he would never touch it while the servant stayed, and at last, after it had stood perhaps an hour, would eat it walking; for he continued his old habit, and was on his feet ten hours a day.

Next year (1742) he had an inflammation in his left eye, which swelled it to the size of an egg, with boils in other parts; he was kept long waking with the pain, and was not easily restrained by five attendants from tearing out his eye.

The tumour at last subsided; and a short interval of reason ensuing, in which he knew his physician and his family, gave hopes of his recovery; but in a few days he sunk into lethargic stupidity, motionless, heedless, and speechless. But it is said, that, after a year of total silence, when his housekeeper, on the 30th of November, told him that the usual bonfires and illuminations were preparing to celebrate his birthday, he answered, "It is all folly; they had better let it alone."

It is remembered, that he afterwards spoke now and then, or gave some intimation of a meaning; but at last sunk into a perfect silence, which continued till about the end of October 1745, when, in his seventy-eighth year, he expired without a struggle.

When Swift is considered as an author, it is just to estimate his powers by their effects. In the reign of Queen Anne he turned the stream of popularity against the Whigs, and must be confessed to have dictated for a time the political opinions of the English nation. In the succeeding reign he delivered Ireland from plunder and oppression; and showed that wit, confederated with truth, had such force as authority was unable to resist. He said truly of himself, that Ireland "was his debtor." It was from the time when he first began to patronise the Irish that they may date their riches and prosperity. He taught them first to know their own interest, their weight, and their strength, and gave them spirit to assert that equality with their fellow-subjects to which they have ever since been making vigorous advances, and to claim those rights which they have at last established. Nor can they be charged with ingratitude to their benefactor; for they reverenced him as a guardian and obeyed him as a dictator.

In his works he has given very different specimens both of sentiments and expression. His *Tale of a Tub* has little resemblance to his other pieces. It exhibits a vehemence and rapidity of mind, a copiousness of images, and vivacity of diction, such as he afterwards never possessed or never exerted. It is of a mode so distinct and peculiar, that it must be considered by itself; what is true of that, is not true of anything else which he has written.

In his other works is found an equable tenor of easy language, which rather trickles than flows. His delight was in simplicity. That he has in his works no metaphor, as has been said, is not true; but his few metaphors seem to be received rather by necessity than choice. He studied purity; and though perhaps all his strictures are not exact, yet it is not often that solecisms can be found; and whoever depends on his authority may generally conclude himself safe. His sentences are never too much dilated or contracted; and it will not be easy to find any embarrassment in the complication of his clauses, any inconsequence in his connections, or abruptness in his transitions.

His style was well suited to his thoughts, which are never subtilised by nice disquisitions, decorated by sparkling conceits, elevated by ambitious sentences, or variegated by far-sought learning. He pays no court to the passions; he excites neither surprise nor admiration; he always understands himself, and his readers always understand him: the peruser of Swift wants little previous knowledge; it will be sufficient that he is acquainted with common words and common things; he is neither required to mount elevations nor to explore profundities;

his passage is always on a level, along solid ground, without asperities, without obstruction.

This easy and safe conveyance of meaning it was Swift's desire to attain, and for having attained he deserves praise, though perhaps not the highest praise. For purposes merely didactic, when something is to be told that was not known before, it is the best mode; but against that inattention by which known truths are suffered to lie neglected, it makes no provision; it instructs, but does not persuade.

By his political education he was associated with the Whigs; but he deserted them when they deserted their principles, yet without running into the contrary extreme; he continued throughout his life to retain the disposition which he assigns to the "Church-of-England Man," of thinking commonly with the Whigs of the State and with the Tories of the Church.

He was a churchman rationally zealous; he desired the prosperity and maintained the honour of the clergy; of the dissenters he did not wish to infringe the toleration, but he opposed their encroachments.

To his duty as dean he was very attentive. He managed the revenues of his church with exact economy; and it is said by Delany that more money was, under his direction, laid out in repairs than had ever been in the same time since its first erection. Of his choir he was eminently careful; and, though he neither loved nor understood music, took care that all the singers were well qualified, admitting none without the testimony of skilful judges.

In his church he restored the practice of weekly communion, and distributed the sacramental elements in the most solemn and devout manner with his own hand. He came to church every morning, preached commonly in his turn, and attended the evening anthem, that it might not be negligently performed.

He read the service "rather with a strong, nervous voice than in a graceful manner; his voice was sharp and high-toned, rather than harmonious."

He entered upon the clerical state with hope to excel in preaching; but complained, that, from the time of his political controversies, "he could only preach pamphlets." This censure of himself, if judgment be made from those sermons which have been printed, was unreasonably severe.

The suspicions of his irreligion proceeded in a great measure from his dread of hypocrisy; instead of wishing to seem better, he delighted in seeming worse than he was. He went in London to early prayers, lest he should be seen at church; he read prayers to his servants every morning with such dexterous secrecy, that Dr. Delany was six months in his house before he knew it. He was not only careful to hide the good which he did, but willingly incurred the suspicion of evil which he did not. He forgot what himself had formerly asserted, that hypocrisy is less mischievous than open impiety. Dr. Delany, with all his zeal for his honour, has justly condemned this part of his character.

The person of Swift had not many recommendations. He had a kind of muddy complexion, which, though he washed himself with Oriental scrupulosity, did not look clear. He had a countenance sour and severe, which he seldom softened by any appearance of gaiety. He stubbornly resisted any tendency to laughter.

To his domestics he was naturally rough; and a man of a rigorous temper, with that vigilance of minute attention which his works discover, must have been a master that few could bear. That he was disposed to do his servants good, on important occasions, is no great mitigation; benefaction can be but rare, and tyrannic peevishness is perpetual. He did not spare the servants of others. Once, when he dined alone with the Earl of Orrery, he said of one that waited in the room, "That man has, since we sat to the table, committed fifteen faults." What the faults were, Lord Orrery, from whom I heard the story, had not been attentive enough to discover. My number may perhaps not be exact.

In his economy he practised a peculiar and offensive parsimony, without disguise or apology. The practice of saving being once necessary, became habitual, and grew first ridiculous, and at last detestable. But his avarice, though it might exclude pleasure, was never suffered to encroach upon his virtue. He was frugal by inclination, but liberal by principle; and if the purpose to which he destined his little accumulations be remembered, with his distribution of occasional charity, it will perhaps appear that he only liked one mode of expense better than another, and saved merely that he might have something to give. He did not grow rich by injuring his successors, but left both Laracor and the Deanery more valuable than he found them.—With all this talk of his covetousness and generosity, it should be remembered that he was never rich. The revenue of his Deanery was not much more than seven hundred a year. His beneficence was not graced with tenderness or civility;

he relieved without pity, and assisted without kindness; so that those who were fed by him could hardly love him.

He made a rule to himself to give but one piece at a time, and therefore always stored his pocket with coins of different value.

Whatever he did, he seemed willing to do in a manner peculiar to himself, without sufficiently considering that singularity, as it implies a contempt of the general practice, is a kind of defiance which justly provokes the hostility of ridicule; he, therefore, who indulges peculiar habits is worse than others, if he be not better:

Of his humour, a story told by Pope may afford a specimen.

"Dr. Swift has an odd, blunt way, that is mistaken, by strangers, for ill-nature.—'Tis so odd, that there's no describing it but by facts. I'll tell you one that just comes into my head. One evening, Gay and I went to see him: you know how intimately we were all acquainted. On our coming in, 'Hey-day, gentlemen (says the Doctor), what's the meaning of this visit? How come you to leave all the great Lords, that you are so fond of, to come hither to see a poor Dean?'—'Because we would rather see you than any of them.'—'Ay, any one that did not know you so well as I do, might believe you. But since you are come, I must get some supper for you, I suppose.'—'No, Doctor, we have supped already.'—'Supped already? that's impossible! why, 'tis not eight o'clock yet.'—'Indeed, we have.'—'That's very strange; but, if you had not supped, I must have got something for you. Let me see, what should I have had? A couple of lobsters; ay, that would have done very well; two shillings —tarts a shilling: but you will drink a glass of wine with me, though you supped so much before your usual time only to spare my pocket?'—'No, we had rather talk with you than drink with you.'—'But if you had supped with me, as in all reason you ought to have done, you must have drank with me. —A bottle of wine, two shillings—two and two is four, and one is five: just two-and-sixpence apiece. There, Pope, there's half a crown for you, and there's another for you, Sir; for I won't save anything by you, I am determined.'—This was all said and done with his usual seriousness on such occasions; and, in spite of everything we could say to the contrary, he actually obliged us to take the money."

In the intercourse of familiar life, he indulged his disposition to petulance and sarcasm, and thought himself injured if the licentiousness of his raillery, the freedom of his censures, or the petulance of his frolics, was resented or repressed. He predominated over his companions with very high ascendency, and probably would bear none over whom he could not predominate. To give him advice was, in the style of his friend Delany, "to venture to speak to him." This customary superiority soon grew too delicate for truth; and Swift, with all his penetration, allowed himself to be delighted with low flattery.

On all common occasions, he habitually affects a style of arrogance, and dictates rather than persuades. This authoritative and magisterial language he expected to be received as his peculiar mode of jocularity: but he apparently flattered his own arrogance by an assumed imperiousness, in which he was ironical only to the resentful, and to the submissive sufficiently serious.

He told stories with great felicity, and delighted in doing what he knew himself to do well; he was therefore captivated by the respectful silence of a steady listener, and told the same tales too often.

He did not, however, claim the right of talking alone; for it was his rule, when he had spoken a minute, to give room by a pause for any other speaker. Of time, on all occasions, he was an exact computer, and knew the minutes required to every common operation.

It may be justly supposed that there was in his conversation, what appears so frequently in his letters, an affectation of familiarity with the great, an ambition of momentary equality sought and enjoyed by the neglect of those ceremonies which custom has established as the barriers between one order of society and another. This transgression of regularity was by himself and his admirers termed greatness of soul. But a great mind disdains to hold anything by courtesy, and therefore never usurps what a lawful claimant may take away. He that encroaches on another's dignity, puts himself in his power; he is either repelled with helpless indignity, or endured by clemency and condescension.

Of Swift's general habits of thinking, if his letters can be supposed to afford any evidence, he was not a man to be either loved or envied. He seems to have wasted life in discontent, by the rage of neglected pride, and the languishment of unsatisfied desire. He is querulous and fastidious, arrogant and malignant; he scarcely speaks of himself but with indignant lamentations, or of others but with insolent superiority when he is gay, and with angry contempt when he is gloomy. From the letters that pass between him and Pope, it might be inferred that they, with Arbuthnot and Gay, had engrossed all the understanding and virtue of mankind; that their merits filled the world, or that there was no hope of more. They show the age involved in darkness, and shade the picture with sullen emulation.

When [1714] the Queen's death drove him into Ireland, he might be allowed to regret for a time the interception of his views, the extinction of his hopes, and his ejection from gay scenes, important employment, and splendid friendships; but when time had enabled reason to prevail over vexation, the complaints, which at first were natural, became ridiculous because they were useless. But querulousness was now grown habitual, and he cried out when he probably had ceased to feel. His reiterated wailings persuaded Bolingbroke that he was really willing to quit his deanery for an English parish; and Bolingbroke procured an exchange, which was rejected; and Swift still retained the pleasure of complaining.

The greatest difficulty that occurs in analysing his character is to discover by what depravity of intellect he took delight in revolving ideas from which almost every other mind shrinks with disgust. The ideas of pleasure, even when criminal, may solicit the imagination; but what has disease, deformity, and filth, upon which the thoughts can be allured to dwell? Delany is willing to think that Swift's mind was not much tainted with this gross corruption before his [first] long visit to Pope. He does not consider how he degrades his hero by making him at fifty-nine the pupil of turpitude, and liable to the malignant influence of an ascendant mind. But the truth is, that Gulliver had described his Yahoos before the visit; and he that had formed those images had nothing filthy to learn.

I have here given the character of Swift as he exhibits himself to my perception; but now let another be heard who knew him better. Dr. Delany, after long acquaintance, describes him to Lord Orrery in these terms:

"My Lord, when you consider Swift's singular, peculiar, and most variegated vein of wit, always rightly intended (although not always so rightly directed), delightful in many instances, and salutary even where it is most offensive; when you consider his strict truth, his fortitude in resisting oppression and arbitrary power; his fidelity in friendship, his sincere love and zeal for religion, his uprightness in making right resolutions, and his steadiness in adhering to them; his care of his church, its choir, its economy, and its income; his attention to all those that preached in his cathedral, in order to their amendment in pronunciation and style; as also his remarkable attention to the interest of his successors, preferably to his own present emoluments; his invincible patriotism, even to a country which he did not love; his very various, well-devised, well-judged, and extensive charities, throughout his life, and his whole fortune (to say nothing of his wife's) conveyed to the same Christian purposes at his death; charities from which he could enjoy no honour, advantage, or satisfaction of any kind in this world; when you consider his ironical and humorous, as well as his serious schemes, for the promotion of true religion and virtue, his success in soliciting for the First Fruits and Twentieths, to the unspeakable benefit of the Established Church of Ireland; and his felicity (to rate it no higher) in giving occasion to the building of fifty new churches in London:

"All this considered, the character of his life will appear like that of his writings; they will both bear to be reconsidered and re-examined with the utmost attention, and always discover new beauties and excellences upon every examination.

"They will bear to be considered as the sun, in which the brightness will hide the blemishes; and whenever petulant ignorance, pride, malignity, or envy interposes to cloud or sully his fame, I will take upon me to pronounce that the eclipse will not last long.

"To conclude—No man ever deserved better of his country than Swift did of his. A steady, persevering, inflexible friend; a wise, a watchful, and a faithful counsellor, under many severe trials and bitter persecutions, to the manifest hazard both of his liberty and fortune.

"He lived a blessing, he died a benefactor, and his name will ever live an honour to Ireland."

In the poetical works of Dr. Swift there is not much upon which the critic can exercise his powers. They are often humorous, almost always light, and have the qualities which recommend such compositions, easiness and gaiety. They are, for the most part, what their author intended. The diction is correct, the numbers are smooth, and the rhymes exact. There seldom occurs a hard-laboured expression, or a redundant epithet; all his verses exemplify his own definition of a good style—they consist of "proper words in proper places."

To divide this collection into classes, and show how some

pieces are gross, and some are trifling, would be to tell the reader what he knows already, and to find faults of which the author could not be ignorant, who certainly wrote not often to his judgment, but his humour.

It was said, in a Preface to one of the Irish editions, that Swift had never been known to take a single thought from any writer, ancient or modern. This is not literally true; but perhaps no writer can easily be found that has borrowed so little, or that in all his excellences and all his defects has so well maintained his claim to be considered as original.

WILLIAM BROOME

1689?–1745

Born at Haslington, in Cheshire—Educated at Eton and Cambridge—Enters into Holy Orders—Introduced to Pope—Assists Pope in the Notes to the Iliad—Assists him in translating the Odyssey—His Quarrel with Pope—His Miscellany of Poems—Marries—Death and Burial in Bath Abbey Church—Works and Character.

WILLIAM BROOME was born in Cheshire, as is said, of very mean parents. Of the place of his birth, or the first part of his life, I have not been able to gain any intelligence. He was educated upon the foundation at Eton, and was captain of the school a whole year, without any vacancy, by which he might have obtained a scholarship at King's College. Being by this delay, such as is said to have happened very rarely, superannuated, he was sent to St. John's College [Cambridge] by the contributions of his friends, where he obtained a small exhibition.

At his college he lived for some time in the same chamber with the well-known Ford, by whom I have formerly heard him described as a contracted scholar and a mere versifier, unacquainted with life, and unskilful in conversation. His addiction to metre was then such, that his companions familiarly called him Poet. When he had opportunities of mingling with mankind, he cleared himself, as Ford likewise owned, from great part of his scholastic rust.

He appeared early in the world as a translator of the Iliads into prose, in conjunction with Ozell and Oldisworth. How their several parts were distributed is not known. This is the translation of which Ozell boasted as superior, in Toland's opinion, to that of Pope: it has long since vanished, and is now in no danger from the critics.

He was introduced to Mr. Pope, who was then visiting Sir John Cotton at Madingley near Cambridge, and gained so much of his esteem, that he was employed, I believe, to make extracts from Eustathius for the notes to the translation of the Iliad; and in the volumes of poetry published by Lintot,

commonly called *Pope's Miscellanies*, many of his early pieces
were inserted.

Pope and Broome were to be yet more closely connected.
When the success of the Iliad gave encouragement to a version
of the Odyssey, Pope, weary of the toil, called Fenton and
Broome to his assistance; and taking only half the work upon
himself, divided the other half between his partners, giving
four books to Fenton, and *eight* to Broome. Fenton's books
I have enumerated in his Life; to the lot of Broome fell the
second, sixth, eighth, eleventh, twelfth, sixteenth, eighteenth,
and twenty-third, together with the burthen of writing all
the notes.

As this translation is a very important event in poetical
history, the reader has a right to know upon what grounds
I establish my narration. That the version was not wholly
Pope's, was always known: he had mentioned the assistance of
two friends in his Proposals, and at the end of the work some
account is given by Broome of their different parts, which, however, mentions only *five* books as written by the coadjutors; the
fourth and twentieth by Fenton; the sixth, the eleventh, and
eighteenth by himself; though Pope, in an advertisement prefixed afterwards to a new volume of his works, claimed only
twelve. A natural curiosity, after the real conduct of so great
an undertaking, incited me once to inquire of Dr. Warburton,
who told me, in his warm language, that he thought the relation
given in the note "a lie"; but that he was not able to ascer-
tain the several shares. The intelligence which Dr. Warburton
could not afford me, I obtained from Mr. Langton, to whom
Mr. Spence had imparted it.

The price at which Pope purchased this assistance was three
hundred pounds paid to Fenton, and five hundred to Broome,
with as many copies as he wanted for his friends, which amounted
to one hundred more. The payment made to Fenton I know
not but by hearsay; Broome's is very distinctly told by Pope
in the notes to *The Dunciad*.

It is evident that, according to Pope's own estimate, Broome
was unkindly treated. If four books could merit three hundred
pounds, eight and all the notes, equivalent at least to four,
had certainly a right to more than six.

Broome probably considered himself as injured, and there
was for some time more than coldness between him and his
employer. He always spoke of Pope as too much a lover of
money, and Pope pursued him with avowed hostility; for he

not only named him disrespectfully in *The Dunciad*, but quoted him more than once in the *Bathos*, as a proficient in the "Art of Sinking"; and in his enumeration of the different kinds of poets distinguished for the profound, he reckons Broome among "the parrots who repeat another's words in such a hoarse odd voice as makes them seem their own." I have been told that they were afterwards reconciled; but I am afraid their peace was without friendship.

He afterwards [1739] published a *Miscellany of Poems*, which is inserted, with corrections, in the late compilation.

He never rose to a very high dignity in the Church. He was some time rector of Sturston in Suffolk, where he married [1716] a wealthy widow; and afterwards, when the King visited Cambridge (1728), became Doctor of Laws. He was (1733) presented by the Crown to the rectory of Pulham in Norfolk, which he held with Oakley Magna in Suffolk, given him by the Lord Cornwallis, to whom he was chaplain, and who added the vicarage of Eye in Suffolk; he then resigned Pulham, and retained the other two.

Towards the close of his life he grew again poetical, and amused himself with translating Odes of Anacreon, which he published [1739–40] in *The Gentleman's Magazine*, under the name of Chester.

He died at Bath, November 16, 1745, and was buried in the Abbey Church.

Of Broome, though it cannot be said that he was a great poet, it would be unjust to deny that he was an excellent versifier; his lines are smooth and sonorous, and his diction is select and elegant. His rhymes are sometimes unsuitable: in his *Melancholy*, he makes *breath* rhyme to *birth* in one place, and to *earth* in another. Those faults occur but seldom; and he had such power of words and numbers as fitted him for translation; but, in his original works, recollection seems to have been his business more than invention. His imitations are so apparent, that it is part of his reader's employment to recall the verses of some former poet. Sometimes he copies the most popular writers, for he seems scarcely to endeavour at concealment; and sometimes he picks up fragments in obscure corners. His lines to Fenton,

> Serene, the sting of pain thy thoughts beguile,
> And make afflictions objects of a smile,

brought to my mind some lines on the death of Queen Mary,

written by Barnes, of whom I should not have expected to find an imitator:

> But thou, O Muse, whose sweet nepenthean tongue
> Can charm the pangs of death with deathless song;
> Canst *stinging plagues* with easy *thoughts beguile*,
> *Make* pains and tortures *objects of a smile*.

To detect his imitations were tedious and useless. What he takes he seldom makes worse; and he cannot be justly thought a mean man whom Pope chose for an associate, and whose co-operation was considered by Pope's enemies as so important, that he was attacked by Henley with this ludicrous distich:

> Pope came off clean with Homer; but they say
> Broome went before, and kindly swept the way.

CHRISTOPHER PITT

1699–1748

Born at Blandford in Dorsetshire—Educated at Winchester and Oxford
—Presented to the Rectory of Pimpern in Dorsetshire—Translates Vida's
Art of Poetry, and Virgil's Æneid—His Miscellany of Poems—Death and
Burial at Blandford.

CHRISTOPHER PITT, of whom whatever I shall relate, more than
has been already published, I owe to the kind communication
of Dr. Warton, was born in 1699, at Blandford, the son of a
physician much esteemed.

He was, in 1714, received as a scholar into Winchester College,
where he was distinguished by exercises of uncommon elegance,
and, at his removal to New College in 1719, presented to the
electors, as the product of his private and voluntary studies,
a complete version of Lucan's poem, which he did not then
know to have been translated by Rowe.

This is an instance of early diligence which well deserves to
be recorded. The suppression of such a work, recommended
by such uncommon circumstances, is to be regretted. It is
indeed culpable to load libraries with superfluous books; but
incitements to early excellence are never superfluous, and from
this example the danger is not great of many imitations.

When he had resided at his college three years, he was presented to the rectory of Pimpern, in Dorsetshire (1722), by
his relation, Mr. Pitt of Strathfieldsaye, in Hampshire; and,
resigning his Fellowship, continued at Oxford two years longer,
till he became Master of Arts (1724).

He probably about this time translated Vida's *Art of Poetry*,
which Tristram's splendid edition had then made popular. In
this translation he distinguished himself, both by its general
elegance and by the skilful adaptation of his numbers to the
images expressed—a beauty which Vida has with great ardour
enforced and exemplified.

He then retired to his living, a place very pleasing by its
situation, and therefore likely to excite the imagination of a

poet, where he passed the rest of his life, reverenced for his virtue, and beloved for the softness of his temper and the easiness of his manners. Before strangers he had something of the scholar's timidity or distrust; but when he became familiar he was in a very high degree cheerful and entertaining. His general benevolence procured general respect, and he passed a life placid and honourable, neither too great for the kindness of the low, nor too low for the notice of the great.

At what time he composed his Miscellany, published in 1727, it is not easy nor necessary to know; those which have dates appear to have been very early productions, and I have not observed that any rise above mediocrity.

The success of his *Vida* animated him to a higher undertaking; and in his thirtieth year he published a version of the first book of the Æneid. This being, I suppose, commended by his friends, he some time afterwards added three or four more, with an advertisement, in which he represents himself as translating with great indifference, and with a progress of which himself was hardly conscious. This can hardly be true, and, if true, is nothing to the reader.

At last, without any further contention with his modesty, or any awe of the name of Dryden, he gave us a complete English Æneid, which I am sorry not to see joined in this publication with his other poems. It would have been pleasing to have an opportunity of comparing the two best translations that perhaps were ever produced by one nation of the same author.

Pitt engaging as a rival with Dryden naturally observed his failures, and avoided them; and as he wrote after Pope's Iliad, he had an example of an exact, equable, and splendid versification. With these advantages, seconded by great diligence, he might successfully labour particular passages, and escape many errors. If the two versions are compared, perhaps the result would be, that Dryden leads the reader forward by his general vigour and sprightliness, and Pitt often stops him to contemplate the excellence of a single couplet—that Dryden's faults are forgotten in the hurry of delight, and that Pitt's beauties are neglected in the languor of a cold and listless perusal—that Pitt pleases the critics, and Dryden the people—that Pitt is quoted, and Dryden read.

He did not long enjoy the reputation which this great work deservedly conferred, for he left the world in 1748, and lies buried under a stone at Blandford, on which is this inscription:

In memory of

CHR. PITT, clerk, M.A.

Very eminent
for his talents in poetrv,
and yet more
for the universal candour of
his mind, and the primitive
simplicity of his manners.
He lived innocent,
and died beloved,
Apr. 13, 1748,
aged 48.

JAMES THOMSON

1700–1748

Born at Ednam in Roxburghshire—Educated at Edinburgh, and designed for the Church—Starts for London—His Poverty— Publishes his *Winter, Summer, Spring,* and other Poems—Writes for the Stage—Is made Tutor to the Son of Lord Chancellor Talbot—Visits Italy—Made Secretary of the Briefs—Loses his Office at Lord Talbot's Death—Patronised by the Prince of Wales and Mr. Lyttelton—Writes *Agamemnon* and other Tragedies—Publishes *Liberty,* a Poem—Death and Burial at Richmond in Surrey—Works and Character.

JAMES THOMSON, the son of [the Rev. Thomas Thomson] a minister well esteemed for his piety and diligence, was born September 11, 1700, at Ednam, in the shire of Roxburgh, of which his father was pastor. His mother, whose name was Trotter, inherited as co-heiress a portion of a small estate. The revenue of a parish in Scotland is seldom large; and it was probably in commiseration of the difficulty with which Mr. Thomson supported his family, having nine children, that Mr. Riccaltoun, a neighbouring minister, discovering in James uncommon promises of future excellence, undertook to superintend his education and provide him books.

He was taught the common rudiments of learning at the school of Jedburgh, a place which he delights to recollect in his poem of *Autumn*; but was not considered by his master as superior to common boys, though in those early days he amused his patron and his friends with poetical compositions; with which, however, he so little pleased himself, that on every New-Year's day he threw into the fire all the productions of the foregoing year.

From the school he was removed to Edinburgh, where he had not resided two years when his father died, and left all his children to the care of their mother, who raised upon her little estate what money a mortgage could afford, and, removing with her family to Edinburgh, lived to see her son rising into eminence.

The design of Thomson's friends was to breed him a minister. He lived at Edinburgh, as at school, without distinction or expectation, till, at the usual time, he performed a probationary exercise by explaining a psalm. His diction was so poetically splendid that Mr. Hamilton, the Professor of Divinity, reproved him for speaking language unintelligible to a popular audience; and he censured one of his expressions as indecent, if not profane.

This rebuke is reported to have repressed his thoughts of an ecclesiastical character, and he probably cultivated with new diligence his blossoms of poetry, which, however, were in some danger of a blast; for, submitting his productions to some who thought themselves qualified to criticise, he heard of nothing but faults; but, finding other judges more favourable, he did not suffer himself to sink into despondence.

He easily discovered that the only stage on which a poet could appear, with any hope of advantage, was London; a place too wide for the operation of petty competition and private malignity, where merit might soon become conspicuous, and would find friends as soon as it became reputable to befriend it. A lady, who was acquainted with his mother, advised him to the journey, and promised some countenance or assistance, which at last he never received; however, he justified his adventure by her encouragement, and came [1725] to seek in London patronage and fame.

At his arrival he found his way to Mr. Mallet, then tutor to the sons of the Duke of Montrose. He had recommendations to several persons of consequence, which he had tied up carefully in his handkerchief; but as he passed along the street, with the gaping curiosity of a newcomer, his attention was upon everything rather than his pocket, and his magazine of credentials was stolen from him.

His first want was a pair of shoes. For the supply of all his necessities his whole fund was his *Winter*, which for a time could find no purchaser; till, at last [1726], Mr. Millan was persuaded to buy it at a low price; and this low price he had for some time reason to regret; but, by accident, Mr. Whatley, a man not wholly unknown among authors, happening to turn his eye upon it, was so delighted that he ran from place to place celebrating its excellence. Thomson obtained likewise the notice of Aaron Hill, whom, being friendless and indigent, and glad of kindness, he courted with every expression of servile adulation.

Winter was dedicated to Sir Spencer Compton, but attracted no regard from him to the author; till Aaron Hill awakened his attention by some verses addressed to Thomson, and published in one of the newspapers, which censured the great for their neglect of ingenious men. Thomson then received a present of twenty guineas, of which he gives this account to Mr. Hill:

"I hinted to you in my last that on Saturday morning I was with Sir Spencer Compton. A certain gentleman, without my desire, spoke to him concerning me: his answer was that I had never come near him. Then the gentleman put the question, If he desired that I should wait on him? He returned, he did. On this the gentleman gave me an introductory letter to him. He received me in what they commonly call a civil manner; asked me some commonplace questions; and made me a present of twenty guineas. I am very ready to own that the present was larger than my performance deserved; and shall ascribe it to his generosity, or any other cause, rather than the merit of the address."

The poem, which, being of a new kind, few would venture at first to like, by degrees gained upon the public; and one edition was very speedily succeeded by another.

Thomson's credit was now high, and every day brought him new friends; among others Dr. Rundle, a man afterwards unfortunately famous, sought his acquaintance, and found his qualities such, that he recommended him to the Lord Chancellor Talbot.

Winter was accompanied, in many editions, not only with a Preface and Dedication, but with poetical praises by Mr. Hill, Mr. Mallet (then Malloch), and Mira, the fictitious name of a lady once too well known. Why the dedications are to *Winter* and the other seasons, contrarily to custom, left out in the collected works, the reader may inquire.

The next year (1727) he distinguished himself by three publications—of *Summer* in pursuance of his plan; of *A Poem on the Death of Sir Isaac Newton*, which he was enabled to perform as an exact philosopher by the instruction of Mr. Gray; and of *Britannia*, a kind of poetical invective against the Ministry, whom the nation then thought not forward enough in resenting the depredations of the Spaniards. By this piece he declared himself an adherent to the Opposition, and had therefore no favour to expect from the Court.

Thomson, having been some time entertained in the family of the Lord Binning, was desirous of testifying his gratitude by making him the patron of his *Summer*; but the same kindness which had first disposed Lord Binning to encourage him, determined him to refuse the Dedication, which was by his advice addressed to Mr. Dodington, a man who had more power to advance the reputation and fortune of a poet.

Spring was published next year [June 1728] with a Dedication to the Countess of Hertford, whose practice it was to invite every summer some poet into the country, to hear her verses and assist her studies. This honour was one summer conferred on Thomson, who took more delight in carousing with Lord Hertford and his friends than assisting her Ladyship's poetical operations, and therefore never received another summons.

Autumn, the season to which the *Spring* and *Summer* are preparatory, still remained unsung, and was delayed till he published (May 1730) his works collected.

He produced in 1729 the tragedy of *Sophonisba,* which raised such expectation, that every rehearsal was dignified with a splendid audience, collected to anticipate the delight that was preparing for the public. It was observed, however, that nobody was much affected, and that the company rose as from a moral lecture.

It had upon the stage no unusual degree of success. Slight accidents will operate upon the taste of pleasure. There is a feeble line in the play:

O Sophonisba, Sophonisba, O!

This gave occasion to a waggish parody:

O, Jemmy Thomson, Jemmy Thomson, O!

which for a while was echoed through the town.

I have been told by Savage that of the Prologue to *Sophonisba,* the first part was written by Pope, who could not be persuaded to finish it; and that the concluding lines were added by Mallet.

Thomson was not long afterwards, by the influence of Dr. Rundle, sent [1730] to travel with Mr. Charles Talbot, the eldest son of the Chancellor. He was yet young enough to receive new impressions, to have his opinions rectified, and his views enlarged; nor can he be supposed to have wanted that curiosity which is inseparable from an active and comprehensive mind. He may therefore now be supposed to have revelled in all the joys of intellectual luxury; he was every day feasted with instructive novelties; he lived splendidly without expense, and might expect when he returned home a certain establishment.

At this time a long course of opposition to Sir Robert Walpole had filled the nation with clamours for liberty, of which no man felt the want, and with care for liberty, which was not in danger. Thomson, in his travels on the Continent, found or fancied so many evils arising from the tyranny of other governments, that he resolved to write a very long poem, in five parts, upon Liberty.

While he was busy on the first book, Mr. Talbot died, and Thomson, who had been rewarded for his attendance by the place of Secretary of the Briefs, pays in the initial lines a decent tribute to his memory.

Upon this great poem two years were spent, and the author congratulated himself upon it as his noblest work; but an author and his reader are not always of a mind. Liberty called in vain upon her votaries to read her praises, and reward her encomiast: her praises were condemned to harbour spiders, and to gather dust: none of Thomson's performances were so little regarded.

The judgment of the public was not erroneous; the recurrence of the same images must tire in time; an enumeration of examples to prove a position which nobody denied, as it was from the beginning superfluous, must quickly grow disgusting.

The poem of *Liberty* does not now appear in its original state; but, when the author's works were collected after his death, was shortened by Sir George Lyttelton, with a liberty which, as it has a manifest tendency to lessen the confidence of society, and to confound the characters of authors, by making one man write by the judgment of another, cannot be justified by any supposed propriety of the alteration, or kindness of the friend: I wish to see it exhibited as its author left it.

Thomson now lived in ease and plenty, and seems for a while to have suspended his poetry; but he was soon called back to labour by the death [1737] of the Chancellor, for his place then became vacant; and though the Lord Hardwicke delayed for some time to give it away, Thomson's bashfulness, or pride, or some other motive perhaps not more laudable, withheld him from soliciting; and the new Chancellor would not give him what he would not ask.

He now relapsed to his former indigence; but the Prince of Wales was at that time [1737] struggling for popularity, and by the influence of Mr. Lyttelton professed himself the patron of wit; to him Thomson was introduced, and being gaily interrogated about the state of his affairs, said, "that they were in a more poetical posture than formerly"; and had a pension allowed him of 100*l.* a year.

Being now obliged to write, he produced (1738) the tragedy of

Agamemnon, which was much shortened in the representation. It had the fate which most commonly attends mythological stories, and was only endured, but not favoured. It struggled with such difficulty through the first night, that Thomson, coming late to his friends with whom he was to sup, excused his delay by telling them how the sweat of his distress had so disordered his wig, that he could not come till he had been refitted by a barber.

He so interested himself in his own drama, that, if I remember right, as he sat in the upper gallery, he accompanied the players by audible recitation, till a friendly hint frighted him to silence. Pope countenanced *Agamemnon* by coming to it the first night, and was welcomed to the theatre by a general clap; he had much regard for Thomson, and once expressed it in a poetical Epistle sent to Italy, of which, however, he abated the value by transplanting some of the lines into his *Epistle to Arbuthnot*.

About this time [1737] the Act was passed for licensing plays, of which the first operation was the prohibition of *Gustavus Vasa*, a tragedy of Mr. Brooke, whom the public recompensed by a very liberal subscription; the next was the refusal of *Edward and Eleonora*, offered by Thomson. It is hard to discover why either play should have been obstructed. Thomson likewise endeavoured to repair his loss by a subscription, of which I cannot now tell the success.

When the public murmured at the unkind treatment of Thomson, one of the ministerial writers remarked, that "he had taken a *Liberty* which was not agreeable to *Britannia* in any *Season*."

He was soon after employed, in conjunction with Mr. Mallet, to write the masque of *Alfred*, which was acted before the Prince at Cliefden House.

His next work (1745) was *Tancred and Sigismunda*, the most successful of all his tragedies; for it still keeps its turn upon the stage. It may be doubted whether he was, either by the bent of nature or habits of study, much qualified for tragedy. It does not appear that he had much sense of the pathetic; and his diffusive and descriptive style produced declamation rather than dialogue.

His friend Mr. Lyttelton was now in power, and conferred upon him the office of surveyor-general of the Leeward Islands; from which, when his deputy was paid, he received about three hundred pounds a year.

The last piece that he lived to publish [1748] was the *Castle of Indolence*, which was many years under his hand, but was at last finished with great accuracy. The first canto opens a scene of lazy luxury that fills the imagination.

He was now at ease, but was not long to enjoy it; for, by taking cold on the water between London and Kew, he caught a disorder, which, with some careless exasperation, ended in a fever that put an end to his life, August 27, 1748. He was buried in the church of Richmond, without an inscription; but a monument has been erected to his memory in Westminster Abbey.

Thomson was of stature above the middle size, and "more fat than bard beseems," of a dull countenance, and a gross, unanimated, uninviting appearance; silent in mingled company, but cheerful among select friends, and by his friends very tenderly and warmly beloved.

He left behind him the tragedy of *Coriolanus*, which was, by the zeal of his patron, Sir George Lyttelton, brought upon the stage for the benefit of his family, and recommended by a Prologue, which Quin, who had long lived with Thomson in fond intimacy, spoke in such a manner as showed him "to be," on that occasion, "no actor." The commencement of this benevolence is very honourable to Quin; who is reported to have delivered Thomson, then known to him only for his genius, from an arrest by a very considerable present; and its continuance is honourable to both; for friendship is not always the sequel of obligation. By this tragedy a considerable sum was raised, of which part discharged his debts, and the rest was remitted to his sisters, whom, however removed from them by place or condition, he regarded with great tenderness, as will appear by the following letter, which I communicate with much pleasure, as it gives me at once an opportunity of recording the fraternal kindness of Thomson, and reflecting on the friendly assistance of Mr. Boswell, from whom I received it.

> HAGLEY, IN WORCESTERSHIRE,
> *October the 4th*, 1747.
>
> MY DEAR SISTER,—I thought you had known me better than to interpret my silence into a decay of affection, especially as your behaviour has always been such as rather to increase than diminish it. Don't imagine, because I am a bad correspondent, that I can ever prove an unkind friend and brother. I must do myself the justice to tell you that my affections are naturally very fixed and constant; and if I had ever reason of complaint against you (of which, by the bye, I have not the least shadow), I am conscious of

so many defects in myself, as dispose me to be not a little charitable and forgiving.

It gives me the truest heart-felt satisfaction to hear you have a good, kind husband, and are in easy, contented circumstances; but, were they otherwise, that would only awaken and heighten my tenderness towards you. As our good and tender-hearted parents did not live to receive any material testimonies of that highest human gratitude I owed them (than which nothing could have given me equal pleasure), the only return I can make them now is by kindness to those they left behind them. Would to God poor Lizy had lived longer, to have been a farther witness of the truth of what I say, and that I might have had the pleasure of seeing once more a sister who so truly deserved my esteem and love! But she is happy, while we must toil a little longer here below; let us, however, do it cheerfully and gratefully, supported by the pleasing hope of meeting yet again on a safer shore, where to recollect the storms and difficulties of life will not perhaps be inconsistent with that blissful state. You did right to call your daughter by her name; for you must needs have had a particular tender friendship for one another, endeared as you were by nature, by having passed the affectionate years of your youth together, and by that great softener and engager of hearts—mutual hardship. That it was in my power to ease it a little, I account one of the most exquisite pleasures of my life. But enough of this melancholy though not unpleasing strain.

I esteem you for your sensible and disinterested advice to Mr. Bell, as you will see by my letter to him: as I approve entirely of his marrying again, you may readily ask me why I don't marry at all. My circumstances have hitherto been so variable and un-certain in this fluctuating world, as induce to keep me from engaging in such a state; and now, though they are more settled, and of late (which you will be glad to hear) considerably improved, I begin to think myself too far advanced in life for such youthful undertakings, not to mention some other petty reasons that are apt to startle the delicacy of difficult old bachelors. I am, however, not a little sus-picious that, was I to pay a visit to Scotland (which I have some thought of doing soon), I might possibly be tempted to think of a thing not easily repaired if done amiss. I have always been of opinion that none make better wives than the ladies of Scotland; and yet, who more forsaken than they, while the gentlemen are continually running abroad all the world over? Some of them, it is true, are wise enough to return for a wife. You see I am beginning to make interest already with the Scots ladies. But no more of this infectious subject. Pray let me hear from you now and then; and, though I am not a regular correspondent, yet perhaps I may mend in that respect. Remember me kindly to your husband, and believe me to be

Your most affectionate brother,
JAMES THOMSON.

(Addressed)   To Mrs. Thomson in Lanark.

The benevolence of Thomson was fervid, but not active: he would give on all occasions what assistance his purse would supply; but the offices of intervention or solicitation he could not conquer his sluggishness sufficiently to perform. The affairs of others, however, were not more neglected than his own. He had often felt the inconveniences of idleness, but he never cured it; and was so conscious of his own character, that he talked of writing an Eastern Tale " of the Man who Loved to be in Distress."

Among his peculiarities was a very unskilful and inarticulate manner of pronouncing any lofty or solemn composition. He was once reading to Dodington, who being himself a reader eminently elegant, was so much provoked by his odd utterance, that he snatched the paper from his hands, and told him that he did not understand his own verses.

The biographer of Thomson has remarked, that an author's life is best read in his works: his observation was not well timed. Savage, who lived much with Thomson, once told me how he heard a lady remarking that she could gather from his works three parts of his character: that he was a "great lover, a great swimmer, and rigorously abstinent"; but, said Savage, he knows not any love but that of the sex; he was perhaps never in cold water in his life; and he indulges himself in all the luxury that comes within his reach. Yet Savage always spoke with the most eager praise of his social qualities, his warmth and constancy of friendship, and his adherence to his first acquaintance when the advancement of his reputation had left them behind him.

As a writer, he is entitled to one praise of the highest kind: his mode of thinking, and of expressing his thoughts, is original. His blank verse is no more the blank verse of Milton, or of any other poet, than the rhymes of Prior are the rhymes of Cowley. His numbers, his pauses, his diction, are of his own growth, without transcription, without imitation. He thinks in a peculiar train, and he thinks always as a man of genius; he looks round on Nature and on life with the eye which Nature bestows only on a poet; the eye that distinguishes, in everything presented to its view, whatever there is on which imagination can delight to be detained, and with a mind that at once comprehends the vast and attends to the minute. The reader of *The Seasons* wonders that he never saw before what Thomson shows him, and that he never yet has felt what Thomson impresses.

His is one of the works in which blank verse seems properly used. Thomson's wide expansion of general views, and his enumeration of circumstantial varieties, would have been obstructed and embarrassed by the frequent intersections of the sense, which are the necessary effects of rhyme.

His descriptions of extended scenes and general effects bring before us the whole magnificence of Nature, whether pleasing or dreadful. The gaiety of Spring, the splendour of Summer, the tranquillity of Autumn, and the horror of Winter, take in their turns possession of the mind. The poet leads us through the appearances of things as they are successively varied by the vicissitudes of the year, and imparts to us so much of his own enthusiasm, that our thoughts expand with his imagery, and kindle with his sentiments. Nor is the naturalist without his part in the entertainment; for he is assisted to recollect and to combine, to arrange his discoveries, and to amplify the sphere of his contemplation.

The great defect of *The Seasons* is want of method; but for this I know not that there was any remedy. Of many appearances subsisting all at once, no rule can be given why one should be mentioned before another; yet the memory wants the help of order, and the curiosity is not excited by suspense or expectation.

His diction is in the highest degree florid and luxuriant, such as may be said to be to his images and thoughts "both their lustre and their shade"; such as invest them with splendour, through which perhaps they are not always easily discerned. It is too exuberant, and sometimes may be charged with filling the ear more than the mind.

These poems, with which I was acquainted at their first appearance, I have since found altered and enlarged by subsequent revisals, as the author supposed his judgment to grow more exact, and as books or conversation extended his knowledge and opened his prospects. They are, I think, improved in general; yet I know not whether they have not lost part of what Temple calls their "race"; a word which, applied to wines in its primitive sense, means the flavour of the soil.

Liberty, when it first appeared, I tried to read, and soon desisted. I have never tried again, and therefore will not hazard either praise or censure.

The highest praise which he has received ought not to be suppressed: it is said by Lord Lyttelton, in the Prologue to his posthumous play, that his works contained

No line which, dying, he could wish to blot.

ISAAC WATTS

1674–1748

Born at Southampton—Educated among the Independents—Becomes Tutor to the Son of Sir John Hartopp—Is received into Sir Thomas Abney's Family—Popularity of his Preaching—His Work on *The Improvement of the Mind*—Death and Burial at Bunhill Fields in London.

THE Poems of Dr. Watts were by my recommendation inserted in the late Collection; the readers of which are to impute to me whatever pleasure or weariness they may find in the perusal of Blackmore, Watts, Pomfret, and Yalden.

Isaac Watts was born July 17, 1674, at Southampton, where his father, of the same name, kept a boarding-school for young gentlemen, though common report makes him a shoemaker. He appears, from the narrative of Dr. Gibbons, to have been neither indigent nor illiterate.

Isaac, the eldest of nine children, was given to books from his infancy; and began, we are told, to learn Latin when he was four years old, I suppose at home. He was afterwards taught Latin, Greek, and Hebrew by Mr. Pinhorne, a clergy-man, master of the free-school at Southampton, to whom the gratitude of his scholar afterwards inscribed a Latin ode.

His proficiency at school was so conspicuous that a subscription was proposed for his support at the university; but he declared his resolution of taking his lot with the Dissenters. Such he was as every Christian Church would rejoice to have adopted.

He therefore repaired in 1690 to an academy taught by Mr. Rowe, where he had for his companions and fellow-students Mr. Hughes the poet, and Dr. Horte, afterwards Archbishop of Tuam. Some Latin Essays, supposed to have been written as exercises at this academy, show a degree of knowledge, both philosophical and theological, such as very few attain by a much longer course of study.

He was, as he hints in his *Miscellanies*, a maker of verses from fifteen to fifty, and in his youth he appears to have paid attention to Latin poetry. His verses to his brother, in the *glyconic* measure, written when he was seventeen, are remarkably easy and elegant. Some of his other odes are deformed by the Pindaric folly then prevailing, and are written with such neglect of all metrical rules as is without example among the ancients; but his diction, though perhaps not always exactly pure, has such copiousness and splendour as shows that he was but at a very little distance from excellence.

His method of study was to impress the contents of his books upon his memory by abridging them, and by interleaving them to amplify one system with supplements from another.

With the congregation of his tutor, Mr. Rowe, who were, I believe, Independents, he communicated in his nineteenth year.

At the age of twenty he left the academy, and spent two years in study and devotion at the house of his father, who treated him with great tenderness; and had the happiness, indulged to few parents, of living to see his son eminent for literature and venerable for piety.

He was then entertained by Sir John Hartopp five years, as domestic tutor to his son; and in that time particularly devoted himself to the study of the Holy Scriptures; and being chosen assistant to Dr. Chauncy, preached the first time on the birthday that completed his twenty-fourth year; probably considering that as the day of a second nativity, by which he entered on a new period of existence.

In about three years, 8th March, 1701-2, he succeeded Dr. Chauncy; but, soon after his entrance on his charge, he was seized by a dangerous illness, which sunk him to such weakness that the congregation thought an assistant necessary, and [June 1703] appointed Mr. Price. His health then returned gradually; and he performed his duty, till (1712) he was seized by a fever of such violence and continuance, that from the feebleness which it brought upon him he never perfectly recovered.

This calamitous state made the compassion of his friends necessary, and drew upon him the attention of Sir Thomas Abney, who received him into his house; where, with a constancy of friendship and uniformity of conduct not often to be found, he was treated for thirty-six years with all the kindness that friendship could prompt, and all the attention that respect could dictate. Sir Thomas died about eight years afterwards; but he continued with the lady and her daughters to the end of his life. The lady died about a year after him.

A coalition like this, a state in which the notions of patronage and dependence were overpowered by the perception of reciprocal benefits, deserves a particular memorial; and I will not withhold from the reader Dr. Gibbons's representation, to which regard is to be paid as to the narrative of one who writes what he knows, and what is known likewise to multitudes besides.

"Our next observation shall be made upon that remarkably kind Providence which brought the Doctor into Sir Thomas Abney's family, and continued him there till his death, a period of no less than thirty-six years. In the midst of his sacred labours for the glory of God and good of his generation, he is seized with a most violent and threatening fever, which leaves him oppressed with great weakness, and puts a stop at least to his public services for four years. In this distressing season, doubly so to his active and pious spirit, he is invited to Sir Thomas Abney's family, nor ever removes from it till he had finished his days. Here he enjoyed the uninterrupted demonstrations of the truest friendship. Here, without any care of his own, he had everything which could contribute to the enjoyment of life, and favour the unwearied pursuits of his studies. Here he dwelt in a family which, for piety, order, harmony, and every virtue, was a house of God. Here he had the privilege of a country recess, the fragrant bower, the spreading lawn, the flowery garden, and other advantages, to soothe his mind and aid his restoration to health; to yield him, whenever he chose them, most grateful intervals from his laborious studies, and enable him to return to them with redoubled vigour and delight. Had it not been for this most happy event, he might, as to outward view, have feebly, it may be painfully, dragged on through many more years of languor, and inability for public service, and even for profitable study, or perhaps might have sunk into his grave under the overwhelming load of infirmities in the midst of his days; and thus the church and world would have been deprived of those many excellent sermons and works which he drew up and published during his long residence in this family. In a few years after his coming hither Sir Thomas Abney dies; but his amiable consort survives, who shows the Doctor the same respect and friendship as before, and most happily for him and great numbers besides; for, as her riches were great, her generosity and munificence were in full proportion; her thread of life was drawn out to a great age, even beyond that of the Doctor's; and thus this excellent man, through her kindness and that of her daughter, the present Mrs. Elizabeth Abney, who in a like degree esteemed and honoured him, enjoyed all the benefits and felicities he experienced at his first entrance into this family, till his days were numbered and finished; and, like a shock of corn in its season, he ascended into the regions of perfect and immortal life and joy."

If this quotation has appeared long, let it be considered that it comprises an account of six-and-thirty years, and those the years of Dr. Watts.

From the time of his reception into this family his life was no otherwise diversified than by successive publications. The series of his works I am not able to deduce; their number and their variety show the intenseness of his industry and the extent of his capacity.

He was one of the first authors that taught the Dissenters to court attention by the graces of language. Whatever they had among them before, whether of learning or acuteness, was commonly obscured and blunted by coarseness and inelegance of style. He showed them that zeal and purity might be expressed and enforced by polished diction.

He continued to the end of his life the teacher of a congregation, and no reader of his works can doubt his fidelity or diligence. In the pulpit, though his low stature, which very little exceeded five feet, graced him with no advantages of appearance, yet the gravity and propriety of his utterance made his discourses very efficacious. I once mentioned the reputation which Mr. Foster had gained by his proper delivery to my friend Dr. Hawkesworth, who told me that in the art of pronunciation he was far inferior to Dr. Watts.

Such was his flow of thoughts, and such his promptitude of language, that in the latter part of his life he did not precompose his cursory sermons, but having adjusted the heads, and sketched out some particulars, trusted for success to his extempory powers.

He did not endeavour to assist his eloquence by any gesticulations; for, as no corporeal actions have any correspondence with theological truth, he did not see how they could enforce it.

At the conclusion of weighty sentences he gave time, by a short pause, for the proper impression.

To stated and public instruction he added familiar visits and personal application, and was careful to improve the opportunities which conversation offered of diffusing and increasing the influence of religion.

By his natural temper he was quick of resentment; but by his established and habitual practice he was gentle, modest and inoffensive. His tenderness appeared in his attention to children and to the poor. To the poor, while he lived in the

family of his friend, he allowed the third part of his annual
revenue, though the whole was not a hundred a year; and
for children he condescended to lay aside the scholar, the philosopher, and the wit, to write little poems of devotion, and
systems of instruction, adapted to their wants and capacities,
from the dawn of reason through its gradations of advance in
the morning of life. Every man acquainted with the common
principles of human action will look with veneration on the
writer who is at one time combating Locke, and at another
making a catechism for children in their fourth year. A voluntary
descent from the dignity of science is perhaps the hardest lesson
that humility can teach.

As his mind was capacious, his curiosity excursive, and his
industry continual, his writings are very numerous, and his
subjects various. With his theological works I am only enough
acquainted to admire his meekness of opposition and his mildness of censure. It was not only in his book but in his mind
that *orthodoxy* was *united* with *charity*.

Of his philosophical pieces, his *Logic* [1724] has been received
into the universities, and therefore wants no private recommendation: if he owes part of it to Le Clerc, it must be
considered that no man who undertakes merely to methodise
or illustrate a system, pretends to be its author.

In his metaphysical disquisitions, it was observed by the
late learned Mr. Dyer, that he confounded the idea of *space*
with that of *empty space*, and did not consider that though
space might be without matter, yet matter being extended
could not be without space.

Few books have been perused by me with greater pleasure
than his *Improvement of the Mind*, of which the radical principles
may indeed be found in Locke's *Conduct of the Understanding*,
but they are so expanded and ramified by Watts, as to confer
upon him the merit of a work in the highest degree useful
and pleasing. Whoever has the care of instructing others,
may be charged with deficience in his duty if this book is
not recommended.

I have mentioned his treatises of Theology as distinct from
his other productions, but the truth is, that whatever he took in
hand was, by his incessant solicitude for souls, converted to
Theology. As piety predominated in his mind, it is diffused
over his works: under his direction it may be truly said, *Theo-
logiæ Philosophia ancillatur*, philosophy is subservient to evan-
gelical instruction; it is difficult to read a page without learning,

or at least wishing, to be better. The attention is caught by indirect instruction, and he that sat down only to reason is on a sudden compelled to pray.

It was therefore with great propriety that, in 1728, he received from Edinburgh and Aberdeen an unsolicited diploma, by which he became a Doctor of Divinity. Academical honours would have more value, if they were always bestowed with equal judgment.

He continued many years to study and to preach, and to do good by his instruction and example; till at last the infirmities of age disabled him from the more laborious part of his ministerial functions, and being no longer capable of public duty, he offered to remit the salary appendant to it; but his congregation would not accept the resignation.

By degrees his weakness increased, and at last confined him to his chamber and his bed; where he was worn gradually away without pain, till he expired Nov. 25, 1748, in the seventy-fifth year of his age.

Few men have left behind such purity of character or such monuments of laborious piety. He has provided instruction for all ages, from those who are lisping their first lessons to the enlightened readers of Malbranche and Locke; he has left neither corporeal nor spiritual nature unexamined; he has taught the Art of Reasoning and the Science of the Stars.

His character, therefore, must be formed from the multiplicity and diversity of his attainments, rather than from any single performance; for it would not be safe to claim for him the highest rank in any single denomination of literary dignity; yet perhaps there was nothing in which he would not have excelled, if he had not divided his powers to different pursuits.

As a poet, had he been only a poet, he would probably have stood high among the authors with whom he is now associated. For his judgment was exact, and he noted beauties and faults with very nice discernment; his imagination, as the *Dacian Battle* proves, was vigorous and active, and the stores of knowledge were large by which his fancy was to be supplied. His ear was well tuned, and his diction was elegant and copious. But his devotional poetry is, like that of others, unsatisfactory. The paucity of its topics enforces perpetual repetition, and the sanctity of the matter rejects the ornaments of figurative diction. It is sufficient for Watts to have done better than others what no man has done well.

His poems on other subjects seldom rise higher than might

be expected from the amusements of a Man of Letters, and have different degrees of value as they are more or less laboured, or as the occasion was more or less favourable to invention.

He writes too often without regular measures, and too often in blank verse: the rhymes are not always sufficiently correspondent. He is particularly unhappy in coining names expressive of characters. His lines are commonly smooth and easy, and his thoughts always religiously pure; but who is there that, to so much piety and innocence, does not wish for a greater measure of sprightliness and vigour? He is at least one of the few poets with whom youth and ignorance may be safely pleased; and happy will be that reader whose mind is disposed by his verses, or his prose, to imitate him in all but his nonconformity, to copy his benevolence to man, and his reverence to God.

AMBROSE PHILIPS

1675-1749

A Native of Shropshire—Educated at Cambridge—Encouraged by the Earl of Dorset—Sides with the Whigs—His Friendship with Addison and Steele—Produces *The Distressed Mother*, a Tragedy—The famous Epilogue to his Tragedy—Publishes his Pastorals—His Quarrel with Pope—Joins in *The Freethinker*—Is patronised by Archbishop Boulter—Death and Burial in Audley Chapel, South Audley Street, London.

OF the birth or early part of the life of Ambrose Philips I have not been able to find any account. His academical education he received at St. John's College in Cambridge, where he first solicited the notice of the world by some English verses, in the collection published by the University on the death of Queen Mary.

From this time how he was employed, or in what station he passed his life, is not yet discovered. He must have published his Pastorals before the year 1708, because they are evidently prior to those of Pope.

He afterwards (1709) addressed to the universal patron, the Duke of Dorset, a *Poetical Letter from Copenhagen*, which was published in *The Tatler* (No. 12), and is by Pope in one of his first letters mentioned with high praise, as the production of a man "who could write very nobly."

Philips was a zealous Whig, and therefore easily found access to Addison and Steele; but his ardour seems not to have procured him anything more than kind words; since he was reduced to translate the *Persian Tales* for Tonson, for which he was afterwards reproached, with this addition of contempt, that he worked for half-a-crown. The book is divided into many sections, for each of which if he received half-a-crown, his reward, as writers then were paid, was very liberal; but half-a-crown had a mean sound.

He was employed in promoting the principles of his party, by epitomising Hacket's *Life of Archbishop Williams*. The original book is written with such depravity of genius, such mixture of the fop and pedant, as has not often appeared.

The epitome is free enough from affectation, but has little spirit or vigour.

In 1712 he brought upon the stage *The Distressed Mother*, almost a translation of Racine's *Andromaque*. Such a work requires no uncommon powers, but the friends of Philips exerted every art to promote his interest. Before the appearance of the play, a whole *Spectator*, none indeed of the best, was devoted to its praise; while it yet continued to be acted, another *Spectator* was written, to tell what impression it made upon Sir Roger; and on the first night a select audience, says Pope, was called together to applaud it.

It was concluded with the most successful Epilogue that was ever yet spoken on the English theatre. The three first nights it was recited twice; and not only continued to be demanded through the run, as it is termed, of the play, but whenever it is recalled to the stage, where by peculiar fortune, though a copy from the French, it yet keeps its place, the Epilogue is still expected, and is still spoken.

The propriety of Epilogues in general, and consequently of this, was questioned by a correspondent of *The Spectator*, whose letter was undoubtedly admitted for the sake of the answer, which soon followed, written with much zeal and acrimony. The attack and the defence equally contributed to stimulate curiosity and continue attention. It may be discovered in the defence, that Prior's Epilogue to *Phædra* had a little excited jealousy; and something of Prior's plan may be discovered in the performance of his rival.

Of this distinguished Epilogue the reputed author was the wretched Budgell, whom Addison used to denominate "the man who calls me cousin"; and when he was asked how such a silly fellow could write so well, replied, "The Epilogue was quite another thing when I saw it first." It was known in Tonson's family, and told to Garrick, that Addison was himself the author of it, and that, when it had been at first printed with his name, he came early in the morning, before the copies were distributed, and ordered it to be given to Budgell, that it might add weight to the solicitation which he was then making for a place.

Philips was now high in the ranks of literature. His play was applauded; his translations from Sappho had been published in *The Spectator*; he was an important and distinguished associate of clubs witty and political; and nothing was wanting to his happiness but that he should be sure of its continuance.

The work which had procured him the first notice from the public was his Six Pastorals, which, flattering the imagination with Arcadian scenes, probably found many readers, and might have long passed as a pleasing amusement, had they not been unhappily too much commended.

The rustic poems of Theocritus were so highly valued by the Greeks and Romans, that they attracted the imitation of Virgil, whose Eclogues seem to have been considered as precluding all attempts of the same kind; for no shepherds were taught to sing by any succeeding poet, till Nemesian and Calphurnius ventured their feeble efforts in the lower age of Latin literature.

At the revival of learning in Italy, it was soon discovered that a dialogue of imaginary swains might be composed with little difficulty; because the conversation of shepherds excludes profound or refined sentiment; and, for images and descriptions, satyrs and fauns, and naiads and dryads, were always within call; and woods and meadows, and hills and rivers, supplied variety of matter, which, having a natural power to soothe the mind, did not quickly cloy it.

Petrarch entertained the learned men of his age with the novelty of modern Pastorals in Latin. Being not ignorant of Greek, and finding nothing in the word *Eclogue* of rural meaning, he supposed it to be corrupted by the copiers, and therefore called his own productions *Æglogues*, by which he meant to express the talk of goatherds, though it will mean only the talk of goats. This new name was adopted by subsequent writers, and amongst others by our Spenser.

More than a century afterwards (1498) Mantuan published his Bucolics with such success, that they were soon dignified by Badius with a comment, and, as Scaliger complained, received into schools, and taught as classical; his complaint was vain, and the practice, however injudicious, spread far, and continued long. Mantuan was read, at least in some of the inferior schools of this kingdom, to the beginning of the present century. The speakers of Mantuan carried their disquisitions beyond the country, to censure the corruptions of the Church; and from him Spenser learned to employ his swains on topics of controversy.

The Italians soon transferred Pastoral Poetry into their own language: Sannazaro wrote *Arcadia* in prose and verse; Tasso and Guarini wrote *Favole Boschareccie*, or Sylvan Dramas; and all nations of Europe filled volumes with Thyrsis and Damon, and Thestylis and Phyllis.

Philips thinks it "somewhat strange to conceive how, in an age so addicted to the Muses, Pastoral Poetry never comes to be so much as thought upon." His wonder seems very unseasonable: there had never, from the time of Spenser, wanted writers to talk occasionally of Arcadia and Strephon; and half the book in which he first tried his powers consists of dialogues on Queen Mary's death, between Tityrus and Corydon, or Mopsus and Menalcas. A series or book of Pastorals, however, I know not that any one had then lately published.

Not long afterwards Pope made the first display of his powers in four Pastorals, written in a very different form. Philips had taken Spenser, and Pope took Virgil for his pattern. Philips endeavoured to be natural, Pope laboured to be elegant.

Philips was now favoured by Addison, and by Addison's companions, who were very willing to push him into reputation. *The Guardian* gave [April 1713] an account of Pastoral, partly critical, and partly historical; in which, when the merit of the modern is compared, Tasso and Guarini are censured for remote thoughts and unnatural refinements; and, upon the whole, the Italians and French are all excluded from rural poetry; and the pipe of the pastoral muse is transmitted by lawful inheritance from Theocritus to Virgil, from Virgil to Spenser, and from Spenser to Philips.

With this inauguration of Philips his rival Pope was not much delighted; he therefore drew a comparison of Philips's performance with his own, in which, with an unexampled and unequalled artifice of irony, though he has himself always the advantage, he gives the preference to Philips. The design of aggrandising himself he disguised with such dexterity, that, though Addison discovered it, Steele was deceived, and was afraid of displeasing Pope by publishing his paper. Published, however, it was (*Guardian*, 40): and from that time Pope and Philips lived in a perpetual reciprocation of malevolence.

In poetical powers, of either praise or satire, there was no proportion between the combatants; but Philips, though he could not prevail by wit, hoped to hurt Pope with another weapon, and charged him, as Pope thought, with Addison's approbation, as disaffected to the Government.

Even with this he was not satisfied; for, indeed, there is no appearance that any regard was paid to his clamours. He proceeded to grosser insults, and hung up a rod at Button's, with which he threatened to chastise Pope, who appears to have been extremely exasperated; for in the first edition of his

Letters he calls Philips "rascal," and in the last still charges him with detaining in his hands the subscriptions for Homer delivered to him by the Hanover Club.

I suppose it was never suspected that he meant to appropriate the money; he only delayed, and with sufficient meanness, the gratification of him by whose prosperity he was pained.

Men sometimes suffer by injudicious kindness; Philips became ridiculous, without his own fault, by the absurd admiration of his friends, who decorated him with honorary garlands, which the first breath of contradiction blasted.

When upon the succession of the House of Hanover [1st Aug. 1714] every Whig expected to be happy, Philips seems to have obtained too little notice: he caught few drops of the golden shower, though he did not omit what flattery could perform. He was only made a Commissioner of the Lottery (1717), and, what did not much elevate his character, a Justice of the Peace.

The success of his first play must naturally dispose him to turn his hopes towards the stage: he did not, however, soon commit himself to the mercy of an audience, but contented himself with the fame already acquired, till after nine years he produced (1722) *The Briton*, a tragedy which, whatever was its reception, is now neglected; though one of the scenes, between Vanoc the British Prince and Valens the Roman General, is confessed to be written with great dramatic skill, animated by spirit truly poetical.

He had not been idle, though he had been silent; for he exhibited another tragedy the same year, on the story of *Humphry Duke of Gloucester*. This tragedy is only remembered by its title.

His happiest undertaking was [1711] of a paper, called *The Freethinker*, in conjunction with associates, of whom one was Dr. Boulter, who, then only minister of a parish in Southwark, was of so much consequence to the Government that he was made first Bishop of Bristol, and afterwards Primate of Ireland, where his piety and his charity will be long honoured.

It may easily be imagined that what was printed under the direction of Boulter would have nothing in it indecent or licentious; its title is to be understood as implying only freedom from unreasonable prejudice. It has been reprinted in volumes, but is little read; nor can impartial criticism recommend it as worthy of revival.

Boulter was not well qualified to write diurnal essays; but

he knew how to practise the liberality of greatness and the fidelity of friendship. When he was advanced to the height of ecclesiastical dignity, he did not forget the companion of his labours. Knowing Philips to be slenderly supported, he took him to Ireland, as partaker of his fortune; and, making him his secretary, added such preferments as enabled him to represent the county of Armagh in the Irish Parliament.

In December 1726 he was made Secretary to the Lord Chancellor; and in August 1733 became Judge of the Prerogative Court.

After the death of his patron he continued some years in Ireland; but at last longing, as it seems, for his native country, he returned (1748) to London, having doubtless survived most of his friends and enemies, and among them his dreaded antagonist Pope. He found, however, the Duke of Newcastle still living, and to him he dedicated his poems collected into a volume.

Having purchased an annuity of 400*l.*, he now certainly hoped to pass some years of life in plenty and tranquillity; but his hope deceived him: he was struck with a palsy, and died June 18, 1749, in his seventy-eighth year.

Of his personal character all that I have heard is, that he was eminent for bravery and skill in the sword, and that in conversation he was solemn and pompous. He had great sensibility of censure, if judgment may be made by a single story which I heard long ago from Mr. Ing, a gentleman of great eminence in Staffordshire. "Philips," said he, "was once at table, when I asked him, How came thy king of Epirus to drive oxen, and to say 'I'm goaded on by love'? After which question he never spoke again."

Of *The Distressed Mother* not much is pretended to be his own, and therefore it is no subject of criticism: his other two tragedies, I believe, are not below mediocrity, nor above it. Among the poems comprised in the late Collection, the *Letter from Copenhagen* may be justly praised; the Pastorals, which by the writer of *The Guardian* were ranked as one of the four genuine productions of the rustic Muse, cannot surely be despicable. That they exhibit a mode of life which did not exist, nor ever existed, is not to be objected: the supposition of such a state is allowed to Pastoral. In his other poems he cannot be denied the praise of lines sometimes elegant; but he has seldom much force, or much comprehension. The pieces that please best are those which, from Pope and Pope's adherents, procured him the name of *Namby Pamby*, the poems of short lines, by which he paid his court to all ages and characters, from Walpole the "steerer of the realm," to Miss Pulteney in the nursery. The numbers are smooth and sprightly, and the diction is seldom faulty. They are not loaded with much thought, yet, if they had been written by Addison, they would have had admirers: little things are not valued but when they are done by those who cannot do greater.

In his translations from Pindar he found the art of reaching all the obscurity of the Theban bard, however he may fall below his sublimity; he will be allowed, if he has less fire, to have more smoke.

He has added nothing to English poetry, yet at least half his book deserves to be read: perhaps he valued most himself that part which the critic would reject.

GILBERT WEST

1700?–1756

Educated at Eton and Oxford—Marries, and retires to Wickham in
Kent—Translates Pindar, and publishes *Observations on the Resurrection*
—His Friendship with Lyttelton and Pitt—Death and Burial at Wickham
—Works and Character.

GILBERT WEST is one of the writers of whom I regret my
inability to give a sufficient account; the intelligence which
my inquiries have obtained is general and scanty.

He was the son of the Reverend Dr. West; perhaps him who
published Pindar at Oxford about the beginning of this century.
His mother was sister to Sir Richard Temple, afterwards Lord
Cobham. His father purposing to educate him for the Church,
sent him first to Eton, and afterwards to Oxford; but he was
seduced to a more airy mode of life, by a commission in a troop
of horse procured him by his uncle.

He continued some time in the army; though it is reasonable
to suppose that he never sunk into a mere soldier, nor ever
lost the love or much neglected the pursuit of learning; and
afterwards, finding himself more inclined to civil employment,
he laid down his commission, and engaged in business under
the Lord Townshend, then Secretary of State, with whom he
attended the King to Hanover.

His adherence to Lord Townshend ended in nothing but a
nomination (May 1729) to be Clerk-Extraordinary of the Privy
Council, which produced no immediate profit; for it only placed
him in a state of expectation and right of succession, and it
was very long before a vacancy admitted him to profit.

Soon afterwards he married, and settled himself in a very
pleasant house at Wickham, in Kent, where he devoted himself
to learning and to piety. Of his learning the late Collection
exhibits evidence, which would have been yet fuller, if the
dissertations which accompany his version of Pindar had not
been improperly omitted. Of his piety the influence has, I hope,
been extended far by his *Observations on the Resurrection*, published in 1747, for which the University of Oxford created him
a Doctor of Laws by Diploma (March 30, 1748), and would

doubtless have reached yet farther had he lived to complete what he had for some time meditated, the Evidences of the Truth of the New Testament. Perhaps it may not be without effect to tell that he read the prayers of the public liturgy every morning to his family, and that on Sunday evening he called his servants into the parlour, and read to them first a sermon, and then prayers. Crashaw is now not the only maker of verses to whom may be given the two venerable names of *Poet* and *Saint*.

He was very often visited by Lyttelton and Pitt, who, when they were weary of faction and debates, used at Wickham to find books and quiet, a decent table, and literary conversation. There is at Wickham a walk made by Pitt; and, what is of far more importance, at Wickham Lyttelton received that conviction which produced [1748] his *Observations on St. Paul*.

These two illustrious friends had for a while listened to the blandishments of infidelity; and when West's book was published, it was bought by some who did not know his change of opinion, in expectation of new objections against Christianity; and as infidels do not want malignity, they revenged the disappointment by calling him a Methodist.

Mr. West's income was not large; and his friends endeavoured, but without success, to obtain an augmentation. It is reported that the education of the young Prince was offered to him, but that he required a more extensive power of superintendence than it was thought proper to allow him.

In time, however, his revenue was improved; he lived to have one of the lucrative clerkships of the Privy Council (1752); and Mr. Pitt at last had it in his power to make him treasurer of Chelsea Hospital.

He was now sufficiently rich; but wealth came too late to be long enjoyed; nor could it secure him from the calamities of life: he lost (1755) his only son; and the year after (March 26) a stroke of the palsy brought to the grave one of the few poets to whom the grave might be without its terrors.

Of his translations I have only compared the first Olympic ode with the original, and found my expectation surpassed both by its elegance and its exactness. He does not confine himself to his author's train of stanzas; for he saw that the difference of the languages required a different mode of versification. The first strophe is eminently happy; in the second he has a little strayed from Pindar's meaning, who says, "If thou, my soul, wishest to speak of games, look not in the desert sky for a planet hotter than the sun, nor shall we tell of nobler games than those of Olympia." He is sometimes too paraphrastical. Pindar bestows upon Hiero an epithet, which, in one word, signifies *delighting in horses*; a word which, in the translation, generates these lines:

> Hiero's royal brows, whose care
> Tends the courser's noble breed,
> Pleas'd to nurse the pregnant mare,
> Pleas'd to train the youthful steed.

Pindar says of Pelops, that "he came alone in the dark to the White Sea"; and West:

> Near the billow-beaten side
> Of the foam-besilver'd main,
> Darkling, and alone, he stood:

which, however, is less exuberant than the former passage.

A work of this kind must, in a minute examination, discover many imperfections; but West's version, so far as I have considered it, appears to be the product of great labour and great abilities.

His *Institution of the Garter* (1742) is written with sufficient knowledge of the manners that prevailed in the age to which it is referred, and with great elegance of diction; but for want of a process of events, neither knowledge nor elegance preserve the reader from weariness.

His *Imitations of Spenser* are very successfully performed, both with respect to the metre, the language, and the fiction; and being engaged at once by the excellence of the sentiments and the artifice of the copy, the mind has two amusements together. But such compositions are not to be reckoned among the great achievements of intellect, because their effect is local and temporary; they appeal not to reason or passion, but to memory, and presuppose an accidental or artificial state of mind. An imitation of Spenser is nothing to a reader, however acute, by whom Spenser has never been perused. Works of this kind may deserve praise, as proofs of great industry and great nicety of observation, but the highest praise, the praise of genius, they cannot claim. The noblest beauties of art are those of which the effect is co-extended with rational nature, or at least with the whole circle of polished life; what is less than this can be only pretty, the plaything of fashion and the amusement of a day.

There is in *The Adventurer* a paper of verses given to one

of the authors as Mr. West's, and supposed to have been written by him. It should not be concealed, however, that it is printed with Mr. Jago's name in Dodsley's Collection, and is mentioned as his in a letter of Shenstone's. Perhaps West gave it without naming the author, and Hawkesworth, receiving it from him, thought it his; for his he thought it, as he told me, and as he tells the public.

WILLIAM COLLINS

1720-1759

Born at Chichester—Educated at Winchester and Oxford—Publishes *Oriental Eclogues* and Odes on several Descriptive and Allegoric Subjects —Publishes Proposals for a *History of the Revival of Learning*—Publishes, a Poem on Thomson's Death—Dies insane, and buried in St. Andrew's Church, Chichester—Works and Character.

WILLIAM COLLINS was born at Chichester on the 25th day of December, 1720. His father was a hatter of good reputation. He was in 1733, as Dr. Warton has kindly informed me, admitted scholar of Winchester College, where he was educated by Dr. Burton. His English exercises were better than his Latin.

He first courted the notice of the public by some verses to a *Lady weeping*, published in *The Gentleman's Magazine*.

In 1740 he stood first in the list of the scholars to be received in succession at New College, but unhappily there was no vacancy. He became a Commoner of Queen's College, probably with a scanty maintenance; but was, in about half a year, elected a Demy of Magdalen College, where he continued till he had taken a Bachelor's degree, and then suddenly left the University, for what reason I know not that he told.

He now (about 1744) came to London a literary adventurer, with many projects in his head, and very little money in his pocket. He designed many works; but his great fault was irresolution, or the frequent calls of immediate necessity broke his schemes, and suffered him to pursue no settled purpose A man doubtful of his dinner, or trembling at a creditor, is not much disposed to abstracted meditation, or remote inquiries. He published proposals for a History of the Revival of Learning; and I have heard him speak with great kindness of Leo the Tenth, and with keen resentment of his tasteless successor. But probably not a page of his history was ever written. He planned several tragedies, but he only planned them. He wrote now and then odes and other poems, and did something, however little.

313

About this time I fell into his company. His appearance was decent and manly; his knowledge considerable, his views extensive, his conversation elegant, and his disposition cheerful. By degrees I gained his confidence; and one day was admitted to him when he was immured by a bailiff that was prowling in the street. On this occasion recourse was had to the book-sellers, who, on the credit of a translation of Aristotle's *Poetics*, which he engaged to write with a large commentary, advanced as much money as enabled him to escape into the country. He showed me the guineas safe in his hand. Soon afterwards his uncle, Mr. Martin, a lieutenant-colonel, left him about two thousand pounds; a sum which Collins could scarcely think exhaustible, and which he did not live to exhaust. The guineas were then repaid, and the translation neglected.

But man is not born for happiness. Collins, who, while he *studied to live*, felt no evil but poverty, no sooner *lived to study* than his life was assailed by more dreadful calamities: disease and insanity.

Having formerly written his character, while perhaps it was yet more distinctly impressed upon my memory, I shall insert it here.

"Mr. Collins was a man of extensive literature, and of vigorous faculties. He was acquainted not only with the learned tongues, but with the Italian, French, and Spanish languages. He had employed his mind chiefly upon works of fiction, and subjects of fancy; and, by indulging some peculiar habits of thought, was eminently delighted with those flights of imagination which pass the bounds of nature, and to which the mind is reconciled only by a passive acquiescence in popular traditions. He loved fairies, genii, giants, and monsters; he delighted to rove through the meanders of enchantment, to gaze on the magnificence of golden palaces, to repose by the waterfalls of Elysian gardens.

"This was, however, the character rather of his inclination than his genius; the grandeur of wildness, and the novelty of extravagance, were always desired by him, but were not always attained. Yet, as diligence is never wholly lost, if his efforts sometimes caused harshness and obscurity, they likewise produced in happier moments sublimity and splendour. This idea which he had formed of excellence led him to Oriental fictions and allegorical imagery; and perhaps, while he was intent upon description, he did not sufficiently cultivate sentiment. His poems are the productions of a mind not deficient in fire, nor unfurnished with knowledge either of books or life, but somewhat obstructed in its progress by deviation in quest of mistaken beauties.

"His morals were pure, and his opinions pious; in a long continuance of poverty, and long habits of dissipation, it cannot be expected that any character should be exactly uniform. There is a degree of want by which the freedom of agency is almost destroyed; and long association with fortuitous companions will at last relax the strictness of truth, and abate the fervour of sincerity. That this man, wise and virtuous as he was, passed always unentangled through the snares of life, it would be prejudice and temerity to affirm; but it may be said that at least he preserved the source of action unpolluted, that his principles were never shaken, that his distinctions of right and wrong were never confounded, and that his faults had nothing of malignity or design, but proceeded from some unexpected pressure, or casual temptation.

"The latter part of his life cannot be remembered but with pity and sadness. He languished some years under that depression of mind which enchains the faculties without destroying them, and leaves reason the knowledge of right without the power of pursuing it. These clouds which he perceived gathering on his intellects, he endeavoured to disperse by travel, and passed into France; but found himself constrained to yield to his malady, and returned. He was for some time confined in a house of lunatics, and afterwards retired to the care of his sister in Chichester, where death, in 1759, came to his relief.

"After his return from France, the writer of this character paid him a visit at Islington, where he was waiting for his sister, whom he had directed to meet him: there was then nothing of disorder discernible in his mind by any but himself; but he had withdrawn from study, and travelled with no other book than an English Testament, such as children carry to the school: when his friend took it into his hand, out of curiosity to see what companion a man of letters had chosen, 'I have but one book,' said Collins, 'but that is the best.'"

Such was the fate of Collins, with whom I once delighted to converse, and whom I yet remember with tenderness.

He was visited at Chichester in his last illness by his learned friends Dr. Warton and his brother, to whom he spoke with disapprobation of his Oriental Eclogues, as not sufficiently expressive of Asiatic manners, and called them his Irish Eclogues. He showed them, at the same time, an ode inscribed to Mr. John Home, on the superstitions of the Highlands;

which they thought superior to his other works, but which no search has yet found.

His disorder was not alienation of mind, but general laxity and feebleness, a deficiency rather of his vital than intellectual powers. What he spoke wanted neither judgment nor spirit; but a few minutes exhausted him, so that he was forced to rest upon the couch, till a short cessation restored his powers, and he was again able to talk with his former vigour.

The approaches of this dreadful malady he began to feel soon after his uncle's death; and with the usual weakness of men so diseased, eagerly snatched that temporary relief with which the table and the bottle flatter and seduce. But his health continually declined, and he grew more and more burthensome to himself.

To what I have formerly said of his writings may be added, that his diction was often harsh, unskilfully laboured, and injudiciously selected. He affected the obsolete when it was not worthy of revival; and he puts his words out of the common order, seeming to think, with some later candidates for fame, that not to write prose is certainly to write poetry. His lines commonly are of slow motion, clogged and impeded with clusters of consonants. As men are often esteemed who cannot be loved, so the poetry of Collins may sometimes extort praise when it gives little pleasure.

Mr. Collins's first production is added here from *The Gentleman's Magazine.*

To Miss Aurelia C——r,
On her Weeping at her Sister's Wedding

Cease, fair Aurelia, cease to mourn;
  Lament not Hannah's happy state;
You may be happy in your turn,
  And seize the treasure you regret.
With Love united Hymen stands,
  And softly whispers to your charms,
"Meet but your lover in my bands,
  You'll find your sister in his arms."

JOHN DYER

1700–1758

Second Son of Robert Dyer, of Aberglasney, in Caermarthenshire—
Educated at Westminster—Studies Poetry and Painting—Publishes
Grongar Hill, a Poem—Enters into Holy Orders—Publishes *The Ruins
of Rome, The Fleece*, etc.—Made Rector of Coningsby, in Lincolnshire—
Death and Burial at Coningsby.

JOHN DYER, of whom I have no other account to give than
his own letters, published with Hughes's correspondence, and
the notes added by the editor, have afforded me, was born
in 1700, the second son of Robert Dyer, of Aberglasney, in
Caermarthenshire, a solicitor of great capacity and note.

He passed through Westminster School under the care of
Dr. Freind, and was then called home to be instructed in his
father's profession. But his father died soon, and he took no
delight in the study of the law, but having always amused
himself with drawing, resolved to turn painter, and became
pupil to Mr. Richardson, an artist then of high reputation, but
now [1780] better known by his books than by his pictures.

Having studied a while under his master, he became, as he
tells his friend, an itinerant painter, and wandered about
South Wales and the parts adjacent; but he mingled poetry with
painting, and about 1727 [in 1726] printed *Grongar Hill* in
Lewis's *Miscellany*.

Being, probably, unsatisfied with his own proficiency, he, like
other painters, travelled to Italy; and coming back in 1740,
published *The Ruins of Rome*.

If his poem was written soon after his return, he did not
make much use of his acquisitions in painting, whatever they
might be; for decline of health and love of study determined
him to the Church. He therefore entered into orders; and, it
seems, married about the same time a lady of the name of
Ensor, "whose grandmother," says he, "was a Shakespeare,
descended from a brother of everybody's Shakespeare"; by
her, in 1756, he had a son and three daughters living.

His ecclesiastical provision was a long time but slender.
His first patron, Mr. Harper, gave him, in 1741, Calthorp, in

Leicestershire, of 80*l.* a year, on which he lived ten years, and then exchanged it for Belchford, in Lincolnshire, of 75*l.* His condition now began to mend. In 1751 Sir John Heathcote gave him Coningsby [in Lincolnshire], of 140*l.* a year; and in 1755 the Chancellor added Kirkby, of 110*l.* He complains that the repair of the house at Coningsby, and other expenses, took away the profit. In 1757 he published *The Fleece,* his greatest poetical work, of which I will not suppress a ludicrous story. Dodsley, the bookseller, was one day mentioning it to a critical visitor, with more expectation of success than the other could easily admit. In the conversation the author's age was asked; and being represented as advanced in life, "He will," said the critic, "be buried in woollen."

He did not indeed long survive that publication, nor long enjoy the increase of his preferments; for in 1758 he died.

Dyer is not a poet of bulk or dignity sufficient to require an elaborate criticism. *Grongar Hill* is the happiest of his productions: it is not indeed very accurately written; but the scenes which it displays are so pleasing, the images which they raise so welcome to the mind, and the reflections of the writer so consonant to the general sense or experience of mankind, that when it is once read, it will be read again.

The idea of *The Ruins of Rome* strikes more, but pleases less, and the title raises greater expectation than the performance gratifies. Some passages, however, are conceived with the mind of a poet; as when, in the neighbourhood of dilapidating edifices, he says,

> ——The Pilgrim oft,
> At dead of night, mid his orison hears
> Aghast the voice of time, disparting tow'rs,
> Tumbling all precipitate down dash'd,
> Rattling around, loud thund'ring to the moon.

Of *The Fleece,* which never became popular, and is now universally neglected, I can say little that is likely to recall it to attention. The woolcomber and the poet appear to me such discordant natures, that an attempt to bring them together is to *couple the serpent with the fowl.* When Dyer, whose mind was not unpoetical, has done his utmost, by interesting his reader in our native commodity, by interspersing rural imagery and incidental digressions, by clothing small images in great words, and by all the writer's arts of delusion, the meanness naturally adhering, and the irreverence habitually annexed to trade and manufacture, sink him under insuperable oppression; and the disgust which blank verse, encumbering and encumbered, super-adds to an unpleasing subject, soon repels the reader, however willing to be pleased.

Let me, however, honestly report whatever may counter-balance this weight of censure. I have been told that Aken-side, who, upon a poetical question, has a right to be heard, said, "That he would regulate his opinion of the reigning taste by the fate of Dyer's *Fleece*; for, if that were well received, he should not think it any longer reasonable to expect fame from excellence."

WILLIAM SHENSTONE

1714-1763

Born at the Leasowes, in Shropshire—Educated at Hales-Owen and Oxford—Publishes a small Miscellany of Poems without his Name—Publishes *The Judgment of Hercules, The Schoolmistress*, and other Poems —His Ferme ornée—His Pecuniary Difficulties—Death and Burial in Hales-Owen Churchyard, Shropshire—Works and Character.

WILLIAM SHENSTONE, the son of Thomas Shenstone and Anne Penn, was born in November 1714, at the Leasowes in Hales-Owen, one of those insulated districts which, in the division of the kingdom, was appended, for some reason not now discoverable, to a distant county; and which, though surrounded by Warwickshire and Worcestershire, belongs to Shropshire, though perhaps thirty miles distant from any other part of it.

He learned to read of an old dame, whom his poem of *The Schoolmistress* has delivered to posterity; and soon received such delight from books, that he was always calling for fresh entertainment, and expected that, when any of the family went to market, a new book should be brought him, which, when it came, was in fondness carried to bed and laid by him. It is said, that when his request had been neglected, his mother wrapped up a piece of wood of the same form, and pacified him for the night.

As he grew older, he went for a while to the grammar-school in Hales-Owen, and was placed afterwards with Mr. Crumpton, an eminent schoolmaster at Solihull, where he distinguished himself by the quickness of his progress.

When he was young (June 1724) he was deprived of his father, and soon after (August 1726) of his grandfather; and was, with his brother, who died afterwards unmarried, left to the care of his grandmother, who managed the estate.

From school he was sent in 1732 to Pembroke College in Oxford, a society which for half a century has been eminent for English poetry and elegant literature. Here it appears that he found delight and advantage; for he continued his name in the book ten years, though he took no degree. After the first four years he put on the civilian's gown, but without showing any intention to engage in the profession.

About the time when he went to Oxford, the death of his grandmother devolved his affairs to the care of the Rev. Mr. Dolman, of Brome in Staffordshire, whose attention he always mentioned with gratitude.

At Oxford he employed himself upon English poetry; and in 1737 published a small *Miscellany*, without his name.

He then for a time wandered about, to acquaint himself with life, and was sometimes at London, sometimes at Bath, or any other place of public resort; but he did not forget his poetry. He published in 1741 his *Judgment of Hercules*, addressed to Mr. Lyttelton, whose interest he supported with great warmth at an election: this was next year [May 1742] followed by *The Schoolmistress*.

Mr. Dolman, to whose care he was indebted for his ease and leisure, died in 1745, and the care of his own fortune now fell upon himself. He tried to escape it awhile, and lived at his house with his tenants, who were distantly related; but, finding that imperfect possession inconvenient, he took the whole estate into his own hands, more to the improvement of its beauty than the increase of its produce.

Now was excited his delight in rural pleasures, and his ambition of rural elegance: he began from this time to point his prospects, to diversify his surface, to entangle his walks, and to wind his waters; which he did with such judgment and such fancy as made his little domain the envy of the great and the admiration of the skilful; a place to be visited by travellers, and copied by designers. Whether to plant a walk in undulating curves, and to place a bench at every turn where there is an object to catch the view; to make water run where it will be heard, and to stagnate where it will be seen; to leave intervals where the eye will be pleased, and to thicken the plantation where there is something to be hidden, demands any great powers of mind, I will not inquire: perhaps a sullen and surly speculator may think such performances rather the sport than the business of human reason. But it must be at least confessed that to embellish the form of nature is an innocent amusement; and some praise must be allowed, by the most supercilious observer, to him who does best what such multitudes are contending to do well.

This praise was the praise of Shenstone; but like all other modes of felicity, it was not enjoyed without its abatements.

Lyttelton was his neighbour and his rival, whose empire, spacious and opulent, looked with disdain on the *petty State* that *appeared behind it*. For a while the inhabitants of Hagley affected to tell their acquaintance of the little fellow that was trying to make himself admired; but when by degrees the Leasowes forced themselves into notice, they took care to defeat the curiosity which they could not suppress, by conducting their visitants perversely to inconvenient points of view, and introducing them at the wrong end of a walk to detect a deception; injuries of which Shenstone would heavily complain. Where there is emulation there will be vanity; and where there is vanity there will be folly.

The pleasure of Shenstone was all in his eye; he valued what he valued merely for its looks; nothing raised his indignation more than to ask if there were any fishes in his water.

His house was mean, and he did not improve it; his care was of his grounds. When he came home from his walks, he might find his floors flooded by a shower through the broken roof; but could spare no money for its reparation.

In time his expenses brought clamours about him, that overpowered the lamb's bleat and the linnet's song; and his groves were haunted by beings very different from fauns and fairies. He spent his estate in adorning it, and his death was probably hastened by his anxieties. He was a lamp that spent its oil in blazing. It is said that if he had lived a little longer, he would have been assisted by a pension: such bounty could not have been ever more properly bestowed; but that it was ever asked is not certain; it is too certain that it never was enjoyed.

He died at the Leasowes of a putrid fever, about five on Friday morning, February 11, 1763; and was buried by the side of his brother in the churchyard of Hales-Owen.

He was never married, though he might have obtained the lady, whoever she was, to whom his *Pastoral Ballad* was addressed. He is represented by his friend Dodsley as a man of great tenderness and generosity, kind to all that were within his influence; but, if once offended, not easily appeased; inattentive to economy, and careless of his expenses: in his person he was larger than the middle size, with something clumsy in his form; very negligent of his clothes, and remarkable for wearing his grey hair in a particular manner; for he held that the fashion was no rule of dress, and that every man was to suit his appearance to his natural form.

His mind was not very comprehensive, nor his curiosity active; he had no value for those parts of knowledge which he had not himself cultivated.

His life was unstained by any crime: the Elegy on Jesse, which has been supposed to relate an unfortunate and criminal amour of his own, was known by his friends to have been suggested by the story of Miss Godfrey in Richardson's *Pamela*.

What Gray thought of his character, from the perusal of his letters, was this:

"I have read too an octavo volume of Shenstone's Letters. Poor man! he was always wishing for money, for fame, and other distinctions; and his whole philosophy consisted in living against his will in retirement, and in a place which his taste had adorned; but which he only enjoyed when people of note came to see and commend it: his correspondence is about nothing else but this place and his own writings, with two or three neighbouring clergymen, who wrote verses too."

His poems consist of elegies, odes, and ballads, humorous sallies, and moral pieces.

His conception of an elegy he has in his Preface very judiciously and discriminately explained. It is, according to his account, the effusion of a contemplative mind, sometimes plaintive, and always serious, and therefore superior to the glitter of slight ornaments. His compositions suit not ill to this description. His topics of praise are the domestic virtues, and his thoughts are pure and simple; but, wanting combination, they want variety. The peace of solitude, the innocence of inactivity, and the unenvied security of an humble station, can fill but a few pages. That of which the essence is uniformity will be soon described: his Elegies have therefore too much resemblance of each other.

The lines are sometimes, such as Elegy requires, smooth and easy; but to this praise his claim is not constant: his diction is often harsh, improper, and affected; his words ill-coined or ill-chosen, and his phrase unskilfully inverted.

The Lyric Poems are almost all of the light and airy kind, such as trip lightly and nimbly along, without the load of any weighty meaning. From these, however, *Rural Elegance* has some right to be excepted. I once heard it praised by a very learned lady; and though the lines are irregular, and the thoughts diffused with too much verbosity, yet it cannot be denied to contain both philosophical argument and poetical spirit.

Of the rest I cannot think any excellent; *The Skylark* pleases me best, which has, however, more of the epigram than of the ode.

But the four parts of his *Pastoral Ballad* demand particular notice. I cannot but regret that it is pastoral: an intelligent reader, acquainted with the scenes of real life, sickens at the mention of the *crook*, the *pipe*, the *sheep*, and the *kids*, which it is not necessary to bring forward to notice, for the poet's art is selection, and he ought to show the beauties without the grossness of the country life. His stanza seems to have been chosen in imitation of Rowe's *Despairing Shepherd*.

In the first part are two passages, to which if any mind denies its sympathy, it has no acquaintance with love or nature:

> I priz'd every hour that went by,
>   Beyond all that had pleas'd me before;
> But now they are past, and I sigh,
>   And I grieve that I priz'd them no more.
> When forc'd the fair nymph to forego,
>   What anguish I felt in my heart!
> Yet I thought—but it might not be so—
>   'Twas with pain that she saw me depart.
> She gaz'd as I slowly withdrew,
>   My path I could hardly discern;
> So sweetly she bade me adieu,
>   I thought that she bade me return.

In the second this passage has its prettiness, though it be not equal to the former:

> I have found out a gift for my fair;
>   I have found where the wood-pigeons breed:
> But let me that plunder forbear,
>   She will say 'twas a barbarous deed:
> For he ne'er could be true, she averr'd,
>   Who could rob a poor bird of its young;
> And I lov'd her the more when I heard
>   Such tenderness fall from her tongue.

In the third he mentions the commonplaces of amorous poetry with some address:

> 'Tis his with mock passion to glow!
>   'Tis his in smooth tales to unfold,
> How her face is as bright as the snow,
>   And her bosom, be sure, is as cold:
> How the nightingales labour the strain,
>   With the notes of his charmer to vie;
> How they vary their accents in vain,
>   Repine at her triumphs, and die.

In the fourth I find nothing better than this natural strain of Hope:

> Alas! from the day that we met,
>   What hope of an end to my woes?

When I cannot endure to forget
The glance that undid my repose.
Yet Time may diminish the pain:
The flower, and the shrub, and the tree,
Which I rear'd for her pleasure in vain,
In time may have comfort for me.

His *Levities* are by their title exempted from the severities of criticism; yet it may be remarked in a few words, that his humour is sometimes gross, and seldom sprightly.

Of the Moral Poems the first is *The Choice of Hercules*, from Xenophon. The numbers are smooth, the diction elegant, and the thoughts just; but something of vigour is still to be wished, which it might have had by brevity and compression. His *Fate of Delicacy* has an air of gaiety, but not a very pointed and general moral. His blank verses, those that can read them may probably find to be like the blank verses of his neighbours. *Love and Honour* is derived from the old ballad, *Did you not hear of a Spanish Lady?*—I wish it well enough to wish it were in rhyme.

The Schoolmistress, of which I know not what claim it has to stand among the Moral Works, is surely the most pleasing of Shenstone's performances. The adoption of a particular style, in light and short compositions, contributes much to the increase of pleasure: we are entertained at once with two imitations, of nature in the sentiments, of the original author in the style, and between them the mind is kept in perpetual employment.

The general recommendation of Shenstone is easiness and simplicity; his general defect is want of comprehension and variety. Had his mind been better stored with knowledge, whether he could have been great, I know not; he would certainly have been agreeable.

EDWARD YOUNG

1681–1765

Born at Upham, in Hampshire—Educated at Winchester and Oxford—His first Poetry—Is patronised by the Duke of Wharton—Publishes his *Universal Passion*—Writes for the Stage—Enters into Holy Orders—Receives a Pension of 200*l.* a year from George I.—Marries—Death of his Wife—Publishes *The Complaint, or Night Thoughts*—Presented to the Living of Welwyn, in Hertfordshire—His only Son—Death and Burial at Welwyn—Works and Character.

THE following Life was written, at my request, by a gentleman who had better information than I could easily have obtained; and the public will perhaps wish that I had solicited and obtained more such favours from him.

DEAR SIR,—In consequence of our different conversations about authentic materials for the Life of Young, I send you the following detail:—

Of great men, something must always be said to gratify curiosity. Of the illustrious author of the *Night Thoughts* much has been told of which there never could have been proofs; and little care appears to have been taken to tell that of which proofs, with little trouble, might have been procured.

Edward Young was born at Upham, near Winchester, in June 1681. He was the son of Edward Young, at that time Fellow of Winchester College and rector of Upham; who was the son of Jo. Young of Woodhay in Berkshire, styled by Wood *gentleman*. In September 1682, the poet's father was collated to the prebend of Gillingham Minor, in the church of Sarum, by Bishop Ward. When Ward's faculties were impaired through age, his duties were necessarily performed by others. We learn from Wood that, at a visitation of Sprat's, July the 12th, 1686, the prebendary preached a Latin sermon, afterwards published, with which the bishop was so pleased, that he told the chapter he was concerned to find the preacher had one of the worst prebends in their church. Some time after this, in consequence of his merit and reputation, or of the interest of Lord Bradford, to whom, in 1702, he dedicated two volumes of sermons, he was appointed chaplain to King William and

Queen Mary, and preferred to the deanery of Sarum. Jacob, who wrote in 1720, says, "He was chaplain and clerk of the closet to the late Queen [Anne], who honoured him by standing godmother to the poet." His Fellowship of Winchester he resigned in favour of a gentleman of the name of Harris, who married his only daughter. The dean died at Sarum, after a short illness, in 1705, in the sixty-third year of his age. On the Sunday after his decease Bishop Burnet preached at the cathedral, and began his sermon with saying, "Death has been of late walking round us, and making breach upon breach upon us, and has now carried away the head of this body with a stroke; so that he, whom you saw a week ago distributing the holy mysteries, is now laid in the dust. But he still lives in the many excellent directions he has left us, both how to live and how to die."

The dean placed his son upon the foundation at Winchester College, where he had himself been educated. At this school Edward Young remained till the election after his eighteenth birthday, the period at which those upon the foundation are superannuated. Whether he did not betray his abilities early in life, or his masters had not skill enough to discover in their pupil any marks of genius for which he merited reward, or no vacancy at Oxford afforded them an opportunity to bestow upon him the reward provided for merit by William of Wykeham, certain it is that to an Oxford fellowship our poet did not succeed. By chance, or by choice, New College cannot claim the honour of numbering among its fellows him who wrote the *Night Thoughts*.

On the 13th of October, 1703, he was entered an independent member of New College, that he might live at little expense in the warden's lodgings, who was a particular friend of his father's, till he should be qualified to stand for a fellowship at All Souls. In a few months the warden of New College died. He then removed to Corpus College. The president of this society, from regard also for his father, invited him thither, in order to lessen his academical expenses. In 1708 he was nominated to a law fellowship at All Souls by Archbishop Tenison, into whose hands it came by devolution. Such repeated patronage, while it justifies Burnet's praise of the father, reflects credit on the conduct of the son. The manner in which it was exerted seems to prove that the father did not leave behind him much wealth.

On the 23rd of April, 1714, Young took his degree of Bachelor of Civil Laws, and his Doctor's degree on the 10th of June, 1719.

Soon after he went to Oxford, he discovered, it is said, an inclination for pupils. Whether he ever commenced tutor is not known. None has hitherto boasted to have received his academical instruction from the author of the *Night Thoughts*.

It is probable that his college was proud of him no less as a scholar than as a poet; for in 1716, when the foundation of the Codrington Library was laid, two years after he had taken his Bachelor's degree, Young was appointed to speak the Latin oration. This is at least particular for being dedicated in English "To the Ladies of the Codrington Family." To these ladies he says, "that he was unavoidably flung into a singularity, by being obliged to write an epistle dedicatory void of commonplace, and such an one as was never published before by any author whatever: that this practice absolved them from any obligation of reading what was presented to them; and that the bookseller approved of it, because it would make people stare, was absurd enough, and perfectly right."

Of this oration there is no appearance in his own edition of his works; and prefixed to an edition by Curll and Tonson, in 1741, is a letter from Young to Curll, if we may credit Curll, dated December the 9th, 1739, wherein he says that he has not leisure to review what he formerly wrote, and adds, "I have not the *Epistle to Lord Lansdown*. If you will take my advice, I would have you omit that, and the oration on Codrington. I think the collection will sell better without them."

There are who relate that, when first Young found himself independent, and his own master at All Souls, he was not the ornament to religion and morality which he afterwards became.

The authority of his father, indeed, had ceased some time before by his death; and Young was certainly not ashamed to be patronised by the infamous Wharton. But Wharton befriended in Young, perhaps, the poet, and particularly the tragedian. If virtuous authors must be patronised only by virtuous peers, who shall point them out?

Yet Pope is said by Ruffhead to have told Warburton, that "Young had much of a sublime genius, though without common sense; so that his genius, having no guide, was perpetually liable to degenerate into bombast. This made him pass a *foolish youth*, the sport of peers and poets: but his having a very good heart enabled him to support the clerical character when he assumed it, first with decency, and afterwards with honour."

They who think ill of Young's morality in the early part of

his life, may perhaps be wrong; but Tindal could not err in his opinion of Young's warmth and ability in the cause of religion. Tindal used to spend much of his time at All Souls. "The other boys," said the atheist, "I can always answer, because I always know whence they have their arguments, which I have read a hundred times; but that fellow Young is continually pestering me with something of his own."

After all, Tindal and the censurers of Young may be reconcileable Young might, for two or three years, have tried that kind of life, in which his natural principles would not suffer him to wallow long. If this were so, he has left behind him not only his evidence in favour of virtue, but the potent testimony of experience against vice.

We shall soon see that one of his earliest productions was more serious than what comes from the generality of unfledged poets.

Young perhaps ascribed the good fortune of Addison to the *Poem to his Majesty*, presented, with a copy of verses, to Somers; and hoped that he also might soar to wealth and honours on wings of the same kind. His first poetical flight was when Queen Anne called up to the House of Lords the sons of the Earls of Northampton and Aylesbury, and added, in one day, ten others to the number of peers. In order to reconcile the people to one, at least, of the new lords, he published, in 1713, *An Epistle to the Right Honourable the Lord Lansdown*. In this composition the poet pours out his panegyric with the extravagance of a young man, who thinks his present stock of wealth will never be exhausted.

The poem seems intended also to reconcile the public to the late peace. This is endeavoured to be done by showing that men are slain in war, and that in peace "harvests wave, and commerce swells her sail." If this be humanity, for which he meant it, is it politics? Another purpose of this epistle appears to have been to prepare the public for the reception of some tragedy he might have in hand. His Lordship's patronage, he says, will not let him "repent his passion for the stage"; and the particular praise bestowed on *Othello* and *Oroonoko* looks as if some such character as Zanga was even then in contemplation. The affectionate mention of the death of his friend Harrison of New College, at the close of this poem, is an instance of Young's art, which displayed itself so wonderfully some time afterwards in the *Night Thoughts*, of making the public a party in his private sorrow.

Should justice call upon you to censure this poem, it ought

at least to be remembered that he did not insert it in his works; and that in the letter to Curll, as we have seen, he advises its omission. The booksellers, in the late body of English poetry, should have distinguished what was deliberately rejected by the respective authors. This I shall be careful to do with regard to Young. "I think," says he, "the following pieces in *four* volumes to be the most excusable of all that I have written; and I wish *less apology* was needful for these. As there is no recalling what is got abroad, the pieces here republished I have revised and corrected, and rendered them as *pardonable* as it was in my power to do."

Shall the gates of repentance be shut only against literary sinners?

When Addison published *Cato* in 1713, Young had the honour of prefixing to it a recommendatory copy of verses. This is one of the pieces which the author of the *Night Thoughts* did not republish.

On the appearance of his poem on *The Last Day* Addison did not return Young's compliment; but *The Englishman* of October 29, 1713, which was probably written by Addison, speaks handsomely of this poem. *The Last Day* was published soon after the peace. The vice-chancellor's *imprimatur* (for it was first printed at Oxford) is dated May the 19th, 1713. From the exordium Young appears to have spent some time on the composition of it. While other bards "with Britain's hero set their souls on fire," he draws, he says, a deeper scene. Marlborough *had been* considered by Britain as her *hero*; but, when *The Last Day* was published, female cabal had blasted for a time the laurels of Blenheim. This serious poem was finished by Young as early as 1710, before he was thirty; for part of it is printed in *The Tatler*. It was inscribed to the Queen [Anne], in a Dedication which, for some reason, he did not admit into his works. It tells her that his only title to the great honour he now does himself is the obligation which he formerly received from her royal indulgence.

Of this obligation nothing is now known, unless he alluded to her being his godmother. He is said indeed to have been engaged at a settled stipend as a writer for the Court. In Swift's *Rhapsody on Poetry* are these lines, speaking of the Court:

> Whence Gay was banish'd in disgrace,
> Where Pope will never show his face,
> Where Y—— must torture his invention
> To flatter knaves, or lose his pension.

That Y—— means Young seems clear from four other lines in the same poem:

> Attend, ye Popes and Youngs and Gays,
> And tune your harps and strew your bays;
> Your panegyrics here provide;
> You cannot err on flattery's side.

Yet who shall say with certainty that Young was a pensioner? In all modern periods of this country have not the writers on one side been regularly called hirelings, and on the other patriots?

Of the Dedication the complexion is clearly political. It speaks in the highest terms of the late peace; it gives her Majesty praise indeed for her victories, but says that the author is more pleased to see her rise from this lower world, soaring above the clouds, passing the first and second heavens, and leaving the fixed stars behind her; nor will he lose her there, he says, but keep her still in view through the boundless spaces on the other side of creation, in her journey towards eternal bliss, till he behold the heaven of heavens open, and angels receiving and conveying her still onward from the stretch of his imagination, which tires in her pursuit, and falls back again to earth.

The Queen was soon called away from this lower world to a place where human praise or human flattery, even less general than this, are of little consequence. If Young thought the Dedication contained only the praise of truth, he should not have omitted it in his works. Was he conscious of the exaggeration of party? Then he should not have written it. The poem itself is not without a glance towards politics, notwithstanding the subject. The cry that the Church was in danger had not yet subsided. *The Last Day*, written by a layman, was much approved by the Ministry and their friends.

Before the Queen's death, *The Force of Religion, or Vanquished Love*, was sent into the world. This poem is founded on the execution of Lady Jane Grey and her husband Lord Guildford, 1554; a story chosen for the subject of a tragedy by Edmund Smith, and wrought into a tragedy by Rowe. The dedication of it to the Countess of Salisbury does not appear in his own edition. He hopes it may be some excuse for his presumption that the story could not have been read without thoughts of the Countess of Salisbury, though it had been dedicated to another. "To behold," he proceeds, "a person *only* virtuous, stirs in us a prudent regret; to behold a person *only* amiable to the sight, warms us with a religious indignation; but to turn our eyes on a Countess of Salisbury, gives us pleasure and improvement; it works a sort of miracle, occasions the bias of our nature to fall off from sin; and makes our very senses and affections converts to religion, and promoters of our duty." His flattery was as ready for the other sex as for ours, and was at least as well adapted.

August the 27th, 1714, Pope writes to his friend Jervas, that he is just arrived from Oxford; that everyone is much concerned for the Queen's death, but that no panegyrics are ready yet for the King. Nothing like friendship had yet taken place between Pope and Young; for, soon after the event which Pope mentions, Young published a poem on the Queen's death, and his Majesty's accession to the throne. It is inscribed to Addison, then secretary to the Lords Justices. Whatever were the obligations which he had formerly received from Anne, the poet appears to aim at something of the same sort from George. Of the poem the intention seems to have been to show that he had the same extravagant strain of praise for a King as for a Queen. To discover, at the very outset of a foreigner's reign, that the gods bless his new subjects in such a King, is something more than praise. Neither was this deemed one of his *excusable pieces*. We do not find it in his works.

Young's father had been well acquainted with Lady Anne Wharton, the first wife of Thomas Wharton, Esq., afterwards Marquis of Wharton; a lady celebrated for her poetical talents by Burnet and by Waller.

To the Dean of Sarum's visitation sermon, already mentioned, were added some verses "by that excellent poetess Mrs. Anne Wharton," upon its being translated into English, at the instance of Waller, by Atwood. Wharton, after he became ennobled, did not drop the son of his old friend. In him, during the short time he lived, Young found a patron, and in his dissolute descendant a friend and a companion. The Marquis died in April 1715. In the beginning of the next year the young Marquis set out upon his travels, from which he returned in about a twelvemonth. The beginning of 1717 carried him to Ireland, where, says the *Biographia*, "on the score of his extraordinary qualities, he had the honour done him of being admitted, though under age, to take his seat in the House of Lords."

With this unhappy character it is not unlikely that Young went to Ireland. From his letter to Richardson on *Original Composition*, it is clear he was, at some period of his life, in that country. "I remember," says he, in that letter, speaking of Swift, "as I and others were taking with him an evening walk, about a mile out of Dublin, he stopped short; we passed on; but perceiving he did not follow us, I went back, and found him fixed as a statue, and earnestly gazing upward at a noble elm, which in its uppermost branches was much withered and decayed. Pointing at it, he said, 'I shall be like that tree, I shall die at top.'" Is it not probable that this visit to Ireland was paid when he had an opportunity of going thither with his avowed friend and patron?

From *The Englishman* it appears that a tragedy by Young was in the theatre so early as 1713. Yet *Busiris* was not brought upon Drury Lane stage till 1719. It was inscribed to the Duke of Newcastle, because "the late instances he had received of his Grace's undeserved and uncommon favour, in an affair of some consequence (foreign to the theatre), had taken from him the privilege of choosing a patron." The Dedication he afterwards suppressed.

Busiris was followed in the year 1721 by *The Revenge*. He dedicated this famous tragedy to the Duke of Wharton. "Your Grace," says the Dedication, "has been pleased to make yourself accessary to the following scenes, not only by suggesting the most beautiful incident in them, but by making all possible provision for the success of the whole."

That his Grace should have suggested the incident to which he alludes, whatever that incident might have been, is not unlikely. The last mental exertion of the superannuated young man in his quarters at Lerida, in Spain, was some scenes of a tragedy on the story of Mary Queen of Scots.

Dryden dedicated *Marriage à la Mode* to Wharton's infamous relation Rochester, whom he acknowledges not only as the defender of his poetry, but as the promoter of his fortune. Young concludes his address to Wharton thus—"My present fortune is his bounty, and my future his care, which I will venture to say will be always remembered to his honour, since he, I know, intended his generosity as an encouragement to merit, though, through his very pardonable partiality to one who bears him so sincere a duty and respect, I happen to receive the benefit of it." That he ever had such a patron as Wharton, Young took all the pains in his power to conceal from the world, by excluding this Dedication from his works. He should have remembered that he at the same time concealed his obligation to Wharton for *the most beautiful incident* in what is surely not his least beautiful composition. The passage just quoted is, in a poem afterwards addressed to Walpole, literally copied:

> Be this thy partial smile from censure free;
> 'Twas meant for merit, though it fell on me.

While Young, who, in his *Love of Fame*, complains grievously how often "dedications wash an Æthiop white," was painting an amiable Duke of Wharton in perishable prose, Pope was, perhaps, beginning to describe the "scorn and wonder of his days" in lasting verse.

To the patronage of such a character, had Young studied men as much as Pope, he would have known how little to have trusted. Young, however, was certainly indebted to it for something material; and the Duke's regard for Young, added to his "Lust of Praise," procured to All Souls College a donation, which was not forgotten by the poet when he dedicated *The Revenge*.

It will surprise you to see me cite second Atkins, Case 136, Stiles *versus* the Attorney-General, 14th March, 1740, as authority for the life of a poet. But biographers do not always find such certain guides as the oaths of the persons whom they record. Chancellor Hardwicke was to determine whether two annuities, granted by the Duke of Wharton to Young, were for legal considerations. One was dated the 24th of March, 1719, and accounted for his Grace's bounty in a style princely and commendable, if not legal—"considering that the public good is advanced by the encouragement of learning and the polite arts, and being pleased therein with the attempts of Dr. Young, in consideration thereof, and of the love I bear him," etc. The other was dated the 10th of July, 1722.

Young, on his examination, swore that he quitted the Exeter family, and refused an annuity of 100*l.* which had been offered him for his life if he would continue tutor to Lord Burleigh, upon the pressing solicitations of the Duke of Wharton, and his Grace's assurances of providing for him in a much more ample manner. It also appeared that the Duke had given him a bond for 600*l.*, dated the 15th of March, 1721, in consideration of his taking several journeys, and being at great expenses, in order to be chosen member of the House of Commons at the Duke's desire, and in consideration of his not taking two livings of 200*l.* and 400*l.* in the gift of All Souls College, on his Grace's promises of serving and advancing him in the world.

Of his adventures in the Exeter family I am unable to give

any account. The attempt to get into Parliament was at Ciren-
cester, where Young stood a contested election. His Grace
discovered in him talents for oratory as well as for poetry. Nor
was this judgment wrong. Young, after he took orders, became
a very popular preacher, and was much followed for the grace
and animation of his delivery. By his oratorical talents he
was once in his life, according to the *Biographia*, deserted.
As he was preaching in his turn at St. James's, he plainly
perceived it was out of his power to command the attention
of his audience. This so affected the feelings of the preacher,
that he sat back in the pulpit and burst into tears. But we
must pursue his poetical life.

In 1719 he lamented the death of Addison, in a Letter
addressed to their common friend Tickell. For the secret history
of the following lines, if they contain any, it is now vain to seek:

> *In joy once join'd, in sorrow, now, for years—*
> Partner in grief, and brother of my tears,
> Tickell, accept this verse, thy mournful due.

From your account of Tickell it appears that he and Young
used to "communicate to each other whatever verses they
wrote, even to the least things."

In 1719 appeared a *Paraphrase on Part of the Book of Job.*
Parker, to whom it is dedicated, had not long, by means of the
seals, been qualified for a patron. Of this work the author's
opinion may be known from his Letter to Curll: "You seem,
in the Collection you propose, to have omitted what I think
may claim the first place in it; I mean *A Translation from part
of Job*, printed by Mr. Tonson." The Dedication, which was
only suffered to appear in Mr. Tonson's edition, while it speaks
with satisfaction of his present retirement, seems to make an
unusual struggle to escape from retirement. But everyone who
sings in the dark does not sing from joy. It is addressed, in no
common strain of flattery, to a Chancellor of whom he clearly
appears to have had no kind of knowledge.

Of his Satires it would not have been possible to fix the
dates without the assistance of first editions, which, as you had
occasion to observe in your account of Dryden, are with difficulty
found. We must then have referred to the poems, to discover
when they were written. For these internal notes of time we
should not have referred in vain. The first Satire laments that
"Guilt's chief foe in Addison is fled." The second, addressing
himself, asks:

> Is thy ambition sweating for a rhyme,
> Thou unambitious fool, at this late time?
> A fool at *forty* is a fool indeed.

The Satires were originally published separately in folio, under the title of *The Universal Passion*. These passages fix the appearance of the first to about 1725, the time at which it came out. As Young seldom suffered his pen to dry, after he had once dipped it in poetry, we may conclude that he began his Satires soon after he had written the *Paraphrase on Job*. The last Satire was certainly finished in the beginning of the year 1726. In December 1725, the King, in his passage from Helvoetsluys, escaped with great difficulty from a storm by landing at Rye; and the conclusion of the Satire turns the escape into a miracle, in such an encomiastic strain of compliment as poetry too often seeks to pay to royalty.

From the sixth of these poems we learn:

> Midst empire's charms, how Carolina's heart
> Glow'd with the love of virtue and of art:

since the grateful poet tells us, in the next couplet:

> Her favour is diffus'd to that degree,
> Excess of goodness! it has dawn'd on me.

Her Majesty had stood godmother and given her name to a daughter of the lady whom Young married in 1731, and had perhaps shown some attention to Lady Elizabeth's future husband.

The fifth Satire, *On Women*, was not published till 1727, and the sixth [on the same subject] not till 1728.

To these poems, when, in 1728, he gathered them into one publication, he prefixed a Preface; in which he observes, that "no man can converse much in the world but, at what he meets with, he must either be insensible or grieve, or be angry or smile. Now to smile at it, and turn it into ridicule," he adds, "I think most eligible, as it hurts ourselves least, and gives vice and folly the greatest offence. . . . Laughing at the misconduct of the world will, in a great measure, ease us of any more disagreeable passion about it. One passion is more effectually driven out by another than by reason, whatever some teach." So wrote, and so of course thought, the lively and witty satirist at the grave age of almost fifty, who, many years earlier in life, wrote *The Last Day*. After all, Swift pronounced of these Satires, that they should either have been more angry or more merry.

Is it not somewhat singular that Young preserved, without any palliation, this Preface, so bluntly decisive in favour of laughing at the world, in the same collection of his works which contains the mournful, angry, gloomy *Night Thoughts*?

At the conclusion of the Preface he applies Plato's beautiful fable of the Birth of Love to modern poetry, with the addition, "that Poetry, like Love, is a little subject to blindness, which makes her mistake her way to preferments and honours; and that she retains a dutiful admiration of her father's family; but divides her favours, and generally lives with her mother's relations." Poetry, it is true, did not lead Young to preferments or to honours; but was there not something like blindness in the flattery which he sometimes forced her, and her sister Prose, to utter? She was always, indeed, taught by him to entertain a most dutiful admiration of riches; but surely Young, though nearly related to Poetry, had no connection with her whom Plato makes the mother of Love. That he could not well complain of being related to Poverty appears clearly from the frequent bounties which his gratitude records, and from the wealth which he left behind him. By *The Universal Passion* he acquired no vulgar fortune, more than 3000*l.* A considerable sum had already been swallowed up in the South Sea. For this loss he took the vengeance of an author. His muse makes poetical use more than once of a South-Sea Dream.

It is related by Mr. Spence, in his *Manuscript Anecdotes*, on the authority of Mr. Rawlinson, that Young, upon the publication of his *Universal Passion*, received from the Duke of Wharton 2000*l.*; and that, when one of his friends exclaimed, "Two thousand pounds for a poem!" he said it was the best bargain he ever made in his life, for the poem was worth four thousand.

This story may be true; but it seems to have been raised from the two answers of Lord Burghley and Sir Philip Sidney in Spenser's Life.

After inscribing his Satires, not perhaps without the hope of preferments and honours, to such names as the Duke of Dorset, Mr. Dodington, Mr. Spencer Compton, Lady Elizabeth Germaine, and Sir Robert Walpole, he returns to plain panegyric. In 1726 he addressed a poem to Sir Robert Walpole, of which the title sufficiently explains the intention. If Young must be acknowledged a ready celebrator, he did not endeavour, or did not choose, to be a lasting one. *The Instalment* is among the pieces he did not admit into the number of his *excusable writings*; yet it contains a couplet which pretends to pant after the power of bestowing immortality!

> Oh how I long, enkindled by the theme,
> In deep eternity to launch thy name!

The bounty of the former reign seems to have been continued, possibly increased, in this. Whatever it might have been, the poet thought he deserved it; for he was not ashamed to acknowledge what, without his acknowledgment, would now perhaps never have been known:

> My breast, O Walpole, glows with grateful fire.
> The streams of royal bounty, turn'd by thee,
> Refresh the dry domains of poesy.

If the purity of modern patriotism will term Young a pensioner, it must at least be confessed he was a grateful one.

The reign of the new monarch [George II.] was ushered in by Young with *Ocean, an Ode*. The hint of it was taken from the Royal speech, which recommended the increase and the encouragement of the seamen; that they might be "invited rather than compelled by force and violence, to enter into the service of their country"—a plan which humanity must lament that policy has not even yet been able, or willing, to carry into execution. Prefixed to the original publication were an *Ode to the King, Pater Patriæ*, and an *Essay on Lyric Poetry*. It is but justice to confess that he preserved neither of them, and that the ode itself, which in the first edition and in the last consists of seventy-three stanzas, in the author's own edition is reduced to forty-nine. Among the omitted passages is a "Wish" that concluded the poem, which few would have suspected Young of forming, and of which few, after having formed it, would confess something like their shame by suppression.

It stood originally so high in the author's opinion that he intituled the poem *Ocean, an Ode. Concluding with a Wish*. This wish consists of thirteen stanzas. The first runs thus:

> O may I *steal*
> Along the *vale*
> Of humble life, secure from foes!
> My friend sincere,
> My judgment clear,
> And gentle business my repose!

The three last stanzas are not more remarkable for just

rhymes; but altogether they will make rather a curious page in the life of Young:

> Prophetic schemes,
> And golden dreams,
> May I, unsanguine, cast away!
> Have what I *have*,
> And live, not *leave*,
> Enamour'd of the present day!
>
> My hours my own!
> My faults unknown!
> My chief revenue in content!
> Then leave one *beam*
> Of honest *fame*!
> And scorn the labour'd monument!
>
> Unhurt my urn
> Till that great TURN
> When mighty Nature's self shall die,
> Time cease to glide,
> With human pride,
> Sunk in the ocean of eternity!

It is whimsical that he, who was soon to bid adieu to rhyme, should fix upon a measure in which rhyme abounds even to satiety. Of this he said, in his *Essay on Lyric Poetry*, prefixed to the poem, "For the more *harmony* likewise I chose the frequent return of rhyme, which laid me under great difficulties. But difficulties overcome give grace and pleasure. Nor can I account for the *pleasure of rhyme in general* (of which the moderns are too fond) but from this truth." Yet the moderns surely deserve not much censure for their fondness of what, by his own confession, affords pleasure, and abounds in harmony.

The next paragraph in his Essay did not occur to him when he talked of "that great turn" in the stanza just quoted. "But then the writer must take care that the difficulty is overcome. That is, he must make rhyme consistent with as perfect sense and expression as could be expected if he was perfectly free from that shackle."

Another part of this Essay will convict the following stanza of, what every reader will discover in it, "involuntary burlesque."

> The northern blast,
> The shatter'd mast,
> The syrt, the whirlpool, and the rock,
> The breaking spout,
> The *stars gone out*,
> The boiling strait, the monster's shock.

But would the English poets fill quite so many volumes if

all their productions were to be tried, like this, by an elaborate essay on each particular species of poetry of which they exhibit specimens?

If Young be not a lyric poet, he is at least a critic in that sort of poetry; and if his lyric poetry can be proved bad, it was first proved so by his own criticism. This surely is candid.

Milbourne was styled by Pope "the fairest of critics," only because he exhibited his own version of Virgil to be compared with Dryden's, which he condemned, and with which every reader had it otherwise in his power to compare it. Young was surely not the most unfair of poets for prefixing to a lyric composition an *Essay on Lyric Poetry*, so just and impartial as to condemn himself.

We shall soon come to a work before which we find indeed no critical essay, but which disdains to shrink from the touch-stone of the severest critic, and which certainly, as I remember to have heard you say, if it contain some of the worst, contains also some of the best things in the language.

Soon after the appearance of *Ocean*, when he was almost fifty, Young entered into orders. In April 1728, not long after he put on the gown, he was appointed chaplain to George the Second.

The tragedy of *The Brothers*, which was already in rehearsal, he immediately withdrew from the stage. The managers resigned it with some reluctance to the delicacy of the new clergyman. The Epilogue to *The Brothers*, the only appendage to any of his three plays which he added himself, is, I believe, the only one of the kind. He calls it an Historical Epilogue. Finding that "Guilt's dreadful close his narrow scene denied," he, in a manner, continues the tragedy in the Epilogue, and relates how Rome revenged the shade of Demetrius, and punished Perseus "for this night's deed."

Of Young's taking orders something is told by a former biographer of Pope, which places the easiness and simplicity of the poet in a singular light. When he determined on the Church, he did not address himself to Sherlock, to Atterbury, or to Hare for the best instructions in theology, but to Pope; who, in a youthful frolic, advised the diligent perusal of Thomas Aquinas. With this treasure Young retired from interruption to an obscure place in the suburbs. His poetical guide to godliness hearing nothing of him during half a year, and apprehending he might have carried the jest too far, sought after him, and found him just in time to prevent what Ruffhead calls "an irretrievable derangement."

That attachment to his favourite study which made him think a poet the surest guide in his new profession, left him little doubt whether poetry were the surest path to its honours and preferments. Not long indeed after he took orders, he published in prose, 1728, *A true Estimate of Human Life*, dedicated, notwithstanding the Latin quotations with which it abounds, to the Queen; and a sermon preached before the House of Commons, 1729, on the martyrdom of King Charles, intituled, *An Apology for Princes, or the Reverence due to Government*. But the *Second Discourse*, the counterpart of his *Estimate*, without which it cannot be called "a true estimate," though in 1728 it was announced as "soon to be published," never appeared; and his old friends the Muses were not forgotten. In 1730 he relapsed to poetry, and sent into the world *Imperium Pelagi : a Naval Lyric, written in Imitation of Pindar's Spirit, occasioned by His Majesty's Return from Hanover, September, 1729, and the succeeding Peace*. It is inscribed to the Duke of Chandos. In the Preface we are told that the Ode is the most spirited kind of Poetry, and that the Pindaric is the most spirited kind of Ode. "This I speak," he adds, with sufficient candour, "at my own very great peril. But truth has an eternal title to our confession, though we are sure to suffer by it." Behold, again, the fairest of poets. Young's *Imperium Pelagi* was ridiculed in Fielding's *Tom Thumb*; but let us not forget that it was one of his pieces which the author of the *Night Thoughts* deliberately refused to own.

Not long after this Pindaric attempt, he published two Epistles to Pope, "concerning the Authors of the Age," 1730. Of these poems one occasion seems to have been an apprehension lest, from the liveliness of his satires, he should not be deemed sufficiently serious for promotion in the Church.

In July 1730 he was presented by his College to the rectory of Welwyn in Hertfordshire. In May 1731 he married Lady Elizabeth Lee, daughter of the Earl of Lichfield, and widow of Colonel Lee. His connection with this lady arose from his father's acquaintance, already mentioned, with Lady Anne Wharton, who was co-heiress of Sir Henry Lee, of Ditchley in Oxfordshire. Poetry had lately been taught by Addison to aspire to the arms of nobility, though not with extraordinary happiness.

We may naturally conclude that Young now gave himself up in some measure to the comforts of his new connection, and to the expectations of that preferment which he thought due to his poetical talents, or, at least, to the manner in which they had so frequently been exerted.

The next production of his Muse was *The Sea-piece*, in two odes.

Young enjoys the credit of what is called an *Extempore Epigram on Voltaire*; who, when he was in England, ridiculed, in the company of the jealous English poet, Milton's allegory of Sin and Death:

> You are so witty, profligate, and thin,
> At once we think thee Milton, Death, and Sin.

From the following passage in the poetical Dedication of his *Sea-piece* to Voltaire, it seems that this extemporaneous reproof, if it must be extemporaneous (for what few will now affirm Voltaire to have deserved any reproof?), was something longer than a distich, and something more gentle than the distich just quoted:

> No stranger, Sir, though born in foreign climes.
> On *Dorset* downs, when Milton's page
> With Sin and Death provok'd thy rage,
> Thy rage provok'd, who sooth'd with *gentle* rhymes?

By "Dorset downs" he probably meant Mr. Dodington's seat. In Pitt's Poems is *An Epistle to Dr. Edward Young, at Eastbury in Dorsetshire, on the Review at Sarum*, 1722.

> While with your Dodington retir'd you sit,
> Charm'd with his flowing Burgundy and wit, etc.

Thomson, in his *Autumn*, addressing Mr. Dodington, calls his seat the seat of the Muses:

> Where, in the secret bower and winding walk,
> For virtuous Young and thee they twine the bay.

The praises Thomson bestows but a few lines before on Philips, the second

> Who nobly durst, in rhyme-unfetter'd verse,
> With British freedom sing the British song,

added to Thomson's example and success, might perhaps induce Young, as we shall see presently, to write his great work without rhyme.

In 1734 he published *The Foreign Address, or the best Argument for Peace, occasioned by the British Fleet and the Posture of Affairs. Written in the Character of a Sailor*. It is not to be found in the author's four volumes.

He now appears to have given up all hopes of overtaking Pindar, and perhaps at last resolved to turn his ambition to some original species of poetry. This poem concludes with a formal farewell to Ode, which few of Young's readers will regret:

> My shell, which Clio gave, which *Kings applaud*,
> Which Europe's bleeding Genius call'd abroad,
> Adieu!

In a species of poetry altogether his own, he next tried his skill, and succeeded.

Of his wife he was deprived in 1741. Lady Elizabeth had lost, after her marriage with Young, an amiable daughter, by her former husband, just after she was married to Mr. Temple, son of Lord Palmerston. Mr. Temple did not long remain after his wife, though he was married a second time to a daughter of Sir John Barnard's, whose son is the present peer. Mr. and Mrs. Temple have generally been considered as Philander and Narcissa. From the great friendship which constantly subsisted between Mr. Temple and Young, as well as from other circumstances, it is probable that the poet had both him and Mrs. Temple in view for these characters; though at the same time some passages respecting Philander do not appear to suit either Mr. Temple or any other person with whom Young was known to be connected or acquainted, while all the circumstances relating to Narcissa have been constantly found applicable to Young's daughter-in-law.

At what short intervals the poet tells us he was wounded by the deaths of the three persons particularly lamented, none that has read the *Night Thoughts* (and who has not read them?) needs to be informed.

> Insatiate Archer! could not one suffice?
> Thy shaft flew thrice; and thrice my peace was slain;
> And thrice, ere thrice yon moon had fill'd her horn.

Yet how is it possible that Mr. and Mrs. Temple and Lady Elizabeth Young could be these three victims, over whom Young has hitherto been pitied for having to pour the "Midnight Sorrows" of his religious poetry? Mrs. Temple died in 1736; Mr. Temple four years afterwards, in 1740; and the poet's wife seven months after Mr. Temple, in 1741. How could the insatiate Archer thrice slay his peace in these three persons, "ere thrice the moon had fill'd her horn"?

But in the short Preface to *The Complaint*, he seriously tells us "that the occasion of this poem was real, not fictitious; and that the facts mentioned did naturally pour these moral reflections on the thought of the writer." It is probable, therefore, that in these three contradictory lines the poet complains more than the father-in-law, the friend, or the widower.

Whatever names belong to these facts, or, if the names be those generally supposed, whatever heightening a poet's sorrow may have given the facts; to the sorrow Young felt from them, religion and morality are indebted for the *Night Thoughts.* There is a pleasure sure in sadness which mourners only know!

Of these poems the two or three first have been perused perhaps more eagerly and more frequently than the rest. When he got as far as the fourth or fifth, his original motive for taking up the pen was answered; his grief was naturally either diminished or exhausted. We still find the same pious poet; but we hear less of Philander and Narcissa, and less of the mourner whom he loved to pity.

Mrs. Temple died of a consumption at Lyons, in her way to Nice, the year after her marriage; that is, when poetry relates the fact, "in her bridal hour." It is more than poetically true, that Young accompanied her to the Continent.

> I flew, I snatch'd her from the rigid North,
> And bore her nearer to the sun.

But in vain. Her funeral was attended with the difficulties painted in such animated colours in Night the Third. After her death, the remainder of the party passed the ensuing winter at Nice.

The poet seems perhaps in these compositions to dwell with more melancholy on the death of Philander and Narcissa than of his wife. But it is only for this reason. He who runs and reads may remember that in the *Night Thoughts* Philander and Narcissa are often mentioned and often lamented. To recollect lamentations over the author's wife, the memory must have been charged with distinct passages. This lady brought him one child, Frederick, now [1780] living, to whom the Prince of Wales was godfather.

That domestic grief is, in the first instance, to be thanked for these ornaments to our language, it is impossible to deny. Nor would it be common hardiness to contend, that worldly discontent had no hand in these joint productions of poetry and piety. Yet am I by no means sure that, at any rate, we should not have had something of the same colour from Young's pencil, notwithstanding the liveliness of his satires. In so long a life, causes for discontent and occasions for grief must have occurred. It is not clear to me that his Muse was not sitting

upon the watch for the first which happened. "Night Thoughts"
were not uncommon to her, even when first she visited the
poet, and at a time when he himself was remarkable neither
for gravity nor gloominess. In his *Last Day*, almost his earliest
poem, he calls her "the melancholy maid,"

> ———— whom dismal scenes delight,
> Frequent at tombs and in the realms of Night.

In the prayer which concludes the second book of the same
poem, he says:

> —Oh! permit the gloom of solemn night
> To sacred thought may forcibly invite.
> Oh! how divine to tread the milky way,
> To the bright palace of Eternal Day!

When Young was writing a tragedy, Wharton is said by
Spence to have sent him a human skull, with a candle in it,
as lamp; and the poet is reported to have used it.

What he calls "The *true* estimate of Human Life," which
has already been mentioned, exhibits only the wrong side of
the tapestry; and being asked why he did not show the right,
he is said to have replied that he could not. By others it has
been told me that this was finished, but that, before there
existed any copy, it was torn in pieces by a lady's monkey.

Still, is it altogether fair to dress up the poet for the man,
and to bring the gloominess of the *Night Thoughts* to prove
the gloominess of Young, and to show that his genius, like
the genius of Swift, was in some measure the sullen inspiration
of discontent?

From them who answer in the affirmative it should not be
concealed that, though "Invisibilia non decipiunt" appeared
upon a deception in Young's grounds, and "Ambulantes in
horto audiêrunt vocem Dei" on a building in his garden, his
parish was indebted to the good humour of the author of the
Night Thoughts for an assembly and a bowling-green.

Whether you think with me I know not; but the famous
"De mortuis nil nisi bonum" always appeared to me to savour
more of female weakness than of manly reason. He that has
too much feeling to speak ill of the dead, who, if they cannot
defend themselves, are at least ignorant of his abuse, will not
hesitate by the most wanton calumny to destroy the quiet,
the reputation, the fortune of the living. Yet censure is not
heard beneath the tomb any more than praise. "De mortuis
nil nisi verum—De vivis nil nisi bonum"—would approach

much nearer to good sense. After all, the few handfuls of remaining dust which once composed the body of the author of the *Night Thoughts* feel not much concern whether Young pass now for a man of sorrow, or for a "fellow of infinite jest." To this favour must come the whole family of Yorick. His immortal part, wherever that now dwell, is still less solicitous on this head.

But to a son of worth and sensibility it is of some little consequence whether contemporaries believe, and posterity be taught to believe, that his debauched and reprobate life cast a Stygian gloom over the evening of his father's days, saved him the trouble of feigning a character completely detestable, and succeeded at last in bringing his "grey hairs with sorrow to the grave."

The humanity of the world, little satisfied with inventing perhaps a melancholy disposition for the father, proceeds next to invent an argument in support of their invention, and chooses that Lorenzo should be Young's own son. The *Biographia* and every account of Young pretty roundly assert this to be the fact; of the absolute impossibility of which the *Biographia* itself, in particular dates, contains undeniable evidence. Readers I know there are of a strange turn of mind who will hereafter peruse the *Night Thoughts* with less satisfaction; who will wish they had still been deceived; who will quarrel with me for discovering that no such character as their Lorenzo ever yet disgraced human nature, or broke a father's heart. Yet would these admirers of the sublime and terrible be offended should you set them down for cruel and for savage.

Of this report, inhuman to the surviving son, if it be true, in proportion as the character of Lorenzo is diabolical, where are we to find the proof? Perhaps it is clear from the poems.

From the first line to the last of the *Night Thoughts* no one expression can be discovered which betrays anything like the father. In the Second Night I find an expression which betrays something else: that Lorenzo was his friend—one, it is possible, of his former companions; one of the Duke of Wharton's set. The poet styles him "gay friend"—an appellation not very natural from a pious incensed father to such a being as he paints Lorenzo, and that being his son.

But let us see how he has sketched this dreadful portrait, from the sight of some of whose features the artist himself must have turned away with horror—a subject more shocking, if his only child really sat to him, than the Crucifixion of Michael

Angelo, upon the horrid story told of which Young composed a short poem of fourteen lines in the early part of his life, which he did not think deserved to be republished.

In the First Night the address to the poet's supposed son is:

> Lorenzo, Fortune makes her court to thee.

In the Fifth Night:

> And burns Lorenzo still for the sublime
> Of life? to hang his airy nest on high?

Is this a picture of the son of the rector of Welwyn? Eighth Night:

> In foreign realms (for thou hast travelled far)—

which even now does not apply to his son.

In Night Five:

> So wept Lorenzo fair Clarissa's fate,
> Who gave that angel-boy on whom he dotes,
> And died to give him, orphan'd in his birth?

At the beginning of the Fifth Night we find:

> Lorenzo, to recriminate is just,
> I grant the man is vain who writes for praise.

But, to cut short all inquiry, if any one of these passages, if any passage in the poems be applicable, my friend shall pass for Lorenzo. The son of the author of the *Night Thoughts* was not old enough, when they were written, to recriminate or to be a father. The *Night Thoughts* were begun immediately after the mournful event of 1741. The first Nights appear in the books of the Company of Stationers as the property of Robert Dodsley, in 1742. The Preface to Night Seven is dated July the 7th, 1744. The marriage, in consequence of which the supposed Lorenzo was born, happened in May 1731. Young's child was not born till June 1733. In 1741 this Lorenzo, this finished infidel, this father to whose education Vice had for some years put the last hand, was only eight years old.

An anecdote of this cruel sort, so open to contradiction, so impossible to be true, who could propagate? Thus easily are blasted the reputation of the living and of the dead.

Who then was Lorenzo? exclaim the readers I have mentioned. If we cannot be sure that he was his son, which would have been finely terrible, was he not his nephew, his cousin?

These are questions which I do not pretend to answer. For the sake of human nature, I could wish Lorenzo to have been

only the creation of the poet's fancy: like the Quintus of Anti-
Lucretius, "quo nomine," says Polignac, "quemvis Atheum
intellige." That this was the case many expressions in the
Night Thoughts would seem to prove, did not a passage in
Night Eight appear to show that he had somebody in his
eye for the groundwork at least of the painting. Lovelace or
Lorenzo may be feigned characters; but a writer does not feign
a name of which he only gives the initial letter.

> Tell not Calista. She will laugh thee dead,
> Or send thee to her hermitage with L——.

The *Biographia,* not satisfied with pointing out the son of
Young, in that son's lifetime, as his father's Lorenzo, travels
out of its way into the history of the son, and tells of his having
been forbidden his college at Oxford for misbehaviour. How
such anecdotes, were they true, tend to illustrate the life of
Young it is not easy to discover. Was the son of the author of
the *Night Thoughts* indeed forbidden his college for a time,
at one of our universities? The author of *Paradise Lost* is
by some supposed to have been disgracefully ejected from the
other. From juvenile follies who is free? But, whatever the
Biographia choose to relate, the son of Young experienced no
dismission from his college, either lasting or temporary.

Yet were nature to indulge him with a second youth, and to
leave him at the same time the experience of that which is past,
he would probably spend it differently—who would not?—he
would certainly be the occasion of less uneasiness to his father.
But, from the same experience, he would as certainly, in the
same case, be treated differently by his father.

Young was a poet: poets, with reverence be it spoken, do
not make the best parents. Fancy and imagination seldom
deign to stoop from their heights—always stoop unwillingly to
the low level of common duties. Aloof from vulgar life, they
pursue their rapid flight beyond the ken of mortals, and descend
not to earth but when compelled by necessity. The prose of
ordinary occurrences is beneath the dignity of poets.

He who is connected with the author of the *Night Thoughts*,
only by veneration for the poet and the Christian, may be
allowed to observe that Young is one of those concerning whom,
as you remark in your account of Addison, it is proper rather
to say "nothing that is false than all that is true."

But the son of Young would almost sooner, I know, pass for
Lorenzo than see himself vindicated, at the expense of his

father's memory, from follies which, if it may be thought blameable in a boy to have committed them, it is surely praiseworthy in a man to lament, and certainly not only unnecessary but cruel in a biographer to record.

Of the *Night Thoughts*, notwithstanding their author's professed retirement, all are inscribed to great or to growing names. He had not yet weaned himself from earls and dukes, from Speakers of the House of Commons, Lords Commissioners of the Treasury, and Chancellors of the Exchequer. In Night Eight the politician plainly betrays himself:

> Think no post needful that demands a knave,
> When late our civil helm was shifting hands,
> So P—— thought: think better, if you can.

Yet it must be confessed that at the conclusion of Night Nine, weary perhaps of courting earthly patrons, he tells his soul:

> Henceforth
> Thy *patron* he, whose diadem has dropt
> Yon gems of heaven; Eternity thy prize;
> And leave the racers of the world their own.

The Fourth Night was addressed by "a much-indebted Muse" to the Honourable Mr. Yorke, now Lord Hardwicke, who meant to have laid the Muse under still greater obligation by the living of Shenfield in Essex, if it had become vacant.

The First Night concludes with this passage:

> Dark, though not blind, like thee, Meonides;
> Or Milton, thee. Ah! could I reach your strain;
> Or his who made Meonides our own!
> Man too he sung. Immortal man I sing.
> Oh had he prest his theme, pursued the track
> Which opens out of darkness into day!
> Oh had he mounted on his wing of fire,
> Soar'd where I sink, and sung immortal man—
> How had it blest mankind, and rescued me!

To the author of these lines was dedicated, in 1756, the first volume of an *Essay on the Writings and Genius of Pope*, which attempted, whether justly or not, to pluck from Pope his "Wing of Fire," and to reduce him to a rank at least one degree lower than the first class of English poets. If Young accepted and approved the dedication, he countenanced this attack upon the fame of him whom he invokes as his Muse.

Part of "paper-sparing" Pope's Third Book of the Odyssey, deposited in the Museum, is written upon the back of a letter signed "E. Young," which is clearly the handwriting of our Young. The letter, dated only May the 2nd, seems obscure; but there can be little doubt that the friendship he requests was a literary one, and that he had the highest literary opinion of Pope. The request was a prologue, I am told.

May the 2nd.

DEAR SIR,—Having been often from home, I know not if you have done me the favour of calling on me. But, be that as it will, I much want that instance of your friendship I mentioned in my last—a friendship I am very sensible I can receive from no one but yourself. I should not urge this thing so much but for very particular reasons; nor can you be at a loss to conceive how a "trifle of this nature" may be of serious moment to me; and, while I am in hopes of the great advantage of your advice about it, I shall not be so absurd as to make any further step without it. I know you are much engaged, and only hope to hear of you at your entire leisure.

I am, Sir, your most faithful and obedient servant,
E. YOUNG.

Nay, even after Pope's death, he says, in Night Seven:

Pope, who could'st make immortals, art thou dead?

Either the *Essay*, then, was dedicated to a patron who disapproved its doctrine, which I have been told by the author [Joseph Warton] was not the case; or Young appears, in his old age, to have bartered for a dedication an opinion entertained of his friend through all that part of life when he must have been best able to form opinions.

From this account of Young, two or three short passages, which stand almost together in Night Four, should not be excluded. They afford a picture, by his own hand, from the study of which my readers may choose to form their own opinion of the features of his mind and the complexion of his life.

Ah me! the dire effect
Of loitering here, of death defrauded long;
Of old so gracious (and let that suffice),
My very master knows me not.

.   .   .   .

I've been so long remember'd, I'm forgot.

.   .   .   .

When in his courtier's ears I pour my plaint,
They drink it as the Nectar of the Great;
And squeeze my hand, and beg me come to-morrow.

.   .   .   .

Twice told the period spent on stubborn Troy,
Court-favour, yet untaken, I *besiege.*

.   .   .   .

If this song lives, Posterity shall know
One, though in Britain born, with courtiers bred,
Who thought ev'n gold might come a day too late;
Nor on his subtle death-bed plann'd his scheme
For future vacancies in church or state.

Deduct from the writer's age "twice told the period spent on
stubborn Troy," and you will still leave him more than forty
when he sat down to the miserable siege of court favour. He
has before told us

> A fool at forty is a fool indeed.

After all, the siege seems to have been raised only in consequence
of what the General thought his "death-bed."

By these extraordinary poems, written after he was sixty, of
which I have been led to say so much, I hope by the wish of
doing justice to the living and the dead, it was the desire of
Young to be principally known. He entitled the four volumes
which he published himself, *The Works of the Author of the
Night Thoughts*. While it is remembered that from these he
excluded many of his writings, let it not be forgotten that
the rejected pieces contained nothing prejudicial to the cause
of virtue or of religion. Were everything that Young ever
wrote to be published, he would only appear perhaps in a less
respectable light as a poet, and more despicable as a dedicator:
he would not pass for a worse Christian, or for a worse man.
This enviable praise is due to Young. Can it be claimed by
every writer? His dedications, after all, he had perhaps no
right to suppress. They all, I believe, speak, not a little to the
credit of his gratitude, of favours received; and I know not
whether the author who has once solemnly printed an acknowledgment of a favour, should not always print it.

Is it to the credit or to the discredit of Young, as a poet,
that of his *Night Thoughts* the French are particularly fond?

Of the *Epitaph on Lord Aubrey Beauclerk*, dated 1740, all
I know is, that I find it in the late body of English poetry, and
that I am sorry to find it there.

Notwithstanding the farewell which he seemed to have
taken in the *Night Thoughts* of everything which bore the least
resemblance to ambition, he dipped again in politics. In 1745
he wrote *Reflections on the Public Situation of the Kingdom,
addressed to the Duke of Newcastle*; indignant, as it appears,
to behold

> —a pope-bred Princeling crawl ashore,
> And whistle cut-throats, with those swords that scrap'd
> Their barren rocks for wretched sustenance,
> To cut his passage to the British throne.

This political poem might be called a "Night Thought." Indeed
it was originally printed as the conclusion of the *Night Thoughts*,
though he did not gather it with his other works.

Prefixed to the second edition of Howe's *Devout Meditations* is a letter from Young, dated January 19, 1752, addressed to Archibald Macauly, Esq.; thanking him for the book, which, he says, "he shall never lay far out of his reach; for a greater demonstration of a sound head and a sincere heart he never saw."

In 1753, when *The Brothers* had lain by him above thirty years, it appeared upon the stage. If any part of his fortune had been acquired by servility of adulation, he now determined to deduct from it no inconsiderable sum, as a gift to the Society for the Propagation of the Gospel. To this sum he hoped the profits of *The Brothers* would amount. In his calculation he was deceived; but by the bad success of his play the Society was not a loser. The author made up the sum he originally intended, which was a thousand pounds, from his own pocket.

The next performance which he printed was a prose publication, entitled, *The Centaur not fabulous, in Six Letters to a Friend on the Life in Vogue.* The conclusion is dated November 29, 1754. In the third Letter is described the death-bed of the "gay, young, noble, ingenious, accomplished, and most wretched Altamont." His last words were—"My principles have poisoned my friend, my extravagance has beggared my boy, my unkindness has murdered my wife!" Either Altamont and Lorenzo were the twin production of fancy, or Young was unlucky enough to know two characters who bore no little resemblance to each other in perfection of wickedness. Report has been accustomed to call Altamont Lord Euston.

The Old Man's Relapse, occasioned by an Epistle to Walpole, if written by Young, which I much doubt, must have been written very late in life. It has been seen, I am told, in a Miscellany published thirty years before his death. In 1758 he exhibited *The Old Man's Relapse,* in more than words, by again becoming a dedicator, and publishing a sermon addressed to the King.

The lively Letter in prose on *Original Composition,* addressed to Richardson, the author of *Clarissa,* appeared in 1759. Though he despair "of breaking through the frozen obstructions of age and care's incumbent cloud, into that flow of thought and brightness of expression which subjects so polite require," yet is it more like the production of untamed, unbridled youth, than of jaded fourscore. Some sevenfold volumes put him in mind of Ovid's sevenfold channels of the Nile at the conflagration:

$$\text{———————— ostia septem}$$
$$\text{Pulverulenta vocant, septem sine flumine valles.}$$

Such leaden labours are like Lycurgus's iron money, which was so much less in value than in bulk, that it required barns for strong-boxes, and a yoke of oxen to draw five hundred pounds.

If there is a famine of invention in the land, we must travel, he says, like Joseph's brethren, far for food; we must visit the remote and rich ancients. But an inventive genius may safely stay at home; that, like the widow's cruse, is divinely replenished from within, and affords us a miraculous delight. He asks why it should seem altogether impossible that Heaven's latest editions of the human mind may be the most correct and fair? And Jonson, he tells us, was very learned, as Sampson was very strong, to his own hurt. Blind to the nature of tragedy, he pulled down all antiquity on his head, and buried himself under it.

Is this "care's incumbent cloud," or "the frozen obstructions of age"?

In this letter Pope is severely censured for his "fall from Homer's numbers, free as air, lofty and harmonious as the spheres, into childish shackles and tinkling sounds; for putting Achilles in petticoats a second time": but we are told that the dying swan talked over an Epic plan with Young a few weeks before his decease.

Young's chief inducement to write this letter was, as he confesses, that he might erect a monumental marble to the memory of an old friend. He who employed his pious pen for almost the last time in thus doing justice to the exemplary death-bed of Addison, might probably, at the close of his own life, afford no unuseful lesson for the deaths of others.

In the postscript he writes to Richardson, that he will see in his next how far Addison is an original. But no other letter appears.

The few lines which stand in the last edition, as "sent by Lord Melcombe to Dr. Young, not long before his Lordship's death," were indeed so sent, but were only an introduction to what was there meant by "The Muse's latest Spark." The poem is necessary, whatever may be its merit, since the Preface to it is already printed. Lord Melcombe called his Tusculum "La Trappe."

> Love thy country, wish it well,
>   Not with too intense a care;
> 'Tis enough that, when it fell,
>   Thou its ruin didst not share.

> Envy's censure, Flattery's praise,
>   With unmov'd indifference view;
> Learn to tread Life's dangerous maze,
>   With unerring Virtue's clue.
>
> Void of strong desire and fear,
>   Life's wide ocean trust no more;
> Strive thy little bark to steer
>   With the tide, but near the shore.
>
> Thus prepar'd, thy shorten'd sail
>   Shall, whene'er the winds increase,
> Seizing each propitious gale,
>   Waft thee to the Port of Peace.
>
> Keep thy conscience from offence
>   And tempestuous passions free,
> So, when thou art call'd from hence,
>   Easy shall thy passage be;
>
> Easy shall thy passage be,
>   Cheerful thy allotted stay,
> Short the account 'twixt God and thee;
>   Hope shall meet thee on the way:
>
> Truth shall lead thee to the gate,
>   Mercy's self shall let thee in,
> Where its never-changing state
>   Full perfection shall begin.

The poem was accompanied by a letter:

> LA TRAPPE, *the 27th of Oct.*, 1761.
>
> DEAR SIR,—You seemed to like the ode I sent you for your amusement; I now send it you as a present. If you please to accept of it, and are willing that our friendship should be known when we are gone, you will be pleased to leave this among those of your own papers that may possibly see the light by a posthumous publication. God send us health while we stay, and an easy journey!
>
> My dear Dr. Young,
>   Yours, most cordially,
>   MELCOMBE.

In 1762, a short time before his death, Young published *Resignation.* Notwithstanding the manner in which it was really forced from him by the world, criticism has treated it with no common severity. If it shall be thought not to deserve the highest praise, on the other side of fourscore, by whom except by Newton and by Waller has praise been merited?

To Mrs. Montagu, the famous champion of Shakespeare, I am indebted for the history of *Resignation.* Observing that Mrs. Boscawen, in the midst of her grief for the loss of the Admiral, derived consolation from the perusal of the *Night Thoughts,* Mrs. Montagu proposed a visit to the author. From conversing with Young, Mrs. Boscawen derived still further consolation; and to that visit she and the world were indebted for this poem. It compliments Mrs. Montagu in the following lines:

> Yet, write I must. A Lady sues,
> How shameful her request!
> My brain in labour with dull rhyme,
> Her's teeming with the best!

And again:

> A friend you have, and I the same,
> Whose prudent, soft address
> Will bring to life those healing thoughts
> Which died in your distress.
> That friend, the spirit of my theme
> Extracting for your ease,
> Will leave to me the dreg, in thoughts
> Too common; such as these.

By the same lady I am enabled to say, in her own words, that Young's unbounded genius appeared to greater advantage in the companion, than even in the author; that the Christian was in him a character still more inspired, more enraptured, more sublime than the poet; and that, in his ordinary conversation,

> —letting down the golden chain from high,
> He drew his audience upward to the sky.

Notwithstanding Young had said, in his *Conjectures on Original Composition*, that "blank verse is verse unfallen, uncurst; verse reclaimed, re-inthroned in the true language of the Gods": notwithstanding he administered consolation to his own grief in this immortal language, Mrs. Boscawen was comforted in rhyme.

While the poet and the Christian were applying this comfort, Young had himself occasion for comfort, in consequence [1761] of the sudden death of Richardson, who was printing the former part of the poem. Of Richardson's death he says:

> When Heaven would kindly set us free,
> And earth's enchantment end,
> It takes the most effectual means,
> And robs us of a friend.

To *Resignation* was prefixed an Apology for its appearance: to which more credit is due than to the generality of such apologies, from Young's unusual anxiety that no more productions of his old age should disgrace his former fame. In his will, dated February 1760, he desires of his executors, *in a particular manner*, that all his manuscript books and writings whatever might be burned, except his book of accounts.

In September 1764, he added a kind of codicil, wherein he

made it his dying entreaty to his housekeeper, to whom he left 1000*l.*, "that all his manuscripts might be destroyed as soon as he was dead, which would greatly oblige her deceased *friend.*"

It may teach mankind the uncertainty of worldly friendships, to know that Young, either by surviving those he loved, or by outliving their affections, could only recollect the names of two *friends*, his housekeeper and a hatter, to mention in his will; and it may serve to repress that testamentary pride which too often seeks for sounding names and titles, to be informed that the author of the *Night Thoughts* did not blush to leave a legacy to his "friend Henry Stevens, a hatter at the Temple-gate." Of these two remaining friends, one went before Young. But, at eighty-four, "where," as he asks in *The Centaur*, "is that world into which we were born?"

The same humility which marked a hatter and a housekeeper for the friends of the author of the *Night Thoughts*, had before bestowed the same title on his footman, in an epitaph in his *Churchyard* upon James Barker, dated 1749; which I am glad to find in the late collection of his works.

Young and his housekeeper were ridiculed with more ill-nature than wit in a kind of novel published by Kidgell in 1755, called *The Card*, under the names of Dr. Elwes and Mrs. Fusby.

In April 1765, at an age to which few attain, a period was put to the life of Young.

He had performed no duty for three or four years, but he retained his intellects to the last.

Much is told in the *Biographia*, which I know not to have been true, of the manner of his burial: of the master and children of a charity-school, which he founded in his parish, who neglected to attend their benefactor's corpse; and of a bell which was not caused to toll as often as upon those occasions bells usually toll. Had that humanity which is here lavished upon things of little consequence either to the living or to the dead, been shown in its proper place to the living, I should have had less to say about Lorenzo. They who lament that these misfortunes happened to Young, forget the praise he bestows upon Socrates, in the Preface to Night Seven, for resenting his friend's request about his funeral.

During some part of his life Young was abroad, but I have not been able to learn any particulars.

In his seventh Satire he says:

> When, after battle, I the field have SEEN
> Spread o'er with ghastly shapes which once were *men.*

It is known also that from this or from some other field he once wandered into the camp, with a classic in his hand, which he was reading intently; and had some difficulty to prove that he was only an absent poet, and not a spy.

The curious reader of Young's life will naturally inquire to what it was owing, that, though he lived almost forty years after he took orders, which included one whole reign uncommonly long, and part of another, he was never thought worthy of the least preferment. The author of the *Night Thoughts* ended his days upon a living which came to him from his college without any favour, and to which he probably had an eye when he determined on the Church. To satisfy curiosity of this kind is, at this distance of time, far from easy. The parties themselves know not often, at the instant, why they are neglected, or why they are preferred. The neglect of Young is by some ascribed to his having attached himself to the Prince of Wales, and to his having preached an offensive sermon at St. James's. It has been told me that he had two hundred a year in the late reign, by the patronage of Walpole; and that, whenever anyone reminded the King of Young, the only answer was, "He has a pension." All the light thrown on this inquiry by the following letter from Secker only serves to show at what a late period of life the author of the *Night Thoughts* solicited preferment:

DEANERY OF ST. PAUL'S, JULY 8, 1758.

GOOD DR. YOUNG,—I have long wondered that more suitable notice of your great merit hath not been taken by persons in power. But how to remedy the omission I see not. No encouragement hath ever been given me to mention things of this nature to his Majesty. And therefore, in all likelihood, the only consequence of doing it would be weakening the little influence which else I may possibly have on some other occasions. Your fortune and your reputation set you above the need of advancement; and your sentiments above that concern for it, on your own account, which, on that of the public, is sincerely felt by

Your loving Brother,
THO. CANT.

At last, at the age of fourscore, he was appointed, in 1761, Clerk of the Closet to the Princess Dowager.

One obstacle must have stood not a little in the way of that preferment after which his whole life seems to have panted. Though he took orders, he never entirely shook off politics. He was always the Lion of his master Milton, "pawing to get free his hinder parts." By this conduct, if he gained some friends, he made many enemies.

Again, Young was a poet; and again, with reverence be it spoken, poets by profession do not always make the best clergymen. If the author of the *Night Thoughts* composed many sermons, he did not oblige the public with many.

Besides, in the latter part of life, Young was fond of holding himself out for a man retired from the world. But he seemed to have forgotten that the same verse which contains "oblitus meorum," contains also "obliviscendus et illis." The brittle chain of worldly friendship and patronage is broken as effectually when one goes beyond the length of it as when the other does. To the vessel which is sailing from the shore, it only appears that the shore also recedes; in life it is truly thus. He who retires from the world will find himself, in reality, deserted as fast, if not faster, by the world. The public is not to be treated as the coxcomb treats his mistress; to be threatened with desertion, in order to increase fondness.

Young seems to have been taken at his word. Notwithstanding his frequent complaints of being neglected, no hand was reached out to pull him from that retirement of which he declared himself enamoured. Alexander assigned no palace for the residence of Diogenes, who boasted his surly satisfaction with his tub.

Of the domestic manners and petty habits of the author of the *Night Thoughts*, I hoped to have given you an account from the best authority: but who shall dare to say, To-morrow I will be wise or virtuous, or to-morrow I will do a particular thing? Upon inquiring for his housekeeper, I learned that she was buried two days before I reached the town of her abode.

In a letter from Tscharner, a noble foreigner, to Count Haller, Tscharner says he has lately spent four days with Young at Welwyn, where the author tastes all the ease and pleasure mankind can desire. "Everything about him shows the man, each individual being placed by rule. All is neat without art. He is very pleasant in conversation, and extremely polite."

This, and more, may possibly be true; but Tscharner's was a first visit, a visit of curiosity and admiration, and a visit which the author expected.

Of Edward Young an anecdote which wanders among readers is not true, that he was Fielding's Parson Adams. The original of that famous painting was William Young, who was a clergyman. He supported an uncomfortable existence by translating for the booksellers from Greek; and, if he did not seem to be his own friend, was at least no man's enemy. Yet the facility with which this report has gained belief in the world argues, were it not sufficiently known, that the author of the *Night Thoughts* bore some resemblance to Adams.

The attention which Young bestowed upon the perusal of books is not unworthy imitation. When any passage pleased him, he appears to have folded down the leaf. On these passages he bestowed a second reading. But the labours of man are too frequently vain. Before he returned to much of what he had once approved, he died. Many of his books, which I have seen, are by those notes of approbation so swelled beyond their real bulk, that they will hardly shut.

> What though we wade in wealth, or soar in fame?
> Earth's highest station ends in *Here he lies !*
> And *dust to dust* concludes her noblest song.

The author of these lines is not without his *Hic jacet*.

By the good sense of his son, it contains none of that praise which no marble can make the bad or the foolish merit; which, without the direction of a stone or a turf, will find its way, sooner or later, to the deserving.

M. S.
Optimi parentis
EDWARDI YOUNG, LL.D.
Hujus Ecclesiæ rect.
Et Elizabethæ
fæm. prænob.
Conjugis ejus amantissimæ
Pio & gratissimo animo
Hoc marmor posuit
F. Y.
Filius superstes.

Is it not strange that the author of the *Night Thoughts* has inscribed no monument to the memory of his lamented wife? Yet what marble will endure as long as the poems?

Such, my good friend, is the account which I have been able to collect of the great Young. That it may be long before anything like what I have just transcribed be necessary for you is the sincere wish of,

Dear Sir,
Your greatly obliged Friend,
HERBERT CROFT, Jun.

LINCOLN'S INN, SEPT. 1780.

P.S. This account of Young was seen by you in manuscript, you know, Sir; and, though I could not prevail on you to make any alterations, you insisted on striking out one passage, because it said, that if I did not wish you to live long for your sake, I did for the sake of myself and of the world. But this post-script you will not see before the printing of it; and I will say here, in spite of you, how I feel myself honoured and bettered by your friendship; and that if I do credit to the Church, after which I always longed, and for which I am now going to give in exchange the Bar, though not at so late a period of life as Young took orders, it will be owing, in no small measure, to my having had the happiness of calling the author of *The Rambler* my friend.

H. C.

Oxford, *Sept.* 1782.

Of Young's poems it is difficult to give any general character; for he has no uniformity of manner: one of his pieces has no great resemblance to another. He began to write early, and continued long; and at different times had different modes of poetical excellence in view. His numbers are sometimes smooth, and sometimes rugged; his style is sometimes con-catenated, and sometimes abrupt; sometimes diffusive, and sometimes concise. His plan seems to have started in his mind at the present moment, and his thoughts appear the effect of chance, sometimes adverse, and sometimes lucky, with very little operation of judgment.

He was not one of the writers whom experience improves, and who, observing their own faults, become gradually correct. His poem on the *Last Day*, his first great performance, has an equability and propriety which he afterwards either never endeavoured or never attained. Many paragraphs are noble, and few are mean, yet the whole is languid; the plan is too much extended, and a succession of images divides and weakens the general conception; but the great reason why the reader is disappointed is, that the thought of the LAST DAY makes every man more than poetical, by spreading over his mind a general obscurity of sacred horror, that oppresses distinction, and disdains expression.

His story of *Jane Grey* was never popular. It is written with elegance enough; but Jane is too heroic to be pitied.

The Universal Passion is indeed a very great performance. It is said to be a series of epigrams; but if it be, it is what the author intended. His endeavour was at the production of striking distichs and pointed sentences, and his distichs have the weight of solid sentiment, and his points the sharpness of resistless truth.

His characters are often selected with discernment, and drawn with nicety; his illustrations are often happy, and his reflections often just. His species of satire is between those of Horace and Juvenal; and he has the gaiety of Horace without his laxity of numbers, and the morality of Juvenal with greater variation of images. He plays, indeed, only on the surface of life; he never penetrates the recesses of the mind, and therefore the whole power of his poetry is exhausted by a single perusal; his conceits please only when they surprise.

To translate he never condescended, unless his *Paraphrase on Job* may be considered as a version, in which he has not, I think, been unsuccessful: he indeed favoured himself by choosing those parts which most easily admit the ornaments of English poetry.

He had least success in his lyric attempts, in which he seems to have been under some malignant influence: he is alway labouring to be great, and at last is only turgid.

In his *Night Thoughts* he has exhibited a very wide display of original poetry, variegated with deep reflections and striking allusions, a wilderness of thought, in which the fertility of fancy scatters flowers of every hue and of every odour. This is one of the few poems in which blank verse could not be changed for rhyme but with disadvantage. The wild diffusion of the sentiments, and the digressive sallies of imagination, would have been compressed and restrained by confinement to rhyme. The excellence of this work is not exactness, but copiousness; particular lines are not to be regarded; the power is in the whole, and in the whole there is a magnificence like that ascribed to Chinese plantation, the magnificence of vast extent and endless diversity.

His last poem was the *Resignation*; in which he made, as he was accustomed, an experiment of a new mode of writing, and succeeded better than in his *Ocean* or his *Merchant*. It was very falsely represented as a proof of decaying faculties. There is Young in every stanza, such as he often was in his highest vigour.

His tragedies not making part of the Collection, I had forgotten, till Mr. Steevens recalled them to my thoughts by remarking that he seemed to have one favourite catastrophe, as his three plays all concluded with lavish suicide; a method by which, as Dryden remarked, a poet easily rids his scene of persons whom he wants not to keep alive. In *Busiris* there are the greatest ebullitions of imagination; but the pride of Busiris is such as no other man can have, and the whole is too remote from known life to raise either grief, terror, or indignation. *The Revenge* approaches much nearer to human practices and manners, and therefore keeps possession of the stage: the first design seems suggested by *Othello*; but the reflections, the incidents, and the diction are original. The moral observations are so introduced, and so expressed, as to have all the novelty that can be required. Of *The Brothers* I may be allowed to say nothing, since nothing was ever said of it by the public.

It must be allowed of Young's poetry, that it abounds in thought, but without much accuracy or selection. When he lays hold of an illustration, he pursues it beyond expectation, sometimes happily, as in his parallel of *Quicksilver* with *Pleasure*, which I have heard repeated with approbation by a lady, of whose praise he would have been justly proud, and which is very ingenious, very subtle, and almost exact; but sometimes he is less lucky, as when, in his *Night Thoughts*, having it dropped into his mind, that the orbs, floating in space, might be called the *cluster* of creation, he thinks on a cluster of grapes, and says that they all hang on the great vine, drinking the "nectareous juice of immortal life."

His conceits are sometimes yet less valuable. In the *Last Day* he hopes to illustrate the reassembly of the atoms that compose the human body at the "Trump of Doom," by the collection of bees into a swarm at the tinkling of a pan.

The Prophet says of Tyre, that "her Merchants are Princes." Young says of Tyre in his *Merchant*:

> Her merchants Princes, and each *deck a Throne*.

Let burlesque try to go beyond him.

He has the trick of joining the turgid and familiar: to buy the alliance of Britain, "Climes were paid down." Antithesis is his favourite: "They for kindness hate": and "because she's right, she's ever in the wrong."

His versification is his own; neither his blank nor his rhyming lines have any resemblance to those of former writers; he picks up no hemistichs, he copies no favourite expressions; he seems to have laid up no stores of thought or diction, but to owe all to the fortuitous suggestions of the present moment. Yet I have reason to believe that, when once he had formed a new design, he then laboured it with very patient industry, and that he composed with great labour and frequent revisions.

His verses are formed by no certain model; he is no more like himself in his different productions than he is like others. He seems never to have studied prosody, nor to have had any direction but from his own ear. But, with all his defects, he was a man of genius and a poet.

DAVID MALLET

1698?–1765

Born in the Highlands of Scotland—Educated at Edinburgh—Made Tutor to the Sons of the Duke of Montrose—Visits London—Publishes *William and Margaret*, a Ballad—Changes his Name—Publishes *The Excursion*, a Poem—Courts Pope by a Poem on *Verbal Criticism*—Writes for the Stage—Made Under-Secretary to Frederick Prince of Wales—Writes a *Life of Bacon*, and undertakes a *Life of the Duke of Marlborough*—Publishes *Amyntor and Theodora*, a Poem—Seeks to blacken the Memory of Pope—Left Bolingbroke's Literary Executor—His Pamphlet against Admiral Byng—Obtains a Pension—Is twice married—Death and Burial —Works and Character.

OF David Mallet, having no written memorial, I am able to give no other account than such as is supplied by the unauthorised loquacity of common fame, and a very slight personal knowledge.

He was, by his original, one of the Macgregors, a clan that became, about sixty years ago, under the conduct of Robin Roy, so formidable and so infamous for violence and robbery that the name was annulled by a legal abolition, and when they were all to denominate themselves anew, the father, I suppose of this author, called himself Malloch.

David Malloch was, by the penury of his parents, compelled to be janitor of the High School at Edinburgh, a mean office, of which he did not afterwards delight to hear. But he surmounted the disadvantages of his birth and fortune; for when [1723] the Duke of Montrose applied to the College of Edinburgh for a tutor to educate his sons, Malloch was recommended, and I never heard that he dishonoured his credentials.

When his pupils were sent to see the world, they were entrusted to his care; and having conducted them round the common circle of modish travels, he returned with them to London, where, by the influence of the family in which he resided, he naturally gained admission to many persons of the highest rank and the highest character, to wits, nobles, and statesmen.

Of his works, I know not whether I can trace the series. His first production was *William and Margaret*, of which, though it contains nothing very striking or difficult, he has

365

been envied the reputation, and plagiarism has been boldly charged, but never proved.

Not long afterwards he published *The Excursion* (1728), a desultory and capricious view of such scenes of Nature as his fancy led him, or his knowledge enabled him, to describe. It is not devoid of poetical spirit. Many of the images are striking, and many of the paragraphs are elegant. The cast of diction seems to be copied from Thomson, whose *Seasons* were then in their full blossom of reputation. He has Thomson's beauties and his faults.

His poem on *Verbal Criticism* (April 1733) was written to pay court to Pope, on a subject which he either did not understand or willingly misrepresented; and is little more than an improvement, or rather expansion, of a fragment which Pope printed in a Miscellany long before he engrafted it into a regular poem. There is in this piece more pertness than wit, and more confidence than knowledge. The versification is tolerable, nor can criticism allow it a higher praise.

His first tragedy was *Eurydice*, acted at Drury Lane in 1731, of which I know not the reception nor the merit, but have heard it mentioned as a mean performance. He was not then too high to accept a Prologue and Epilogue from Aaron Hill, neither of which can be much commended.

Having cleared his tongue from his native pronunciation so as to be no longer distinguished as a Scot, he seems inclined to disencumber himself from all adherences of his original, and took upon him to change his name from Scotch *Malloch* to English *Mallet*, without any imaginable reason of preference which the eye or ear can discover. What other proofs he gave of disrespect to his native country, I know not; but it was remarked of him, that he was the only Scot whom Scotchmen did not commend.

About this time Pope, whom he visited familiarly, published his *Essay on Man*, but concealed the author; and when Mallet entered one day, Pope asked him slightly what there was new. Mallet told him that the newest piece was something called an *Essay on Man*, which he had inspected idly, and seeing the utter inability of the author, who had neither skill in writing nor knowledge of his subject, had tossed it away. Pope, to punish his self-conceit, told him the secret.

A new edition of the works of Bacon being prepared (1740) for the press, Mallet was employed to prefix a Life, which he has written with elegance, perhaps with some affectation;

but with so much more knowledge of history than of science, that when he afterwards undertook the Life of Marlborough, Warburton remarked that he might perhaps forget that Marlborough was a general, as he had forgotten that Bacon was a philosopher.

When [1737] the Prince of Wales was driven from the palace, and setting himself at the head of the Opposition, kept a separate court, he endeavoured to increase his popularity by the patronage of literature, and made [June 1742] Mallet his under-secretary, with a salary of 200*l*. a year. Thomson likewise had a pension, and they were associated in the composition of the masque of *Alfred*, which in its original state was played at Cliefden in 1740; it was afterwards almost wholly changed by Mallet, and brought upon the stage at Drury Lane in 1751, but with no great success.

Mallet, in a familiar conversation with Garrick, discoursing of the diligence which he was then exerting upon the *Life of Marlborough*, let him know that in the series of great men, quickly to be exhibited, he should *find a niche* for the hero of the theatre. Garrick professed to wonder by what artifice he could be introduced, but Mallet let him know that, by a dexterous anticipation, he should fix him in a conspicuous place. "Mr. Mallet," says Garrick, in his gratitude of exultation, "have you left off to write for the stage?" Mallet then confessed that he had a drama in his hands. Garrick promised to act it, and *Alfred* was produced.

The long retardation of the Life of the Duke of Marlborough shows, with strong conviction, how little confidence can be placed in posthumous renown. When he died, it was soon determined that his story should be delivered to posterity; and the papers supposed to contain the necessary information were delivered to the Lord Molesworth, who had been his favourite in Flanders. When Molesworth died, the same papers were transferred with the same design to Sir Richard Steele, who, in some of his exigences, put them in pawn. They then remained with the old Duchess, who in her will assigned the task to Glover and Mallet, with a reward of a thousand pounds, and a prohibition to insert any verses. Glover rejected, I suppose, with disdain the legacy, and devolved the whole work upon Mallet, who had from the late Duke of Marlborough [died 1758] a pension to promote his industry, and who talked of the discoveries which he had made, but left not, when he died, any historical labours behind him.

While he was in the Prince's service he published [1739] *Mustapha*, with a Prologue by Thomson, not mean, but far inferior to that which he had received from Mallet for *Agamemnon*. The Epilogue, said to be written by a friend, was composed in haste by Mallet, in the place of one promised, which was never given. This tragedy was dedicated to the Prince, his master. It was acted at Drury Lane in 1739, and was well received, but was never revived.

In 1740 he produced, as has been already mentioned, the masque of *Alfred*, in conjunction with Thomson.

For some time afterwards he lay at rest. After a long interval, his next work was *Amyntor and Theodora* (1747), a long story in blank verse; in which it cannot be denied that there is copiousness and elegance of language, vigour of sentiment, and imagery well adapted to take possession of the fancy. But it is blank verse. This he sold to Vaillant for 120*l*. The first sale was not great, and it is now lost in forgetfulness.

Mallet, by address or accident, perhaps by his dependence on the Prince, found his way to Bolingbroke; a man whose pride and petulance made his kindness difficult to gain, or keep, and whom Mallet was content to court by an act which, I hope, was unwillingly performed. When it was found [1744] that Pope had clandestinely printed an unauthorised pamphlet, called *The Patriot King*, Bolingbroke, in a fit of useless fury, resolved to blast his memory, and employed Mallet (1749) as the executioner of his vengeance. Mallet had not virtue, or had not spirit, to refuse the office; and was rewarded, not long after [1751], with the legacy of Lord Bolingbroke's works.

Many of the political pieces had been written during the opposition to Walpole, and given to Francklin, as he supposed, in perpetuity. These, among the rest, were claimed by the will. The question was referred to arbitrators; but when they decided against Mallet, he refused to yield to the award, and by the help of Millar, the bookseller, published all that he could find, but with success very much below his expectation.

In 1755, his masque of *Britannia* was acted at Drury Lane, and his tragedy of *Elvira* in 1763; in which year he was appointed keeper of the Book of Entries for ships in the Port of London.

In the beginning of the last war, when the nation was exasperated by ill-success, he was employed to turn the public vengeance upon Byng, and wrote a letter of accusation under the character of a " Plain Man." The paper was with great industry circulated and dispersed; and he, for his seasonable intervention, had a considerable pension bestowed upon him, which he retained to his death.

Towards the end of his life he went with his wife to France; but after a while, finding his health declining, he returned alone to England, and died in April 1765.

He was twice married, and by his first wife had several children. One daughter, who married an Italian of rank, named Cilesia, wrote a tragedy, called *Almida*, which was acted at Drury Lane. His second wife was the daughter of a nobleman's steward, who had a considerable fortune, which she took care to retain in her own hands.

His stature was diminutive, but he was regularly formed; his appearance, till he grew corpulent, was agreeable, and he suffered it to want no recommendation that dress could give it. His conversation was elegant and easy. The rest of his character may, without injury to his memory, sink into silence.

As a writer, he cannot be placed in any high class. There is no species of composition in which he was eminent. His dramas had their day, a short day, and are forgotten: his blank verse seems to my ear the echo of Thomson. His *Life of Bacon* is known as it is appended to Bacon's volumes, but is no longer mentioned. His works are such as a writer, bustling in the world, showing himself in public, and emerging occasionally from time to time into notice, might keep alive by his personal influence; but which, conveying little information and giving no great pleasure, must soon give way, as the succession of things produces new topics of conversation and other modes of amusement.

MARK AKENSIDE

1721–1770

Born at Newcastle-on-Tyne—Educated at Edinburgh and Leyden—
Determines to study Physic—Publishes *The Pleasures of Imagination*—
His Quarrel with Warburton—Writes a Poem against Pulteney—Pub-
lishes a Volume of Odes—Mr. Dyson's Friendship for him—His small
Practice as a Physician—Death, and Burial in St. James's Church,
Piccadilly, London.

MARK AKENSIDE was born on the 9th of November, 1721, at
Newcastle-upon-Tyne. His father Mark was a butcher, of the
Presbyterian sect; his mother's name was Mary Lumsden. He
received the first part of his education at the grammar-school
of Newcastle, and was afterwards instructed by Mr. Wilson,
who kept a private academy.

At the age of eighteen he was sent to Edinburgh, that he
might qualify himself for the office of a dissenting minister, and
received some assistance from the fund which the Dissenters
employ in educating young men of scanty fortune. But a wider
view of the world opened other scenes and prompted other
hopes: he determined to study physic, and repaid that contri-
bution, which, being received for a different purpose, he justly
thought it dishonourable to retain.

Whether, when he resolved not to be a dissenting minister,
he ceased to be a Dissenter, I know not. He certainly retained
an unnecessary and outrageous zeal for what he called and
thought liberty; a zeal which sometimes disguises from the
world, and not rarely from the mind which it possesses, an
envious desire of plundering wealth or degrading greatness,
and of which the immediate tendency is innovation and anarchy,
an impetuous eagerness to subvert and confound, with very
little care what shall be established.

Akenside was one of those poets who have felt very early the
motions of genius, and one of those students who have very
early stored their memories with sentiments and images. Many
of his performances were produced in his youth; and his greatest
work, *The Pleasures of Imagination*, appeared in 1744. I have
heard Dodsley, by whom it was published, relate, that when

the copy was offered him, the price demanded for it, which was 12*l*., being such as he was not inclined to give precipitately, he carried the work to Pope, who, having looked into it, advised him not to make a niggardly offer, for "this was no everyday writer."

In 1741 he went to Leyden in pursuit of medical knowledge, and three years afterwards (May 16, 1744) became doctor of physic, having, according to the custom of the Dutch Universities, published a thesis or dissertation. The subject which he chose was *The Original and Growth of the Human Fœtus*; in which he is said to have departed, with great judgment, from the opinion then established, and to have delivered that which has been since confirmed and received.

Akenside was a young man, warm with every notion that by nature or accident had been connected with the sound of liberty, and by an eccentricity which such dispositions do not easily avoid, a lover of contradiction, and no friend to anything established. He adopted Shaftesbury's foolish assertion of the efficacy of ridicule for the discovery of truth. For this he was attacked by Warburton, and defended by Dyson: Warburton afterwards reprinted his remarks at the end of his Dedication to the *Freethinkers*.

The result of all the arguments which have been produced in a long and eager discussion of this idle question may easily be collected. If ridicule be applied to any position as the test of truth, it will then become a question whether such ridicule be just; and this can only be decided by the application of truth as the test of ridicule. Two men fearing, one a real and the other a fancied danger, will be for a while equally exposed to the inevitable consequences of cowardice, contemptuous censure, and ludicrous representation; and the true state of both cases must be known before it can be decided whose terror is rational, and whose is ridiculous—who is to be pitied, and who to be despised. Both are for a while equally exposed to laughter, but both are not therefore equally contemptible.

In the revisal of his poem, which he left unfinished at his death, he omitted the lines which had given occasion to Warburton's objections.

He published, soon after his return from Leyden (1745), his first collection of odes; and was impelled by his rage of patriotism to write [1744] a very acrimonious epistle to Pulteney, whom he stigmatises, under the name of Curio, as the betrayer of his country.

Being now to live by his profession, he first commenced [1744] physician at Northampton, where Dr. Stonehouse then practised, with such reputation and success, that a stranger was not likely to gain ground upon him. Akenside tried the contest awhile; and having deafened the place with clamours for liberty, removed [1747] to Hampstead, where he resided more than two years, and then fixed himself in London, the proper place for a man of accomplishments like his.

At London he was known as a poet, but was still to make his way as a physician; and would perhaps have been reduced to great exigences, but that Mr. Dyson, with an ardour of friendship that has not many examples, allowed him 300*l.* a year. Thus supported, he advanced gradually in medical reputation, but never attained any great extent of practice, or eminence or popularity. A physician in a great city seems to be the mere plaything of Fortune; his degree of reputation is, for the most part, totally casual: they that employ him know not his excellence; they that reject him know not his deficience. By any acute observer, who had looked on the transactions of the medical world for half a century, a very curious book might be written on the "Fortune of Physicians."

Akenside appears not to have been wanting to his own success: he placed himself in view by all the common methods; he became [1753] a Fellow of the Royal Society; he obtained a degree at Cambridge, and was admitted [1754] into the College of Physicians; he wrote little poetry, but published, from time to time, medical essays and observations; he became [1759] Physician to St. Thomas's Hospital; he read [1755] the Gulstonian Lectures in Anatomy; but began to give, for the Croonian Lecture, a history of the Revival of Learning, from which he soon desisted; and, in conversation, he very eagerly forced himself into notice by an ambitious ostentation of elegance and literature.

His Discourse on the Dysentery (1764) was considered as a very conspicuous specimen of Latinity, which entitled him to the same height of place among the scholars as he possessed before among the wits; and he might perhaps have risen to a greater elevation of character, but that his studies were ended with his life, by a putrid fever, June 23, 1770, in the forty-ninth year of his age.

Akenside is to be considered as a didactic and lyric poet. His great work is the *Pleasures of Imagination*; a performance

which, published as it was at the age of twenty-three, raised
expectations that were not very amply satisfied. It has undoubtedly a just claim to very particular notice, as an example
of great felicity of genius, and uncommon amplitude of acquisitions, of a young mind stored with images, and much exercised
in combining and comparing them.

With the philosophical or religious tenets of the author I
have nothing to do; my business is with his poetry. The subject
is well chosen, as it includes all images that can strike or please,
and thus comprises every species of poetical delight. The only
difficulty is in the choice of examples and illustrations; and
it is not easy in such exuberance of matter to find the middle
point between penury and satiety. The parts seem artificially
disposed, with sufficient coherence, so as that they cannot
change their places without injury to the general design.

His images are displayed with such luxuriance of expression,
that they are hidden, like Butler's Moon, by a "Veil of Light";
they are forms fantastically lost under superfluity of dress.
Pars minima est ipsa puella sui. The words are multiplied till
the sense is hardly perceived; attention deserts the mind, and
settles in the ear. The reader wanders through the gay diffusion,
sometimes amazed, and sometimes delighted; but, after many
turnings in the flowery labyrinth, comes out as he went in.
He remarked little, and laid hold on nothing.

To his versification justice requires that praise should not be
denied. In the general fabrication of his lines he is perhaps
superior to any other writer of blank verse; his flow is smooth,
and his pauses are musical; but the concatenation of his verses
is commonly too long continued, and the full close does not
recur with sufficient frequency. The sense is carried on through
a long intertexture of complicated clauses, and as nothing is
distinguished, nothing is remembered.

The exemption which blank verse affords from the necessity
of closing the sense with the couplet betrays luxuriant and
active minds into such self-indulgence, that they pile image
upon image, ornament upon ornament, and are not easily persuaded to close the sense at all. Blank verse will therefore, I
fear, be too often found in description exuberant, in argument
loquacious, and in narration tiresome.

His diction is certainly poetical as it is not prosaic, and
elegant as it is not vulgar. He is to be commended as having
fewer artifices of disgust than most of his brethren of the blank
song. He rarely either recalls old phrases or twists his metre

into harsh inversions. The sense, however, of his words is strained, when "he views the Ganges from Alpine heights"; that is, from mountains like the Alps. And the pedant surely intrudes (but when was blank verse without pedantry?) when he tells how "Planets *absolve* the stated round of Time."

It is generally known to the readers of poetry that he intended to revise and augment this work, but died before he had completed his design. The reformed work as he left it, and the additions which he had made, are very properly retained in the late Collection. He seems to have somewhat contracted his diffusion; but I know not whether he has gained in closeness what he has lost in splendour. In the additional book, the "Tales of Solon" is too long.

One great defect of his poem is very properly censured by Mr. Walker, unless it may be said in his defence, that what he has omitted was not properly in his plan. "His picture of man is grand and beautiful, but unfinished. The immortality of the soul, which is the natural consequence of the appetites and powers she is invested with, is scarcely once hinted throughout the poem. This deficiency is amply supplied by the masterly pencil of Dr. Young; who, like a good philosopher, has invincibly proved the immortality of man, from the grandeur of his conceptions, and the meanness and misery of his state; for this reason, a few passages are selected from the *Night Thoughts*, which, with those from Akenside, seem to form a complete view of the powers, situation, and end of man."

His other poems are now to be considered; but a short consideration will dispatch them. It is not easy to guess why he addicted himself so diligently to lyric poetry, having neither the ease and airiness of the lighter, nor the vehemence and elevation of the grander ode. When he lays his ill-fated hand upon his harp, his former powers seem to desert him; he has no longer his luxuriance of expression, nor variety of images. His thoughts are cold, and his words inelegant. Yet such was his love of lyrics, that, having written with great vigour and poignancy his *Epistle to Curio*, he transformed it afterwards into an ode disgraceful only to its author.

Of his odes nothing favourable can be said: the sentiments commonly want force, nature, or novelty; the diction is sometimes harsh and uncouth, the stanzas ill-constructed and unpleasant, and the rhymes dissonant, or unskilfully disposed, too distant from each other, or arranged with too little regard to established use, and therefore perplexing to the ear, which in a short composition has not time to grow familiar with an innovation.

To examine such compositions singly, cannot be required; they have doubtless brighter and darker parts: but when they are once found to be generally dull, all further labour may be spared; for to what use can the work be criticised that will not be read?

LORD LYTTELTON

1709-1773

Son of Sir Thomas Lyttelton, of Hagley, in Worcestershire—Educated at Eton and Oxford—Visits France and Italy—Obtains a seat in Parliament—Made Secretary to Frederick Prince of Wales—His Friendship with Pope and Thomson—Is twice married—Publishes his *Observations on the Conversion of St. Paul*—Inherits his Father's Baronetcy—Is created a Peer—Writes *The History of the Reign of Henry II.*—Death, and Burial at Hagley.

GEORGE LYTTELTON, the son of Sir Thomas Lyttelton, of Hagley in Worcestershire, was born in 1709. He was educated at Eton, where he was so much distinguished, that his exercises were recommended as models to his schoolfellows.

From Eton he went to Christ-Church, where he retained the same reputation of superiority, and displayed [1728] his abilities to the public in a poem on *Blenheim*.

He was a very early writer, both in verse and prose. His *Progress of Love* [1732], and his *Persian Letters*, were both written when he was very young; and indeed the character of a young man is very visible in both. The verses cant of shepherds and flocks, and crooks dressed with flowers; and the letters have something of that indistinct and headstrong ardour for liberty which a man of genius always catches when he enters the world, and always suffers to cool as he passes forward.

He stayed not long at Oxford; for in 1728 he began his travels, and saw France and Italy. When he returned, he obtained [April 1735] a seat in Parliament, and soon distinguished himself among the most eager opponents of Sir Robert Walpole, though his father, who was Commissioner of the Admiralty, always voted with the Court.

For many years the name of George Lyttelton was seen in every account of every debate in the House of Commons. He opposed the standing army; he opposed the Excise; he supported the motion for petitioning the King to remove Walpole. His zeal was considered by the courtiers not only as violent, but as acrimonious and malignant; and when Walpole was at last hunted from his places, every effort was made by his friends, and many friends he had, to exclude Lyttelton from the secret committee.

The Prince of Wales, being (1737) driven from St. James's, kept a separate court, and opened his arms to the opponents of the ministry. Mr. Lyttelton became [Oct. 1737] his secretary, and was supposed to have great influence in the direction of his conduct. He persuaded his master, whose business it was now to be popular, that he would advance his character by patronage. Mallet was made under-secretary, with 200*l.*, and Thomson had a pension of 100*l.* a year. For Thomson Lyttelton always retained his kindness, and was able at last to place him at ease.

Moore courted his favour by an apologetical poem, called *The Trial of Selim,* for which he was paid with kind words, which, as is common, raised great hopes, that were at last disappointed.

Lyttelton now stood in the first rank of opposition; and Pope, who was incited, it is not easy to say how, to increase the clamour against the ministry, commended him among the other patriots. This drew upon him the reproaches of Fox, who, in the House, imputed to him as a crime his intimacy with a lampooner so unjust and licentious. Lyttelton supported his friend, and replied, that he thought it an honour to be received into the familiarity of so great a poet.

While he was thus conspicuous, he married (1741) Miss Lucy Fortescue, of Devonshire, by whom he had a son, the late Lord Lyttelton, and two daughters, and with whom he appears to have lived in the highest degree of connubial felicity: but human pleasures are short; she died in childbed about five years afterwards, and he solaced his grief by writing a long poem to her memory.

He did not, however, condemn himself to perpetual solitude and sorrow; for, after a while, he was content to seek happiness again by a second marriage [10 Aug. 1749] with the daughter of Sir Robert Rich; but the experiment was unsuccessful.

At length, after a long struggle, Walpole gave way, and honour and profit were distributed among his conquerors. Lyttelton was made (December 1744) one of the Lords of the Treasury, and from that time was engaged in supporting the schemes of the ministry.

Politics did not, however, so much engage him as to withhold his thoughts from things of more importance. He had, in the pride of juvenile confidence, with the help of corrupt conversation, entertained doubts of the truth of Christianity; but he thought the time now come when it was no longer fit to doubt or believe by chance, and applied himself seriously to the great question. His studies being honest, ended in conviction. He found that religion was true, and what he had learned he endeavoured to teach (1747), by *Observations on the Conversion of St. Paul;* a treatise to which infidelity has never been able to fabricate a specious answer. This book his father had the happiness of seeing, and expressed his pleasure in a letter which deserves to be inserted:

I have read your religious treatise with infinite pleasure and satisfaction. The style is fine and clear, the arguments close, cogent, and irresistible. May the King of kings, whose glorious cause you have so well defended, reward your pious labours, and grant that I may be found worthy, through the merits of Jesus Christ, to be an eye-witness of that happiness which I don't doubt he will bountifully bestow upon you. In the mean time I shall never cease glorifying God for having endowed you with such useful talents, and giving me so good a son.

Your affectionate father,

THOMAS LYTTELTON.

A few years afterwards (1751), by the death of his father, he inherited a baronet's title with a large estate, which, though perhaps he did not augment, he was careful to adorn by a house of great elegance and expense, and by much attention to the decoration of his park.

As he continued his activity in parliament, he was gradually advancing his claim to profit and preferment, and accordingly was made in time (1754) cofferer and privy councillor: this place he exchanged next year for the great office of Chancellor of the Exchequer,—an office, however, that required some qualifications which he soon perceived himself to want.

The year after his curiosity led him into Wales, of which he has given an account, perhaps rather with too much affectation of delight, to Archibald Bower, a man of whom he had conceived an opinion more favourable than he seems to have deserved, and whom, having once espoused his interest and fame, he never was persuaded to disown. Bower, whatever was his moral character, did not want abilities; attacked as he was by an universal outcry, and that outcry, as it seems, the echo of truth, he kept his ground; at last, when his defences began to fail him, he sallied out upon his adversaries, and his adversaries retreated.

About this time Lyttelton published his *Dialogues of the Dead*, which were very eagerly read, though the production rather, as it seems, of leisure than of study, rather effusions than compositions. The names of his persons too often enable the reader to anticipate their conversation; and when they have met, they too often part without any conclusion. He has copied Fenelon more than Fontenelle.

When they were first published, they were kindly commended by the "Critical Reviewers"; and poor Lyttelton, with humble gratitude, returned, in a note which I have read, acknowledgments which can never be proper, since they must be paid either for flattery or for justice.

When, in the latter part of the last reign, the inauspicious commencement of the war made the dissolution of the ministry unavoidable, Sir George Lyttelton, losing with the rest his employment, was [19th Nov. 1757] recompensed with a peerage, and rested from political turbulence in the House of Lords.

His last literary production was his *History of Henry the Second*, elaborated by the searches and deliberations of twenty years, and published with such anxiety as only vanity can dictate.

The story of this publication is remarkable. The whole work was printed twice over, a great part of it three times, and many sheets four or five times. The booksellers paid for the first impression; but the charges and repeated operations of the press were at the expense of the author, whose ambitious accuracy is known to have cost him at least a thousand pounds. He began to print in 1755. Three volumes appeared in 1764, a second edition of them in 1767, a third edition in 1768, and the conclusion in 1771.

Andrew Reid, a man not without considerable abilities, and not unacquainted with letters or with life, undertook to persuade Lyttelton, as he had persuaded himself, that he was master of the secret of punctuation; and, as fear begets credulity, he was employed, I know not at what price, to point the pages of *Henry the Second*. The book was at last pointed, and printed and sent into the world. Lyttelton took money for his copy, of which, when he had paid the printer, he probably gave the rest away, for he was very liberal to the indigent.

When time brought the *History* to a third edition, Reid was either dead or discarded; and the superintendence of typography and punctuation was committed to a man originally a combmaker, but then known by the style of Doctor. Something uncommon was probably expected, and something uncommon was at last done; for to the Doctor's edition is appended, what the world had hardly seen before, a list of errors in nineteen pages.

But to politics and literature there must be an end. Lord Lyttelton had never the appearance of a strong or of a healthy man; he had a slender, uncompacted frame, and a meagre face; he lasted, however, sixty years, and was then seized with his last illness. Of his death a very affecting and instructive account has been given by his physician, which will spare me the task of his moral character.

"On Sunday evening the symptoms of his Lordship's disorder, which for a week past had alarmed us, put on a fatal appearance, and his Lordship believed himself to be a dying man. From this time he suffered by restlessness rather than pain; though his nerves were apparently much fluttered, his mental faculties never seemed stronger when he was thoroughly awake.

"His Lordship's bilious and hepatic complaints seemed alone not equal to the expected mournful event; his long want of sleep, whether the consequence of the irritation in the bowels, or, which is more probable, of causes of a different kind, accounts for his loss of strength and for his death very sufficiently.

"Though his Lordship wished his approaching dissolution not to be lingering, he waited for it with resignation. He said, 'It is a folly, a keeping me in misery, now to attempt to prolong life'; yet he was easily persuaded, for the satisfaction of others, to do or take anything thought proper for him. On Saturday he had been remarkably better, and we were not without some hopes of his recovery.

"On Sunday, about eleven in the forenoon, his Lordship sent for me, and said he felt a great hurry, and wished to have a little conversation with me, in order to divert it. He then proceeded to open the fountain of that heart from whence goodness had so long flowed, as from a copious spring. 'Doctor,' said he, 'you shall be my confessor; when I first set out in the world, I had friends who endeavoured to shake my belief in the Christian religion. I saw difficulties which staggered me, but I kept my mind open to conviction. The evidences and doctrines of Christianity, studied with attention, made me a most firm and persuaded believer of the Christian religion. I have made it the rule of my life, and it is the ground of my future hopes. I have erred and sinned, but have repented, and never indulged any vicious habit. In politics and public life, I have made public good the rule of my conduct. I never gave

counsels which I did not at the time think the best. I have
seen that I was sometimes in the wrong, but I did not err
designedly. I have endeavoured, in private life, to do all the
good in my power, and never for a moment could indulge
malicious or unjust designs upon any person whatsoever.'

"At another time he said, 'I must leave my soul in the same
state it was in before this illness; I find this a very inconvenient
time for solicitude about anything.'

"On the evening, when the symptoms of death came on, he
said, 'I shall die, but it will not be your fault.' When Lord
and Lady Valentia came to see his Lordship, he gave them his
solemn benediction, and said, 'Be good, be virtuous, my Lord;
you must come to this.' Thus he continued giving his dying
benedictions to all around him. On Monday morning a lucid
interval gave some small hopes, but these vanished in the
evening, and he continued dying, but with very little uneasiness, till Tuesday morning, August 22, when, between seven
and eight o'clock, he expired, almost without a groan."

His Lordship was buried at Hagley, and the following
inscription is cut on the side of his Lady's monument:

This unadorned stone was placed here
By the particular desire and express
Directions of the Right Honourable

GEORGE Lord LYTTELTON,

Who died August 22, 1773, aged 64.

Lord Lyttelton's Poems are the works of a man of literature
and judgment devoting part of his time to versification. They
have nothing to be despised, and little to be admired. Of his
Progress of Love, it is sufficient blame to say that it is pastoral.
His blank verse in *Blenheim* has neither much force nor much
elegance. His little performances, whether Songs or Epigrams,
are sometimes sprightly, and sometimes insipid. His epistolary
pieces have a smooth equability, which cannot much tire, because they are short, but which seldom elevates or surprises.
But from this censure ought to be excepted his *Advice to Belinda*,
which, though for the most part written when he was very
young, contains much truth and much prudence, very elegantly
and vigorously expressed, and shows a mind attentive to life,
and a power of poetry which cultivation might have raised
to excellence.

THOMAS GRAY

1716–1771

Born in Cornhill, London—Educated at Eton and Cambridge—Accompanies Horace Walpole into Italy—His Quarrel with Pope—Publishes his *Elegy written in a Country Churchyard*—Its immediate Popularity—Publishes his Odes—Refuses the Laurel—Made Professor of Modern History at Cambridge—Death, and Burial at Stoke Poges in Buckinghamshire—Works and Character.

THOMAS GRAY, the son of Mr. Philip Gray, a scrivener of London, was born in Cornhill, November 26, 1716. His grammatical education he received at Eton under the care of Mr. Antrobus, his mother's brother, then assistant to Dr. George; and when he left school, in 1734, entered a pensioner at Peterhouse in Cambridge.

The transition from the school to the college is, to most young scholars, the time from which they date their years of manhood, liberty, and happiness; but Gray seems to have been very little delighted with academical gratifications; he liked at Cambridge neither the mode of life nor the fashion of study, and lived sullenly on to the time when his attendance on lectures was no longer required. As he intended to profess the Common Law, he took no degree.

When he had been at Cambridge about five years, Mr. Horace Walpole, whose friendship he had gained at Eton, invited him to travel with him as his companion. They wandered through France into Italy; and Gray's letters contain a very pleasing account of many parts of their journey. But unequal friendships are easily dissolved: at Florence they quarrelled, and parted; and Mr. Walpole is now content to have it told that it was by his fault. If we look, however, without prejudice on the world, we shall find that men whose consciousness of their own merit sets them above the compliances of servility, are apt enough in their association with superiors to watch their own dignity with troublesome and punctilious jealousy, and in the fervour of independence to exact that attention which they refuse to pay. Part they did, whatever was the

383

quarrel, and the rest of their travels was doubtless more unpleasant to them both. Gray continued his journey in a manner suitable to his own little fortune, with only an occasional servant.

He returned to England in September 1741, and in about two months afterwards buried his father; who had, by an injudicious waste of money upon a new house, so much lessened his fortune, that Gray thought himself too poor to study the law. He therefore retired to Cambridge, where he soon after became Bachelor of Civil Law; and where, without liking the place or its inhabitants, or professing to like them, he passed, except a short residence in London, the rest of his life.

About this time [1742] he was deprived of Mr. West, the son of a chancellor of Ireland, a friend on whom he appears to have set a high value, and who deserved his esteem by the powers which he shows in his letters and in the *Ode to May* which Mr. Mason has preserved, as well as by the sincerity with which, when Gray sent him part of *Agrippina*, a tragedy that he had just begun, he gave an opinion which probably intercepted the progress of the work, and which the judgment of every reader will confirm. It was certainly no loss to the English stage that *Agrippina* was never finished.

In this year (1742) Gray seems first to have applied himself seriously to poetry; for in this year were produced the *Ode to Spring*, his *Prospect of Eton*, and his *Ode to Adversity*. He began likewise a Latin poem, *De principiis cogitandi*.

It may be collected from the narrative of Mr. Mason, that his first ambition was to have excelled in Latin poetry: perhaps it were reasonable to wish that he had prosecuted his design; for though there is at present some embarrassment in his phrase, and some harshness in his lyric numbers, his copiousness of language is such as very few possess; and his lines, even when imperfect, discover a writer whom practice would quickly have made skilful.

He now lived on at Peterhouse, very little solicitous what others did or thought, and cultivated his mind and enlarged his views without any other purpose than of improving and amusing himself; when Mr. Mason being elected Fellow of Pembroke Hall, brought him a companion who was afterwards to be his editor, and whose fondness and fidelity has kindled in him a zeal of admiration which cannot be reasonably expected from the neutrality of a stranger, and the coldness of a critic.

In this retirement he wrote (1747) an ode on the *Death of Mr. Walpole's Cat*; and the year afterwards attempted a poem of more importance, on *Government and Education*, of which the fragments which remain have many excellent lines.

His next production (1751) was his far-famed *Elegy in the Churchyard*, which, finding its way into a magazine, first, I believe, made him known to the public.

An invitation from Lady Cobham about this time gave occasion to an odd composition called *A Long Story*, which adds little to Gray's character.

Several of his pieces were published (1753), with designs by Mr. Bentley, and, that they might in some form or other make a book, only one side of each leaf was printed. I believe the poems and the plates recommended each other so well, that the whole impression was soon bought. This year he lost his mother.

Some time afterwards (1756) some young men of the college, whose chambers were near his, diverted themselves with disturbing him by frequent and troublesome noises, and, as is said, by pranks yet more offensive and contemptuous. This insolence, having endured it a while, he represented to the governors of the society, among whom perhaps he had no friends; and, finding his complaint little regarded, removed himself to Pembroke Hall.

In 1757 he published *The Progress of Poetry* and *The Bard*, two compositions at which the readers of poetry were at first content to gaze in mute amazement. Some that tried them confessed their inability to understand them, though Warburton said that they were understood as well as the works of Milton and Shakespeare, which it is the fashion to admire. Garrick wrote a few lines in their praise. Some hardy champions undertook to rescue them from neglect, and in a short time many were content to be shown beauties which they could not see.

Gray's reputation was now so high, that, after the death of Cibber [1757], he had the honour of refusing the laurel, which was then bestowed on Mr. Whitehead.

His curiosity, not long after, drew him away [1759] from Cambridge to a lodging near the Museum, where he resided near three years, reading and transcribing; and, so far as can be discovered, very little affected by two odes on *Oblivion* and *Obscurity*, in which his lyric performances were ridiculed with much contempt and much ingenuity.

When [1762] the Professor of Modern History at Cambridge died, he was, as he says, "cockered and spirited up" till he asked it of Lord Bute, who sent him a civil refusal; and the place was given to Mr. Brocket, the tutor of Sir James Lowther.

His constitution was weak, and believing that his health was promoted by exercise and change of place, he undertook (1765) a journey into Scotland, of which his account, so far as it extends, is very curious and elegant: for, as his comprehension was ample, his curiosity extended to all the works of art, all the appearances of nature, and all the monuments of past events. He naturally contracted a friendship with Dr. Beattie, whom he found a poet, a philosopher, and a good man. The Mareschal College at Aberdeen offered him the degree of Doctor of Laws, which, having omitted to take it at Cambridge, he thought it decent to refuse.

What he had formerly solicited in vain was at last given him without solicitation. The Professorship of History became again vacant, and he received (1768) an offer of it from the Duke of Grafton. He accepted, and retained it to his death; always designing lectures, but never reading them; uneasy at his neglect of duty, and appeasing his uneasiness with designs of reformation, and with a resolution which he believed himself to have made of resigning the office, if he found himself unable to discharge it.

Ill health made another journey necessary, and he visited (1769) Westmoreland and Cumberland. He that reads his epistolary narration wishes that to travel, and to tell his travels, had been more of his employment; but it is by studying at home that we must obtain the ability of travelling with intelligence and improvement.

His travels and his studies were now near their end. The gout, of which he had sustained many weak attacks, fell upon his stomach, and, yielding to no medicines, produced strong convulsions, which (July 30, 1771) terminated in death.

His character I am willing to adopt, as Mr. Mason has done, from a letter written to my friend Mr. Boswell by the Rev. Mr. Temple, rector of St. Gluvias in Cornwall; and am as willing as his warmest well-wisher to believe it true.

"Perhaps he was the most learned man in Europe. He was equally acquainted with the elegant and profound parts of science, and that not superficially, but thoroughly. He knew every branch of history, both natural and civil; had read all the original historians of England, France, and Italy; and was a great antiquarian. Criticism, metaphysics, morals, politics, made a principal part of his study; voyages and travels of all sorts were his favourite amusements; and he had a fine taste in painting, prints, architecture, and gardening. With such a fund

of knowledge, his conversation must have been equally instructing and entertaining; but he was also a good man, a man of
virtue and humanity. There is no character without some
speck, some imperfection; and I think the greatest defect in
his was an affectation in delicacy, or rather effeminacy, and a
visible fastidiousness, or contempt and disdain of his inferiors
in science. He also had, in some degree, that weakness which
disgusted Voltaire so much in Mr. Congreve: though he seemed
to value others chiefly according to the progress they had made
in knowledge, yet he could not bear to be considered himself
merely as a man of letters; and though without birth, or fortune, or station, his desire was to be looked upon as a private
independent gentleman, who read for his amusement. Perhaps
it may be said, What signifies so much knowledge, when it produced so little? Is it worth taking so much pains to leave no
memorial but a few poems? But let it be considered that Mr.
Gray was to others at least innocently employed; to himself,
certainly beneficially. His time passed agreeably; he was every
day making some new acquisition in science; his mind was
enlarged, his heart softened, his virtue strengthened; the world
and mankind were shown to him without a mask; and he was
taught to consider everything as trifling, and unworthy of the
attention of a wise man, except the pursuit of knowledge and
practice of virtue in that state wherein God hath placed us."

To this character Mr. Mason has added a more particular
account of Gray's skill in zoology. He has remarked, that
Gray's effeminacy was affected most "before those whom he
did not wish to please"; and that he is unjustly charged with
making knowledge his sole reason of preference, as he paid his
esteem to none whom he did not likewise believe to be good.

What has occurred to me from the slight inspection of his
letters in which my undertaking has engaged me, is, that his
mind had a large grasp; that his curiosity was unlimited, and
his judgment cultivated; that he was a man likely to love much
where he loved at all, but that he was fastidious and hard to
please. His contempt, however, is often employed, where I hope
it will be approved, upon scepticism and infidelity. His short
account of Shaftesbury I will insert.

"You say you cannot conceive how Lord Shaftesbury came
to be a philosopher in vogue; I will tell you: first, he was a
lord; secondly, he was as vain as any of his readers; thirdly,
men are very prone to believe what they do not understand;
fourthly, they will believe anything at all, provided they are

under no obligation to believe it; fifthly, they love to take a
new road, even when that road leads nowhere; sixthly, he was
reckoned a fine writer, and seems always to mean more than
he said. Would you have any more reasons? An interval of
above forty years has pretty well destroyed the charm. A dead
lord ranks with commoners; vanity is no longer interested in
the matter, for a new road is become an old one."

Mr. Mason has added, from his own knowledge, that though
Gray was poor, he was not eager of money; and that out of the
little that he had he was very willing to help the necessitous.

As a writer he had this peculiarity, that he did not write his
pieces first rudely and then correct them, but laboured every
line as it arose in the train of composition; and he had a notion
not very peculiar, that he could not write but at certain times,
or at happy moments; a fantastic foppery, to which my kindness for a man of learning and of virtue wishes him to have
been superior.

Gray's poetry is now to be considered; and I hope not to
be looked on as an enemy to his name, if I confess that I
contemplate it with less pleasure than his life.

His ode on *Spring* has something poetical, both in the language and the thought; but the language is too luxuriant,
and the thoughts have nothing new. There has of late arisen
a practice of giving to adjectives derived from substantives,
the termination of participles; such as the *cultured* plain, the
daisied bank; but I was sorry to see, in the lines of a scholar
like Gray, the *honied* Spring. The morality is natural, but too
stale; the conclusion is pretty.

The poem *On the Cat* was doubtless by its author considered as a
trifle, but it is not a happy trifle. In the first stanza "the azure
flowers *that* blow," show how resolutely a rhyme is sometimes
made when it cannot easily be found. Selima, the Cat, is called
a nymph, with some violence both to language and sense; but
there is good use made of it when it is done; for of the two lines,

> What female heart can gold despise?
> What cat's averse to fish?

the first relates merely to the nymph, and the second only to
the cat. The sixth stanza contains a melancholy truth, that
"a favourite has no friend"; but the last ends in a pointed
sentence of no relation to the purpose: if *what glistered* had
been *gold*, the cat would not have gone into the water; and if
she had, would not less have been drowned.

The *Prospect of Eton College* suggests nothing to Gray which every beholder does not equally think and feel. His supplication to Father Thames, to tell him who drives the hoop or tosses the ball, is useless and puerile. Father Thames has no better means of knowing than himself. His epithet "buxom health" is not elegant; he seems not to understand the word. Gray thought his language more poetical as it was more remote from common use: finding in Dryden "honey redolent of Spring," an expression that reaches the utmost limits of our language, Gray drove it a little more beyond common apprehension by making "gales" to be "redolent of joy and youth."

Of the *Hymn to Adversity*, the hint was at first taken from "O Diva, gratum quæ regis Antium"; but Gray has excelled his original by the variety of his sentiments, and by their moral application. Of this piece, at once poetical and rational, I will not by slight objections violate the dignity.

My process has now brought me to the *wonderful* "Wonder of Wonders," the two Sister Odes; by which, though either vulgar ignorance or common sense at first universally rejected them, many have been since persuaded to think themselves delighted. I am one of those that are willing to be pleased, and therefore would gladly find the meaning of the first stanza of the *Progress of Poetry*.

Gray seems in his rapture to confound the images of "spreading sound and running water." A "stream of music" may be allowed; but where does "music," however "smooth and strong," after having visited the "verdant vales, roll down the steep amain," so as that "rocks and nodding groves rebellow to the roar"? If this be said of music, it is nonsense; if it be said of water, it is nothing to the purpose.

The second stanza, exhibiting Mars's car and Jove's eagle, is unworthy of further notice. Criticism disdains to chase a school-boy to his commonplaces.

To the third it may likewise be objected that it is drawn from mythology, though such as may be more easily assimilated to real life. Idalia's "velvet-green" has something of cant. An epithet or metaphor drawn from nature ennobles art: an epithet or metaphor drawn from art degrades nature. Gray is too fond of words arbitrarily compounded. "Many-twinkling" was formerly censured as not analogical; we may say "many-spotted," but scarcely "many-spotting." This stanza, however, has something pleasing.

Of the second ternary of stanzas, the first endeavours to tell

something, and would have told it had it not been crossed by
Hyperion: the second describes well enough the universal prevalence of poetry; but I am afraid that the conclusion will not
rise from the premises. The caverns of the North and the plains
of Chili are not the residences of "glory and generous shame."
But that poetry and virtue go always together is an opinion so
pleasing, that I can forgive him who resolves to think it true.

The third stanza sounds big with "Delphi," and "Egean,"
and "Ilissus," and "Meander," and "hallowed fountains," and
"solemn sound"; but in all Gray's odes there is a kind of
cumbrous splendour which we wish away. His position is at
last false: in the time of Dante and Petrarch, from whom we
derive our first school of poetry, Italy was overrun by "tyrant
power" and "coward vice"; nor was our state much better
when we first borrowed the Italian arts.

Of the third ternary, the first gives a mythological birth of
Shakespeare. What is said of that mighty genius is true; but
it is not said happily: the real effects of this poetical power are
put out of sight by the pomp of machinery. Where truth is
sufficient to fill the mind, fiction is worse than useless; the
counterfeit debases the genuine.

His account of Milton's blindness, if we suppose it caused
by study in the formation of his poem—a supposition surely
allowable—is poetically true, and happily imagined. But the
car of Dryden, with his *two coursers*, has nothing in it peculiar;
it is a car in which any other rider may be placed.

The Bard appears at the first view to be, as Algarotti and
others have remarked, an imitation of the prophecy of Nereus.
Algarotti thinks it superior to its original, and if preference
depends only on the imagery and animation of the two poems,
his judgment is right. There is in *The Bard* more force, more
thought, and more variety. But to copy is less than to invent,
and the copy has been unhappily produced at a wrong time.
The fiction of Horace was to the Romans credible; but its
revival disgusts us with apparent and unconquerable falsehood.
Incredulus odi.

To select a singular event, and swell it to a giant's bulk by
fabulous appendages of spectres and predictions, has little difficulty; for he that forsakes the probable may always find the
marvellous. And it has little use: we are affected only as we
believe; we are improved only as we find something to be
imitated or declined. I do not see that *The Bard* promotes
any truth, moral or political.

His stanzas are too long, especially his epodes; the ode is finished before the ear has learned its measures, and consequently before it can receive pleasure from their consonance and recurrence.

Of the first stanza the abrupt beginning has been celebrated; but technical beauties can give praise only to the inventor. It is in the power of any man to rush abruptly upon his subject that has read the ballad of *Johnny Armstrong*:

Is there ever a man in all Scotland.

The initial resemblances, or alliterations, "ruin, ruthless, helm or hauberk," are below the grandeur of a poem that endeavours at sublimity.

In the second stanza the Bard is well described; but in the third we have the puerilities of obsolete mythology. When we are told that "Cadwallo hush'd the stormy main," and that "Modred made huge Plinlimmon bow his cloud-topp'd head," attention recoils from the repetition of a tale that, even when it was first heard, was heard with scorn.

The *weaving* of the *winding sheet* he borrowed, as he owns, from the Northern bards; but their texture, however, was very properly the work of female powers, as the act of spinning the thread of life in another mythology. Theft is always dangerous; Gray has made weavers of slaughtered bards, by a fiction outrageous and incongruous. They are then called upon to "weave the warp, and weave the woof," perhaps with no great propriety; for it is by crossing the *woof* with the *warp* that men *weave* the *web* or piece; and the first line was dearly bought by the admission of its wretched correspondent, "Give ample room and verge enough." He has, however, no other line as bad.

The third stanza of the second ternary is commended, I think, beyond its merit. The personification is indistinct. *Thirst* and *hunger* are not alike; and their features, to make the imagery perfect, should have been discriminated. We are told in the same stanza how "towers are fed." But I will no longer look for particular faults; yet let it be observed that the ode might have been concluded with an action of better example; but suicide is always to be had without expense of thought.

These odes are marked by glittering accumulations of ungraceful ornaments; they strike, rather than please; the images are magnified by affectation; the language is laboured into harshness. The mind of the writer seems to work with unnatural violence. "Double, double, toil and trouble." He has a kind of strutting dignity, and is tall by walking on tiptoe. His art and his struggle are too visible, and there is too little appearance of ease and nature.

To say that he has no beauties, would be unjust: a man like him, of great learning and great industry, could not but produce something valuable. When he pleases least, it can only be said that a good design was ill directed.

His translations of Northern and Welsh poetry deserve praise; the imagery is preserved, perhaps often improved; but the language is unlike the language of other poets.

In the character of his Elegy I rejoice to concur with the common reader; for by the common sense of readers uncorrupted with literary prejudices, after all the refinements of subtilty and the dogmatism of learning, must be finally decided all claim to poetical honours. The *Churchyard* abounds with images which find a mirror in every mind, and with sentiments to which every bosom returns an echo. The four stanzas beginning "Yet even these bones" are to me original: I have never seen the notions in any other place; yet he that reads them here, persuades himself that he has always felt them. Had Gray written often thus, it had been vain to blame, and useless to praise him.

THE END